Comparative Federalism

Comparative Federalism

A Systematic Inquiry

THOMAS O. HUEGLIN
AND
ALAN FENNA

broadview press

LIBRARY AND ARCHIVES CANADA CATALOGUING IN PUBLICATION

Hueglin, Thomas O. (Thomas Otto), 1946–
Comparative federalism: a systematic inquiry / Thomas O. Hueglin and Alan Fenna.

Includes bibliographical references and index.
ISBN 1–55111–410–0

1. Federal government–Textbooks.   I. Fenna, Alan, 1958-   II. Title.

JC355.H82 2005   321.02   C2005–905779–3

Broadview Press Ltd. is an independent, international publishing house, incorporated in 1985. Broadview believes in shared ownership, both with its employees and with the general public; since the year 2000 Broadview shares have traded publicly on the Toronto Venture Exchange under the symbol BDP.

We welcome comments and suggestions regarding any aspect of our publications—please feel free to contact us at the addresses below or at broadview@broadviewpress.com.

North America
Post Office Box 1243,
Peterborough, Ontario, Canada K9J 7H5

Post Office Box 1015,
3576 California Road, Orchard Park,
NY, USA 14127
TEL (705) 743–8990; FAX (705) 743–8353
EMAIL customerservice@broadviewpress.com

UK, Ireland, and continental Europe
NBN Plymbridge,
Estover Road, Plymouth, UK PL6 7PY
TEL 44 (0) 1752 202301;
FAX 44 (0) 1752 202331
FAX ORDER LINE 44 (0) 1752 2023333
CUST. SERVICE cservs@nbnplymbridge.com
ORDERS orders@nbnplymbridge.com

Australia and New Zealand
UNIREPS, University of New South Wales
Sydney, NSW, Australia 2052
TEL 61 2 9664 0999; FAX 61 2 9664 5420
EMAIL info.press@unsw.edu.au
www.broadviewpress.com

Broadview Press Ltd. gratefully acknowledges the financial support of the Government of Canada through the Book Publishing Industry Development Program for our publishing activities.

Edited by Betsy Struthers.

Typeset by Infoscan Collette, Quebec City

Printed in Canada

Contents

Acknowledgements

I am grateful to the Division of Humanities, Curtin University, for funding overseas study leave to research and write my share of this book. It is a book that has been a long time in the writing, and I am also grateful to the publishers, specifically Michael Harrison, for their patience, and my family for their endurance. Finally, I must thank my co-author, Thomas, for a great experience in collaborative work.

AF

In turn, my gratitude goes to the Social Sciences and Humanities Research Council of Canada for research grant funding, and to the Forum of Federations for the opportunity to be part of a world-wide dialogue on federalism. Michael Harrison has been a friend and mentor for many years. I also want to thank the Department of Political Science at Wilfrid Laurier University, which has become such a collegial and stimulating place, and my family for years of putting up with pipe smoke behind the closed doors of my study. The friendship and intellectual symbiosis with Alan have been the reward for writing this book.

TH

1 The Relevance of Federalism in a Changing World

In the nineteenth century, the French theorist of socialist federalism, Pierre-Joseph Proudhon, wrote that "the twentieth century will open the age of federations, or else humanity will undergo another purgatory of a thousand years."[1] After the purgatory of two world wars (and countless other wars) in the twentieth century, the eminent American scholar of federalism Daniel Elazar wrote of an ongoing "federalist revolution" as the only safeguard for peace and stability in a rapidly changing world.[2] In this introductory chapter, we explore some of the developments indicating that the age of federations might finally be upon us at the outset of the twenty-first century.

THE CASE FOR FEDERALISM

The reality is that federalism is here to stay, and for good reason. As we shall explore later, more than half of the world's space and nearly half of its population are governed by some form of federal arrangement. While some of the classic federations may be showing signs of intergovernmental fatigue, there has been an outburst of federalization elsewhere. The most important case may be the European Union, even though its future character as a federal system is still subject to debate. Some of the older unitary nation-states such as Belgium, Spain, and South Africa, have recently adopted federal forms of governance in order to establish or regain democratic stability. In developing countries such as Mexico and Brazil economic modernization and democratic accountability have been tied to federal reform. Federal arrangements have also been proposed for the resolution of some of the world's most intractable conflicts such as in the Middle East and Northern Ireland.

---

1. Pierre-Joseph Proudhon, *The Principle of Federation* (Toronto, ON: University of Toronto Press, 1973; originally published in 1863 as *Du Principe fédératif et de la nécessité de reconstituer le parti de la révolution*) 68–69. For discussion of Proudhon's interest in federalism, see Chapter 4.
2. Daniel J. Elazar, *Federalism and the Road to Peace* (Kingston, ON: Institute of Intergovernmental Relations, Queen's University, 1994) esp. 21–25.

And last but not least, the growing debate about the future of democratic governance in a globalizing world is increasingly cast in federal terms.

Persons and Places

Within nation-states as well as in the international arena, we can observe processes of integration and fragmentation. Above the level of the nation-state, a growing number of international organizations with far-reaching regulatory powers have begun to influence the lives of people everywhere. Below the level of the nation-state, various regional and social movements continue to challenge the exclusive exercise of power by national governments.

These ongoing processes of integration and fragmentation are not likely to produce a world of individualized citizenship. Regional and associational organizations of social life remain important and are perhaps even getting stronger. Alongside persons and their individual interests, places and their collective interests remain a principal focus of politics. In such a world the importance of federalism as a structured institutional approach to political participation, decision-making and problem-solving is likely to increase.

Governance Beyond the State

In political science, a paradigmatic change is taking place from the government of states to multi-level governance beyond the state. Federalism is an obvious institutional response to this transformation for two main reasons.
- It has a long history and tradition in political thought and practice. In search of new and more adequate forms of governance for a changing world, therefore, the wheel does not have to be invented all over again.
- Because it is by definition a form of divided or shared governance, federalism allows flexible solutions to complex situations of overlapping jurisdiction and contested sovereignty.

The International State System

Until recently, there was a seemingly clear division of politics. On the one hand, there was the territorial nation-state, ruled by **sovereign** governments. On the other, there was the international state system, ruled entirely by international relations. Admittedly, the division of these political arenas was never quite so clear cut in practice. International organizations such as the United Nations (UN) or the World Bank have existed for some time, and they were preceded by other similar institutions. And the internal sovereignty of nation-state governments has always been challenged by regionalist and other social movements striving for autonomy or a larger share of the national pie. But, in principle, nation-states were expected to maintain control over such movements internally and be subjected to international regulation only on the basis of their voluntary agreement registered in international treaties.

Federal states were not treated any differently in this modern system of politics. Externally, they were considered to be sovereign entities as much as unitary states. Internally, it was recognized that sovereignty was constrained or shared by the legislative powers of two levels of government. Generally, however, the 'federal' or, as we shall refer to it in this book, the 'national' level of government was assigned or gradually established constitutional supremacy over the most important policy fields.

New Realities

This traditional view of modern politics has become challenged by a number of recent developments that do not fit the picture.

- The **European Union** (EU) gradually evolved into a quasi-federal system of regional integration that goes far beyond the scope of international relations.
- More generally, **globalization** increasingly constrains the sovereign powers of nation-states by the autonomous regulatory powers of international organizations.
- At the same time, a number of existing nation-states had to resort to varying degrees of **federalization** in order to maintain unity and democratic stability.
- Conventional politics also proved unable to contain the most violent **cultural and micro-nationalist crises.**

A common denominator in all instances has been the ability or inability to reach federal solutions to these problems of integration and fragmentation.

EMERGING FEDERALISM IN THE EUROPEAN UNION

The EU is of particular significance for several reasons. With 25 member countries as of 2004, it is by far the largest economic and political bloc in the world. Its institutions and decision-making procedures constitute a novel type of federal system somewhere between federation and confederation. While some policy areas remain in the domain of member-state sovereignty, others have reached a level of full political integration. This resembles the division of powers in federal states. It differs from these in that the ultimate source of authority allocating powers and determining their scope and dimension is not a constitutional document but a series of treaties based on mutual agreement. In contrast to the American model of **constitutional federalism,** it is this dimension of European **treaty federalism** that may serve as a new model of multilevel governance in a globalizing world.

European Integration

The process of European integration began after World War II. It was driven by both a pervasive desire for peace and a realization that economic integration was necessary in order to defend European interests against the world's two superpowers of the time, the United States of America and the Soviet Union.[3]

In contrast to the fully bicameral model of American federalism, however, European governance remained essentially tied to intergovernmental agreement in the Council of Ministers, even though the original treaties had foreseen the introduction of majority voting in the Council for most market- and trade-related policy areas. In the early phase of integration, France rejected the idea of a supranational European federal state. Later, after its entry to the Community in 1973, it was Britain that most stubbornly defended national sovereignty.

A dramatic change began to take shape in the mid-1980s. Confronted with years of economic stagnation and unemployment, Europe was propelled into a phase of intensified integration under the leadership of a new president of the European Commission, Jacques Delors. The transformation of the common market into a single market providing free movement of people, goods, services, and capital in 1987 and the adoption of most legislation pertaining to this transformation by majority vote in the Council was only the first significant step.

The Maastricht Treaty

The decisive turning point was the Maastricht Treaty of 1993 which created the EU as a novel type of polity based on three so-called pillars. The first of these completed the supranational project of economic and monetary union; the second established intergovernmental cooperation on foreign and security policy; and the third involved cooperation in matters of justice and home affairs. Two additional treaty provisions provided the Union with a more clearly discernible federal character.

- The limited powers of the European Parliament were strengthened by a **co-decision right** alongside the Council in a number of important policy areas. This meant that the European system of governance was given more of a bicameral character even though the intergovernmental Council would continue to be the principal legislator.
- The **subsidiarity principle** was introduced as a yardstick for a European division of powers. Under this principle, the EU would be able

---

3. See Desmond Dinan, "How Did We Get Here?" in Elizabeth Bomberg and Alexander Stubb, eds., *The European Union: How Does It Work?* (Oxford: Oxford University Press, 2003); also Mark Gilbert, *Surpassing Realism: The Politics of European Integration since 1945* (Lanham, MD: Rowman and Littlefield, 2003).

to adopt new powers only if there was agreement that the continued exercise of these powers by the member states was not sufficient for the realization of likewise agreed-upon policy goals.

For all practical purposes, then, the EU had become a novel type of federal system,[4] with a flexible provision for the division of powers and an emerging system of bicameral majority governance. Yet its primary legal basis remained a series of consecutive treaties rather than a clear constitutional document. With more amending treaties added during the 1990s, and significant enlargement in the offing, enthusiasm grew for a firmer and more symbolically powerful constitutional basis.

A Constitution for Europe

In a memorable speech at Humboldt University in Berlin on 12 May 2000, the German foreign minister, Joschka Fischer, launched the idea of a European constitution that would transform what he called a European confederacy into a federation of European nation-states. He argued that such a constitution would have to clarify the division of powers between the EU and the member states, but he also reaffirmed Europe's reliance on the principle of **subsidiarity** to protect against an erosion of nation-state autonomy and identity.

Two years later, a European Constitutional Convention was formally inaugurated. It was composed of representatives from governments and parliaments not only of the existing member states but from all future membership candidates as well. Headed by a former French president and a former Italian prime minister, and aided by numerous working groups as well as broad public involvement, it produced a first constitutional outline within six months and a first set of draft articles within a year. In July 2003, work on the draft treaty was completed. An intergovernmental conference (IGC) was established to resolve several outstanding issues, and after an earlier false start, the Treaty Establishing a Constitution for Europe was signed by the member states on 29 October 2004.[5]

At this point, it is far from clear that the European Constitution will be ratified by 2006 as foreseen in the Treaty. The ratification procedure has been left to the member states, and most will resort to a national referendum. If eventually adopted, however, the Constitution will replace all previous treaties and mark another important step in Europe's journey from fratricidal statehood to federal comity. It will contain a European Charter of Fundamental Rights as well as a consolidated framework for the operation of the Union. The co-decision right of the

---

4. See also David McKay, *Designing Europe: Comparative Lessons from the Federal Experience* (Oxford: Oxford University Press, 2001).

5. For this and other EU matters see the Gateway to the European Union website at <http://europa.eu.int/index_en.htm>.

European Parliament will be strengthened, eventually covering about 95 per cent of all European legislation.

The current division of powers, on the other hand, will not be substantially altered. Most powers will be shared, and who gets to do what and to what extent will be decided in accordance with the subsidiarity principle (see Chapter 6). Most importantly, the Constitution did not take the quantum leap towards a fully democratic federal state in the conventional sense.[6] The legitimacy of European governance will continue to hinge on procedures of civic participation and consultation as well as policy efficiency and fairness rather than direct parliamentary accountability. The Constitution will also remain a treaty in character: amendments will continue to require unanimous intergovernmental agreement.

This is an exciting development nonetheless—and not just for students of federalism. It can only be compared to the Philadelphia Convention of 1787 which crafted the Constitution of the United States. While it seems safe to predict that the EU will never become a conventional federal state, in many ways it will be federal in nature, governed on the basis of a complex matrix of power-sharing and compromise among different political actors and levels of governance. Again, this is what eventually lies ahead for the emerging world system of globalized interdependence.

FEDERALISM AND GLOBALIZATION

Globalization often evokes images of a world without borders. Free trade and universal citizenship are conjured up as a global opportunity structure for everyone. More than ever, it is argued, people are establishing world-wide connexions through travel, business, and the Internet. Increasingly, this raises questions about international governance.

Pluralistic Realities

These images provide a rather inaccurate picture of the world; continental trade blocs seem to be a more likely scenario. Among these, the EU is obviously the most advanced system. But there are several others: NAFTA, the North American Free Trade Agreement; AFTA, the ASEAN Free Trade Area of south-east Asia; and MERCOSUR, a similar organization promoting free trade in South America.

Despite much wishful thinking after the collapse of Soviet communism, it is also inaccurate more generally to see the world as a uniformly capitalist system of states and markets. The world in fact appears to be divided into several capitalisms reflecting established cultural differences

---

6.   See Renaud Dehousse, "Beyond Representative Democracy: Constitutionalism in a Polycentric Polity," in Joseph H.H. Weiler and Marlene Wind, eds., *European Constitutionalism Beyond the State* (Cambridge: Cambridge University Press, 2003) esp. 144.

and following different rules and practices. In contrast to the liberal model of American individualistic free market capitalism, for instance, continental European welfare capitalism at least for the time being has retained a stronger commitment to social equality. Post-communist Russia, on the other hand, struggles to emerge from an abyss of mafia capitalism. And Asian tiger economy capitalism emerged as a combination of market practice and social authoritarianism. The developing world, finally, seems to be divided between those seeking access to the global marketplace by adhering to the impositions of foreign investors and international regulatory agencies and those left behind as the world's hapless periphery. Much of Africa falls into this most unfortunate category.

International Organizations

The federalist argument points to integration and fragmentation as the real face of globalization. The North American and European trade blocs regularly clash over competition issues. Asian countries show continuing resistance to Western financial impositions and trade rules.

International organizations such as the World Trade Organization (WTO), the International Monetary Fund (IMF), and the World Bank have not always been sensitive to such differences. They are driven by ambitions of economic liberalization which in turn are dominated by the strongest players. This is particularly evident in the case of money-lending institutions such as the IMF where decision-making powers are apportioned according to financial strength.

Loan packages are not only designed for economic stabilization. They typically come with strings attached requiring far-reaching changes to domestic political culture and practice such as social deregulation or opening doors to foreign direct investment. While many poor countries have few options other than accepting such conditions, Asian countries, on the basis of their relative economic strength, are more resentful about what they see as impositions of "ideological change."[7]

Even in the UN a new divisiveness is evident. After the end of the Cold War and the demise of the Soviet Union as the world's other superpower, there were expectations for a 'new world order' led by the United States and uniform in its adoption of liberal principles of political and economic governance. These expectations simply ignored the deep cultural and ideological divisions that continued to exist, not only between the Western world and the world of Islam, for instance, but also within the West between those accepting unquestioned American leadership and those insisting on a plurality of principles and approaches.

---

7. Richard Higgott, "Regionalism in the Asia-Pacific: Two Steps Forward, One Step Back?" in Richard Stubbs and Geoffrey R.D. Underhill, eds., *Political Economy and the Changing Global Order* (Don Mills, ON: Oxford University Press, 2000).

Global Governance

The inescapable overall impression is that a common approach to an efficient regime of world governance is nowhere in sight. Globalization remains very much a project pursued by some and resented by others.[8] A new reality of rapidly increasing global interdependence clashes with old territorial structures of political power. At the same time, a patchwork of international organizations reflects this clash than it provides a genuine forum for negotiated settlement. As a result, the new world order is fraught with new conflicts.

It may be that only a federal solution can accommodate these conflicts. This would mean that even in a world of globalizing free trade, there must be recognition of different communities and their autonomous right to decide upon the kind of principles they want to live by. This is a matter of adequate joint decision-making mechanisms—a matter of deciding, by means of carefully negotiated compromise and on the basis of fair representation, what can be 'free' in free trade and what cannot be subjected to universal rules.

OLD NATION-STATES AND NEW FEDERALISM

In international relations or on the European stage, federalism is still a concept and term that is introduced only reluctantly. In his Berlin speech, Fischer almost apologized for using it, adding that he simply could not think of another term that would describe what he had in mind. The reason for such hesitancy is that, for many, federalism is associated with the creation of central power—as in the American historical experience—and consequently with a loss of nation-state sovereignty. In domestic politics, however, federalism has gained new currency in exactly the opposite sense: as a structural device of devolution. This devolutionary federalization has come to the rescue of a number of unitary states such as Spain, Belgium, and South Africa, which otherwise might have fallen apart or become enmeshed in civil conflict. In some formally constituted federal states such as Brazil and Mexico, federalism has helped the process of democratization. And finally, even some of the most notorious unitary nation-states—notably Britain, France and Italy—have embarked upon a path of regional devolution.[9]

---

8.   For an overview of the main positions, see David Held and Anthony McGrew, eds., *The Global Transformations Reader* (Cambridge: Polity, 2002).

9.   For an initial overview, consult Ann L. Griffiths and Karl Nerenberg, eds., *Handbook of Federal Countries 2002* (Montreal, QC and Kingston, ON: McGill-Queen's University Press, 2002); also Mark Kesselman, Joel Krieger, Christopher S. Allen, Stephen Hellman, David Ost, and George Ross, eds., *European Politics in Transition*, 4th ed. (Boston, MA: Houghton Mifflin, 2002).

Reconstructing Unitary States

Later on in the book we discuss the way that the forcible creation of unitary nation states in early modern Europe established the dominant model of state formation, to the exclusion of more pluralistic development paths. Some of these unitary states have had to acknowledge their inherently pluralistic nature and adopt new state forms reflecting those social and political realities.

Democratization and Federalization in Spain

Among the most dramatic and successful cases of recent federalization is Spain. Its three historic regions—Catalonia, Galicia, and the Basque Country—had been brutally suppressed under the Franco dictatorship that lasted from 1939 to Franco's death in 1975. In 1978, a democratic constitution established Spain as a state composed of 17 Autonomous Communities. The three historic regions were put on a fast track towards self-government, and all other regional communities were given the opportunity to follow suit.

What is equally remarkable, although perhaps not surprising, is the fact that the attack on centralism was led by the Spanish Left, Communists and Socialists alike. Ever since the French Revolution, the European Left had supported centralism because decentralization was historically seen as synonymous with the existence of undemocratic local fiefdoms. In Spain, however, the centre had been occupied by the forces of the authoritarian Right, and calls for decentralization became a strategic weapon for the democratic Left. History was essentially turned on its head. The Spanish State of the Autonomous Communities is not formally constituted as a federation because regional autonomies do not enjoy full constitutional protection. To revoke these autonomies, however, would be politically suicidal. On that basis, we must judge modern Spain to be a *de facto* federal system.

Belgium's Innovative Solution

Another interesting case is Belgium. Created as a unitary state in 1831 from leftover territory in between France and the Netherlands, Belgium is composed primarily of a Flemish (Dutch-speaking) majority and a Walloon (French-speaking) minority. In addition, there is a small but significant German-speaking community. Some sort of balance was maintained as long as Wallonia in the south was the economically stronger region. When this changed with the decline of its mining and heavy industries, linguistic and socio-economic tensions brought the country to the brink of break-up. Various constitutional reforms establishing regional autonomy were introduced between 1970 and 1993 in an attempt to re-establish political stability. The amendment of 1994 re-constituted Belgium as a particularly innovative federal state. It not only recognizes three autonomous regions—Wallonia, Flanders, and the bilingual capital region of Brussels—but it also provides self-governing autonomies to the three French, Flemish, and German-speaking cultural communities on a non-territorial basis.

Democratization and Federalization in South Africa

Of particular importance, finally, is the case of South Africa because it provides an example of successful federalization in a wider global context of democratic stabilization among deeply divided ethnic groups. The adoption of constitutional federalism in post-apartheid South Africa is surprising given the centralist bias of the African National Congress (ANC) as well as the association of federalism in South Africa with the disgraced policy of "homelands" for the suppressed African population.

The new constitution of 1996 not only distinguishes national, provincial, and local spheres of government with their respective powers, it also contains a formal mandate for cooperation as well as provisions for the protection of cultural communities, including the minority of formerly ruling white Afrikaners. South African federalism has yet to stand the test of socio-economic stability, but, in principle, it has quickly become the accepted form of democratic governance.

Federalism in Africa has not been a success story generally. South Africa is in many ways a unique case because federalism was both a survival strategy for the white minority and a common rallying point for a black majority united for the occasion. Ethnic divisions in countries with artificial post-colonial boundaries combined with extreme levels of poverty do not make for a spirit of power-sharing and compromise. The only other federation in all of Africa is Nigeria, which has recently emerged from military dictatorship; however, Nigeria has a long way to go to qualify as a genuine federation.

Rejuvenated Federations

The story in Central and South America is a different one. At the beginning of the twentieth century, four of the nine existing federations in the world were located south of the United States. While closely following the American model in design, these federations experienced long periods of political instability and various forms of military dictatorship under which both democracy and federalism were suppressed. More recently, however, a transition to stable democracy has begun, and the existing federal structures and traditions have played a significant role in this transition.[10]

Constitutional Reform in Brazil

Brazil has been a federal state since 1891. After a long and turbulent history of military dictatorship and presidential authoritarianism, the reformed federal constitution of 1988 has opened up a new chapter in the country's history. Traditionally, the structures of federalism had been used as transmission belts for central control and top-down clientelist relationships. The constitution of 1988 for the first time combined political and financial decentralization, giving real power to state and local governments. This happened without much upheaval because a federal system was already in place and unfamiliar new structures of governance did not have to be superimposed. Corruption and clientelism are still endemic in Brazil, but in the overall dynamic of the federal system there is now also a new bottom-up dynamic that may yet succeed in the process of democratic stabilization.

Injecting Life into Mexican Federalism

Mexico is an even older federal state, dating back to 1824. For much of the twentieth century, the country was in the authoritarian grip of the Institutional Revolutionary Party (PRI) for which federalism also served as a top-down transmission belt of central control. As in the Brazilian case, too, this may be the principal reason why the federal system was never formally dissolved. Federalism, however, is a two-way street, and since the 1980s opposition parties have gained ground, first at the municipal level and then, beginning with the 1989 victory in the Baja California gubernatorial elections, at the state level as well. The victorious party there was the conservative National Action Party (PAN) whose leader, Vicente Fox, finally ended more than 70 years of PRI rule by winning the 2000 presidential election.

The Right Conditions

Federalism in Central and South America did not automatically or inevitably lead to democratization, but it provided opportunity structures that could be used by democratic forces when the conditions were right. In Brazil and Mexico, socio-economic modernization eventually forced ruling elites to loosen their grip on political control. In contrast to the situation in South Africa, another factor has been the relative absence

---

10. For example of recent discussion, see Edward L. Gibson, ed., *Federalism and Democracy in Latin America* (Baltimore, MD: Johns Hopkins University Press, 2004).

of deep ethnic divisions, because the plight of the relatively small numbers of Indigenous peoples has been almost entirely neglected thus far. The revolt of the Zapatistas in the Mexican Chiappas region is a reminder that the business of democratic federalism remains unfinished.

Devolution

Finally, we turn our attention to a number of established unitary states that have more recently embarked upon a path of decentralization without, however, committing themselves to wholesale federalization. Each of these countries has a history of containing—and in several cases actively suppressing—regional and cultural identities.

The United Kingdom

The most startling example is the United Kingdom of Great Britain and Northern Ireland (UK). For centuries it has suppressed regional and cultural difference to enforce a unitary state, though Scotland has always enjoyed some special privileges. Yet precisely at the moment when many British politicians across partisan lines appeared to be so worried about their country being absorbed into the EU, the Parliament at Westminster finally gave the green light for a devolution of powers to Scotland and Wales. In 1999, both elected their own parliaments. Given the limited range of political power given to these parliaments, and particularly their lack of financial autonomy, these acts of devolution do not warrant us speaking of the UK as a federation, but they have put it at the top of what critics see as the beginning of a slippery slope towards federalization. The main reason for these developments has been mounting regional pressure, especially in Scotland. There, and elsewhere, the perception has been that European integration offers an unprecedented chance of pursuing regional interests directly at the European level of governance rather in London. In a complex world of economic integration and multilevel governance, regional differentiation may open up improved and diversified access points to agenda-setting and policy formulation.

The Italian Case

While the 'F-word' is generally avoided in the UK, it has enjoyed great popularity in Italy more recently. In Britain, federalism is widely feared as a dual threat to nation-state sovereignty: through European centralization from above and by regional decentralization from below. In Italy, it is celebrated for almost precisely the same reasons: from above as a European opportunity structure for more autonomous regional development and from below as a strategy of democratic control over the clientelist networks of central governance.

In a country with strong regionalist traditions like Italy, though, federalism means different things to different people. In the prosperous north, it is synonymous with a new selfishness that wants to end the redistributive policies for southern regional development it has to pay for. In the less developed south, it stands for the opposite, a more egalitarian access to the political and economic system. In practice, a modest constitutional change has strengthened the regions whose presidents are now directly elected. While it is unlikely that Italy will become a fully developed federal system any time soon, an intense debate about federalism has taken root almost everywhere in the country. This will be reflected in future political reforms.

France

Our final and most unlikely case is the notoriously centralized 'jacobin state' of France.[11] In 2000, the government split when the minister of the interior resigned over plans to grant partial autonomy to the Mediterranean island of Corsica, which had been under French administration since 1797 and haunted by violent separatism for more than 20 years. The program was to have been implemented by 2004, bringing Corsica a modest form of self-government. The Corsican language was to gain equal status to French and was to be taught in school. That offer was rejected, however, by Corsicans themselves in a 2003 referendum, in part because it fell short of full self-determination and, apparently, in part also because a traditional male-dominated society would not accept the imposition of a quota requirement for the participation of women in an elected island assembly.

French nationalists saw these concessions not only as a shameful surrender to armed struggle—only two years earlier, the French prefect of the island had been assassinated by the separatists—they also saw it as a dangerous precedent for autonomy claims elsewhere, for example, in Brittany or along the French-Spanish border with its Catalonian and Basque populations.

Federalism is not a popular political concept in France and quite possibly never will be. The significance of the French case lies in the realization that even the most famously unitary state of Europe would benefit from some form of shared or divided governance. France is often portrayed as the classical case of unitary state- and nationhood. Yet surprisingly, it contains a number of cultural minorities who have never accepted entirely their assimilation into a uniform ethno-linguistic state-building project. And at least in one case, Corsica, there seems to have been a

---

11. So-called after the concerted effort by the French revolutionaries to create a modern centralized state apparatus governing the entire country.

belated realization that a modest concession for autonomy and divided governance would be a promising strategy of conflict management.

FEDERALISM AND MULTINATIONAL CONFLICT MANAGEMENT

Our final consideration in favour of federalism points to its potential for managing multinational conflict. The concepts and rules of indivisible territorial nation-state sovereignty have proven inadequate to deal with some of the world's most violent and debilitating conflicts. More often than not, such conflicts have to do with multi-ethnic or multinational diversity within states or regions. They appear to be fuelled by a new intensity of integration *and* fragmentation in an interdependent world. As the boundaries of nation-states become more porous and their claims to sovereignty more dubious in the face of economic internationalization and migration, more and more national minorities may want to cash in on the promise of self-determination first made by American president Woodrow Wilson at the beginning of the last century.

Within the confines of territorial nation-state politics and ideology, parties to these conflicts have no other strategic perspective than victory over the other side. Peaceful accommodation inevitably requires some measure of mutual toleration and compromise for which federalism offers some well-practised institutional models and procedural techniques.[12] In this section we explore cases that range from cautious optimism (Northern Ireland) to wishful thinking (Middle East) and apparent failure (Yugoslavia).

Northern Ireland

In principle, the conflict lines in Northern Ireland are quite simple. They have been fuelled by the intransigence of two parties, Protestant Unionists and Catholic Republicans. Federalism as a form of shared governance had never been a serious option because the ultimate Republican goal was reunification with Ireland and because the Unionists, not wanting to abandon the ultimate authority of Westminster in any matter whatsoever, preferred devolved governance to federalized self-government.

A dramatic change came with the Belfast, or so-called Good Friday, Agreement of 1998. It is still unclear whether this agreement will finally bring peace and political stability back to Northern Ireland, and it has already been on the brink of collapse on more than one occasion. The point is, however, that it provided for the first time a formula of power

---

12. See, critically, John McGarry, "Federal Political Systems and the Accommodation of National Minorities," in Griffiths and Nerenberg, *Handbook of Federal Countries.*

sharing that involved not only the two conflicting parties but the governments of the UK and Ireland as well. The Agreement rests on three pillars or "strands."[13]

- The first re-establishes Northern Irish parliamentary self-government on the basis of proportional inclusion of "all sections of the community." Parliamentary rule is, moreover, complemented by a consultative second chamber, the Civic Forum. The range of powers is to be specified in a treaty and therefore not constitutionally guaranteed, a concession to the Unionists' preference for devolution. However, it would be politically impossible to revoke these powers as long as self-governance proved stable.

- The second strand sets up a Ministerial Council between Northern Ireland and the Republic of Ireland, which is essentially an intergovernmental body for the administration of trans-border issues. This is a major concession to the Republicans because it acknowledges and strengthens legitimate north-south ties.

- The third strand, finally, sets up a British-Irish Council consisting of representatives of these two governments, as well as representatives from Scotland, Wales, the Isle of Man, the Channel Islands, and, if eventually established, the regional assemblies of England.

It is of course too early to assess or even guess how all these new institutions may function in practice and what powers they may end up with effectively. But it should be clear that the Good Friday Agreement has been the first sign of hope in a conflict that seemed hopeless. And it is equally clear that its acceptance in principle by all participants is owed to its quasi-federal multilevel design. The idea that there must be one ultimate source of sovereignty—Irish, Northern Irish, or British—is given up. Governance in Northern Ireland becomes embedded in a cooperative matrix involving all surrounding national and regional governing bodies.

The Middle East

Even more so than in the case of Northern Ireland, the conflict between Israelis and Palestinians in the Middle East has been predicated upon a history of injustice, territorial occupation, religious orthodoxy, and civilian as well as military terrorism. For a long time, Israel's territorial expansionism stood against the Palestinian vow to eradicate the Jewish state altogether.

But even under the assumption that both sides recognize in principle each other's rights to one and the same territory, a federal solution seems

---

13. See Elizabeth Meehan, "The Belfast Agreement: Its Distinctiveness and Points of Cross-fertilization in the UK's Devolution Programme," *Parliamentary Affairs* 52:1 (1999).

improbable. Federalism conventionally is about shared sovereignty on the basis of divided territorial jurisdiction. Sharing requires trust—something that cannot be said to exist on either side. Divided territorial jurisdiction in turn requires divisions with clear boundaries that allow each to exercise powers in a practical and unmistakable way. Because of Israel's settlement policies on Palestinian land and because the city of Jerusalem contains, in closest proximity, holy religious sites for both peoples, this seems way out of reach.

Is it? Except for outmoded concepts of territorial statehood, there is no reason why governance could not be relocated into a localized network of neighbourhoods, villages, towns and settlements. Such a **patchwork federalism** would of course also require some form of cooperation and policy coordination in joint councils. The federalist assumption is that such cooperation is more likely among those directly affected by the outcome than at the level of national politics. As in the case of Northern Ireland, it would have to be underwritten by outside political forces, both neighbouring states and the world community. And, as in most conventional federal systems, it would have to be backed up by a commitment to social equalization. Without such a commitment, stable federalism is not possible.

Political realists will be quick to point out the practical limits of federal norms and principles in a world driven by power, self-interest, and sheer despair. But as in the case of 'democracy' or 'liberalism,' federalism is not just a structural design, it also contains normative goals. Without such goals, any form of progress would be impossible.

Federal Failure in Yugoslavia?

The final test case for federalism as a promising tool of conflict management is Yugoslavia. Once hailed as an exemplary socialist federation, it came apart at the seams as soon as the end of the Cold War removed the strategic need for unity in the face of the ideological superpower blocs. The atrocities committed in Bosnia and Kosovo against their ethnic and religious minorities provide all the evidence one needs of the depth of existing divisions. And even after two wars with massive outside intervention, the nations and peoples of the region remain deeply divided. If federalism was meant to provide lasting accommodation among them, political realists would argue, it failed miserably.

The counter-argument is that the Yugoslavian tragedy has had little or nothing to do with federalism. The state that Tito forged out of the ashes of World War II was a personalized dictatorship. When Tito died, it was not the country that continued as a federation but the Communist Party which instituted a joint leadership, bridging the regional and ethnic cleavages through proportional participation and the rotation of leadership functions. The fundamental differences of political culture, history, and religion, were never addressed at the societal level because of the pretence, under socialism, that they were no longer an issue. Finally Yugoslavia was not a union of states that had chosen to federate. "The Yugoslav experience supports the thesis ... that one of the basic conditions for a viable federal state is that all of its constituent parts must have passed through the historical stage of nation statehood."[14]

When the communist regime collapsed and capitalism came, some parts were better prepared for it than others. Freedom was quickly associated with selfish disrespect for others. Vying for economic advantage and expanding markets, the outside world encouraged dissociative behaviour rather than helped forge a new consensus. When Croatia and Slovenia broke away, with the encouragement of Germany in particular, Yugoslavia lost much of its economic base. Federalism cannot be a panacea for economic, social, or political pathologies in general.

Yugoslavia for now has been reduced to a federation of two remaining states, Serbia and Montenegro. It is an unloved union that may eventually fail as well. But the case of Yugoslavia is not one of federal failure; it is one of missed federal chances. Only Slovenia has been accepted into the EU. Had they been encouraged and helped to form a democratic federal union, all the peoples and ethnic groups of former Yugoslavia might have qualified. And none of this means that federalism is not relevant to the future of democratizing or newly democratic Eastern Europe more broadly.[15]

THE FEDERAL EXPERIENCE

All of this begs a number of important questions about the experience of 'actually existing' federal systems. How has federalism worked in those several countries where it is already well-established, even long established? What has federal theory contributed to our understanding of federalism? The United States, Switzerland, Canada, Australia, and Germany are major liberal democracies that have accumulated substantial experience in operating the system of divided and shared rule that is federalism. In some cases, they have learned from one another and taken common paths; in others, they have taken different approaches and had to cope with different circumstances. Although well-established federations, they all continue to face challenges in making federalism work efficiently and effectively. How to regard and manage powerful

---

14. Mihailo Markovic, "The Federal Experience in Yugoslavia," in Karen Knop, Sylvia Ostry, Richard Simeon, and Katherine Swinton, eds., *Rethinking Federalism: Citizens, Markets, and Governments in a Changing World* (Vancouver, BC: University of British Columbia Press, 1995) 83.

15. See Jürgen Rose and Johannes Ch. Traut, eds., *Federalism and Decentralization: Perspectives for the Transformation Process in Eastern and Central Europe* (Basingstoke: Palgrave Macmillan, 2002).

forces of centralization, respond to devolutionary or even secessionist demands, avoid problems of duplication or conflict—these are the sorts of issues that continue to confront the older federations.

Themes

This book explores the federal experience in terms of the following themes. The existing range of practices and experiences can teach us something about the problems and possibilities of federalism.

- *Intentions and outcomes*. Federations are the result of a conscious process of institutional design intended to strike and perpetuate a particular balance of interests, forces, and objectives. Those choices influence subsequent developments, though not necessarily in the direction envisaged or intended. In making choices about institutional design, the framers of federal systems engage in a process of social learning that may or may not be accurate or successful.

- *Separating governments*. The central defining feature of federalism is the way it shares sovereignty and divides powers between two or more levels of government. This presents a challenge of institutional design: how to divide powers in a sustainable, efficient, and effective manner? This has proven to be the great problem of federalism, particularly in the era of modern industrial society when the growth of govern-ment has greatly magnified the complexities of governance. These complexities create an ongoing tension between constitutional plans, constitutional change, and practical adjustment in federal systems.

- *Connecting governments*. Having divided government, federalism must connect the governments it has created to share rule over a common territory. Federalism is a negotiated union, both in its act of creation and in its ongoing maintenance and operation. Federa-tions that provided limited constitutional anticipation of this typically need to find other, sub-constitutional *modus vivendi* between the different levels of government.

- *Constitutionality, constitutional permanence, and constitutional adju-dication*. Federalism has contributed significantly to the rise of cod-ified constitutions as the binding fundamental law governing the operation of modern liberal democracies. As an express agreement based on compromise between different forces and elements creating a system in which those forces are expected to exist in a dynamic relationship, federalism is inherently constitutional. It requires the overriding authority of a single authoritative document to regulate the highly implausible relationship it has invented, the relationship of shared sovereignty. By their nature, constitutions in turn require a permanence, an inflexibility, a resistance to change. Federalism has characteristic ways of granting that permanence, but a delicate and varying balance must be sought between flexibility and rigidity. Constitutional rules in turn entail constitutional adjudication, and the elevated role that adjudication has given to the courts has long made federalism seem an innately legalistic political order. The federal experience, however, shows important variance in that regard.

- *Harmony and diversity.* The underlying assumption of federalism—and the premise on which federations were often established in the first place—is that it allows for the coexistence of substantial difference. The union can impose homogeneity in policy areas where broad agreement regards such homogeneity is necessary or desirable, while the constituent jurisdictions can go their own way in other respects. This can allow regional populations to retain specific cultural practices specific to their local 'identity'; choose the style of government and policy they desire, and promote their own economic welfare. Federal theory differs, though, in the emphasis it places on the diversity-enhancing requirement and in the policy spheres or domains it should operate. In practice, federalism has struggled to maintain such a diversity-enhancing framework, and modern federations harbour notably less diversity than these underlying assumptions might lead one to expect.

2 Federal Principles, Federal Organization

Having begun this book by suggesting some of the reasons we might be interested in federalism, we focus in this chapter on how to think about such a form of political organization, drawing some definitional boundaries, identifying a few key concepts, and noting some of their implications. Federalism has a reasonably well-defined meaning and can be distinguished quite clearly from more centralized unitary government on the one hand and more decentralized confederal arrangements on the other. More philosophically, federalism can be understood as a way of approaching politics that acknowledges group identity alongside individual identity. However, it is a particular form of group identity—a spatial, locational, or territorial one. It gives rise to a set of normative issues about the virtues and vices of a system of multiple governments, and it raises practical questions about how powers are to be divided and how relations between governments are to be defined and conducted.

WHAT IS FEDERALISM?

Federal states are most obviously characterized by their different levels of government. Federations comprise both an overarching national or central government and a set of regional or sub-national governments: provinces in Canada, states in the United States, *Länder*[1] in Germany, cantons in Switzerland. But France also has its departments, Italy its regions, and Britain its local governments—and these are **unitary**, not federal, states. What, then, distinguishes federal from unitary political systems?

Federal Versus Unitary States

In 1963, the UK Parliament passed the *London Government Act* creating the Greater London Council (GLC) as a new level of local government for the huge metropolitan area of London. In 1985, the Conservative

---

1.   Literally: 'lands'—equivalent to states or provinces elsewhere.

government of Prime Minister Margaret Thatcher abolished the GLC to eradicate a bastion of persistent Labour opposition.[2]

In 1980, the Canadian government introduced an ambitious new National Energy Program that fixed domestic oil prices and secured a larger share of the rapidly growing oil and gas revenues for itself. This unilateral move infuriated the government of Alberta, Canada's major oil-producing province, which retaliated by imposing punitive cuts in oil shipments destined for the consumers in central Canada. Much as he might have liked to, Prime Minister Trudeau could not simply abolish the renegade western province as Thatcher had the GLC. Instead, he had to relent and negotiate a compromise. The difference separating these two cases is federalism.

Delegated Versus Sovereign Powers

The United Kingdom is a unitary state. Parliament holds supreme legislative power. Local government—of which the GLC was the largest and most important example—has traditionally been entrusted with significant administrative and regulatory responsibilities. However, these powers exist only as long as and to the extent that Parliament so decides; they are **delegated** powers that can be withdrawn at any time.

By contrast, Canada is a federal state. Legislative powers are divided between the national government and the provincial governments, and this division of powers is guaranteed by the Constitution. Neither level of government can unilaterally alter the powers of the other. *In a federal system of government, sovereignty is shared and powers divided between*

FIGURE 2.1
Contrasts: Some Unitary and Federal States

Unitary	Federal
United Kingdom	United States
France	Germany
Sweden	Switzerland
Netherlands	Belgium
Italy	Spain
New Zealand	Australia
China	India
Chile	Brazil

2.   The GLC was reinstated in 2000, after the Labour Party had returned to power under Prime Minister Tony Blair.

two or more levels of government each of which enjoys a direct rela-
tionship with the people.[3] Some of these divided powers can be shared
or delegated to another level. But they are sovereign powers, and such
arrangements require mutual consent and cannot be imposed by one
level of government.

Two Tiers or Three?

In most federations there are three, not just two, levels or tiers of
government. Typically, though, this privileged constitutional status does
not apply to the third level. Local government is subordinate—existing
and operating on the basis of delegated powers as if in a unitary system.
This is the case in such federations as Canada, Australia, and Germany,
where local governments are periodically reshuffled and where the
actions of local government are always liable to be overridden by their
provincial, state, or *Länder* governments. Even in Switzerland, where
local government has long been the foundation of political life, the
communes—as they are called—do not enjoy a constitutional status on
par with the cantons. At the other extreme, India remained a two-tiered
federation until constitutional amendments in 1992 addressed this most
un-Gandhian neglect of local self-government.[4] Over the last century
and a half, many of the US states have entrenched the status of their
local governments within their own constitutions; however, those local
governments remain entirely outside the federal union itself, which recognizes only the state and national governments.[5]

Appearance Versus Reality

In Figures 2.1 and 3.1 we identify various of the world's federations.
Some federations are, however, a good deal less federal than others, and
indeed some are federations in little more than name. Argentina, Nigeria,

---

3. Scholars of federalism have shown a surprising difficulty over the years in agreeing
   on the definition of their subject. For some discussion, see William H. Riker, "Federalism," in Fred I. Greenstein and Nelson W. Polsby, eds., *Handbook of Political
   Science*, Vol. 5 (Reading, MA: Addison-Wesley, 1975).

4. Amendments 73 and 74 introduced a requirement into the Constitution that the
   states establish and maintain systems of rural (the *panchayats*) and urban local
   government. This occurred as part of a general shift away from a top-down philosophy of economic development.

5. The American Constitution does not acknowledge the existence of local government.
   The subordinate status of municipal government in the United States was most
   famously expressed in "Dillon's rule," an 1868 decision of the Iowa Supreme Court
   that quickly established itself as authoritative. Under the movement for so-called
   Home Rule, the majority of states have created constitutional space within their
   systems of government for formal recognition of local government authority.

Malaysia, and even Austria[6] describe themselves as federations while being so centrally dominated in design and practice as to be little short of unitary states. In a number of cases, federal appearances were erected on a non-democratic base. Under such circumstances a large gap between appearance and reality is inevitable; democracy is a necessary condition, a *sine qua non*, of federalism. "In a strict sense, only a system that is a constitutional democracy can provide *credible guarantees* and the institutionally embedded mechanisms that help ensure that the lawmaking prerogatives of the subunits will be respected."[7]

Federal or Confederal?

The genius of federalism is that it creates a balance between national and subnational governments. As we shall explore later in this book, such a balance typically evolved out of experiences with much looser associations between constituent units. In those looser, **confederal**, arrangements member states remained the locus of sovereignty and retained the bulk of their powers, assigning a minimum of powers and responsibilities to their common government.[8] Confederations are more than alliances or leagues, but they fall short of being federations. Typically such confederal arrangements leave the central government dependent on the member states for revenue and with little scope for making domestic policy. Some confederations were highly successful and impressively long-lived. The United Provinces of the Netherlands endured for two centuries, 1581–1795, and the Swiss Republic functioned effectively for half a millennium, 1291–1803. Not all worked so well. The short-lived first US Constitution—the *Articles of Confederation and Perpetual Union* (the *Articles*)—survived less than a decade from its ratification in 1781 to its replacement in 1789 and was dysfunctional for much of that time.[9] The regime established by the *Articles* exemplified the weaknesses of such one-sidedness and, by exposing those shortcomings,

6.   See Reinhard Rack, "Austria: Has the Federation Become Obsolete," in Joachim Jens Hesse and Vincent Wright, eds., *Federalizing Europe? The Costs, Benefits, and Preconditions of Federal Political Systems* (Oxford: Oxford University Press, 1996).

7.   Alfred Stepan, "Toward a New Comparative Politics of Federalism, (Multi)Nationalism, and Democracy: Beyond Rikerian Federalism," in Alfred Stepan, ed., *Arguing Comparative Politics* (New York: Oxford University Press, 2001) 318.

8.   Murray Forsyth, *Unions of States: The Theory and Practice of Confederation* (Leicester: Leicester University Press, 1981); Frederick K. Lister, *The Later Security Confederations: The American, Swiss, and German Unions* (Westport, CT: Greenwood Press, 2001).

9.   Individual states acquiesced to congressional requisitions of soldiers and money, for instance, only insofar as they judged it to be in their own material interests to do so and by 1786 had all but ceased supplying Congress with essential funds. Keith L. Dougherty, *Collective Action Under the Articles of Confederation* (Cambridge: Cambridge University Press, 2001).

FIGURE 2.2
The Constitutional Continuum

Sovereignty most centralized		Sovereignty most dispersed	
Unitary state —— Federation ——	Confederation ——	League ——	Alliance

paved the way for more durable arrangements. "Confederations ... are usually stepping stones to a federal state."[10]

Hybrid Qualities

An interestingly ambiguous case is the European Union. The EU is more than a confederation because significant powers have been transferred to a European level of governance. Moreover, these powers do not just regulate the conduct and relationship of the member states, as they are known; rather, they apply directly to individual citizens and businesses and can be enforced by the European Court of Justice. At the same time, the EU is not a fully developed or conventional federation because the member states still retain most traditional powers over domestic and foreign policy and dominate revenue collection. In addition, the union treaties that establish the scope and dimension of supranational authority cannot be changed without the consent of all member states. Thus, the EU has been called a case of "confederal federalism."[11]

Confederal tendencies can also be detected in more conventional federal systems. In Canada, for instance, certain amendments to the Constitution require unanimous approval by all provinces. One of the characteristics of confederations as distinct from federations is that they deviate little from the unanimity principle. If the constituent member units remain the locus of sovereignty, then coercion is scarcely an option. Unanimity imposes a very high level of constraint, though, and once sovereignty is shared between the two levels of government and a federation is created, the unanimity requirement is generally superceded by a more practical majority principle.

Centralization and Decentralization

This fundamental difference between unitary, federal, and confederal states must be distinguished from **centralization** and **decentralization**. The UK, for example, has traditionally been a very decentralized unitary state, leaving the regulation and administration of many policy areas to local self-government. Sweden is another example of a decentralized unitary state. France, on the other hand, has been the very embodiment

---

10. Forsyth, *Unions of States* 208.
11. John Kincaid, "Confederal Federalism and Citizen Representation in the European Union," *West European Politics* 22:2 (1999).

of a unitary and centralized state, keeping administration of the regional departments under strict national supervision.

Centralization and decentralization are likewise to be found among federal states. In the Federal Republic of Germany, most legislative powers are concentrated at the national level and, for this reason, Germany has even been called a "unitary federal state." Another of the classic federations, Australia, has also become highly centralized. By comparison, Canada is a notably decentralized federation. Provincial governments have aggressively resisted any erosion of their constitutional powers, and they have even been able to extend them in a number of policy areas. The EU, finally, must be considered as an even more decentralized federal system. Important political powers are still held entirely by the member states, and the process of integration depends on their agreement.

In short, while federal systems are distinguished from unitary states by their constitutional division of powers, centralization and decentralization describe the character and dynamic of power allocation. More generally, the basic difference between a decentralized federal system and a confederal system is this: decentralization denotes a condition, or a process, whereby the distribution of powers between the two levels of government tilts in favour of the lower level; confederalism denotes a constitutional form in which the member states retain constitutional primacy. At some point, though, this distinction breaks down. When centralization reaches the point that the sub-national governments are little more than administrative units—as is largely the case in Malaysia for instance—then federalism has assumed the status of a veneer.

FIGURE 2.3
An Indicative Centralization Continuum

Centralized	De-Centralized
India — South Africa — Germany — Australia — United States — Switzerland — Canada	

NB: It is important to emphasize that this is indicative only. There are various indices of centralization/decentralization and they will rank countries differently.

Principles and Practice

What should have become clear by now is that federalism is something both quite simple and rather complicated. On the one hand, it simply means divided government and power-sharing in countries or larger political communities which, for whatever reason, do not possess a unitary form of government. These relatively simple principles then translate into a few typical forms of organization. On the other hand, there is an almost infinite variety of federal states and federal arrangements similar to the considerable variety of unitary parliamentary regimes and arrangements.

What is confusing is that there is only one term, federalism, which comprises both a commitment to federal principles (like liberalism, which denotes a commitment to liberal principles) and the existence of complex federal arrangements in practice. Collapsing these two meanings into one discourages a critical examination of how well federal practices live up to their principles.

GROUP IDENTITY

Modern democratic states are universally constructed on the principle of **liberal individualism**—the proposition that individuals rather than groups or communities are the bearers of rights and duties and that individual liberty is the primary objective of policy. Federalism presents an alternative to that principle by giving status to communities. In doing so, however, it privileges one form of collective identity over others.

Relationships and Communities

What liberal individualism cannot explain is why there should be nations and states in the first place. The existence of such powerful collective identities is simply taken for granted, and, except for a radically libertarian position according to which all human beings are world citizens, individual freedom and identity find their limits within the boundaries of the nation-state.

Federalism as a broad social philosophy challenges this position by assuming that forming relationships and communities is part of human nature. Belonging to one or several communities is regarded as part of individual liberty and identity. In other words, the most general principle of federalism holds that human beings possess by nature individual as well as group identities. The purpose of politics, then, is to organize and protect both individual and group liberties. The nation-state is one—and obviously one very important—community in which citizens find their group identity, but it is by no means the only one. Federalism responds to these assumptions by constructing political systems in which a balance is maintained between different forms of identity, individual, local, regional, national and, increasingly, transnational.

Territorial Bias and Historical Logic

One critical weakness of the federal position already becomes apparent here. Primarily conceived as an alternative to, and critique of, the unitary territorial nation-state, federalism typically recognizes only group identities that are *territorial* in nature.

Historically, this is understandable because in the past, localities and regions were also social communities where people were *at home*, formed most of their social relationships including marriage and kin-ship, and engaged in the economic exchange of goods and services. In the modern world, however, identities have begun to extend beyond, or cut across, such spatial communities. In modern political discourse, they are usually identified as communities of class, gender, and ethnicity, but one can easily think of others such as environmental groups or the entire range of plural interest organizations more generally.

Federalism and Pluralism

Federalism then differs from pluralism in two significant ways. On the one hand, it is *more* than pluralism by formally recognizing group iden-tities as legitimate and autonomous participants in the political process. On the other hand, it is *less* than pluralism by limiting this recognition to spatial communities only. Political organization, it has been said, is the "mobilization of bias. Some issues are organized into politics while others are organized out."[12] Federalism, in its classical territorial form, tends to organize issues and conflicts of territoriality into politics, while organizing out issues and conflicts that are social in nature.

The federalist recognition of group identity in the organization of politics is therefore incomplete. It can accommodate the social concerns and identities of citizens only when these happen to coincide with regional boundaries, by pitting, for example, richer and poorer regions against one another within a federation. It does not adequately deal with the inequalities and differences that exist within regions or across regions. In other words, territorial federalism usually disregards groups of citizens who may have a common interest or identity but live dispersed across territory rather than concentrated in one part of it.

Bridging the Gap

One way classical federal states have dealt with this problem is to universalize social policy in national welfare programs, leaving to regional self-government only those issues that are considered regional in nature, such as education and culture. But, given the mobility of modern life, the regional boundaries of such issues increasingly appear unclear, and the assumption of a clean separation between social and cultural issues becomes contested.

Functional Representation

Another way of dealing with this problem of social and spatial incon-gruity is to extend the federalist recognition of group identity to social

---

12. E.E. Schattschneider, *The Semisovereign People: A Realist's View of Democracy in America* (New York: Holt, Rinehart and Winston, 1960) 71.

constituencies. This has been considered occasionally in theory and practice, but it certainly is not part of the mainstream tradition of federalism.[13]

The essence of this idea is one of **functional** rather than territorial representation. The standard argument against it is that territorial representation is all-inclusive by definition and therefore democratic at least in a formal sense, whereas functional representation either includes some groups and leaves out others, opening the door to conflicts over who is in and who is out, or becomes unmanageable because unlimited numbers of groups will claim collective identity and special representative status.

Recent Innovations

It need not necessarily be so. In Belgium, for instance, there are three cultural communities: Walloon (French), Flemish (Dutch), and German. These have been recognized by the new constitution, and they have been given self-governing powers over matters of education, language, and culture. For the exercise of these powers, the members of each community elect their own governing bodies regardless of where they live. Similarly, the idea of some form of non-territorial federalism has been proposed for Indigenous people in Canada.

In the EU, governance by the Council of Ministers is complemented not only by a Committee of the Regions but by an Economic and Social Committee comprising representatives of business, labour, and other civic organizations appointed by their national governments. These committees have only a consultative role in European decision-making, but at least they are being heard. Nowhere is it suggested that functional representation could or should entirely replace territorial representation, and it is not recognized as a conventional or even desirable institutional element of federal systems. Yet it may become an inevitable solution for problems of fair representation and inclusion in divided societies.

DIVIDED POWERS

In pre-modern times, most people lived in small communities that were relatively autonomous and isolated from one another. There was no concept of exclusive territorial sovereignty. This situation changed with the rise of territorial absolutism from the seventeenth century onward. The process of territorial state-building occurred gradually over several centuries. Only the Industrial Revolution eventually provided the means for effective centralization in the second half of the nineteenth century,

---

13. See David J. Elkins, *Beyond Sovereignty: Territory and Political Economy in the Twenty-first Century* (Toronto, ON: University of Toronto Press, 1995).

and only then did it become necessary to redefine the plurality of peoples, regions, and communities as one homogenous body politic. Citizenship came to be defined in terms of individual rights and duties regardless of social class, region, or any other form of group identity. A powerful ideology of nationalism was forged, making one people out of societies that in reality still continued to live in relatively autonomous spheres of social life. For the first time in history, they had to speak the same language; abide by the same laws; and use the same currency, weights, and measures. The centralized territorial state had finally become the centralized territorial nation-state. Group identities continued to exist, of course, but they were no longer recognized as units of political self-determination.

It is this notion of unitary centralized territorial governance that federalism rejects. This should not be surprising given the federalist commitment to group identity as a principle of social organization. As in the pre-modern political tradition, political power remains divided among different levels of government. Typically, the constituent units—provinces, states, or cantons—retain 'traditional' powers over culture, language, education, and welfare. The national level of government, on the other hand, assumes responsibility for the more 'modern' tasks of regulating trade and commerce, alongside such traditional ones as foreign policy and defence.

Self-Determination and Democratic Control

Dividing powers and responsibilities between two levels of government has been supported as desirable on a number of grounds. These propositions constitute one side of a normative debate about the virtues of federalism.

Self-Governance Arguments

One set of these arguments might be summed up in the adage that 'the government closest to the people governs best.' It is an argument about governmental and democratic efficacy and comprises the following claims:

- In a large and complex modern polity, decisions should be made at the level of government with the best local knowledge. Not everything is most effectively managed from the centre.
- Citizens have more control over the governments that are closer to them and thus democratic accountability is greatest.

A second set of arguments is based on the principle of local or regional **self-determination**. This comprises the following claims:

- More locally based governments can tailor policies to local tastes. Historically different regions, for example, can have different sets of cultural policy while still being equal parts of one large national market.
- More locally based government gives subnational communities greater ability to protect and advance their local economic interests.

Constitutionalist Arguments

A third set of arguments are constitutionalist in nature. Federalism disperses power between two levels of government in a way that gives citizens much greater protection against the tyranny of any one government. It also creates multiple jurisdictions within one nation-state, thereby creating what Hirschman described as "exit" options for citizens and businesses.[14] In parliamentary regimes, federalism contributes a major mechanism for the dispersal of power. Indeed it may contribute *the* major mechanism. The fusion of executive and legislative branches in parliamentary systems may mean, depending on its form, that there is little constraint on the **majoritarian** exercise of power. A federal division of powers can address that problem. In presidential regimes, the vertical division of powers complements and reinforces the existing horizontal **separation of powers** between the executive, legislative, and judicial branches of government—providing a "double security." When ratification was being sought for the US Constitution and the "compound republic" it was creating in 1788–89, this was exactly the argument made by those who called themselves "Federalists"—most notably by James Madison:

> In the compound republic of America, the power surrendered by the people, is first divided between two distinct governments, and then the portion allotted to each subdivided among distinct and separate departments. Hence a double security arises to the rights of the people. The different governments will control each other; at the same time that each will be controled by itself. [*sic*][15]

Entanglement, Duplication, and Obstruction

What sounds like a great idea in principle, though, contains a number of problems in practice and what shows up as an attribute from one point of view looks like a deficiency from another. Federalism has generated its share of criticisms.

Virtually everything identified as a virtue of divided jurisdiction may also be viewed as a vice. While subnational governments may be closer to their citizens, they are also in a position to divert criticism on to external scapegoat. In addition, policy making and administration are burdened with coordination and duplication problems, and governments

---

14. Albert O. Hirschman, *Exit, Voice, and Loyalty: Responses to Decline in Firms, Organizations and States* (Cambridge, MA: Harvard University Press, 1970).

15. Alexander Hamilton, John Jay, and James Madison, The Federalist (various publishers), 1787–88, No. 51. Here we use the edition edited by George W. Carey and James McClellan (Indianapolis, IN: Liberty Fund, 2001).

may jealously guard their jurisdictional prerogatives rather than compromise their powers for the larger good. Accountability, transparency and efficiency may all be impaired as a consequence.[16] While federalism allows accommodation of local tastes it may also protect parochialism—and permit local majorities to tyrannize over local minorities. While federalism may help local communities advance their own economic interests, it may also make possible an unproductive balkanization of the national economy. And the Madisonian argument for **limited government** through separation and division of powers is only attractive to those opposed to majoritarian democracy.

Modernization and the Balance of Powers

If federalism means that each level of government limits the other, powers must be roughly equal. Over time, however, most new political problems arising from processes of economic modernization have come to be defined as national problems requiring national solutions.

As a consequence, most federal systems have become more centralized during the era of modern nation-state politics. Rather than insisting on changes in the existing divisions of power, national governments made use of constitutional clauses assigning to them the general responsibility for welfare and good government. In this, they were often aided by judicial decisions interpreting such clauses broadly in their favour. But they also found support in the national media competing for the largest possible readership and audience, and from increasingly national societies and nationally oriented businesses that had come to rely on national policies.

Canada is somewhat of an exception to this. The sustained vigour of Québec nationalism has prevented a wholesale erosion of provincial powers in the name of modernized socio-economic efficiency, and the ownership of natural resources has provided the provinces with additional political clout more generally. To the extent that the Canadian political economy still relies heavily on the extraction and export of natural resources, one could argue that centralization did not occur precisely because delayed economic modernization did not render these traditional regional powers as insignificant as the constitutional designers might have thought.

Only a short while ago, this provincial resistance against the centralizing dynamic of modernization could be denounced as an "unprecedented betrayal of the national interest."[17] In the meantime, a change of mind

---

16. For example, see Fred Cutler, "Government Responsibility and Electoral Accountability in Federations," *Publius* 34:2 (2004).
17. Garth Stevenson, *Unfulfilled Union: Canadian Federalism and National Unity*, 2nd ed. (Toronto, ON: Gage, 1982) Preface.

has taken place, and not only in Canada. As economic internationalization begins to curtail the sovereign powers of nation-states, regions and localities are rediscovered as important socio-economic actors in their own right. They are the ones most directly affected by the investment and location decisions of multinational corporations and are therefore in need of strengthened rather than diminished powers over economic and social policy.

CONSTITUTIONAL GUARANTEES

Because it provides a legal point of reference for the division of powers as agreed to among the constituent members of a federation, a codified ('written') constitution is an essential part of a federal system. The particular purpose of constitutions in federal systems is to spell out as precisely as possible how the powers are allocated to different levels of government and the procedures to be followed for this allocation to be altered. These principles and provisions are meant to safeguard political stability in federal systems. As we shall discuss in Chapter 10, this reliance on constitutional regulation has invited an equally strong reliance on the courts for adjudication. One issue, finally, that defies all principles of balanced political stability is secession: is federation a one-way street or can member units revoke their commitment?

Allocation of Powers

As we shall discuss at greater length in Chapter 6, there are a number of basic ways in which powers can be divided. In the American case, only the powers given to Congress are listed, with the assumption that all other powers remain the preserve of the states. The Canadians chose separate lists for both levels of government and added a provision that intended, by contrast, to give **residual powers** to the central government.

Earlier constitutions—the American and the Canadian—enumerated only a relatively small number of general powers. This created problems of interpretation and unintended **concurrency**. Later constitutions such as the German and Indian learned from this by making lists much more detailed and by adding specifically enumerated lists of joint or concurrent powers. Typically, in these cases, the courts have been much less involved in adjudicating power conflicts.

An Alternative to Enumeration

Finally, the principle of **subsidiarity**, as particularly developed and practised in the EU, intends to replace concurrency—the idea that both levels of government can freely and competitively legislate within the same policy field—with a political process of negotiated and flexible power-sharing within each policy field and according to specific criteria of democracy (as close as possible to the people) and efficiency (the policy goal cannot be attained by individual member-state action). This again opens up room for judicial interpretation in case an agreement cannot be found.

Principles of Amendment

The most intricate question in any federal system is that of constitutional amendment—the question of who has the power to change the existing division of powers, to alter the terms on which the union was established. Typically in federal systems, constitutional change requires agreement of both levels of government. Powers cannot be taken away or modified without consent.

High Thresholds

In most federal systems, this means that a majority or even **super majority** of the provinces, states, cantons, or *Länder* have to agree to the change—three-fourths of them in the case of the United States. In other words, constitutional change can be brought about against the will of one or a few constituent member units, but it cannot be achieved by simple majority. In particularly asymmetrical federations such as Canada, not even that is good enough, and unanimity is required for particularly sensitive issues pertaining to the preservation of language and culture. In Switzerland and Australia, **double majority** requirements are in place instead. All constitutional changes have to be decided by the people themselves, in a referendum requiring not only a majority of the national population as a whole, but majorities in a majority of the cantons or states.

Prohibitions

Federal constitutions do not guarantee the continued existence of federalism itself, though they seek to guarantee that a derogation from federal principles and even the abandonment of those principles will only occur on the basis of a broad 'federal' consensus. The West German Constitution ("Basic Law") of 1949 is an interesting example in this respect. It laid down, in Article 79, that the federal nature of the German republic cannot be altered under any circumstances. Federalism in Germany, in other words, acquired the status of a fundamental and inalienable political right. In all other federations, in theory agreement could be reached to change the constitutional form of the country from a federal to a unitary one. Given both the vested interests and powers of the governments involved and the commitment to federalism among most populations, that is an unlikely eventuality.

Right of Secession

There is one issue that seems to defy the legal wisdom of constitutional guarantees: separatism or secession, the desire and right of one part of a country to sever political ties with the rest. This is not a problem restricted to federal systems, but it is a problem more innate to federations. In federal systems, the region in question already possesses rights of political autonomy; its government can promote, fuel, and channel the separatist agenda; and there may be a sense that having entered a union voluntarily, a member should have the right to withdraw.

The federal constitution of the old Soviet Union was the only one to recognize a formal right of secession. Within the context of Soviet totalitarianism this was a meaningless provision because in reality such decisions would be made by the supreme leaders of the Communist Party. Regionalist and separatist movements have sprung up everywhere since the late 1960s, and the question of whether a democratic federal system must allow secession as a last resort is a very real one. If Québec can argue, for example, that the existing division of powers, or in fact any conceivable division of powers short of full sovereignty, will not be able to protect the constitutionally guaranteed autonomy of francophone culture and society, then on what grounds can such separation be denied in a modern democratic world?

Force of Words, Force of Arms

These questions have been played out for as long as federal associations of any sort have existed. One of the distinguishing features of federal as distinct from confederal unions is that the presumption of permanence or irrevocability is much stronger in the former. Logically, if member states retain the great proportion of their sovereignty in a confederation, then they are as free to undo the ties as they were to make them in the first place.[18] In a series of debates and conflicts that culminated in the murderous Civil War of the 1860s, the Americans were forced to confront the question of whether such confederal liberties had been carried over into the new union or whether it was now indeed a "perpetual union." The secessionist view, as foreshadowed by John Taylor and expounded by John C. Calhoun, insisted that the Constitution be interpreted according to 'original intent'; that it operated on the basis of a **concurrent majority** whereby national majorities could not steamroller local majorities; and that the union had been created through

---

18. Forsyth, *Unions of States* 141–43.

a revocable **compact** between the states.[19] Quite deliberately, then, the procedure for secession replicated the original procedure for ratification—with the Confederate states electing constitutional conventions to decide the issue.[20] A thoroughly worked-out philosophical position provided the necessary underpinnings for drastic action, but in the end, it was military force, not intellectual reason, that decided the issue. Victory in the Civil War allowed the Supreme Court to rule that the Confederate governments had no legal basis, since "the Constitution, in all its provisions, looks to an indestructible union, composed of indestructible States."[21] Winners get to write the rules.

Constitutional Conundrums

The war between the American states is an extreme case, but not the only one. In 1933, Western Australians voted overwhelmingly for secession in a state-wide plebiscite. Philosophical claims took a back seat to practical grievances in Western Australia's campaign for secession from the Commonwealth, and there was never any suggestion that extra-parliamentary or extra-constitutional methods would be employed.[22] The conundrum faced by discontented Western Australians was: how do you secede from a federation constitutionally when constitutional provision for secession does not exist? Since the covering clauses of the Australian Constitution are actually outside that constitution but within the Imperial *Constitution Act*, secession required British endorsement if it was to be conducted legally. Without the support of the Australian government, however, such endorsement could not be, and was not, forthcoming.[23] Again, then, the move was defeated by force, though this time political, not military.

---

19. John Taylor, *Construction Construed and the Constitution Vindicated* (Richmond, VA, 1820) and *New Views of the Constitution of the United States* (Washington, DC, 1823); John C. Calhoun, *Disquisition on Government* (1840; Indianapolis, IN: Bobbs-Merrill Educational, 1953).
20. Forrest McDonald, *States Rights and the Union: Imperium in Imperio, 1776–1876* (Lawrence, KS: University Press of Kansas, 2000) 190.
21. *The State of Texas v. White* et al., 74 U.S. 700 (1869).
22. See Parliament of Western Australia, *The Case of the People of Western Australia in support of their desire to withdraw from the Commonwealth of Australia established under the Commonwealth of Australia Constitution Act (Imperial), and that Western Australia be restored to its former status as a separate self-governing colony in the British Empire* (Perth: Government of Western Australia, 1934).
23. See Gregory Craven, *Secession: The Ultimate States Right* (Carlton: Melbourne University Press, 1986).

Principles and Procedures for Secession

The philosophical incompatibility between principles of liberal democracy on the one hand, and practices of forcible inclusion on the other, has provoked considerable recent attempts to build a normative 'theory of secession.'[24] A right of secession is strongly implied by the liberal principle of national self-determination: a people have the right to ascribe to themselves a national identity and to govern themselves on that basis.[25] If it is a moral right, though, it follows that it must be conducted morally. Secession must follow procedures that protect the national majority against blackmail (that is, reduce the scope for 'strategic bargaining'), ensure that the democratic basis is indeed there, and protect minorities who may be part of the collateral damage. One procedural element might be a requirement for some sort of referendum super majority.[26]

Secession is legitimate if it is moral, and moral if it is constitutional. This in turn begs the question of whether federal constitutions should contain an exit clause to provide for such contingencies. No democratic federal constitution has ever made place for such a device. Even the constitution of the secessionist Confederate states in the American South made no allowance for secession from their secessionist union—though that was in all likelihood because the right was regarded as implicit or self-evident.[27] Generally, federal constitutions are construed as precluding secession and contain references to such things as the "indissoluble"[28] nature of the union they are creating. This was unequivocally expressed in the debates over the Indian Constitution, where it was asserted that since the new system of government was being created out of an existing union and was not being created by a compact between the States, "no State has the right to secede from it."[29] At the other extreme, though, one must note the radically new stance taken by the new EU Constitution which not only expressly grants a right of secession, but does so in unconditional terms. Section I-60(1) reads: "Any member state may decide to withdraw from the European Union in accordance with its own constitutional requirements."

---

24. For example: Allen Buchanan, *Secession: The Morality of Political Divorce from Fort Sumter to Lithuania and Quebec* (Boulder, CO: Westview Press, 1991); Percy B. Lehnig, ed., *Theories of Secession* (London: Routledge, 1998); Margaret Moore, ed., *National Self-Determination and Secession* (New York: Oxford: Oxford University Press, 1998).

25. For example: Kai Nielsen, "Liberal Nationalism and Secession," in Moore, *National Self-Determination and Secession*.

26. See: Buchanan, *Secession*; and Daryl J. Glazer, "The Right to Secession: An Antisecessionist Defence," *Political Studies* 51:2 (2003).

27. McDonald, *States' Rights* 204.

28. Preamble to the *Commonwealth of Australia Constitution Act* 1900 (UK).

29. Quoted in Granville Austin, *The Indian Constitution: Cornerstone of a Nation* (Oxford: Oxford University Press, 1966) 192.

However, the EU remains, as we have noted, a singular case. It is fair to say that a new benchmark for constitutions was set by the Supreme Court of Canada in its ruling in the 1998 *Reference re Secession of Quebec*, which we shall discuss in Chapter 9. There the Court asserted that the rest of Canada has an obligation to negotiate with Québec if a clear majority of voters in that province elects unambiguously to separate. Under such conditions, secession could be effected through the existing procedures for constitutional amendment. These recent intellectual and political developments serve to remind us that federalism is about negotiation; the federal state is a negotiating state.

NEGOTIATING COMPROMISE

Permanent deliberation among multiple participants is not just a practical consequence of the federal division of powers, it is a basic federal principle in its own right. To talk about matters of mutual concern is of course a basic principle in any political system. The very word parliament for instance, means a 'place to talk.' Yet while modern parliaments talk a lot, they do not have to negotiate seriously as long as a clear governing majority is in place. Parliamentary debates serve all kinds of useful democratic purposes—for example, providing information for the public about the opinions of government and opposition or facilitating the openness and accountability of government action to the people's elected representatives. But this type of parliamentary talking does not typically influence legislative outcomes to any great extent. That matter is decided behind closed cabinet doors or in coalition agreements among several governing parties, and it is often preconfigured in promises made during election campaigns. There may be formalized hearings with a multitude of interest groups as well. In the end, however, the one government in power decides and is held accountable.

Overlapping Authority

Federalism is based on the division of powers among several governments. If these all legislate without regard for the others, the result would be political chaos more often than not. The powers of federalism can hardly ever be organized into watertight compartments; they typically overlap, compete, and sometimes contradict one another.

Negotiations among the different governments of a federation are obviously necessary for coordination in practice. They are also part and parcel of the federal creed. If the governments of a federation represent different group identities with different sets of preferences, these can only be **harmonized** through negotiation, not through the administering of majority votes on the basis of rights. The question is of course whether there are substantively different sets of preferences in modern mass societies, and whether what is being negotiated are in fact the interests of different group identities or just the power interests of different governments.[30]

Bicameralism

There are again two principal ways in which federal negotiations can be organized. One is through participation of the subnational units in national law-making. Federal systems characteristically have **bicameral** legislatures at the national level. A lower house or chamber represents the national population, and an upper house or second chamber represents regional populations by province, state, *land*, or canton. Bills have to be passed by both houses. If there are conflicting national and regional interests, negotiations about some form of compromise have to take place in order to pass any legislation at all. In Germany, a Mediation Committee plays the central role in negotiating legislative compromise between the lower house, the *Bundestag*, and the upper house, the *Bundesrat*.

Bilevel Bicameralism?

Bicameralism is not reciprocal; that is to say, there is no participation of the national government in law-making at the subnational level. The reason is easy to see: according to the rationale of power division in federal systems, the subnational units are supposed to pass legislation on matters that pertain only to themselves, whereas the national level passes general legislation pertinent to all parts of the country.

Bicameralism may or may not be practised at the subnational level of federal systems. Neither the German *Länder*, nor the Canadian provinces, nor the Swiss cantons have upper houses; they are all **unicameral**. Subnational governments of that type are usually less restrained by the need of negotiating compromise than federal governments. On the other hand, with the sole exception of Nebraska, all the American states have an upper house; similarly, with the sole exception of Queensland, all the Australian states are bicameral.

In light of the responsibilities that municipalities carry in modern urbanized societies, it would be very much in line with the idea and principles of federalism to extend bicameralism to the regional level more fully. Municipalities and rural districts could find representation in provincial second chambers, and neighbourhoods reflecting the ethnic and social mix of urban society would be represented more formally in city councils.

---

30. As, for instance, argued in Canada by Alan C. Cairns, "The Governments and Societies of Canadian Federalism," *Canadian Journal of Political Science* 10:4 (1977).

Intergovernmental Relations

The other way of negotiating compromise is based on **intergovernmental relations**. This is the very term that has given federalism much of its bad name. In Canada, it is associated with grandstanding in front of television cameras, highly politicized conferences among first ministers, last-minute deals behind closed doors, and public disenchantment with the entire process. In the United States, it stands for a near-chaotic degree of incoherence in distributive pork-barrel politics. In Germany, it has been deplored as a decision-making trap because the political interlocking of decision-makers at different government levels will result in second best solutions or even indecision.

Ties that Bind

Nevertheless, intergovernmental negotiation is one of the indispensable tools of political practice in federal systems. Governance on the basis of divided powers would be unthinkable without cooperation, coordination, and negotiated compromise. In all federal systems, there is an ongoing process of intergovernmental relations at all levels of government and administration from the lower echelons of the civil service all the way up to first ministers. In Canada, this has been called **executive federalism.**

Communication and meetings at the staff level and among professional policy experts are the functional basis of this form of governance. Typically there are hundreds of contacts of this kind every year. It is when the ongoing intergovernmental relationships become politicized by more general disputes over the division of powers that executive federalism becomes problematic.

Such is the case in Canada where special ministries of intergovernmental relations have been added at both levels of government, and First Ministers' Conferences have become the focal point of intergovernmental disagreement and conflict. By comparison, American intergovernmental relations have remained at the pragmatic level of professional cooperation. An entirely different case is Germany where the *Länder* governments directly participate in national law-making. This leads to another distinction of the way in which federal systems organize cooperation and compromise.

Alternative Approaches to the Dividing of Powers

The character and importance of intergovernmental cooperation very much depends on how divided governance is conceived and thought of in the first place. One idea is that different government levels get discrete sets of powers and are then expected to operate more or less independently of one another or even to compete with one another. In this approach, little consideration is given to the participation of subnational governments in national policy-making. Policy coordination has to be organized after the fact, thus potentially in a more confrontational manner.

- *Divided federalism.* Since at least 1913, when the direct popular election of U.S. senators was introduced, this form of **divided federalism** has become the hallmark of the American model. Because senators represent state *voters* and not state *governments*, the latter have little if any input into congressional decision-making. Divided federalism is characteristic of American, Canadian, and Australian government, with none of those countries having a conduit in place for subnational governments to participate in national law-making.

- *Integrated federalism.* An alternative way of organizing cooperation in federal systems is to give the constituent units a direct voice in the national law-making process. This form of **integrated federalism** is the hallmark of the German model. The members of the second chamber, the *Bundesrat*, are delegates of the German *Länder* governments, often the prime ministers themselves. Since most national legislation requires *Bundesrat* approval, it already contains the kind of cooperative and coordinated compromises that intergovernmental relations elsewhere have to achieve afterwards.

SOCIAL SOLIDARITY

Perhaps the most far-reaching yet often least appreciated dimension of federalism is its inherent commitment to social solidarity. The word federalism itself comes from the Latin *foedus* which means league, treaty, or **compact**. A social compact is not a liberal contract. It means partnership, mutual aid, and protection regardless of which part is stronger or weaker. It means compassion rather than competition. A contract in turn means exchange on the basis of market competition. Typically, you only get what you can pay for. What is liberal about it is that you can choose whether you want to share or not.

A Compact of Sharing

The idea that different parts, endowed with different fortunes and resources, are to share in a federal 'commonwealth,' implies that social sharing is not excluded from the political process but is an essential part of the original federal compact. It is also different from the idea of the modern welfare state because social solidarity is not extended to individuals but to spatial collectivities—regions, provinces, states, *Länder*, or cantons. This is not a trivial distinction. What the social compact dimension of federalism guarantees is the collective social and cultural well-being of the people living in different parts of the country. The constituent members of a federal system acquire a right to economic viability and social stability.

Greater Wealth, Common Wealth

We might ask why such a commitment would be made among members of a federation in the first place. The answer lies in the original federalist compromise between the retention of regional autonomy and the development of a national market economy. Larger markets allocate resources and generate growth more efficiently but also unevenly. The desire to enter into a federal union, and the continued support for such a union, depend on a fair distribution of its benefits for all. Inherent in the federal principle, therefore, is a basic commitment to a common good.

Modern unitary welfare states are committed to such a common good as well. And, as in the case of the Scandinavian welfare states in particular, they may even be more egalitarian because of an individual and social rather than territorial bias. In federal states, by comparison, there may be policies of regional development and fiscal redistribution without much attention being paid as to how such policies affect income distribution and welfare within the subnational member units.

Regional Equalities

The idea and principle of federal social solidarity is an important one nevertheless. Take a unitary welfare state like France, for instance. It has only one dominant cultural, economic, and political centre: Paris. Everything else is provincial periphery, or, as in the case of the industrial region around the city of Lyon, it is closely connected to that centre through intensive channels of communication and high-speed transit. Almost inevitably, a successful education and career requires relocation to Paris.

By comparison, social solidarity and sharing in a federalist sense is based on a multi-centred approach to the distribution of public services and career opportunities. In federal Germany, for instance, there is no dominant centre at all, and personal careers are not dependent on whether they begin at universities in Hamburg, Frankfurt, Munich, Bonn, or Berlin. To varying degrees, federal systems are committed to the provision of equitable life chances and living conditions in all parts.

Equitable Living Conditions

Horizontal Fiscal Equalization

This provision of equitable living conditions constitutes one of the central tasks of **fiscal equalization** policies. Within reasonable limits citizens in all parts of a federation must have comparable access to public services, universities, hospitals, or cultural institutions. Because these are typically and traditionally in the power domain of subnational governance, financial resources have to be shared and redistributed. The commitment to such measures of fiscal redistribution are not equally strong in all federations, being weakest in the United States and strongest in Australia and Germany.

Regional Policy

The principle of social solidarity goes beyond fiscal equalization schemes. It comprises a general commitment to even out the differences of regional economic strength resulting from uneven resource endowment, peripheral location, and differences in population size. But it is also a commitment to correct the imbalances and inequalities arising from resources allocation in capitalist market systems. It therefore finds expression in specific regional development policies and/or the sharing and joint financing of social policy tasks. The ultimate goal, however, is not individual income stabilization but the socio-economic empowerment and stabilization of subnational collectivities.

This is also likely the most controversial aspect of federalism. Spatial equalization policies in federal systems are seen as inefficient because they override the comparative advantage principle in the market allocation of resources. Moreover, critics argue that the commitment to substantive regional transfer payments on a guaranteed regular basis creates **transfer dependency.** Peripheral governments and populations will be less compelled to find autonomous development solutions, even indulging in a kind of self-inflicted culture of poverty.

As in the case of individual welfare transfers, there is little evidence that regional populations and their governments would not want to improve on their own a situation that constrains their life chances. From a federalist perspective, however, the point is a different one. Without equalizing transfers, migration away from places of social and cultural belonging would likely be the only option. The original federal compact, however, comprises a guarantee of spatial integrity. Within reasonable limits, at least, social solidarity in federal systems is therefore an entitlement.

SUMMARY

By sharing sovereignty and dividing powers between two or more levels of government, each of which enjoys a direct relationship with the people, federalism occupies a middle position between the single sovereignty of a unitary state and the multiple sovereignties of a confederacy.

- Like unitary states, federations vary significantly in the degree to which their forms of governance and distribution of effective powers are centralized or dispersed.
- Federalism introduces a form of group representation based on territorial identity to the otherwise individualistic nature of modern liberal democracy. This does little for the wide range of other group identities existent in society unless they happen to be territorially based.
- Arguments in favour of federalism as a system of government begin with the proposition that for many functions, government closer to its citizens is most responsive, capable, and accountable. From the Madisonian point of view, federalism carries the additional benefit that it disperses power in the polity and thus neutralizes democratic excesses. In practice, many of these putative virtues may be nullified by the political skirmishing, administrative entanglements, and judicial obstruction that results from the inevitably intertwined nature of the relationship between different levels of sovereign government within a single country.
- Federalism almost necessarily entails a codified constitution to specify the relationship between the different levels of government. Among the questions this raises is how the powers will be divided, what the rules of amendment will be, and whether a constituent unit has the right to 'back out' or secede from the union.
- There is a strong affinity between federalism and bicameralism, with federations characteristically employing upper houses to provide regional representation to counterbalance the majoritarianism of the lower house. The more effectively that second chamber integrates the concerns of subnational governments into the national law-making process, the less that federation will have to rely on intergovernmental relations to resolve differences.
- While federalism creates separate territorial compartments within one country, it does not do so to the exclusion of social solidarity. The principle of federalism contains within it the principle of common welfare that is embodied in such practices as horizontal fiscal equalization between richer and poorer jurisdictions.

3 Federal Systems

A century ago, there were a mere nine federations in the world; there are now 26 (see Figure 3.1). Much of what has been called the 'federalist revolution' of the twentieth century had to do with the breakdown of colonial empires and the formation of a multitude of newly independent states after 1945. As a consequence of the opportunistic and arbitrary way in which colonial powers had assembled their possessions, most of these states brought together disparate cultures and communities. Federalism seemed to be the most promising way to accommodate this incongruence of colonial territory and plural identity.

While there were some success stories (notably India), not all of these post-colonial creations endured as stable federal systems. Some—such as the United Arab States or the Federations of the West Indies—broke apart. Others—such as Libya or Indonesia—were transformed into unitary and often autocratic systems of governance. Nigeria has only recently reemerged from military dictatorship as a fragile and very much incomplete democratic federation. A belated success story is the constitutional transformation of South Africa into a racially inclusive democratic federation after decades of apartheid.

The twentieth century also saw the rise and fall of communism. Three of the communist states—the Soviet Union, Czechoslovakia, and Yugoslavia—had been formally constituted as federations, but they were in reality held together by party dictatorships, and they disintegrated after 1989. While the Czech Republic and Slovakia divorced peacefully, the breakup of Yugoslavia with its multiple ethnic, religious, linguistic, and national divisions plunged the entire region into war and ongoing instability. Two new and fragile federations emerged—Bosnia and Herzegovina—and the union of Serbia and Montenegro. Stripped of its former satellite republics, Russia still remained the world's largest federation. In all three cases, however, the jury is still out on federalism as a stabilizing factor in a difficult phase of democratic transition and ethnic conflict.

In the Western world of industrialized nations, new federations emerged in Spain and Belgium; devolution has set the UK on the slippery slope to federalization; and the European Community became the European Union and escalated its process of federalization. Because some of its member states are themselves federations, the EU also can be understood as a partial federation of federations. Such is the case with the Republic of Bosnia and Herzegovina which comprises the Federation of Bosnia and Herzegovina as well as the *Republika Srpska*.

FIGURE 3.1
The World's Current 26 Federations in Order of Formation

Formed Pre-Twentieth Century	Formed Twentieth Century
1789 United States of America	1920 Austria
1824 Mexico	1948 Germany (Federal Republic)
1830 Venezuela	1950 India
1848 Switzerland	1958 European Community (EU 1993)
1853 Argentina	1963 Malaysia
1867 Canada	1963 Nigeria
[1871 Germany (2nd Reich)]	1971 United Arab Emirates
1889 Brazil	1973 Pakistan
1901 Australia	1978 Spain
	1979 Micronesia
	1983 St. Kitts and Nevis
	1993 Russia
	1993 Belgium
	1995 Ethiopia
	1995 Bosnia and Herzegovina
	1996 Comoros
	1997 South Africa
	2003 Serbia and Montenegro

NB: This is not to say that all of these qualify as true or genuine federations.

How do we begin to make sense of such a rich diversity of federal experiences both new and old? The basic organizational and normative principles that set federalism apart from unitary political systems cannot be sufficient to describe and explain this bewildering array of federal systems in practice. In this chapter, therefore, we want to provide some analytical order. First, we shall introduce some categories or criteria of federal organization. These will then be used to focus on the analytical description of a small number of basic models of federalism. Finally, we consider some contextual variables affecting institutional choices as well as the dynamic and stability of the political process in federal systems.

FIGURE 3.2
Failed Federations

Dismembered	Became unitary states
Soviet Union (1918–91)	Libya
Czechoslovakia (1948–92)	Indonesia
Yugoslavia (1946–91)	
United Arab States (1958–61)	
West Indies (1958–62)	

ANALYTIC CRITERIA

Observation suggests a number of binary distinctions that can be used to classify federations. Since these are ideal types, their purpose is heuristic, and they cannot be assumed to provide a precise empirical template.

- *Rationale.* The world's federal systems have their basis in either cultural diversity or merely a territorial division of powers.
- *Form of government.* A federation may have either a presidential or parliamentary form of government.
- *Bicameralism.* Second chamber representation can be based either on the senate or on the council principle. Senators represent regional populations; council members represent regional governments.
- *Division of powers.* The mode in which powers are divided between the two levels of government is either legislative or administrative, according to whether subnational governments make their own laws or mainly implement and administer overarching national laws.

The different ways in which these features are combined in any federation will in turn influence the pattern of intergovernmental relations that prevails. Some federations are characterized by a more competitive relationship between the levels of government, others by a more cooperative one.

Cultural or Territorial Basis?

Most federal systems have been the result of compromise among competing elites. In some federations, that compromise was about different cultural interests such as language, religion, or, more generally, distinct cultural histories. In these cases of **cultural federalism**, federalization has arisen out of the desire to build a strong union without giving up regional cultural autonomies. Examples are Switzerland, Canada, Belgium, and India.

Switzerland, for instance, is subdivided into 17 German, four French, one Italian, and four plurilingual cantons. In Canada, the dividing line runs between nine Anglophone provinces and the Francophone province of Québec. The Belgian Constitution recognizes four linguistic regions: French, Dutch, German, and the bilingual capital region of Brussels. In

India, some of the original territorial divisions have had to be revised along linguistic lines—a contingency allowed for in the Indian Constitution.

The rationale of cultural federalism is the establishment and maintenance of cultural peace. While most federations were based initially on a compromise between modernizers seeking economic advantages in a national market economy and traditionalists adamant about the retention of regional cultural autonomy, cultural differences have ceased to be the driving force of compromise in a number of federal systems. Instead, such federations have simply retained a territorial division of government.

These are cases of **territorial federalism**. In Germany, for instance, traditional cultural cleavages between the Protestant north and Catholic south are no longer relevant political factors. The 50 states of the United States of America are culturally diverse, to be sure, but at least in comparative perspective, this diversity is not a prime factor in American federalism. The Australian federation was constructed on the basis of territorial rather than cultural principles of autonomy from its very inception. There are many unitary states with greater regional differences than Australia.

The rationale for the retention of territorial federalism is both democratic and pragmatic. Americans, for instance, insist that the vertical division of powers brings government closer to the people. They also simply accept federalism as a fact of political life.

Presidential or Parliamentary?

While a number of hybrids now exist, the distinction between presidential and parliamentary forms of government remains fundamental to the understanding of modern systems of representative government. In parliamentary systems, the executive branch is formed in and responsible to the legislative branch. Thus 'fused' with the legislative branch, the executive also plays a strong and quite possibly dominant role in the legislative process. In presidential systems, the executive branch is formed separately from, and is not accountable to, the legislature. Thus separated, the executive branch does not enjoy a direct role in the legislative process.

The Separation and Division of Powers in the United States

The American constitutional framers strongly believed in the idea of dispersing power among different branches of government. Constructing a system of checks and balances at the national level of government, they created a bicameral Congress with co-equal powers vested in the House of Representatives and the Senate and an executive branch that would derive its legitimacy directly from popular election as well. Together with the vertical division of powers between the national and state governments, this separation of powers creates a combination of multiple horizontal and vertical checks and balances that Alexander Hamilton, John Jay, and James Madison dubbed the compound republic when extolling the virtues of the new Constitution in *The Federalist* papers of 1787–88. It allows us to speak of American federalism as a case of **plural federalism**. The dispersal of power is generally regarded as the ultimate source and guarantee of democratic stability. This was the model followed by the Latin American federations.

Parliamentary Fusion and Division of Powers

Federalism also operates in tandem with parliamentary rule—though the affinity is weaker—and several federations are embedded in the tradition of Westminster or British parliamentary government. These cases of parliamentary federalism are characterized by the fusion of executive and legislative powers. Prime minister and cabinet sit on the front benches of Parliament and are supported by a party majority. Typically, the upper house of the legislature is weaker by virtue of the fact that the government is formed in the lower house. The main examples of this type of government are Canada, Australia, and India. Germany also falls within the category of parliamentary federalism, although it has some variant characteristics deriving from the strong role of its second chamber, as we shall discuss below.

Contrasts

The dispersal of powers in presidential federal systems leads to a more pragmatic governing style within a pluralized configuration of overlapping or cross-cutting interest cleavages. The federal division of powers and the dispersal of power in the presidential form of government can be seen as complementing operational principles. The fusion of power at both levels of government in parliamentary federal systems can lead to a more confrontational governing style because parliamentary majorities at both levels of government are vested with exclusive political legitimacy. Federalism and parliamentary majority rule therefore can be seen as potentially conflicting operational principles.

Senate or Council Representation?

One of the basic principles of federalism is bicameral representation at the national level of government. Typically, there is a lower house or first chamber representing the population of the entire federation and an upper house or second chamber representing the constituent member units—states, provinces, cantons, or *Länder*. But there are two very different kinds of second chamber organization.

The Senate Approach

One is based on the **senate principle**, whereby the people of the constituent units rather than their governments are represented in the upper house. This is the American approach, though it was arrived at somewhat ambiguously in the United States. Direct election was chosen for the upper house in Australia and adopted shortly thereafter by the Americans.[1] In such systems, two forms of popular representation operate in parallel. The members of the lower house jointly represent the entire population of the federation on a straightforward **majoritarian** basis; the members of the upper house, on the other hand, represent regional populations. They have a mandate that is as free as the mandate of lower house members. In particular, they are not bound by instructions or any other form of guidance from state governments. The principles of vertical power division and **divided federalism** are maintained.

The underlying rationale of the senate principle is to complement the democratic principle of individual equality (one person, one vote, one value) with the principle of member unit equality. The constituent units of the federation are to be given *equal weight* in national law-making regardless of whether they are large or small. Consequently, they are represented equally in the second chamber. By comparison, representation in the lower house follows the principle of proportionality. The more populous states have more representatives and votes than smaller states. The senate form of second chamber representation can also be found in the Latin American presidential federations.

The Council Approach

The other method of second chamber representation is based on the **council principle** which has its roots in the distinctive German federal tradition. The members of the German *Bundesrat*, or Federal Council, are instructed representatives of the *Länder* executive governments. In accordance with the principle of **integrated federalism**, these representatives of the *Länder* participate directly in national law-making. In doing so, however, they represent the people only indirectly.

Council representation also does not follow the American example of equal representation regardless of population. Instead, it is based on a formula of **weighted** representation. The larger *Länder* get more votes than smaller ones. The underlying rationale is a compromise between principles of proportionality and equality. The larger *Länder* have more voting power than the smaller ones, but even smallest *Länder* still have more votes than they would be accorded on a proportional basis of population.

---

1.   In 1913, ratification of the Seventeenth Amendment introduced direct election for the American Senate.

The German approach to federal bicameralism has been historically unique. However, its distinctively federal quality makes it enormously important. From a comparative perspective, its principal significance stems from the fact that it has become the chosen form of governance in the EU where the Council of Ministers dominates the decision-making process. Its strongly federal character has also given it broader appeal and been the reason for its adoption in the new South African Constitution. In both Germany and South Africa, it is intrinsically associated with a particular approach to the division of powers between the two levels of government (see below, administrative federalism).

Half-Way House: Legislative Election

Until 1913, US senators were elected by their respective state legislatures. In a presidential system, where legislatures are quite separate from the executive branch, this falls into the category of popular rather than governmental representation. In parliamentary systems, such a practice is more ambiguous. Legislative election is widely practised in modern federations and falls somewhere in between the senate and the council models. Austria, India, and Spain have all retained legislative election for their upper houses. In cases of strong regional political cultures— that is, when regional politics differs substantively from that of the country as a whole—this form of second chamber representation can be seen as a hybrid of popular and government representation. To the extent that legislatively elected senators are not instructed how to vote, this compromise approach more closely approximates the senate rather than the council model.

How are Powers Divided?

Given that federalism is first and foremost about creating multiple levels of government sharing powers and responsibilities, one of the most important distinctions between federations must be the approach they take to dividing those powers and responsibilities. It turns out that there are two basic alternatives: dividing powers or dividing functions.

Legislative Federalism: Division of Powers

In the original American design of **divided federalism**, once again, the idea was to separate national and subnational policy domains. The responsibilities of the central government included such overarching national concerns as monetary policy, trade and commerce, and foreign and defence policies. The responsibilities of the subnational governments included such local concerns as culture, education, physical infrastructure, and social policy.

Under this system constructed in terms of a **legislative division of powers,** each level of government is responsible for policy-making in its entirety—from policy initiation and formulation to legislation and on to implementation and administration. Citizens are therefore confronted with two separate strands of public administration (or three in instances of local government jurisdiction). Most federations have followed this pattern of legislative federalism

Administrative Federalism: Division of Functions

While American or Canadian citizens must establish which level of government to go to for any particular public service, German citizens have no such need. With few exceptions, German federalism involves only one strand of public administration. Nearly all administrative tasks in the federation are carried out by the *Länder*. As in more orthodox federations, the *Länder* are autonomous in the administration of their own exclusive legislative power. However, they also are responsible for applying most national laws and delivering most services. In doing so, they possess considerable discretion for policy implementation and execution.

In general terms, then, Germany adopted a quite different **administrative division of powers.**[2] Most legislative powers are concentrated at the national level, and most administrative powers have been given to the *Länder*. National legislation is framework legislation specifying general policy goals. On the basis of these, *Länder* legislation is focussed on implementation and administration.

This division between national legislation and *Länder* administration does not render the original federalist idea of divided powers obsolete or even weakened. The rationale is one of **integrated federalism.** By directly participating in national framework legislation, via the *Bundesrat,* the *Länder* governments can insist on formulations and provisions that leave considerable flexibility for adoption and execution across the country. One could see this as a backward linkage in intergovernmental relations: program coordination happens before the legislative dice have been cast. Divided federal systems, by comparison, are limited to forward linkages in this sense: program coordination has to be achieved on the basis of already existing legislation. In a desire to accommodate the realities of modern federal governance, the South Africans expressly chose this German path of integrated federalism with an administrative division of powers and a council-style second chamber. The South

---

2. Germans speak of *Verwaltungsföderalismus* (administrative federalism); see Thomas Elwein and Joachim J. Hesse, *Das Regierungssystem der Bundesrepublik Deutschland* (Opladen: Westdeutscher Verlag, 1987) 80.

African Constitution stipulates that a system of "cooperative federalism" should prevail.[3]

MODELS AND VARIATIONS

In the real world of the 26 existing federal systems, these categories of federal organization combine in many different ways, and it would be a daunting task to sort them all in systematic fashion. Fortunately, it is possible to focus on a few cases which have served as basic models for most others.[4]

- *The American model* was deliberately designed as a radical break with the British parliamentary tradition. As the oldest model of modern federalism, the United States also became an important template and the principal comparative yardstick for all others.
- *The Canadian model* is characterized by its retention of the parliamentary form of government. Such has been the case in all other British colonies that became federations subsequently, such as Australia and India in particular.
- *The German model* is distinguished by the design of its second chamber as a council rather than senate. Rather than a deliberate departure from the American model, it has its roots in a continental European tradition that is considerably older than the American.
- *The EU* may be considered a model in its own right. While it is not yet a fully developed federation in the conventional sense, its inclusion is warranted insofar as it may indeed be a model character for a new type of federalism in a globalizing world.

FIGURE 3.3
Basic Models and Categories

Model	Rationale	Form of Government	Second Chamber	Division of Powers	Inter governmental Relations
American	territorial	presidential	senate	legislative	cooperative
Canadian	cultural	parliamentary	nominal	legislative	competitive
German	territorial	parliamentary	council	administrative	cooperative
EU	cultural	[council governance]	council	administrative	cooperative

3. Nicholas Haysom, "Federal Features of the Final Constitution," in Penelope Andrews and Stephen Ellman, eds., *The Post-Apartheid Constitutions: Perspectives on South Africa's Basic Law* (Johannesburg, SA and Athens, OH: Witwatersrand University Press and Ohio University Press, 2001).

4. This schema differs somewhat from Daniel Elazar's suggestion that "There are three principal models of modern federalism; [*sic*] the American system, the Swiss system, and the Canadian system." See his *Exploring Federalism* (Tuscaloosa, AL: University of Alabama Press, 1987) 42.

The American Model

Beginning with the American model poses some analytical danger. For good historical reasons, on the one hand, it is the model for all federal systems it was the pioneer, the innovator. Although federalist ideas and concepts had been developed much earlier, it was the American success in transcending the conundrum of confederal government that gave the world a simple and practical blueprint to be followed in theory as well as in practice. On the other hand, American federalism has in many ways remained an exceptional case. To treat it as the main model and principal yardstick, and to judge all other federations as variations which either fulfill or fall short of the criteria it established, bears the danger of shortchanging the significance of the other models in their own right.

Specificities

In no other federation is there such a strong ideological commitment to individual liberalism. In most other cases, the relationship between individualism and federalism is typically perceived as an ongoing tension between individual freedom and the regional autonomy of provinces, cantons, states or *Länder*. In the United States, federalism is mainly seen as a governmental mechanism in which all powers play their constitutionally assigned part of promoting individual freedom.

For this reason, American federalism is predominantly **territorial federalism**, with its emphasis on plural power dispersal and not on the balance of power among two different territorial constituencies, nation and states. The horizontal division of powers between the two congressional chambers and the presidency is more jealously watched politically than the balance of power between national and state governments. Final adjudication of the latter is left to the courts.

The Presidential System of Government

The American model also provides the prime example of **presidential federalism**, a system of government that combines the separation of powers between the branches of government with the division of powers between levels of government. By some interpretations the strong congruity between the separation and the division of powers qualifies the United States as the one example of true federalism. Federalism, in this view, is a full package of "interlocked" principles whose purpose is to ensure limited government though the fragmentation and dispersion of power.[5] Certainly, two features of the separation of powers do have a strong affinity with federalism's multi-level governance. One is the way an executive government not dependent on the legislative branch facilitates strong bicameralism (see Chapter 7). The other is the way a powerful judiciary exercising the function of judicial review is intrinsic to both the logic of separation of powers and division of powers (see Chapter 10).

Direct popular election removes the American president from the federalist power equation. The president is both the governing chief executive and the representative head of state. By comparison, the status and power of prime ministers in parliamentary federations appear more limited because of the fusion of their executive powers with those of the national parliament. The horizontal separation of powers among the branches of government in presidential federations makes it easier to suggest federal reforms affecting the balance of powers between the two levels. Such suggestions are not immediately perceived as politically self-serving. The primary concern of American presidents is not their relationship with the states, but their relationship with Congress.

Senate Bicameralism

The institutional core element of American federalism is the bicameral Congress. The country as a whole is represented according to population in the House of Representatives. The states are equally represented in the Senate. The two houses have co-equal powers in all matters of domestic legislation. Since the introduction of direct popular elections in 1913, senators are elected by state populations and not state legislatures. For this reason, senate representation in the American model maintains the divided form of federalism. It modifies the democratic principle by adding a second manifestation of the popular will to the legislative process. But it does not contribute to intergovernmental coordination, since state governments have no direct access to the process of national law-making.

Legislative Division of Powers

The American model is one of legislative federalism. Each level of government legislates in its own sphere of jurisdiction. However, the relatively simple formula of dividing powers in a constitution dating back to 1787 has lost much of its originally intended meaning. That meaning had been to give to Congress a limited number of explicitly enumerated

---

5.   Douglas C. Verney, "Are All Federations Federal? The United States, Canada and India," in Balveer Arora and Dougles C. Verney, eds., *Multiple Identities in a Single State: Indian Federalism in Comparative Perspective* (New Delhi: Konark, 1995).

powers: over trade and commerce, the monetary system, foreign affairs, and defence. Everything else was to be left to the states.

With the rise of modern socio-economic complexity and the welfare state, Congress absorbed more and more responsibilities. Since the Constitution was not changed, and could only be changed with great difficulty, it had to rely on expansive interpretations of its existing powers by the Supreme Court. With the help of these, and on the basis of its superior revenue-raising capacities, Congress began to govern by means of a proliferating grant system that transferred funds to states and localities. Most of these were conditionally tied to compliance with federal policy goals and objectives. The American model in its current form therefore must be characterized as one of congressional legislative supremacy.

Intergovernmental Relations

As a corollary, governance came to rely on an intensive network of **intergovernmental relations,** an expression often used coterminously with American federalism itself. Hundreds of grant programs require interaction and coordination at all levels of government. Inevitably, American federalism is **cooperative federalism.** Historically, the design had been focussed on the constitutional separation of legislative powers as well as on competition among the two levels of government in the use of their exclusive responsibilities. But precisely because of this strictly divided constitutional form, pragmatic and cooperative intergovernmental relations had to become the hallmark of American federalism in practice.

It is important to emphasize again that this cooperation almost entirely takes place under the aegis of congressional supremacy. In return for grant money, the states cooperate in the implementation and administration of national policies. There is no formal cooperation or state participation at the level of congressional law-making. Because of this dependency of state finances on congressional regulatory impositions, some observers have even suggested that American intergovernmental relations have moved from cooperative to coercive federalism.[6]

Despite this constant meddling of congressional policy-making in the affairs of states and municipalities, the American model remains the most decentralized and unregulated among the major federal systems. In particular, there is no formal commitment to providing American citizens with a common standard or level of public services across the country. Despite their dependence on hundreds of mostly conditional grants, the states have remained free to legislate with great variability in all areas not pre-empted by the Congress in the name of national interest.

6.   See John Kincaid, "From Cooperative to Coercive Federalism," *The Annals of the American Academy of Political and Social Science* 509 (May 1990).

The Canadian Model

American federalism started with a bang, as a deliberate break with the political traditions of the British Empire, and as an exercise in constitutional invention. Federalism in the British Dominions emerged later, in an evolutionary rather than revolutionary fashion, and as constitutional adaptation. Most importantly, the Canadian case involved an integration of federalism with the conventions of responsible parliamentary government that, by the mid-nineteenth century, had been established as the Westminster system. Canada provided the first example of the uneasy relationship between parliamentary majority rule and federalism.

Cultural Rationale

The main purpose of federation was the creation of a British North American union. Federalism was the only option for a political settlement between English Canada and Québec. Federal rather than consolidated union was unavoidable in Canada for cultural reasons—reasons that remain fundamental to Canadian federalism. Not unlike Americans, English Canadians tend to regard federalism as a structural device either promoting or inhibiting their individualist aspirations. Individual liberalism among French Canadians may be as strong as anywhere else, but it is complemented by a much stronger commitment to collective cultural identity. Federalism is only acceptable to them if it succeeds in the promotion of individual opportunity as well as collective identity. It is the accommodation of this ambiguity which has made Canada such a difficult case of successful federal governance.

There is a strong sense of regional identity in other parts of the federation as well, and it is compounded by socio-economic asymmetry. The western provinces have resented their historical role as resource hinterlands. Piggy-backing to some extent on Québec's persistent quest for autonomy, the two westernmost provinces—Alberta and British Columbia—developed an aggressive strategy of province-building that includes efforts at emphasizing cultural differences more in line with American values south of the border than with the rest of the country.[7]

A final and perhaps most significant indicator of a cultural-regionalist rationale at the core of the Canadian federal dynamic is the lack of a national party system. Regionalist party formations competing both at the provincial and the national level have not only sprung up in Québec but also and even earlier in the west. In the case of Québec, their agenda is clearly linked to the cause of cultural self-determination. In the West,

---

7.   See Keith Brownsey and Michael Howlett, eds., *The Provincial State in Canada* (Peterborough, ON: Broadview Press, 2001).

they have been expressions of protest against national policy choices dominated by the larger electoral base in central Canada.[8]

Weak Bicameralism

What about the second chamber—how was it designed to provide federal as distinct from majoritarian representation? The designers of the Canadian model ostensibly did provide for that by according to each of the four principal regions—Ontario, Québec, the Maritimes, and the West—the same number of senators. But the Canadian Senate is a government-appointed body lacking any real political legitimacy in a democratic age. This oddity of incomplete bicameralism, with a **senate** construction more reminiscent of the British House of Lords than its American counterpart, leaves the Canadian federation without any authoritative form of provincial representation at the national level.

In this respect, therefore, the model character of Canadian federalism is limited. It has provided the first historical instance of combining federalism with parliamentary majority governance. Yet it has done so by giving legislative powers to a federal parliament unchecked by a horizontal separation of powers. This loyalty to the British tradition has been one of the main sources of regional discontent within the Canadian federation. Ironically, it has weakened rather than strengthened the forces of centralization in Canadian federalism because it provided the Canadian provinces with a legitimate reason to pursue their own legislative options more aggressively.

Legislative Division of Powers

In principle, the Canadian model follows the American approach of legislative federalism. Each level of government is responsible for legislation, implementation, and administration within its respective sphere of jurisdiction. In order to avoid any ambiguity, however, there are two lengthy lists of powers for each level of government, and residual powers are assigned to Parliament rather than to the provinces. In design, this was intended to make Canada a more centralized federation than the American approach was intended to be; however, for reasons we shall explore later, this proved not to be the case.

Intergovernmental Relations

For two main reasons, intergovernmental relations play a much more politicized role in Canada than in the United States. One is the lack of

---

8.   See Lisa Young and Keith Archer, eds., *Regionalism and Party Politics in Canada* (Don Mills, ON: Oxford University Press, 2002).

legitimate regional representation and participation at the national level. The other has to do with the much more regionalized nature of the federation. Despite the centralist intentions of its designers, the Canadian Constitution has not provided Parliament with anything resembling legislative supremacy. As a consequence, the Canadian model is characterized by a need for direct political negotiations about common goals and objectives at the executive leadership level. Most prominently, these are conducted in so-called First Ministers' Conferences, chaired by the prime minister and attended by the provincial premiers. The results of these meetings then have to be approved by the respective legislatures.

This style of intergovernmental policy-making is for the most part competitive. There are competing visions about the true nature of the Canadian model, one more centralist and the other more regionalist. These fundamental differences tend to infuse First Ministers Conferences with a sense of political drama. The competitive nature of the Canadian model is further intensified by the asymmetry of overlapping conflict lines—between the central government and the provinces; between English Canada and Québec; and between the resource-rich provinces in the West, the manufacturing heartland, and the transfer-dependent provinces in Atlantic Canada.

This is not to suggest that intergovernmental relations are entirely competitive or conflictual. There are also notable areas of cooperation. In contrast to the American case, the operation of Canadian federalism essentially relies on intergovernmental agreements on tax collection and program and cost sharing. For some national government programs, there are so-called opting-out provisions whereby individual provinces can run their own programs in return for a greater share of tax revenues.

Such flexibility is characteristic for the Canadian model more generally. It combines a high degree of provincial autonomy with an equally high commitment to the provision of universal social policy services and a constitutional requirement for fiscal equalization.

The German Model

That there is a German model of federalism at all is somewhat of a surprise. The federal union of 1871 was an arrangement among territorial princes under Imperial Prussian hegemony. The democratic Weimar Constitution of 1919, while maintaining the federal form, hollowed out much of the traditional *Länder* autonomy. Then, under Hitler and the Nazis after 1933, Germany was transformed into a totalitarian dictatorship. And finally, when West Germany was reconstructed as a federal republic after 1945, the new Constitution was crafted under Allied supervision and American control in particular.

A new beginning under such conditions, one might assume, should have led to the adoption of the American model. For two main reasons, it did not. First, the Constitution was essentially drafted by representatives of the already re-established *Länder* governments. Secondly, these constitutional designers were influenced by a German federal tradition that went back much further than 1919 or even 1871. It is a tradition that is in fact older than American federalism. It is also significantly different.

Territorial Rationale

Germany's first federal rather than merely confederal arrangement, the Second Reich of 1871, had strong cultural underpinnings. The continued popularity of Germany's dynastic rulers was closely linked to their role as benefactors of regional bourgeois societies.[9]

The reconstruction of West German federalism after 1945 clearly followed a rationale of territorial federalism. Cut off from the Prussian, more Protestant, and more agricultural regions in East Germany, the West German republic became very homogeneous, socially as well as economically. Most of the new *Länder* boundaries were redrawn artificially. While following an old tradition as well as the demands of the Western Allied powers occupying the country, West German federalism was clearly meant to serve as a structural tool for democratic consolidation as well as against any new attempts to centralize power. Despite some initial fears to the contrary, the predominantly territorial character of the German federal model was not challenged by reunification and reincorporation of East Germany after 1990, even though there is now a more significant split of interests between rich and poor *Länder*.

Parliamentarism

Over time, the German model also found its own way of combining federalism with parliamentary majority rule. Under Bismarck's federal scheme, the Imperial (*Reich*) Parliament had only limited powers. In particular, the Chancellor, Bismarck himself, was appointed by, and accountable to, the Emperor, and not to Parliament. During the Weimar Republic, the introduction of full parliamentary democracy proved unstable. The pure proportional electoral system produced a superfluity of parties, and government majorities were defeated from one day to the next.

In order to provide more stability, a system of modified parliamentary federalism was established in 1949. Its most innovative feature was the so-called constructive vote of non-confidence. In between elections, the government can be defeated only if the Parliament elects a new federal chancellor—defeating government bills is not enough. Chancellor and

---

9.   Because of these vested interests in the preservation of decentralized plurality, every major city in Germany still today has, for instance, its own government-subsidized concert hall and opera house, some 95 altogether.

cabinet also do not sit with their parliamentary colleagues but face a semicircle of all parliamentarians.

Council Representation

By far the most significant characteristic of the German model, however, is establishment of the second chamber as a council rather than senate. The linchpin of federalism in the Bismarck Constitution had been the *Bundesrat* (Federal Council), a dynastic upper chamber with full legislative powers. In the West German *Bundesrat*, these dynastic rulers have been replaced by representatives of the democratically elected *Länder* governments. The German *Bundesrat* therefore directly represents government interests and popular interests only indirectly. This does not necessarily mean that it is less democratic than a directly elected senate, though. German voters have learned very well to understand the impact of *Länder* elections on the composition of the *Bundesrat* and, consequently, on party competition and policy choice in Germany's bicameral system of administrative federalism.

Administrative Division of Functions

This system of administrative federalism also has historical origins. From the very beginning, the Bismarckian arrangement had been more centralized than those of the other three federations at the time—the United States, Switzerland, and Canada. Under Prussian hegemonic pressure and Bismarck's leadership, the territorial princes consented to an ever-growing list of Imperial powers. In exchange, they received or retained nearly all powers of policy implementation, allowing them to establish impressively growing *Land* administrations which in turn sustained the respect and loyalty of their subjects.[10]

In addition, of course, they also had joint control over all Imperial legislation. During the years of the Weimar Republic, this control was reduced to those legislative acts particularly affecting constitutionally protected *Länder* interests, and this is how it was taken over into the postwar West German Constitution.

It is this system of interlocking powers in the national legislative process that more than anything else distinguishes the German model of **integrated federalism** from American- or British Dominion-style divided federalism. Most national legislation requires approval of the *Länder* governments in the *Bundesrat* before it is then implemented by the *Länder* administrations.

---

10. See Gerhard Lehmbruch, "Party and Federation in Germany: A Developmental Dilemma," *Government and Opposition* 13:2 (1978).

The integrated nature of the German model finally also accounts for its highly cooperative style of policy-making, the central institution of which is Parliament's **mediation committee** (see Chapter 7).

Intergovernmental Relations

There are no fundamentally conflicting visions about German federalism between the *Länder* and national governments. The high level of centralized regulation with regard to such major policy domains as taxation and social and environmental standards also makes interregional competition less pronounced than in most other federations. Serious intergovernmental conflict erupts only occasionally when different party majorities exist at the two levels of government. The opposition can then block legislation by using its combined majority of votes in the *Bundesrat*. Only on occasion have German federal governments succeeded in breaking such blockages by striking deals with individual *Länder* governments across partisan lines.[11] Given the increased heterogeneity of *Länder* interests since reunification, such tactics may prove successful more often.

The combination of a highly integrated form of federalism with the parliamentary practice of party competition in the German model is not always conducive to the promotion and articulation of specific *Länder* interests. The *Bundesrat* is not so much a second chamber of regional representation as it is an alternative chamber for the articulation of national policy priorities. Even *Länder* elections are more often than not fought over national issues. Voters know that a partisan change of government at the *Land* level may result in a change of the *Bundesrat* majority which in turn may decide the fate of the national government's policy agenda.

The German model is the most tightly regulated and centralized. Given the integrated nature of the legislative process, national standards prevail in most policy fields. Tax sharing and extensive fiscal equalization are not left to political commitment but enshrined as constitutional obligations. The *Länder* governments and administrations have nevertheless maintained or even increased their status as important partners in the system.

The EU Model

At first glance, the EU's institutional arrangements look like those of a federation. There are two legislative chambers—a European Parliament representing European populations on a majoritarian basis and a Council of Ministers representing European governments. There is an executive European Commission composed and functioning much like a cabinet, and there is an independent European Court of Justice. There are also elements

---

11.   Current Federal Chancellor Schroeder scored one such success in 2000 over tax reform.

of a conventional division of powers, assigning matters of trade and commerce to the EU while leaving social policy to the member states.[12]

However, even a quick glance behind this institutional façade reveals a picture very different from the workings of conventional federalism. The European Parliament still has more limited powers than the Council of Ministers, which has the last word in all legislative matters. The Commission is a government-appointed body of policy experts. And the powers given to the EU do not include what would be considered to be the core element of federal statehood: foreign policy and defence.[13]

Nevertheless, because of its unique institutional setup, and because of its genuine supranationality in a number of core policy areas, the EU can be described and appreciated as an emerging federal system in its own right.

Cultural Rationale

Since the EU is currently composed of a growing number of member states with different histories, large variations in their social, legal and economic systems, and different languages, it can only be regarded as a case of **cultural** federalism. Its formation resembles at the European level the history of federal union at the national level in the nineteenth century. Its rationale has been based on a historical compromise between a shared desire to build a large integrated market and an equally strong commitment to the retention of cultural autonomy and self-governance. As in the case of nation-state federations, the question is whether the homogenizing forces of the market will eventually transform the federal system from a predominantly cultural one into an increasingly territorial one, or whether the EU will become the prototype of a transnational federal system that essentially remains multicultural in nature.[14]

What Form of Government?

Because it evolved from international treaty agreement, the European form of government falls into neither the presidential nor the parliamentary tradition. It can perhaps be best described as an eclectic mix

---

12. See McKay, *Designing Europe*.
13. If and when ratified, the European Constitution will change this picture even more towards federalization: there will be a common foreign minister, for example, and the European Parliament will gain co-decision rights in about 95 per cent of all European legislation.
14. The eventual membership of Turkey will give this multicultural character of the EU an even more unprecedented dimension: across continents (Europe-Asia Minor) and across world religions (Christian-Muslim).

of plural powers. The European Parliament is increasingly gaining co-decision powers alongside with the Council of Ministers. The Commission operates as a supranational executive without direct instructions from Member State governments. It holds a near-exclusive right of policy initiative and is not directly accountable to the European Parliament. The Commission President is appointed by the Council. If elected directly at some point in the future, the EU would begin to look more like a presidential federal system. Under the proposed constitution, the European Council,[15] is to be made a formal component of the EU system of government, complete with an appointed president. The European Council clearly demonstrates the treaty character of the EU and the continued reliance on negotiated agreements for its future development.

Council Representation, Council Governance

It is the construction of the Council of Ministers as a second legislative chamber representing the constituent member states of the Union that gives the European model its uniqueness. In presidential systems, as we saw in the American case, checks and balances are constructed between two equally powerful legislative chambers and a directly elected chief executive. In parliamentary systems, legislative and executive powers are fused in parliament, and second or regional chambers usually are weaker. In the case of the EU, the Council is by far the most powerful decision-making body. It is the only body with full legislative powers under the Treaties, and it controls the composition of the executive Commission. The European model is therefore one of **council** or **second chamber governance**.

The composition and operation of the Council have been patterned after the German model: a chamber of emissaries rather than a chamber of elected representatives. Member state votes are weighted according to a scale ranging from three to 29 following the ambitious enlargement that took the EU from 15 Member States to 25 in 2004. Most decisions require a super majority of some 74 per cent of these votes, which means obversely that decisions can be blocked by a minority of some 27 per cent. Moreover, there is in addition a double majority requirement that the Member States accounting for a minimum of 62 per cent of the EU population vote in favour.[16]

---

15. That is, the regular practice of European summit meetings among the heads of government—not to be confused with the Council of Ministers meetings.
16. See Table 3.2 in Elizabeth Bomberg and Alexander Stubb, eds., *The European Union: How Does It Work?* (Oxford: Oxford University Press, 2003) 53.

Procedural Flexibility

Offsetting these rather rigid requirements is the treaty-based flexibility of the European approach—another one of its distinctive features. Different matters are decided by different decision-making rules. While matters of economic and monetary union are left to qualified majority voting, other areas such as foreign and security policy still require unanimous agreement. It is also possible for individual member states to opt out of certain agreements. This flexibility also prevails in the Council itself. Typically, qualified majority voting (QMV) is avoided in cases of serious disagreement. Instead, the participants will try to achieve some compromise or package deal that is eventually supported by all.

Division of Powers and Subsidiarity

The question of power division is more complicated than in conventional federations. The EU can become active in any policy field covered by the broad objectives of the Treaties. This means that most powers are potentially shared powers. The Member States continue to legislate, but the EU can regulate as well. If and to what extent it can is a matter of the **principle of subsidiarity** whereby decisions ought to be made at the lowest possible level. To this end, before the EU can become active in any particular policy field it needs to demonstrate, by means of a political process of deliberation and negotiation, that individual member-state action cannot reach the common objective in a sufficient or satisfactory manner. The implementation and administration of European laws and regulations adopted in this fashion is then left to the member states. In this respect, the EU is a clear case of German-style administrative federalism.

Intergovernmental Relations

Given these characteristics, the spirit of European member state relations is bound to be cooperative. Of course, there are also competing national interests at work in the EU, and these are the ones that usually make the headlines in the international media. Yet at the core of the European success story lies a tremendous predisposition for cooperation and compromise, facilitated by the partial nature of the European project. While the general goals and objectives of market integration enjoy broad support in all parts of Europe, supranationality has to date stopped short of most nationally sensitive policy fields including foreign, security, and social policy.

More importantly, again, the cooperative spirit of the European Union is secured organizationally by an intensive network of intergovernmental committees and conferences involving the most senior levels of the national civil services. The purpose is to reach compromise before an issue becomes politicized at the leadership level. Cooperation at the leadership level in turn is enhanced by the institutionalization of regular summit meetings among the European heads of government. It is at these European Council meetings that agreements have been reached on the far-reaching treaty changes that have transformed the original Common Market into a federal system comprising economic and monetary union.

Limitations

The European model can be appreciated as an innovative and promising form of federal union for other processes and institutions of transnational integration and cooperation. The economically weaker members of the EU have certainly been given a stronger voice than in other and comparable international organizations such as the International Monetary Fund. This has resulted in a stronger focus on balancing economic integration with regional economic development and stabilization objectives than in comparable international trade organizations such as NAFTA.

At the same time, the partial and economic character of the European model has failed to provide a European public space in which Europeans can exercise their rights as responsible citizens. Matters of economic and monetary union have been removed from the member states' national scrutiny and accountability without re-embedding them in a comprehensive set of European political goals and civic objectives. The European model thus becomes subservient to the mutual accommodation of narrow economic interests only.

Imitations and Variations

The United States, Canada, and Germany provide the main models of federal systems; the others can now be considered as instances of imitation and variation. They have either adapted one particular model to their specific needs, or they have combined elements from different models. The EU is an exception in this context. Its system of council governance is itself a variation of the German *Bundesrat* model, but it remains to be seen to what extent its idiosyncratic mix of institutions and procedures will provide a model character in a globalizing world of integration and fragmentation.

Variations of the US Model

The US model has been adopted and imitated most extensively in Latin America. In terms of the institutional setup, the federal systems of Mexico, Venezuela, Brazil, and Argentina are strongly American in character—as is their choice of presidentialism rather than parliamentarism. **Hispanic federalism,** however, has been driven by a much more centralist dynamic owing to these countries' colonial tradition of authoritarianism, Catholicism, and clientelism. Authoritarian parties and military dictatorships used the federal structures of regional administration as transmission belts for their nationalist projects. However, the same federalist structures have more recently become opportunity structures for democratization from below.

A surprising case of imitation is Switzerland. Although by far the oldest federation in the world, with a lineage extending back to the thirteenth century, modernizing elites essentially adopted the American model of second chamber representation when Switzerland changed from confederal to federal governance in the nineteenth century. Swiss federalism then evolved as a mix of American constitutionalism, direct democracy, consociational power-sharing, and German-style administrative division of powers. All constitutional changes require approval in a popular referendum. The system of governance is not based on party competition but instead on a grand coalition of all major parties representing different ideologies as well as the linguistic and regional diversity of the country.

Variations of the Canadian Model

We speak of a Canadian model because Canada was the first federation established in the British Dominions and because it was the first to combine a federal division of powers with the retention of Westminster-style parliamentary governance. The two most prominent and subsequent cases are Australia and India. Both followed Canada's example of parliamentary federalism, yet both rejected Canada's choice of a government-appointed senate. While the members of India's upper house are chosen by the state legislatures, Australia opted for a popularly elected upper house.

Variations of the German Model

Significant elements of the German model are found in the Austrian system, notably the preference for an administrative rather than legislative division of powers. As already explained, the German model of council representation has found its way into the design of council governance in the EU. More recently, South Africa has adopted it in its first post-apartheid democratic constitution as well. The reason is similar for all three cases. In Germany, the *Bundesrat* model first evolved from agreement among dynastic rulers. In the EU, council governance similarly was the outcome of intergovernmental agreement among its sovereign Member States. And in South Africa, the choice of a National

Council of Provinces rather than a senate-type regional chamber reflected the need to reconcile the continued presence of strong tribal leadership at the regional level with the desire to give the country a unified policy framework.

CONTEXTUAL VARIABLES

These categories and models of federalism provide important information about how federal systems work, how stable they are, and what their major critical weaknesses might be.

- A competitive style of policy-making based on cultural difference and combined with a lack of regional participation in the federal legislative process as in Canada, for instance, may inevitably be a weak formula for stability.
- By comparison, the combination of interlocking legislative powers with a functionally divided system of administrative federalism in a culturally homogeneous country such as Germany may produce too much of the opposite, a formula for creeping unitarism undermining the federal balance.

But of course there are other features that affect the stability and performance of federalism.[17] A few of these contextual variables will be discussed briefly in this section: the **geographical size** of a federation, the **number** of constituent units, and the degree of demographic and socio-economic **asymmetry**.

Size and Population

Federations vary enormously in geographic and demographic size, and there seems to be no general pattern that would make stability predictable. There are or have been large stable federations (United States, Australia), large unstable federations (Soviet Union, Pakistan), small stable federations (Switzerland, Austria), and small unstable federations (Czechoslovakia, Yugoslavia). An argument can be made, however, that large countries are more likely to adopt a federal form of governance.

Of the world's eight largest states—Russia, Canada, China, the United States, Brazil, India, Australia, and Argentina—seven are formally constituted as federations. Intuitively, one would assume that countries of this magnitude cannot be governed, at least not democratically, without some form of federalism. Conversely, however, one might argue that for the very same reasons—size and diversity—federalism is not enough. Federalism is based on a balance of powers between two levels of

---

17. For one discussion, see Jonathon Lemco, *Political Stability in Federal Systems* (New York: Praeger, 1991).

government. Across vast distances and differences of continental dimensions, even the most perfect setup of a constitutional balance of powers may be upset by centrifugal forces.

But what are the other means holding these federal systems together? In the case of the Hispanic federations in the Americas, the long-standing practices of administrative centralism and clientelism may have provided the glue. A similar argument can be made for India. While closely following the Canadian model, the cohesion of Indian federalism has in no small part depended on corrupted and clientelist central party governance. In the old Soviet Union, formal federalism was superimposed by Marxist-Leninist party centralism. When communism collapsed, so did the Soviet Union. Whether the Russian successor federation will be able to break away from authoritarian centralism without a permanent loss of stability remains to be seen.

It may come as a surprise that similar arguments can be—and must be—made with regard to two of the most indisputably democratic large federations, the United States and Canada. In the American case, much of its political stability may be owed, just as the constitutional framers envisioned (see Chapter 4), to the plural character of the constitutional design, breaking the pattern of competing majority rule by multiple checks and balances. The establishment of a powerful and popularly elected national president in particular has proven to be a unifying factor. In addition, however, the stability of the American polity rests on the exceptionally conformist ideological mix of liberal individualism and nationalism that permeates the institutions and processes of federalism at all levels of government.

Maybe it is because most if not all of these additional variables are weaker or missing in Canada that its stability has been periodically threatened. However, as we shall see below, problems arising from its number of constituent units and socio-economic asymmetry have probably been more profound.

Number of Units

The number of constituent units of which federations are composed has ranged from two (the former Czechoslovakia) to 50 (the United States). Some of the geographically largest federations are subdivided into only a few units (six states and two self-governing territories in Australia); some of the smallest federations contain a large number of units (26 cantons in Switzerland). There is no general correlation between size and number of units. But there may be one between number of units and stability.

Stability Considerations

The main argument has been that a large number of units contributes to the overall stability of a federal system because it facilitates fluid coalition-building. The obvious example is the United States. At least since the Civil War, there have been no deeply entrenched regional cleavages, nor have the 50 states ever challenged the central government collectively. They are simply too many and too diverse for a unified stance against congressional supremacy. Conversely, from the perspective of the central government, it is easier to play a game of divide-and-rule. The patterns of fiscal grant transfers are so diffuse that a general sentiment of 'you win some, you lose some' prevails.

Proliferation and Centralization

By the same token, the argument can be made that a small number of units tends to strengthen their influence upon the overall system. They can gang up on the central government more easily. Consider in this instance Canada, where the ten provinces have succeeded—against the original constitutional intent—in wresting considerable amounts of power from the federal government. Another case may be the EU. The original Community of Six had retained a rule of unanimity in most policy areas affecting vital member state interests. Subsequent rounds of enlargement forced the increased use of qualified majority decisions and consequently a more serious decline of nation-state sovereignty.

Too Few

A final and related argument pertains to so-called 'bicommunal federa-tions' in which the number of the constituent interest parties is essentially reduced to two. The numbers game cannot be used for cross-cutting coalitions and compromises at all.

Czechoslovakia has been the most extreme case of this kind because there were indeed only two constituent units, the Czech and Slovak Socialist Republics, inhabited by two different cultural groups who were, moreover, at different stages of economic development. Soon after the end of communist rule over both parts, the federation broke up, even though the bicommunal differences were by no means extreme. Belgium is a country similarly divided between two cultural communities. In this case, however, the development led from a unitary state on the brink of a break-up, to the creation of a bicommunal federation recog-nizing both linguistic regions and cultural communities.

And finally, there is Canada again, not a bicommunal federation in terms of numbers, but deeply divided between the anglophone commu-nity mainly living in nine provinces and the francophone community predominantly living in Québec. The fact that there are more than two constituent member units has not helped to disperse the bicommunal conflict. On the contrary, Québec's main grievance in the Canadian federation is that is permanently outnumbered. This, however, is as much a problem of asymmetry as of bicommunalism.

Asymmetry

To have the constitutional status of equals assumes some underlying equalities. Where imbalances are too great, federations face ongoing challenges.

Demographic Relations

In most cases, the size and population of the constituent units in federal systems are very uneven. The size of the smallest Canadian province, Prince Edward Island, amounts to less than 0.5 per cent of the largest province, Québec. The population in the smallest German *Land*, Bremen, barely reaches 4 per cent of the most populous *Land*, *Nordrhein-Westfalen*. If such unevenness is the norm rather than the exception, it can hardly serve as a telling indicator of stability or instability.

What does constitute a problem is the concentration of nearly or more than half of the population in one part or even one constituent unit of the federation. The overpowering role of Russia in the Soviet Union was the most extreme case of this kind, as it dominated all aspects of Communist party rule and was deeply resented by all others.

But asymmetrical demographic domination is by no means a problem unknown to democratic federations. The western provinces of Canada, for instance, routinely and rightly complain that federal elections are already decided before the polling stations in the westernmost province of British Columbia have even closed. This has to do with the time zone differences in a vast country, but also with the fact that more than 60 per cent of Canadians live in the two central Canadian provinces of Ontario and Québec. The metropolitan areas of Toronto and Montreal alone have more inhabitants than the three prairie provinces of Manitoba, Saskatchewan, and Alberta taken together. Québec, of course, feels outnumbered both by demographic (some 25 per cent of the Canadian population) and cultural-provincial asymmetries (nine English against one French province).

Economic Relations

Equally significant are asymmetries of regional economic resources. Canada is the most conspicuous case again. Most of its manufacturing industries are located in central Canada, while the economies of the western and eastern provinces mainly rely on the extraction and export of natural resources. Agreeing upon a national industrial or energy policy under such circumstances is virtually impossible.

Economic disparities are affecting the stability of many federations, including such emerging federal systems as Spain and the EU. In Spain, one of the 17 so-called Autonomous Communities, Catalonia, produces nearly a quarter of the national Gross Domestic Product (GDP). Admired for its leadership role in the process of democratic federalization after the end of General Franco's long-lasting dictatorship, Catalonia's role in Spanish politics is now increasingly resented for its domineering and micro-nationalist overtones.

The dominant economic position of Germany in the EU is also watched jealously by other countries. But the real problem of asymmetry in the EU is the widening disparity gap between north and south. It will be compounded by an east-west dimension when some or most of the central and eastern European states have gained access and membership. Without a serious commitment of fiscal redistribution and equalization, a standard feature in most federal systems (see Chapter 8), the European project of market integration might yet fail.

This last section has pointed to federal systems like Canada, Spain, and the EU as particularly problematic cases of federal stability and balance. Yet the argument can also be turned around to take on a more positive note. In an increasingly globalized and interdependent world, different size, uneven numbers, and glaring asymmetries more than ever will be the contextual norm for the conduct of politics and the design of policy. If federalism can keep these polities together in cooperation or at least peaceful competition, they may indeed present a model character for the next century.

SUMMARY

This chapter has sought to identify some of the defining characteristics that distinguish different federations and some of the contextual factors that influence their operation.

- Three components of institutional design create a range of permutations and combinations. Federal systems of government can be built around either presidential or parliamentary forms of government, have either a senate-style or a council-style federal chamber, and can take primarily a legislative or an administrative approach to the division of powers.
- The American system is presidential, senatorial, and legislative. The Canadian system is parliamentary and legislative. The German system is parliamentary, council-based, and administrative.
- While the EU cannot be classified as either presidential nor parliamentary, there is no doubt that it has adopted both the system of

council governance and the system of administrative federalism that originated in the German model.

- Switzerland is an interesting variation in the way it combines an American-style senatorial bicameralism with a German-style administrative division of powers. Australia is an interesting variation in the way it combines parliamentarism with strong, senate-style bicameralism.
- The reality is that how a federal system functions is going to be as much a consequence of factors other than constitutional design. The number of units, their relative size and economic basis, and underlying cultural identities will all affect the dynamics of the system.

4 Three Traditions of Federal Thought

Where did the idea of federalism come from? Federalism is not only a description of the way power and governance are sometimes organized, it is also a set of values and prescriptions about the way communities should be structured. It thus has its own intellectual history. At the opposite ends of a wide spectrum of opinions about those origins there are two basic positions. One holds that federalism is an American invention, a unique idea and form of government ingeniously developed out of necessity for joint survival and the organization of independent political life among the 13 colonies that had won their independence from Britain in the New World. The other insists that the idea of federalism is as old as Western civilization and that federalism in practice existed throughout the ages, from ancient Israel and Greece down to the present day.

As usual, the truth probably lies somewhere in between these two extremes. There can be no doubt that the Americans came up with something new. The combination of institutionalized division of power between different levels of government, the dual representation of the people in separate legislative chambers, and the popular election of a president was without precedent. The history of modern federal government in this sense begins with the adoption of the US Constitution in 1789.

However, some of the basic ideas implemented in this constitution were much older. Federal principles and practices can indeed be traced through most of human history. Some of the city states of ancient Greece had formed quasi-federal leagues with their military allies and trade partners. Even earlier than that, according to the Old Testament, the 12 tribes of Israel united in a covenant or federal pact after their exodus from Egypt.[1] Governance in the Holy Roman Empire of the Middle Ages very much resembled that of a confederation with overlapping powers and responsibilities. And before the Americans designed their epochal

---

1. According to Daniel J. Elazar, "The principles of strong national federalism were first applied by the ancient Israelites beginning in the thirteenth century BCE to maintain their national unity by linking their several tribes under a single national constitution and confederal political institutions." *Exploring Federalism* 117.

model of federalism, some of the Indigenous peoples of North America were living under systems of multilevel governance that were federal in character.

More generally, the world of political thought can be divided into two strands. One is based on the idea of empire, power concentration, and uniformity of rule, the other on the idea of federation, power dispersal, and plurality of rule. Historical examples of the former include Persia, the Chinese and Roman Empires, and the early modern absolutist states of Western Europe. Examples of the latter include ancient Israel, Mediæval Europe, and the federal states emerging since the end of the eighteenth century.

However, it would be quite misleading to pretend that these two strands have played a parallel and equally important role in the history of political thought. Federal ideas were almost always overshadowed by those of absolutism and the exclusivity of state authority. Since the triumphant rise of the modern centralized nation-state in particular, political ideas of the past that were not seen as supportive of the modern state have for the most part been neglected.

This chapter draws out some of these federal ideas of the past. We do not need to go back to ancient Greece or Biblical Israel, but instead shall focus on those intellectual traditions more directly associated with the rise of modern federal practice. As it turns out, these traditions tend to have emerged from moments in history when groups of people felt threatened by an existing or imminent regime of centralization and/or exclusion. In this vein, we shall examine the following three quite different traditions:

- **consociational federalism** in the seventeenth century as the main political heritage of the Protestant Revolution;
- **republican federalism** in the eighteenth century as the great political invention of the American Revolution; and
- **socio-economic federalism** in the nineteenth century and beyond as one of the logical consequences of the French Revolution.

CONSOCIATIONAL FEDERALISM IN EARLY MODERN EUROPE

The early modern period in European history was a period of transition. During the Middle Ages, most people lived in small communities, and collective survival was more important than individual aspiration. There were many rulers with competing and often overlapping powers. The system was held together by a grand ideology of Christian universality. For ordinary people this meant that they were not to question their place in society and that whatever happened to them was beyond their control; misery on earth would be rewarded in the kingdom to come.

The Reformation and the ensuing religious wars destroyed this complex and fragile balance of powers. The idea of a universal Christian empire with overlapping and shared spheres of authority *across* territories gave way to the idea of exclusive authority *within* territories. In the Augsburg Religious Peace Treaty of 1555, the main territorial rulers gave themselves the right to determine what should be the exclusive religious faith in their realms. Eventually, they claimed absolute authority over all public affairs. Local autonomies were eroded as sovereign kings and princes began to reorganize their powers in absolutist states.

The Protestant Revolution

To this rise of state absolutism, Protestant minorities—in particular the Calvinists—had to take objection. It was a matter of survival. During the St. Bartholomew Day Massacre of 1572, some 20,000 Calvinist Huguenots were murdered in France. Calvinists were brutally repressed in the Spanish Netherlands. Even across the Channel, under the new Church of England, Puritans were persecuted.

These Protestant minorities became Europe's first exiled emigrant societies. They gathered in the few places that offered them security and shelter: the Calvinist Swiss cities of Basle and Geneva, the Netherlands after the success of the Dutch Revolt against Spain, and a number of smaller German territories whose dynastic rulers had turned to the Reformed faith as well. More importantly, Protestants had to find moral and political justification for survival and recognition. This meant that they had to break with the entire tradition of hierarchically organized authority. According to that tradition, there was only one God who had in turn made the Pope his sole representative on earth, and, insofar as they ruled with the Pope's blessing, kings and princes represented a divine authority that could not be called into question by their subjects.

Protestants did not immediately question the divine authority of kings as such. They argued instead that a reformed world without the Pope's supreme authority had in fact become a plural world in which all communities shared in the responsibility of defending the Christian faith. Consequently, if a ruler persecuted them, he could be seen as a tyrant disobeying God's will and forfeiting his divine right of governance. He therefore could be resisted, even deposed by force. In the second part of the sixteenth century, pamphlets were published and distributed all over Europe calling for a *right of resistance* against tyrants.

The Jewish Covenant

In order to make their claim, Calvinists had to demonstrate that plurality and control of unlawful governance were consistent with Christian scripture. They found their evidence in the biblical story of the Jewish covenant. After their exodus from Egypt, the 12 tribes of Israel gathered at Mount Sinai and concluded a covenant with God who would protect them in return for their faith. In the interpretation of the Protestants, this covenant was a federal pact between God, people, and rulers. Rulers thus gained a right to govern the people, but the people likewise gained a right to control their rulers. Both were equally responsible for ensuring that the covenant would be upheld.

The Ideology of Absolutism

This idea—that governance is shared and mutually controlled among rulers and people—constituted a dramatic turnabout in political thought. Throughout the Middle Ages there had been the idea of one universal Christian empire. When this empire fell apart, the dominant assumption was that political stability could only be established by granting each territorial ruler the kind of absolute authority pope and emperor had claimed for so long over the whole.

In Florence, Niccolò Machiavelli had written as early as 1513 that only a "new prince" empowered with ruthless leadership qualities could force the city's divided factions back together again.[2] In France, Jean Bodin—himself almost a victim of the St. Bartholomew Day Massacre—gave to the world the modern definition of sovereignty by declaring, in 1576, that for the sake of peace and stability all governing power had to be "absolute and perpetual."[3] And in England a century later Thomas Hobbes responded to the turmoil of the English Civil War by conjuring, in 1651, the powerful image of a mighty Leviathan with "indivisible" powers.[4]

The Practice and Philosophy of Pluralistic Rule

In other words, these political thinkers took the idea of empire, of universal supremacy, and reapplied it internally, as a new doctrine of exclusive sovereignty within particular territorial polities. By comparison, the Protestants were compelled to search for a more complex solution. They insisted that peaceful and stable government was possible on the basis of a pact or covenant among a plurality of autonomous groups sharing the rights of sovereignty. In doing so, they could also point to a long tradition of political practice. Despite its name, the Holy Roman Empire of the Middle Ages had been a loose confederation among a

---

2.   Niccolò Machiavelli, *The Prince* (1532; Cambridge: Cambridge University Press, 1988) XXVI.

3.   Jean Bodin, *The Six Bookes of a Commonweale*: a facsimile reprint of the English translation of 1606, corrected and supplemented in the light of a new comparison with the French and Latin texts (1576, Cambridge, MA: Harvard University Press, 1962) I.8. Originally published as *Les Six Livres de la République*.

4.   Thomas Hobbes, *Leviathan* (1651; Cambridge: Cambridge University Press, 1992) XVIII.

plurality of dynastic rulers, kings, princes, bishops, and free cities—
neither holy, nor Roman, nor an empire, as it is often said. Each entity
had its privileges and responsibilities that could not be withdrawn. This
meant, for example, that kings or princes had authority over large
territories in certain matters but that cities within these territories had
their own authority to govern themselves. Citizenship and governance
were plural and overlapping. Negotiation and compromise were the
order of the day.

But it was this idea of the biblical covenant as a federal pact that
became the backbone of the Reformed defence strategy. If the people
were directly responsible for ensuring that the covenant with God was
not violated, and therefore had a duty to control the lawful governance
of the ruler, then the primary task was to organize the people in such
a way as to put them into a position in which they could in fact perform
this duty. Apart from the covenant with God, there had to be a political
pact establishing the plurality of villages, towns, cities, and provinces
into an organized body politic. And, since it was the duty of this body
politic to watch over the lawfulness of governance right from the moment
a ruler assumed his or her position, the organization of the people into
a political body had to come before the establishment of government.
In fact, it would be up to the organized body of the people to determine
the conditions and limits of lawful governance.

Johannes Althusius (1557–1638)

A new college for the study of federal theology was founded by a
brother of William of Orange in the German town of Herborn in 1584,
the same year that William, the leader of the Dutch Revolt against
Spain, was assassinated. The school quickly became one of the leading
Reformed centres of academic learning in Europe, attracting students
from across the continent.

One of the professors at this college was **Johannes Althusius**.[5] Althusius
had studied at the main centres of Calvinist learning in Basle and Geneva.
Once appointed to teach at Herborn, he managed to get himself into
trouble with his colleagues by insisting that insofar as the second table
of the Decalogue—commandments six through ten—was about justice,
its interpretation was a matter of politics and not theology. In 1603, he
published a book on politics, the *Politica*,[6] which took up all the major
issues of the time. It justified the revolt of the Reformed Netherlands
against Catholic Spain and defended the plural structures of governance

---

5. See Thomas O. Hueglin, *Early Modern Concepts for a Late Modern World: Althusius
on Community and Federalism* (Waterloo, ON: Wilfrid Laurier University Press, 1999).
6. Johannes Althusius, *Politica* (Indianapolis, IN: Liberty Fund, 1995).

in the Holy Roman Empire. In particular, it attacked Jean Bodin's definition of sovereignty by declaring that anybody's right to govern was "neither supreme and perpetual, nor above the law."[7]

A year later, in 1604, Althusius left Herborn to become legal advisor and chief executive officer of the city council in the northern German seaport of Emden. This wealthy city wanted him to help in their struggle against the provincial ruler, a Lutheran count, whereas the city was staunchly Calvinist. Moreover, the count aspired to transform his province into a modernized state under absolutist rule, and for this he needed the taxes of his wealthiest subjects. Emden's burghers did not want to pay these taxes.

Althusius stayed in Emden for the rest of his long life, as a church elder as well as combative city politician. During one particularly turbulent episode, he had the count effectively imprisoned in his own city residence. During another, he had the count's chancellery raided. At the same time, he published several expanded editions of his book, which soon became a kind of early modern bestseller in Reformed circles all across Europe.

During the following age of absolutism, Althusius was largely forgotten, and his book was condemned as incendiary and poison for the youth by the powerful in church and state. In the late nineteenth century a German scholar, Otto von Gierke, rediscovered Althusius as the first modern theorist of federalism. From then on, his fame has grown slowly but steadily. Federalism in Germany and in the EU can be linked to some of the principles of political organization he formulated.

The First Modern Theory of Federalism

At first glance, Althusius's theory contained only a systematic account of the old plural order that was still pretty much in existence everywhere. Within the Holy Roman Empire there were independent kingdoms and principalities, and within these there were provinces and cities which also had their own statutes of privileges and self-governing rights. The emperor was superior to all this only insofar as he alone had the right to convoke Imperial assemblies. At these periodic sessions, general laws were made that held the Empire together as a whole. The main participants were the three estates—nobility, clergy, and those cities enjoying an Imperial charter. Each of these estates deliberated and voted separately. The emperor's main role was to bring them to a common understanding or consent. Majority decisions were avoided, and the emperor could not prevail over the collective will of the estates. Similar assemblies existed for the smaller territories and provinces. In the cities, there were municipal councils composed of representatives of the major guilds and professional colleges.

---

7.   Althusius, *Politica* IX.21.

This resembled a multi-tiered federal system, not unlike the EU today. There were states, provinces, and municipalities; above them was the empire as an overarching commonwealth for specific and limited purposes. A crucial difference was that the governing rights of provinces and cities depended on imperial privilege and statutes granted from above. Another difference was that not every territory and city was included with the same set of rights.

When this system became unstable in the aftermath of the Reformation and religious wars, it was the kings and princes in the larger territories who began to transform their lands into modern states. Imperial privileges were transformed into divine and absolute rights, and the autonomies of the smaller territories and cities were eroded and replaced with principles and practices of central administration.

This is what the Protestants objected to, and this is also where Althusius had to go beyond a merely systematic description of his time. Essentially, he had to demonstrate that the self-governing powers of all smaller and larger territories were natural entitlement rights, not privileges granted from above, and that they could not be changed or rescinded without their approval.

Althusius's *Politica* is a complex work eluding easy interpretation. We shall confine ourselves to an examination of three concepts that are particularly important in order to understand the federal quality of the commonwealth he had in mind: consociation, communication, and consensus.

Consociation

The *Politica* begins with a simple statement: "Politics is the art of consociating men for the purpose of establishing, cultivating, and conserving social life among them."[8] This may be simple but it has far-reaching consequences for the entire conceptualization of politics.

By Comparison: Bodin and Hobbes

Most early modern political thinkers including Bodin and Hobbes defined politics as the establishment of government authority. Of course, they were also concerned about social stability and peace, which they thought that could be brought about only by undiluted state sovereignty. Consequently, the organization of society became subservient to the principles of sovereign government. Society could develop freely only insofar as these principles were not challenged. In essence, these thinkers

---

8.   Althusius, *Politica* 1.1. The English translation of the original Latin text uses the word association instead of consociation—which, given the central importance of this concept, is regrettably misleading.

introduced the modern distinction and separation of state and society. They saw politics as a vertical relationship between public authority and private social life.

The Althusian View

In sharp contrast, Althusius conceptualized the essence of politics as a horizontal process of bringing people together in social harmony. He did not harbour naïve views about human nature, though. Conflict is inevitable, and it is the role of government to manage and moderate it. But Althusius was convinced that human beings will find reasonable ways of living together if they are provided with appropriate institutions allowing them to do so. And these he found in a plurality of smaller and larger communities with self-governing authority which he called **consociations.**

The entire commonwealth is a federal consociation of consociations. Families are kinship consociations. In cities, we find professional consociations of guilds and colleges. Provinces are made up of many such cities and the rural areas in between. The universal commonwealth finally is composed of a plurality of provinces. Thus far, this is not terribly original, and, indeed, we can easily recognize these structures and institutions in all modern societies.

The Federal Construction of the Polity

The specific federal quality of Althusius's construction comes from a number of qualifying observations. Because consociation is the most general principle of political organization, all such consociations are alike in nature. Families and guilds are as important building blocs of society as are cities or provinces. Therefore, all consociations must be recognized politically. Family interests are represented in the governing bodies of guilds and colleges; guilds and colleges are represented in city councils; cities and rural areas are represented in provincial assemblies; cities and provinces are the constituent members of the universal council or assembly of the commonwealth.

Most importantly, the entire political process is determined as *bottom-up* rather than top-down. There is no supreme ruler with the right to decide the scope and dimension of particular rights of self-governance; nor is the extent of such self-governance *a priori* limited by a superior reason of state or, in modern terms, national interest. Such reason and interest can only be determined by the constituent members of a consociation themselves.

Because "families, cities, and provinces are prior to realms, and gave birth to them,"[9] and because "every constituting body is prior and superior to what is constituted by it," Althusius came to the conclusion that by "nature and circumstance the people ... is superior to its governors."[10] What Althusius meant by "the people," however, is not a modern electorate of individual citizens. It is what he called the organized body of the people and the ascending order of smaller and larger communities or consociations which determine the political process by interacting as collectivities.

Each level of consociation has a governing council. Its members are representatives of the smaller consociations. At the city level, for instance, they are representatives of guilds and colleges. At the provincial level, they are representatives of cities and rural districts. Provincial and city representatives in turn make up the governing assembly of the universal commonwealth.

This tradition of **indirect representation** still lives on in the German model of federalism where the members of the second chamber, the *Bundesrat*, represent the governments of the *Länder*. At the time of Althusius, of course, before the advent of modern parliamentary democracy, there was no first or popular legislative chamber equivalent to the German *Bundestag*. The Althusian model therefore can be characterized as one of **second chamber council governance**.

Communication

In the second paragraph of his book, Althusius continues his explanation of the purpose of politics as the art of consociation. The members of a consociation "pledge themselves each to the other, by explicit or tacit agreement, to mutual communication of whatever is useful and necessary for the harmonious exercise of social life."[11] And a few paragraphs later, he defined communication as the mutual sharing of things, services, and rights.[12]

Specific and General Laws

By things and services, Althusius meant the activities and products of the social and economic life of peasants, carpenters, teachers, public servants, and everyone else. By rights, he meant the law of consociation including the law of governance. For each level of consociation, there

---

9. Althusius, *Politica*, IX.3.
10. Althusius, *Politica*, XVIII.8.
11. Althusius, *Politica*, I.2.
12. Althusius, *Politica*, I.7.

are general principles of lawfulness common to all and then particular bodies of law specific to the nature of the consociation.

This, too, is a tradition that lived on in the German model of administrative federalism. By contrast with the American model, powers are not divided in such a way as to create autonomous spheres of jurisdiction for each level of government. Instead, powers are divided by degree of generality. Within one and the same policy field, general or framework laws are made by the larger consociational units, while more detailed executive laws and regulations are left to the smaller units according to their specific needs and circumstances.

Communication in this context denotes a political process whereby these smaller units participate in the formulation of the more general laws governing them collectively. This is the essence of the council principle for which the EU provides the most obvious example today. In the Council of Ministers, the member states collectively decide upon the scope and dimension of European framework legislation.

Politics by Deliberation and Agreement

Communication gives expression to a deliberative character of the political process more generally. By contrast with the American model of federalism, rights and obligations are not inscribed in constitutional stone. They remain more fluid arrangements based on agreement, and they can be adapted more flexibly to changing times and circumstances. Federations such as Germany and Switzerland that have followed this tradition tend to amend their constitutions more frequently and pragmatically.

Procedural Legitimacy

Finally, communication in the Althusian sense points to an understanding of political legitimacy that is quite distinct from the modern notion of procedural legality. The legitimacy of a particular political decision or behaviour is not primarily tied to preconceived norms and procedures even if these are widely recognized and traditionally accepted. Instead, political legitimacy requires a particular quality of such norms and procedures. They must allow for a common understanding among a plurality of participants with distinct interests and needs. And this common understanding requires a continuous process of communication and deliberation.

For Althusius, politics is not a superstructure of norms and institutions separate from social life; it is part of the communication of goods, services, and rights. Politics is communicative action embedded in the entirety of social life. This is particularly important for federalism, which is based on the assumption that particular communities—or consociations—continue to exist autonomously within a larger union.

According to Althusius, they can only do so if they are actively involved in the decisions governing that union.

Consensus

Ultimately, consensus means that a particular community cannot be overruled by a majority of others. Modern federal systems have responded to this consensus requirement by means of bicameralism. In a second legislative chamber, subnational units are represented regardless of size and population, either equally or at least by giving the smaller ones additional weight. In addition, constitutional change typically requires some form of super majority in both houses and/or ratification by a substantive majority of subnational legislatures.

At the time of Althusius, consensus was a much more fundamental prerequisite for autonomy and survival. The Empire was a very heterogeneous community of communities, and there was no overriding national interest in the modern sense. Cultural and religious differences alone did not permit majority decisions on most matters. Collective action, including such matters as raising taxes for the imperial administration in particular, could come about peacefully only on the basis of agreement.

The situation can be compared to the francophone province of Québec in Canada where constitutional amendments to certain matters of language and culture require the consent of the provincial legislature. In these matters, in other words, Québec cannot be overruled. Similarly, in the EU, where the interests of the Member States still prevail over a sense of European identity, constitutional amendments are in reality treaty changes requiring the approval of all members.

Althusius had a very simple explanation for this consensus requirement: "What touches all ought also to be approved by all."[13] This is in fact an old formula borrowed from Roman Law, but Althusius gave it new and more precise meaning by distinguishing between two types of political decisions: "The decision may be made according to the judgments of the more numerous or larger part in the things that concern all... [constituent members of a federation] together, but not in those that concern them separately."[14] And, if the latter principle appears violated in a substantive and existential sense, a particular community may even have the right of secession.[15]

This distinction of what is common to all from what is particular to each is one of the fundamental principles distinguishing federal from unitary states. In the latter is embedded a modern assumption that 'the people' is essentially a homogeneous body of individual citizens who

---

13. Althusius, *Politica*, I.20.
14. Althusius, *Politica*, VIII.70.
15. Althusius, *Politica*, VIII.92.

can therefore tolerate majority decisions as the most efficient way of conducting politics. Federal systems are more complex because the general will of the majority has to be balanced with the particular interests of different constituencies.

Back to the Future?

Because he lived in an early modern world not yet steeped in modern notions of state and society, Althusius still placed more emphasis on diversity than on unity. To put it differently, his federalism was more *confederal* than federal. With his insistence on a deliberative political process, Althusius also introduced an early modern understanding of subsidiarity—the principle that governance be carried out at the lowest practical level. Because it is up to the smaller consociations to decide which powers should be delegated to the larger one, decisions are likely to remain at the lowest practical level. The Althusian concepts of communication and consensus also suggest that the question of who should do what in a federal system cannot be decided, once and for all, by a final constitutional allocation of powers. Instead, it requires a permanent political process of negotiation and compromise according to changing times and circumstances.

In an emerging modern world of sovereign nation-states, including federal ones, this emphasis on consensus and compromise would soon be dismissed as anachronistic and inefficient. Althusius was quickly forgotten. But there are at least three arguments why his consociational federalism may become more important again.

First, political scientists have pointed out more recently that consociational practices of consensus democracy have continued to exist all along in a number of countries, including those which provided the historical evidence for Althusius such as Germany, the Netherlands, and Switzerland.[16] Moreover, they have provided compelling evidence that at least some of these consensus democracies can boast a public policy record at least as efficient if not superior to that found in typical majority systems such as Britain or the United States.

Secondly, the EU has emerged as a political system demonstrating a number of Althusian characteristics. These include governance by the Council of Ministers, adherence to the principle of subsidiarity, and reliance on consensus as the method of changing the founding treaties. The EU can be interpreted as a case of consociational federalism.[17]

---

16. See Thomas O. Hueglin, "Majoritarianism—Consociationalism," in Roland Axtman, ed., *Understanding Democratic Politics* (London: Sage, 2003).

17. Matthew J. Gabel, "The Endurance of Supranational Governance: A Consociational Interpretation of the European Union," *Comparative Politics* 30:4 (1998): 463–75.

And thirdly, it seems that—notwithstanding globalization—the world continues to be divided into distinct communities of culture and religion. These communities will not tolerate having their particular interests overruled by global or even regional majority rule. Peaceful coexistence will only be possible on the basis of consensus and compromise, very much as Althusius suggested.

REPUBLICAN FEDERALISM IN THE EIGHTEENTH CENTURY

There is no evidence that a copy of Althusius's book sailed to the New World on the Mayflower. That voyage was largely financed, however, by the House of Orange who employed Althusius in Herborn. Althusius had also published the second edition of the *Politica* in the Netherlands at precisely the time when many of the original Pilgrim fathers had stayed there in exile. Indeed, one of the first political documents of the New World, the New England Confederation of 1643, contained a pledge to "cosociation [*sic*]" for mutual help and cooperation.[18]

Some of the radical spirit of early modern Protestantism arrived in America. It lived on in a new world of small settlement communities. More than a century later, the founding fathers of the United States of America were confronted with a much more volatile situation. The settlements had grown into populous colonies often at odds with one another. Their common ties with Britain had been severed by the War of Independence. Trade wars with European powers threatened their economies. The existing confederal union had proven dysfunctional. And there was grave concern about the quality of government in the individual states. A more efficient way of administering and financing their newly independent enterprise had to be found. This in turn required the creation of an enhanced central government. Out of the quest for independence grew the first modern federal state.

The American Revolution

As we know by now, the idea of a federal union was not new. The framers of the US Constitution were men of great learning, familiar with both the existing alternatives to the British unitary state in Germany, the Netherlands, and Switzerland and with historical confederacies. However, they did not like what they saw in any of those examples because all seemed to have displayed the same inefficiency and instability of government that had plagued their own confederation since independence. So, when they came together at Philadelphia in 1787, they were searching for something new.

---

18. Hueglin, *Early Modern Concepts* 16.

They were very much aware that theirs was a new world requiring new solutions. For Althusius, the main motivation had been to secure particular autonomy within an existing European social order. For the Americans, it was the establishment of a new order. The framers may also have been inspired by an already existing example of federal new world governance, the Six Nations Confederacy of the *Haudenosaunee*, or Iroquois, which several of them had visited in upstate New York. As early as 1751, Benjamin Franklin had written to his publishing partner James Parker that:

> It would be a very strange thing if Six Nations of Ignorant Savages should be capable of forming a Scheme for such a Union and be able to execute it in such a manner, as that it has subsisted Ages, and appears indissoluble, and yet a like Union should be impracticable for ten or a dozen English colonies.[19]

Many Americans admired the Six Nations for their communal spirit and the collective discipline with which they conducted business around the council fire. But for their own union, they chose a different path. The Six Nations, after all, lived in tribal communities without the concept or practice of private property or the complex economic institutions of modern trade and commerce.

The American framers were all men of property, and they were faced with a dilemma. On the one hand, they had invoked popular sovereignty as their collective right to break away from Britain. On the other hand, they feared that the common people, empowered by the vote and by the will of the majority, would threaten individual status and wealth. They found the solution in the writings of a French aristocrat who provided them with a formula of political organization that would safeguard individual freedom as well as collective security.

Montesquieu (1689–1755)

This aristocrat was Charles de Secondat, Baron de Montesquieu. Half a century before the French Revolution, he, too, had recognized the mounting bourgeois pressure towards representative inclusion in the body politic. In his celebrated and influential book *de L'esprit des lois* (*The Spirit of the Laws*) published in 1748,[20] he combined his conservative instincts of status protection with a liberal spirit of accepting both the

---

19. Quoted in Robert W. Venables, "The Founding Fathers: Choosing to be Romans," in Jose Barreiro, ed., *Indian Roots of American Democracy* (Ithaca, NY: Akwe:Kon Press, 1992) 81. Also see Donald S. Lutz, "The Iroquois Confederation Constitution: An Analysis," *Publius* 28:2 (1998).

20. The original English translation, the one used by those Americans who were not reading Montesquieu in the original, is reprinted as *The Spirit of Laws* (Berkeley, CA: University of California Press, 1977).

inevitability and legitimacy of the new bourgeois political claims. In absolutist France, such thoughts were not tolerated, and the book was in fact published in the Swiss city of Geneva. But among the liberal circles of Europe, it became a bestseller nevertheless and one of the decisive intellectual sources for the eventual development of liberal constitutionalism in the nineteenth century.

For the Americans, it became required reading, although it provided scant guidance for their federalist project. Three principles were particularly relevant for the American constitution-makers in general. The first of these was recognition of **intermediate powers** between people and government as necessary for political stability. The second was the constitutional **separation of powers** among the branches of government. And the third was the organization of a large state as a **federal republic** subdivided into smaller units on the basis of mutual agreement.

Societal Pluralism

The first principle, about the necessity of intermediate powers, was the most conservative one. Montesquieu liked neither absolute monarchies nor democracies. He referred to nobility, clergy, and cities as the traditional carriers of intermediate power in pre-absolutist times, and he pointed out that the nobility is the most "natural" such power, providing "intermediate channels" of administration, law, and order in large empires or states.[21] Without such channels, he insisted, there can only be despotism. But the very idea of intermediate powers does contain an element of thought which is also important to federalism because it recognizes that societies are plurally structured and that this structure needs to be built into the form of governance. In other words, Montesquieu was opposed to the idea of a society composed of uniform citizens without group identities.

Power Checking Power

The second set of principles—and the one Montesquieu is most famous for—concerns the importance of separating the legislative, executive, and judicial branches of government. Inspired by what he understood to be the British Constitution, the only one then existing whose purpose was, in his view, to protect liberty, Montesquieu made the following influential pronouncements:

- When legislative power is united with executive power in a single person or in a single body of the magistracy, there is no liberty....

---

21. Charles de Secondat, Baron de Montesquieu, *The Spirit of the Laws* (Cambridge: Cambridge University Press, 1989) Bk 2, Chapter 4: "On Laws in their Relation to the Nature of Monarchical Government."

- Nor is there liberty if the power of judging is not separate from legislative power and from executive power.
- All would be lost if the same man or the same body of principal men, either of nobles, or of the people, exercised these three powers....[22]
- A monopoly of power would be tyranny, while a separation of powers would create countervailing powers and thereby protect the citizen from oppression. "So that one cannot abuse power, power must check power...."[23]

It is easy to see how the Americans seized upon these principles as the inspiration for their constitutional system. However, Montesquieu's doctrine of the separation of powers was only obliquely related to federalism because it referred to mutual power control among the branches of government at one and the same level of governance. It offered no direct solution to the problem whose solution had so far eluded them, the problem of constructing a viable balance between distinct levels of government.

Federalism and Democracy

Montesquieu's final principle was the only one directly related to federalism. Because large republics succumb to the internal cancer of despotism and small ones succumb to external aggression, he suggested that several small states should form a larger and **federal republic**.[24] Such an arrangement would provide the best of both worlds—the smallness necessary in his view for democracy to function and the largeness necessary for both internal and external security. Not only would external aggressors face the collective strength of the member states, but so would aggressors internal to any one of the member states. Should sedition or usurpation take root in one, it could be quarantined there by the others and stamped out. And, finally, should the union prove unable to deliver the intended benefits, it could simply be dissolved and the member states resume their independent existence.

By referring to the same examples of early modern federalism as did Althusius—the Netherlands, Germany, and Switzerland—he pointed out that governance must be based on mutual agreement among members regardless of their size and power. He even mentioned the example of the ancient Lycian town confederacy and its practice of weighted voting rights in the common council: three for the large towns, two for the middling ones, and one for the small ones.[25] Beyond this, and by

---

22. Montesquieu, *The Spirit of the Laws* Book 11, Chapter 6.
23. Montesquieu, *The Spirit of the Laws*, Book 11, Chapter 4 (*le pouvoir arrête le pouvoir*).
24. Montesquieu, *The Spirit of the Laws*, Book 9, Chapter 1 (*république fédératif*).
25. Montesquieu, *The Spirit of the Laws*, Book 9, Chapter 3.

contrast with Althusius, though, he did not provide an elaborated theory of federalism.

Montesquieu's main motivation was not to explore the universal principles of political organization in a plural society, but to propose a compromise among different classes that would lead to necessary cooperation rather than social polarization. Realizing that such cooperation was more likely to succeed on a small scale than within a large state or empire, he suggested federalism as a means of combining the republican virtues of social balance in small republics with the security and prosperity of large states.

The Federalist Papers

Out of the compromises negotiated in the Philadelphia Convention emerged modern federalism—a blueprint for a system of shared sovereignty that promised to transcend the problems of confederalism. Not everyone was convinced of the wisdom of this blueprint, however. When the constitutional draft of 1787 had to be ratified in the individual states, there was considerable opposition. This opposition focussed precisely on the innovative attempt to transfer a substantial share of the sovereignty to what they referred to as the "general government." In New York during the winter months following the Philadelphia Convention, therefore, a series of 85 newspaper essays were published in defence of the draft by three of those who had championed a consolidation of national power. These essays were the *Federalist* Papers, written by Alexander Hamilton (1757–1804), John Jay (1745–1829), and James Madison (1751–1836) under the pseudonym Publius.

Although written with the immediate purpose of political persuasion in mind, these essays nevertheless constitute a profound theoretical exposition of American government. They not only elaborate thoroughly on the chosen institutional design but, moreover and more importantly, lay out the major basic principles underpinning the chosen system of government.

The Original Challenge

The central challenge the Convention delegates had faced was how to surmount the disabilities of the confederal arrangement existing under the *Articles of Confederation and Perpetual Union* without going to the other extreme of creating the Frankenstein's monster of a dominant central government that would bring about a *de facto* unitary regime. Prevailing wisdom said that the choice was either a confederal arrangement, where sovereignty was retained by the member states, or a unitary arrangement, where sovereignty was abandoned by the member states and delivered over to the new central government. Sovereignty was regarded as indivisible, and a compromise or middle ground position was ruled out. The Convention, however, produced a blueprint that rejected this assumption—sharing sovereignty between the two levels of government, each enjoying a direct relationship with the people, neither one subservient to the other. To sceptics this was asking the impossible and could only be unitary government by stealth.

A Viable Republicanism

In rationalizing this provocative new proposal, Hamilton, Jay, and Madison—and indeed many of the founders—cast the issue in terms of what they saw as the central problem of governance at the time: how to make **republicanism** viable. Republicanism was a concept widely used at the time then by all those, in Europe as well as in America, who were opposed to monarchical rule, and it generally meant elective representative government. The problem with popular rule, though, was its potential radicalism. Thus, if it were to be made viable, it had to be tamed. The general approach was as conservative as Montesquieu's. There had to be a strong central government for the union, but it had to be constructed in such a way as to prevent the majority from assuming unchecked power over individual property rights. The main source of political conflict is the tendency toward "faction" arising from the unequal distribution of property, Madison wrote, and he declared that the ultimate purpose of government would be to "secure the public good and private rights against the danger of such faction."[26] To this end, he explained later, mutual checks and balances were needed. By following the pattern of Montesquieu's separation of powers, and by repeating the exercise at two different levels of government, "society itself will be broken into so many parts, interests and classes of citizens, that the rights of individuals, or of the minority, will be in little danger from interested combinations of the majority."[27]

This is the most dramatic transformation of federalist thought that the Americans accomplished. For Althusius as much as for Montesquieu, federalism had been an institutional device to safeguard the integrity of particular communities. In the view of the Federalists, such communities had to be broken up, procedurally, by the political process in order to protect individual rights.[28]

Of course, the states were powerful communities, and their fears of usurpation by the central government were assuaged by their co-equal participation in the Senate. But Hamilton at least was quite frank about their status in the larger union. They would continue to exist "for local

---

26. Hamilton *et al.*, *Federalist* 10.
27. Hamilton *et al.*, *Federalist* 51.
28. See Thomas O. Hueglin, "Federalism at the Crossroads: Old Meanings, New Significance," *Canadian Journal of Political Science* 36:2 (June 2003).

purposes" and "in perfect subordination to the general authority of the union."[29] This was a far cry from Althusius's bottom-up construction of power delegation on the basis of consensus.

Competing Visions

It must be remembered that not only was the 1787 Constitution the result of a compromise between opposed visions, but that the exact nature and meaning of this compromise itself immediately became a disputed matter. Hamilton, Jay, and Madison were not just supplying a defence of that compromise, they were also asserting a particular interpretation of what it was—putting their 'spin' on it, so to speak. A more Althusian view of federalism was in fact held by the so-called "states righters" or **anti-federalists.** It was later brought to the point more precisely by John Taylor[30] and later John C. Calhoun, the most prominent spokesman of southern discontent. In almost the same words as Althusius, Calhoun argued in 1853 that a state should have the right to veto national legislation when such legislation affected the interests of that state "separately."[31] The issue was eventually settled on the field of battle.

Dual Governments

The Federalists strongly rejected any constitutional design that would have given the states collective superiority over the Union. They did so because this had been the crucial weakness of the preceding confederation, which they likened to the "imbecility" and chronic instability of the European confederacies. They did so also, however, for far more principled reasons. As Hamilton wrote, the "great and radical vice in the existing confederation" was that it recognized only states in their "collective capacities" and not the "individual citizens of America."[32]

Under the *Articles*, as with all other confederacies, only the member states enjoyed a direct relationship with the people. The central government was a mere agent of the states. This meant that although it might have the power to requisition funds from the member states, it had little means to enforce that requisition, and although it might have the power to legislate in a number of fields, it had little means to enforce those laws either.

The new constitution decisively broke those shackles and granted the new general government a direct relationship to the people, both in

---

29. Hamilton *et al.*, *Federalist* 9; in Hamilton *et al.*, *Federalist* 32, he puts forward a more balanced view.
30. In Taylor, *Construction Construed* and *New Views of the Constitution*.
31. See Calhoun, *A Disquisition on Government*, esp. 20.
32. Hamilton *et al.*, *Federalist* 15.

raising revenue and in passing laws—a genuine existence and potency of its own. It was no longer reliant on the states, but part of a new dual system of government with the two levels enjoying a separate and parallel relationship with the people. This led to the first of the serious objections that the authors of *The Federalist* had to contend with: invigorated with such new authority and powers, would the central government not eventually come to overawe the states? A good part of *The Federalist* papers is taken up with defending that augmentation of powers, indicating why the voters should see the more sweeping grants of power as really quite innocuous and in suggesting reasons for thinking the danger would remain one of state rather than Union dominance. These arguments may have been disingenuous (particularly those of Hamilton, who fervently hoped and campaigned for a decisively stronger union throughout his career) or simply unprescient.[33] In Hamilton's views, opponents of the new constitution were the ones wanting to have it both ways—agreeing that a more effective union was necessary, but refusing to countenance any diminution in state sovereignty. As he put it in *Federalist* 15, they were proposing the "political monster of an *imperium in imperio*"—a sovereignty over sovereigns.

The Extended and Compound Republic

The second challenge was to convince voters that it was possible to have a successful system of republican government across such a large territory as would be spanned by the 13 states and whatever new ones were subsequently added. Madison's answer to this was a clever one.

As Madison explained to his readers in *Federalist* 10, the disease of popular government was conflict between factions. If the faction was a minority, this was not a problem because it could be reined in by the majority. But if the faction was a majority, the minority was in danger of having its rights trampled upon. Because of social inequality, there would always be factions of interest, and, therefore, the "regulation of these various and interfering interests forms the principal task of modern legislation." Such legislation would be made by the people's representatives, and it is at this point that Madison begins to combine republicanism with federalism.

Here the authors of *The Federalist* turned Montesquieu on his head. Whereas Montesquieu and others took as axiomatic the idea that democracy could only function in small republics, Madison, Jay, and Hamilton argued in *Federalist* 9 and 10 that it could only succeed in large ones. In small republics, they argued, there would be less diversity of interests, and, consequently, much more chance that majority decisions would

---

33. See Hamilton *et al.*, *Federalist* 31–33.

oppress the minority. In Hamilton's somewhat overheated prose of *Federalist* 9, left to their own, the states would be "wretched nurseries of unceasing discord." In a large republic, on the other hand, there would a greater fragmentation of interests and hence less of a danger of majoritarian tyranny. An **extended republic** was thus the primary solution to the problem of popular rule.[34] However, an extended unitary republic was not seen as practicable and this is where federalism entered the argument. Federalism, or a **compound republic** as they called it, would be the means to the end of creating the necessary scale to submerge local majorities and prevent democratic tyranny. Thus for Hamilton, Jay, and Madison, federalism was first and foremost an expedient device for making possible the extension of one political system across a broad geographic area.

The Double Security of the Compound Republic

Moreover, as *Federalist* 51 suggests, federalism also complemented the horizontal separation of powers with a vertical division of powers that would provide an additional protection to property and other rights. The system of checks and balances allows "ambition to counteract ambition" and thus neutralizes the threat of tyranny to as great an extent as Montesquieu argued. Should this fail, governments can counteract each other:

> In the compound republic of America, the power surrendered by the people is first divided between two distinct governments, and then the portion allotted to each subdivided among distinct and separate departments. Hence a double security arises to the rights of the people. The different governments will control each other, at the same time that each will be controlled by itself.

While serving as a means to an end and helping to defuse dangers of a tyranny of the majority through facilitating the extended republic, federalism also provides a protective mechanism in itself through the potential counterweight effect of one level of government against another.

Successful Conclusion

A streak of genius it was, this transformation and amalgamation of various strands of previously existing political thought—federalism, republicanism, and individualism—into a coherent system of modern governance. Notwithstanding the great catharsis of the Civil War, the

---

34. George W. Carey, *The Federalist: Design for a Constitutional Republic* (Urbana, IL: University of Illinois Press, 1989) 23.

compounded nature of the constitutional design would produce in the end what the Federalists had expected—a stable polity safeguarding the rights of individuals. At the same time, the divided and competitive nature of the political process would foster a mentality of 'you win some, you lose some,' often falling short of the kind of consensus-oriented solidarity among autonomous communities that had been the essence of previous federalist thought in the older and Althusian tradition.

SOCIO-ECONOMIC FEDERALISM IN THE NINETEENTH CENTURY AND BEYOND

Essentially, the history of federalist thought can be defined in terms of these two traditions: the Althusian tradition with its emphasis on agreement among autonomous communities and the American tradition with its emphasis on individual competition within and across such communities. Because of the tumultuous social transformations during the nineteenth century, however, at least some variations to these models need mentioning.

The French Revolution

Only a couple of years after the Americans drafted their constitutional document, the French Revolution changed the European world of politics in a much more dramatic way. Although ending in abject failure— a regime of terror, Bonapartism, and the eventual restoration of the French monarchy—its declaration of universal human rights in the name of liberty, equality, and brotherhood galvanized all European societies in an unprecedented way.

Though sweeping away the regional fiefdoms of the old regime, the French Revolution's contribution to the history of political institutions was the centralized unitary nation-state. In the wake of industrial modernization and the formation of large working classes, socialists in particular placed their hopes for an egalitarian political order in a new era of democratic centralism. Federalism was rejected as reactionary. Certainly, Bismarck's German federation appeared to Karl Marx as an attempt at preserving the power of territorial dynastic princes against the tidal wave of democratization.[35]

Pierre-Joseph Proudhon (1809–1865)

There were only a few socialist thinkers who seized the idea of federalism as an opportunity for political and economic equality. One of

---

35. Karl Marx, "Moralizing Criticism and Critical Morality," in Karl Marx and Friedrich Engels, *Collected Works*, Vol. 6 (London: Lawrence and Wishart, 1976).

them was **Pierre-Joseph Proudhon** who rejected the centralism inherent in both the French and the Industrial Revolutions and argued for a kind of federal socialism in which agricultural and industrial workers would become self-governing producers in a radically decentralized social order. After Althusius, therefore, for whom the idea of the separation of state and market simply did not exist at the very beginning of the modern age, Proudhon was the first theorist of federalism who explicitly included the organization of economic production in his conception of federalism.[36]

Proudhon rejected all concentrated power, whether it be in the hands of a prince, a liberal bourgeoisie, or a revolutionary proletariat. Instead, he suggested a form of political organization based on pluralized self-governance among local and regional constituencies. Such a federal structure would be incomplete and useless, however, if it did not extend to socio-economic organization as well. Otherwise, the centralism inherent in modern capitalism would triumph over decentralized political powers. Parallel to political federation, Proudhon therefore insisted on an **agro-industrial federation** constituted from autonomous enterprises and the associations of the producers of goods and services.

Like Althusius, Proudhon conceived governance as an ascending order of indirect **council representation**. Municipal or local councils would elect representatives for the regional councils which in turn would elect representatives for the national council. Members of these territorially organized councils were to be representatives of the associations of producers of goods and services as well as of consumer associations.

The state, as embodied by a national council at the top of this ascending pyramid, would retain only two essential functions: foreign policy and national economic planning. In the latter function, the state would provide producers with necessary information about economic needs and trends. Well into the twentieth century, indicative planning was a central motif of French economic and industrial policy. The government provided macro-economic data that could help producers to make the right decisions in their own best interest.

Like Montesquieu, Proudhon did not develop an elaborate theory of federalism, but he added an important socio-economic dimension to federalist thought. He foresaw the enormous concentration of power in modern capitalism, and, like other socialists, he believed that economic power would come to dominate the political system. He therefore insisted that it was the economic system of production itself that had to be federalized.

This was not an idea popular with capitalists. At the same time, it was also rejected by most socialists who harboured dreams about economic equality planned and dispensed by a powerful central state. It

---

36. Proudhon, *The Principle of Federation*.

was taken up, however, by a number of schools and movements that rejected both capitalism and socialism as two sides of the same coin—power concentration at the expense of democratic citizenship.

Integral Federalism

In the 1930s, an international group of intellectuals gathered in Paris around Alexandre Marc, a Russian emigrant socialist philosopher and publicist, who followed Proudhon rather than Marx. In what they would later call a philosophy of **integral federalism**, these intellectuals wanted to provide Europe with a new political order based neither on bourgeois nationalism nor on socialist internationalism. Because they anticipated that the unfinished business of World War I would soon lead to another war, they called for a "real" or "integral" system of European federalism that would have to include political and economic integration.[37]

Faithful to their Proudhonian roots, these integral federalists based their vision on three closely related principles. First, they argued that individual freedom could exist only if it was supported by a structure of self-governing communities tied together by common interests and identities. They called this "personalism," a view of human nature as embedded in plural relationships and therefore at odds with radical individual liberalism. Secondly, they held that the only legitimate role of the state was to serve these community interests. And thirdly, they proposed a mixed economy in which basic consumer needs would be safeguarded through cooperative public planning, while additional consumer interests could be satisfied by a free market. As Proudhon had suggested, the entire system would be primarily based on self-organization and federated coordination among producer and consumer groups. The state would play only an auxiliary role of providing information and guidance.

The utopian idealism of these integral federalists stood little chance of being heard during the interwar years. World War II entirely destroyed their dreams. Both individual and group liberty became casualties of nationalism and state totalitarianism. While the group dispersed, several of its members remained active in various European resistance movements against the Nazi regime, and even during these darkest hours of European history, they continued to campaign for reconciliation between France and Germany in a postwar European federal order.

---

37. See Lutz Roemheld, *Integral Federalism: A Model for Europe* (New York: Peter Lang, 1990).

European Federalism

After the war, integral federalism did provide some inspiration for the architects of European integration. A peaceful European political order, it was generally assumed, would naturally follow from economic integration. In order to prevent a new surge in economic nationalism, however, committed federalists such as Denis de Rougemont, a former member of the integral federalism group, argued that the principal building blocs of a European federal order should be the European regions and not the nation-states.[38]

The Socio-economic Dimension

It soon became clear that nation-states would remain the unavoidable building blocs of the new Europe. Moreover, economic integration would follow the model of individualized market relations and not the kind of socio-economic federalism among producer and consumer groups the integral federalists had championed.

Yet, at least in principle, the evolving process of European integration did incorporate a number of ideas owed to what can be called a European tradition of socio-economic federalism. In 1957, an Economic and Social Committee, which included representatives from producer and consumer organizations, was added to the institutional set-up of the European Community. Although not vested with voting rights, it must be consulted before decisions in most areas of economic policy can be taken.

Subsidiarity

In 1993, when the Maastricht Treaty transformed the European Community into the European Union, a similarly consultative Committee of the Regions was established. At the same time, funding for regional development and cohesion was increased dramatically, and the regions became more directly involved in the process of designing their own development programs. The insertion of the **principle of subsidiarity** into the Treaty acknowledged more generally that decisions should be taken at the lowest possible level of governance.

One of the principal driving forces behind the Maastricht Treaty was Jacques Delors, a French socialist who served as president of the European Commission from 1985 to 1995. He was well acquainted and associated with the personalist circles of the integral federalism school. It was his research team that also discovered and acknowledged the Althusian roots of subsidiarity.

---

38. See Etienne Tassin, "Europe: A Political Community?" in Chantal Mouffe, ed., *Dimensions of Radical Democracy: Pluralism, Citizenship, Community* (London: Verso, 1992).

Emergence of a New Model

It is too early for a precise positioning of the EU in the history of federalist traditions. It would appear, however, that federalist thought and practice have come full circle. Althusius had proposed federalism as a regime of confederal agreements among autonomous communities or consociations. For the Americans, federalism became a tool for state- and nation-building with much more emphasis on the efficiency of central governance. With the EU, the focus has shifted back to a more confederal perspective. The member states remain the principal actors, and changes to the scope and dimension of EU governance can only be made by means of treaty changes requiring unanimous approval.

SUMMARY

Federal traditions and ideas constitute an important alternative strand in the history of political thought. They are the antidote to the idea of empire and the tradition of the modern unitary nation-state. In this chapter, we have drawn attention to three different traditions of federal thought: consociational federalism, republican federalism, and socioeconomic federalism. The emergence of each of these traditions can be linked to revolutionary change: the Protestant revolution in early modern Europe, the American Revolution in the eighteenth century, and the French Revolution at the beginning of the nineteenth century.

- After the Reformation, consociational federalism had its beginnings in the quest of Protestant minorities for survival in a new age of territorial sovereignty. Drawing inspiration from the biblical Jewish covenant and from the tradition of pluralistic rule in the Holy Roman Empire, Calvinists in particular argued that they had a right to live in autonomous communities. Together, these communities would share the rights of sovereignty and determine the conditions and limits of lawful governance. Johannes Althusius (1557–1638) called these communities consociations and constructed the first modern theory of federalism on the basis of shared sovereignty and negotiated agreement. More confederal than federal, the Althusius theory proposed a system of multilevel council governance. At each level, governing councils would be composed of representatives from the lower level consociations.

- The American tradition of republican federalism emerged as a response to the question of how to combine elective representative (i.e., republican) government in a large union both with individual and minority protection and with the retention of state autonomy. The result was the American model of constitutional federalism based on multiple checks and balances, horizontally between the different branches of government, and vertically between the two levels of government. In sharp contrast to Montesquieu (1689–1755), from whom they drew much inspiration nevertheless, the authors of the *Federalist* (1787–88) laid the theoretical foundation for a stable federal polity in which individual rights competition would override the autonomy of social and territorial communities.

- In the wake of industrial modernization and in response to the equality promises of the French Revolution, only a few socialist thinkers of the nineteenth century and beyond applied the idea of federalism to the realm of economic production. Rejecting the centralism inherent in both modern politics and economics, Pierre-Joseph Proudhon (1809–65) advanced a theory of federal socialism in which workers would become self-governing producers in a radically decentralized social order. In the early twentieth century, the French school of integral federalism extended this idea into a system of federated cooperation among self-organized producer and consumer groups.

- After World War II, some of these ideas were incorporated in the evolving process of European integration. The consultative Economic and Social Committee included producer and consumer organizations, and the principle of subsidiarity generally acknowledged that decisions should be taken at the lowest possible level of governance.

5 The Formation of Federal States

Why did some of the modern world's nation-states take a federal form and others not? In the previous chapter, we explored the ideas of social philosophers and political theorists. Their enthusiasm and endorsement of federalism can be explained quite easily. Generally speaking, they were concerned with the mismatch between the complexities and threats of real social life and the simplicity of the modern state construction imposed upon it. They also had more personal motivations. Althusius worried about the autonomy and survival of Protestant minorities under a regime of imposed state religions. Montesquieu's advocacy of mutual checks and balances arose out of his fear that aristocratic class privileges would be wiped out by bourgeois majorities. And Proudhon, finally, stemming from a humble background of craftsmen and tavern-keepers, saw himself as a defender of their interests against the overwhelming forces of industrial capitalism.

However compelling these ideas and motivations may appear, they do not explain why federalism became a practical option for the organization of modern states. With the exception of Montesquieu's influence on American thinking, these theorists did not have a lasting impact on politics in theory and practice. In this chapter, we want to explain why federal solutions to political problems were applied in practice.

In attempting to do so, we first note that while the world's libraries are full of books on modern state formation, the rise of popular sovereignty, and parliamentary democracy, federalism has by comparison been treated with neglect. In fact, it is not an exaggeration to say that a general theory of federal state formation does not exist. Instead, we find country-specific explanations and a few systematic comparisons of institutional arrangements. Anything more general is usually based on the argument that federalism somehow 'naturally' corresponds to the plural nature of social life or that federalism was invented by the Americans and then more or less copied by everyone else.

Both arguments contain some truth, but they hardly suffice as explanations for the remarkable proliferation of federal systems in the nineteenth and twentieth centuries. We take for granted a universal drive

113

towards democratic elections and responsible government, but we have no general explanation as to why some countries, ranging from Germany and Australia to India and Brazil, have chosen a federal form of statehood, or why previously unitary states such as Spain or even the UK have been thrust upon a trajectory of federalization more recently.

In this chapter, we begin by considering a number of factors accounting for the adoption of federal rather than unitary statehood. With the help of these, we then turn to the country-specific design of basic models. We finally discuss some variations of these models in the rest of the world.

THE FEDERAL COMPROMISE: EXPLANATORY PERSPECTIVES

Modern states came about, in the words of a prominent historian, when "small groups of power-hungry men fought off numerous rivals and great popular resistance in the pursuit of their own ends, and inadvertently promoted the formation of national states and wide-spread popular involvement in them."[1] The easiest answer to our question then is this: when no single group of power-hungry men was strong enough to defeat all others, a federalist compromise became necessary for the mutual benefit of stability. However, this begs further questions: under what historical and contextual circumstances was the hegemonic victory of one party improbable, and what compelled rival parties to seek some form of federal union nevertheless? The formation of unitary nation-states was much less likely in cases where

- **late state formation** was bringing together already defined communities;
- **colonial impositions** created pluri-national territories and regional settler societies; or
- interests were deeply divided between **modernizers and traditionalists**.

Meanwhile, disparate units were driven to form some kind of a union by a mixture of pressures, notable among them being:

- **external threat**, which provided an incentive for common defence and action among otherwise independent entities; and
- **economic advantages**, which provided an incentive for a larger and more open market.

Late State Formation

Federations generally came into existence relatively late in the game of modern state-building. Historical reasons for this lateness help to explain why state-building efforts resulted in a federal rather than unitary system.

---

1. Charles Tilly, "Western State-Making and Political Transformation," in Charles Tilly, ed., *The Formation of National States in Western Europe* (Princeton, NJ: Princeton University Press, 1975) 635.

In the Old World

Despite all the modern state-building going on around them, Switzerland and Germany remained loose confederacies. Before the modern age of accelerated transportation and communication, the Swiss Alpine valleys were almost as separated from one another, and from the rest of Europe, as were the settlements in the New World. Meanwhile, the German princes jealously maintained their territorial sovereignty against the fading appeal and power of the Holy Roman Empire. When inevitable modernization came, in the nineteenth century, it strengthened already existing particular societies. Hence, as in the settler societies of the New World, a federal solution and answer to the challenges of modernization and state-building was the obvious answer.

In the New World

The factor of late state formation also played itself out in the New World. The settler colonies of the Americas and Australia were new societies that did not exist when modern state formation began in Europe. Federalism was almost unavoidable because these new societies were settled piecemeal, creating separate societies, economies, and colonial units of responsible self-government across a vast territorial expanse. While these separate societies and their "power-hungry men" eventually agreed on the need for some form of union, they were quite unwilling to abandon their previous achievements and status altogether.

Typically, this federal solution was fraught with ambiguity. In earlier cases of state formation, sovereignty passed from the older and smaller territories to the larger and newer one. In the later cases of negotiated federal state formation, the contentious issue of regional versus national sovereignty was settled in a calculated compromise over divided powers. Inevitably, what looked like a tidy constitutional solution on paper proved to be a messy arena for competing legal interpretations in practice.

Colonial Impositions

The federalist compromise among the British settler colonies of the New World was a compromise among Europeans only. The Indigenous populations, to the extent that they still played a numerical role, were neither consulted nor taken into consideration. There were, however, cases of colonial conquest elsewhere, in Asia and in Africa, where diverse tribal societies within arbitrary colonial boundaries came under the administrative rule of European elites. When these conquest (rather than settler) colonies eventually gained independence, some form of federalism was the only option for political accommodation within the inherited territory.

Only a few of these newly created countries—notably India—managed to develop into relatively stable and democratic federal republics.

Artificial boundaries were not the only imposition upon conquered territories. Government style was another. British colonial administrations left a legacy of responsible self-government. In the Hispanic Americas, on the other hand, authoritarianism, Catholicism, and bureaucratic centralism generated regimes of clientelist provincial administrations dominated by powerful regional settler elites. After independence, federal governments were set up as arenas for competitive struggles among these regional elites who were more interested in the continued exploitation of the land under their control than in national modernization schemes. The instability of such oligarchic federations typically not only retarded modernization but also and almost regularly resulted in military dictatorships imposing national modernization programs from above. Instead of a true federalist compromise, the political development of these countries oscillated between extreme regionalism and authoritarian centralism.

Modernizers and Traditionalists

Modern state-building went hand in hand with economic modernization, economy-of-scale production, and standardized means of communication, transportation, and administration as well as secure and free access to international trade. The efforts of economic modernizers, however, routinely met with the resistance of traditionalists who wanted to protect their regional and class privileges and cultural identities.

Unitary states emerged where traditionalist resistance was successfully submerged. In the English Civil War of 1642–51, the new propertied classes fought against old privileges and monopolies in trade and commerce. A clear regional division of interests can be discerned as well. While support for economic modernization and parliamentary control came from the economically more advanced south and east, economically backward regions in the north and west supported the King.[2] In due course, the monarchy became constitutionally constrained, and Parliament emerged as the absolute sovereign. When the century began, England was still a traditional society of yeomen. When it ended, it had become the first modern commercial empire. "The wealth of the nation," wrote Jonathan Swift, "that used to be reckoned by the value of land, is now computed by the rise and fall of stocks."[3] England had become the first instance of modern and unitary state formation.

---

2.   Christopher Hill, *The Century of Revolution 1603–1714* (New York: Norton, 1982) 103.

3.   Quoted in Hill, *Century of Revolution* 234.

One or two centuries later, economic modernizers in the British settler colonies as well as in the fragmented territories of Switzerland and Germany also pressed for economic modernization, and their efforts were again met with resistance by traditionalists opposed to the standardization of socio-economic and cultural life. Yet traditional societies and their governing elites had become too strong by that point, and their vested interests too deeply entrenched in regional politics and culture. A unilateral victory of one camp over the other was no longer an option. Even where military conflict ensued, as in the American Civil War of 1861–65, or in the brief Swiss war of secession in 1847, the outcome retained a federalist compromise.

This compromise typically gave the modernizers what they wanted: centralized powers over trade and commerce as the essential tools to build national markets. It assuaged traditionalists with local control over social and cultural matters.

External Threat

The most parsimonious theory of the formation of federal systems is William Riker's theory of external compulsion:

> In every successfully formed federalism it must be the case that a significant external or internal threat or a significant opportunity for aggression is present, where the threat can be forestalled and the aggression carried out only with a bigger government. This is what brings union at all and is the main feature, the prospective gain, in both giving and accepting the bargain.[4]

Supportive evidence is not hard to find. Both the early Dutch and the original Helvetic or Swiss confederations were a direct response to strategic threat; they were, indeed, "security confederations."[5] The Swiss confederation of the thirteenth century took shape when the ruling families controlling the Swiss Alpine passes concluded a compact for the mutual defence of their interests against outside forces. Nineteenth-century German state-building was closely associated with European power politics and the attempt to establish strategic dominance. The original US confederation was forged out of the War of Independence and within the context of ongoing trade embargos and diplomatic isolation. In Canada and Mexico, union was in no small part occasioned by the threat or reality of American expansionism.

---

4.   Riker, "Federalism" 116.
5.   Frederick K. Lister, *The Early Security Confederations: From the Ancient Greeks to the United Colonies of New England* (Westport, CT: Greenwood Press, 1999).

Economic Welfare

Parsimony, however, is not the only criterion of good theory and Riker may well be over-simplifying. German political union of the nineteenth century was preceded by important steps toward economic integration, the *Zollverein* or customs union. The drive towards larger markets by modern capitalism, in other words, constitutes a strong incentive for federal union in its own right. Britain's Australasian colonies were not subjected to any significant threat at all—though some warned that Germany's colonialist ventures in the Pacific were a harbinger of danger. And the EU is the epitome of federal integration occurring out of a desire for economic rather than military advantage. Any theory of federal formation must account for these developments. Even Riker, who believed that economic motives were at best secondary to military ones, in the end acknowledged that the relative importance of the two factors might be reversing in the modern world:

> Today the question is: can this once secondary motive for federation become the primary motive that generates a federal Europe? In a world where trade is vastly more important than it was a generation ago, perhaps the answer is affirmative.[6]

EMERGENCE OF THE BASIC MODELS

With these macro-historical and theoretical approaches in mind, we can now look at how the basic models of federalism were designed. As we shall see, caution is required in applying these theoretical criteria too narrowly or too literally. They are only broad guidelines helping to understand the general thrust of federal state formation.

The United States of America

As we have noted in earlier chapters, the American model was the federal prototype, the original example that then stood as model to be imitated or avoided by others. Between the launching of the independence movement in 1775 and the ratification of the final Constitution in 1789, the Americans worked their way towards a viable federal arrangement. It was a process that involved both very practical or empirical trial and error and very theoretical ratiocination of the principles of government. They began with the Continental Congress through which they conducted the War of Independence. That union was formalized by the establishment of a loose confederal arrangement under the *Articles of Confederation and Perpetual Union*. The practical inadequacies

---

6.   William H. Riker, "European Federalism: The Lessons of Past Experience," in Hesse and Wright, eds., *Federalizing Europe?* 23.

of the system of government created by the *Articles* led to the successful attempt at the Philadelphia Constitutional Convention in 1787 to recast the union in a more robust and effective form. In so doing, they arrived at the compromise arrangement that is the essence of federalism.

Initial Union

Agreed upon by the Continental Congress in 1777 but only fully ratified in 1781, the first US Constitution established for the 13 states a classic confederation—a "league of friendship" as Article III described it. The very first substantive clause (Article II) in the document asserted unequivocally that:

> Each state retains its sovereignty, freedom, and independence, and every power, jurisdiction, and right, which is not by this Confederation expressly delegated to the United States, in Congress assembled.

The sole institution of the new United States government was that of the state delegates meeting "in congress." There was no president, no judiciary, and no administrative structures. Congress had a range of powers to make collective decisions; however, each and every one of these decisions had to be ratified by nine of the 13 states. Congress had no power to raise its own revenue, but instead had to rely on the states. By thus having no direct relationship with the people—either in representative terms or in policy and taxation terms—and no autonomous policy power, this newly created central government was without any basis for effective existence. It suffered from the fatal collective action problem that member states contributed their share of resources only to the extent that they calculated was proportional to the direct benefit they would receive. Once the immediate external threat had been dealt with, they contributed very little at all.[7]

A Closer Union

There were then many reasons why the Americans wanted to enter into a closer federal union. Lacking a firm commitment to fiscal contributions from the states, Congress was unable to regulate the domestic economy. External difficulties were very much on the minds of the delegates assembling in Philadelphia. The confederation was threatened by trade embargos and diplomatic isolation. The peace treaty with Britain that had ended the War of Independence was only four years old when

---

7.   Dougherty, *Collective Action*. See also Ben Baack, "Forging a Nation State: The Continental Congress and the Financing of the War of American Independence," *American Economic Review*, LIV:4 (2001).

the Constitution was drafted. However, the war was over, and the United States had been doubly victorious: the British threat had been not only repulsed but entirely removed. What thus appear prominently in the concerns animating the founders were fears of internal threats and disabilities, particularly relating to economic matters.[8] Most studies highlight the deep concern of America's political elites with the instability and dangerous populism of the state governments:

> by the winter of 1786–1787, the American republic was in peril, and the institutional safeguards for liberty and property that had been erected had proved inadequate.... They had learned ... that there were threats to liberty and property that were peculiar to republics.... They had become convinced ... that if American government were not radically and immediately reconstructed, anarchy and then tyranny were soon to come.[9]

This instability and populism they decided would best be curtailed much as Montesquieu had suggested—by having an overarching authority that could quarantine disorders at the local level and bring superior authority to bear.

These were all reasons calling for a strong central government. Yet a unitary state modelled after Britain, Spain, or France was out of the question. The differences among the states were too great, and there was no ruling elite or majority faction strong enough to impose its will on all others.

Proposals, Options, Compromises, and Unfinished Business

The delegates at the Convention all agreed that union governance had to be strengthened, but that was about as far as agreement went. The so-called "Virginia Plan"—spear-headed by Virginia delegate James Madison—intended to create a national republic the powers of which would be superior to those of the states, ultimately perhaps reducing them to the status of dependent administrative units. In response, the "New Jersey Plan" sought to retain a regime of confederal state sovereignty while making some concessions to the need for a more "energetic" central government.

---

8. As, for instance, argued by Roger H. Brown, *Redeeming the Republic: Federalists, Taxation, and the Origins of the Constitution* (Baltimore, MD: Johns Hopkins University Press, 1993).

9. Forrest McDonald, *Novus Ordo Seclorum: The Intellectual Origins of the Constitution* (Lawrence, KS: University Press of Kansas, 1985). See also Brown, *Redeeming the Republic*.

Out of this emerged a series of compromises by which a novel form of government was created, as the modernizers wanted, without abolishing or even seriously touching some of the old ways the traditionalists wanted to retain. The first compromise was about representation in the Congress: was it to be on the old confederal principle or according to population? As we shall discuss in Chapter 7, the "Connecticut Compromise" squared this circle by means of bicameralism. A second compromise had to do with the retention, for the time being, of slavery, that "peculiar institution" on which the social, economic, and cultural traditions of the south hinged. A third and related compromise, as we shall discuss in Chapter 6, pertained to policy-making and the division of powers, giving to the economic modernizers the national tools of trade and commerce regulation while leaving social policy and education with the traditionalists.

The final package transformed the union from something referred to in the plural—"The United States *are* ..."—to something that could be referred to in the singular, a nation-state—"The United States *is*...." However, it left a number of unanswered questions that were the subject of great issue in the ratification debates between so-called Federalists and so-called Anti-Federalists and which remained unresolved until at least the end of the Civil War.

The "Bill of Rights"

As we discussed in the previous chapter, the Federalists placed their faith in the system of multiple checks and balances as the chief mechanism securing individual rights. Moreover, since they saw these rights endangered by local tyrannies of the majority, the constitutional draft also contained, in Article VI, a **supremacy clause** for national legislation. The Anti-Federalists argued that since there could then be only one sovereign legislature, the powers of the union would eventually annihilate states rights.[10] To ensure ratification, therefore, the Federalists had to promise that once the government was established, initiative would be taken to amend the Constitution.

The result was the first ten amendments of 1791, generally known as the Bill of Rights. Under the leadership of Madison in the House of Representatives, these amendments were overwhelmingly concerned

---

10. As evidenced by the great lengths to which Hamilton and Madison went in trying to neutralize this criticism in *Federalist* 17 through 46. See also Jackson Turner Main, *The Antifederalists: Critics of the Constitution, 1781–1788* (1961; Chapel Hill, NC: University of North Carolina Press, 2004) 9; Herbert J. Storing, *What the Anti-Federalists Were For: The Political Thought of the Opponents of the Constitution* (Chicago: University of Chicago Press, 1981); and David J. Siemers, *Ratifying the Republic: Antifederalists and Federalists in Constitutional Time* (Stanford, CA: Stanford University Press, 2002).

with the rights of individuals. The Tenth Amendment, though, acknowl-edged the rights of the states. It gave express indication of the **residual powers** (see Chapter 6) whereby the states would retain all powers not expressly granted to Congress. Although this was transferred from the decidedly confederal constitution that the Americans were replacing, any hopes that the Tenth Amendment would carry over that spirit have proven illusory. As we shall discuss in Chapter 11, judicial interpretation has established rather a different balance between national supremacy and states rights.

The Dominion of Canada

In 1867, three of the remaining British North American colonies—the Province of Canada, New Brunswick, and Nova Scotia—agreed to a federal union. The resulting Dominion of Canada comprised just four "provinces" as the constituent units were called: Québec, Ontario, New Brunswick, and Nova Scotia. Subsequently, neighbouring colonies joined (the last being Newfoundland in 1949); new western provinces were created; and self-governing territories added (the most recent being the far north territory of Nunavut in 1999).

Loyalty

In sharp contrast to the American revolutionary experience, the Canadian agreement was based on continued loyalty, not defiance, to the British institutions of parliamentary rule. The Canadian founders did not like federalism and saw the raging Civil War south of the border as a clear sign of its failure. But all previous attempts at some form of common governance for the two provinces of British North America, French Lower Canada and English Upper Canada, had proven unstable, and some form of federal union became inevitable. And agreement existed that a union had to be forged for all the reasons already explored in the American case: external threat; the desire for a large national market economy; and, most importantly in this case, the accommodation of social and cultural differences.

Conquest Colony

Canada was not just a British settler colony; it was also a conquest colony, a colony imposed on an already existing colony. Ever since their defeat on the Plains of Abraham in 1759, French Canadians had resented British domination. In 1841, the English colony of Upper Canada (Ontario) and the dominantly French colony of Lower Canada (Québec) were united to form the Province of Canada. Canada East and Canada West were granted equal representation in one assembly and, eventually, responsible government as well as (reluctantly) bilingualism. However, the amalgamation did little to ease the tensions. On the English side, equal representation was resented and cries for representation by population became louder once the population of Canada West came to exceed that of Canada East. On the French side, both "rep-by-pop" as well as plans for a larger continental union were seen as a plot to marginalize the French once again. Confederation then "was driven and drawn by the inability of French and English to live together in the unitary state imposed by the British a quarter of a century earlier."[11]

"Confederation"

By 1858, the proposal to solve these problems through the formation of a larger union was on the table. Strategically and economically, these plans were given a powerful thrust by developments south of the border. The end of the Civil War greatly increased the annexationist threat (not least because the defeat of the South now made it possible for new non-slave states to be added without requiring a balancing addition of slave states). It also led to the abrogation of free trade relations and the need for the British North American colonies to turn from a north-south axis to an east-west one. Another facet of this external threat was the fact of American expansionism in the west, not only to the mostly tiny British settlements there, but also to the merchant dreams of a continental economy. Moreover, both the declining commitment to mercantilism in Britain and the imminent annulment of the reciprocity treaty with the Americans threatened foreign trade security and fostered ideas of a national economy with a resource hinterland joined to a manufacturing heartland.

For francophone supporters of "Confederation," as it was peculiarly called, the new federal union offered the space for autonomous development of Québec as a linguistic and cultural island. Francophone opponents—the *Rouge* party—challenged this optimism much as the American Anti-Federalists challenged the proposition that federalism could create an effective central government without eclipsing the states.[12]

Modernizers and Traditionalists

As in the American case, the federal compromise had to accommodate the interests of economic modernizers and traditionalists. In essence,

---

11. John T. Saywell, *The Lawmakers: Judicial Power and the Shaping of Canadian Federalism* (Toronto, ON: University of Toronto Press, 2002) 4.

12. See Robert C. Vipond, *Liberty and Community: Canadian Federalism and the Failure of the Constitution* (Albany, NY: State University of New York Press, 1991).

anglophone merchants wanted to build a union with a strong central government that would facilitate economic integration and western expansion. Francophone *seigneurs* wanted to preserve the autonomy of their land-based privileges under the tutelage of the Catholic church.

The resulting ambiguity of the Canadian federalist compromise[13] was not really all that different from the initial constitutional outcome in the United States. Despite the grand rhetoric of "We the People," the US Constitution did not immediately or automatically succeed in the creation of one nation-state and one national economic system. As in the Canadian case, the conflictive issue of national sovereignty versus the sovereignty of the constituent units remained unresolved. Only the Civil War almost a century later initiated a long and traumatic process of eventual closure in favour of national sovereignty.

Initially, the decisive issue putting Canadian federalism on a trajectory of decentralization rather than centralization was the issue of Québec's cultural-linguistic minority status within the federation. The original settlement was essentially understood among the two Canadas, one French and one English, as a federal union treaty whereby sectional equality would overrule majoritarianism.[14] When the original union of four gradually expanded to a union of ten, Québecers increasingly felt that sectional equality did not suffice to safeguard their differences. Eventually, however, the added western provinces compounded the decentralist thrust with their own quests for greater autonomy, both for the management of the natural resources they owned and for social experimentation more generally.[15]

Germany from Reich to Republic

In the case of Germany, the story of federal state formation has to be told in two instalments. First came Bismarck's Imperial federation of 1871 and then, after the interruptions of the Weimar Republic and Hitler's Third Reich, came the Federal Republic of Germany (West Germany) in 1949. Despite catastrophic discontinuities, German federalism reveals important underlying continuities between its more autocratic nineteenth-century and its democratic postwar twentieth-century versions. The distinguishing features of modern German federalism are legacies of the original Imperial federation and late unification. "In Western Europe

---

13. See Richard Simeon and Ian Robinson, *State, Society, and the Development of Canadian Federalism* (Toronto, ON: University of Toronto Press, 1990) 19–30.
14. See Janet Ajzenstat, Paul Romney, and William D. Gairdner, eds., *Canada's Founding Debates* (Toronto, ON: Stoddart, 1999) 278.
15. See John F. Conway, *The West: The History of a Region in Confederation* (Toronto, ON: James Lorimer, 1983).

Germany stands out as a society which achieved political unification late and on unusual terms."[16]

Historical Background

As we noted in Chapter 4, though, Germany's federal origins can be traced much further back than the unification of 1871. Under the loose and diverse arrangements of the Holy Roman Empire, German territories practised some type of federalism for 800 years. That tradition carried over into the dynamic period of industrialization and nation-building in the nineteenth century.

Economic and Political Union

Under the post-Napoleonic restoration of Europe in 1815, the German states—including the two main contending powers, Prussia and Austria—re-established a confederal structure, the *Deutscher Bund*. Within that loose political framework, Prussia initiated a free trade area, the *Zollverein* or customs union,[17] in 1834 as industrialization created pressure for larger and more open markets. The *Zollverein* unified weights and measures and abolished protective duties limiting trade between the separate German states. Within a decade most German states had joined the union, with the notable exception of Prussia's rival Austria, while continuing to belong to the larger confederacy; "the Zollverein was a confederation within a confederation, a Bund within a Bund."[18] In 1866, Germany took a decisive step towards federation with the reassertion of Prussian hegemony. Austria was defeated militarily and excluded from membership in the newly created North German Confederation. The essential character of the German model was established at this point and carried over into the larger union established following the defeat of France in 1871 and the absorption of the states of southern Germany.

The Imperial German Federation 1871–1918

In 1871, most of the German princes did not particularly desire to unite or form a federal union. Only Prussia and its chancellor (prime minister)

---

16. Nevil Johnson, "Territory and Power: Some Historical Determinants of the Constitutional Structure of the Federal Republic of Germany," in Charlie Jeffrey, ed., *Recasting German Federalism: The Legacies of Unification* (London: Pinter, 1999) 25.

17. A customs union entails the abolition of all tariffs or formal restraints on the exchange of goods between participating jurisdictions and their replacement with a common external tariff. It is the second most minimal form of economic association two or more countries can have a free trade area—which requires only the abolition of internal customs barriers and allows jurisdictions to retain their own tariffs on external trade.

18. Forsyth, *Unions of States*, p. 167.

Otto von Bismarck did. There were two main ambitions: to resurrect German national glory in a second empire, or *Reich*, and to press ahead with a national economy led by the industrializing Prussian Rhineland.

The new Imperial Constitution was proclaimed in the French palace of Versailles, crowning Prussia's victory over France and symbolizing the strategic impetus behind federal union. The Empire was formally constituted as a federation among 25 territorial units: four kingdoms, six grand duchies, four duchies, eight principalities, and three free cities. The border region of Alsace and Lorraine was also appropriated from France as an Imperial territory. Notwithstanding the dynastic and strongly autocratic nature of the Imperial union, late state formation forced it to take a federal form to win acceptance among the established local states.

The federalist compromise was very much one among economic modernizers and cultural traditionalists. The division of powers between the Empire and its constituent units, the *Länder*, followed the usual pattern. While Berlin became the new hub of modernization, the *Länder* continued to provide most services that affected people's everyday lives. By the turn of the century, Germany's overall industrial production was second only to that of the United States. Although deprived of most real powers, the *Länder* thrived as cultural centres. Kings and princes were for the most part admired and imitated by the anti-democratic bourgeois establishment. While Berlin became a centre of world politics, culture and tradition flourished at the periphery.

Bismarck's federal construction of the Empire included a directly elected lower house, the *Reichstag* (Imperial Assembly[19]) and an upper house, the *Bundesrat* (Federal Council) composed of the governing German princes. Voting rights in the crucially important upper house were weighted according to population—not surprisingly since a more confederal equality of votes would leave dominant Prussia heavily outvoted by the minor states. Ultimately, the Empire was dominated by Prussia, but Bismarck could count usually on his powers of persuasion and consensus-building. Parallel to the tensions between national modernizers and regional culturalists, there was a general fault line of authority versus majority between the two chambers. In the *Reichstag*, Bismarck had to secure majority support from the people, and in the *Bundesrat* he had to orchestrate consent among dynastic rulers.[20]

The Federal Republic of Germany 1949

West Germany was reconstructed from the ashes of Hitler's "Third Reich" as a democratic federation. Why did it do so in this form and

---

19. Often translated, rather unhelpfully, as "Diet."
20. See Lehmbruch, "Party and Federation in Germany."

not as a unitary state? Bismarck's Second Reich had not been particularly democratic. The Weimar Republic that replaced it was democratic but not particularly federal. The Nazi dictatorship was neither democratic nor federal. It would have been feasible to have reconstructed liberal democracy on a unitary basis; however, postwar Germany represented a triumph of federalism. We can imagine at least two significant reasons why this occurred.

First, and despite the fact that the old *Länder* boundaries had been redrawn quite arbitrarily after the war, federalism had remained part of Germany's identity and political culture. In fact, if there was one realm of politics where Hitler's totalitarian approach had failed, it was in his attempt at supplanting the age-old colourful plurality of German regional cultures with a bland national culture of brown uniforms. It was only during the formative years of the West German Federal Republic that economic success established a relatively high degree of socio-economic homogeneity, which in turn made Germany a case of territorial rather than cultural federalism. Second, federalism was explicitly seen by the Western powers as affiliated with and supportive of democracy. Imposition of a federal system was thus both natural and desirable. By contrast, the reconstruction of East Germany—the German Democratic Republic—under Soviet supervision occurred in a unitary fashion. As we shall discuss in Chapters 6 and 7, the legacy of Germany's long federal history was evident in the distinctive approach taken to both the division of powers and the design of modern Germany's second chamber.

Unification

The success of Germany's postwar federal system was aided and sustained by the relative homogeneity of the *Länder* and their enormous success in rebuilding the West German economy. When reunification came in 1990, and five rather impoverished *Länder* were recreated out of the old East Germany and added to the system,[21] there were some fears of de-stabilization. Although the worst of these fears proved unfounded, the introduction of an unprecedented degree of regional economic inequality placed strains on the system—particularly Germany's arrangements for revenue sharing or fiscal equalization (see Chapter 11)—that opened up larger questions about the design and workings of German federalism.

---

21. In fact, the decision to recreate the five East German *Länder* had already been taken by the last East German government before reunification.

The European Union

Europe's path towards federal union does not fit smoothly into this survey of federal state formation for several reasons. The EU is not a classical federal state, nor does its formation date back to the nineteenth century. The process of European integration is not finished, and the final outcome is by no means clear. Yet the EU qualifies as a novel kind of federal system among sovereign nation-states, and the history of its formation may be as important for politics in a globalizing twenty-first century as that of the United States was for the nineteenth and twentieth centuries.[22] Its formation also can be explained quite well with the theoretical approaches chosen for federal state formation in general.

Plans for a European federation had already surfaced in various resistance movements against Nazi occupation during World War II. The idea was to tie the European nation-states, including a postwar democratic Germany, into a peaceful union of political, economic, and social cooperation.[23] After that war, and with the onset of the Cold War, external threat also played a significant role. Europeans were afraid of being squeezed by the geopolitical and economic interests of the two superpowers.

Initially, at least, some may have harboured dreams of a United States of Europe in analogy to the United States of America. But soon traditionalist views of nation-state sovereignty reasserted themselves, leaving for Europe only a functional blueprint of economic integration. The modernizers, in other words, were once again interested chiefly in the creation of an integrated market economy while leaving most other policy areas to traditional nation-state governance.[24]

Phase I: The Common Market

Three distinct "communities" were formed by 1958: the European Coal and Steel Community (ECSC); the European Economic Community (EEC); and Euratom, an agency for the joint development and regulation of nuclear energy. Of these, it was the EEC that became the centrepiece of European integration. Later renamed simply the European Community (EC), but referred to as the Common Market, it was very

---

22. See Daniel J. Elazar, "The United States and the European Union: Models for their Epochs," in Kalypso Nicolaïdis and Robert Howse, eds., *The Federal Vision: Legitimacy and Levels of Governance in the United States and the European Union* (Oxford: Oxford University Press, 2001) 31–53; compare Christopher K. Ansell and Giuseppe di Palma, eds., *Restructuring Territoriality: Europe and the United States Compared* (Cambridge: Cambridge University Press, 2004).

23. See Walter Lipgens, ed., *Documents on the History of European Integration: continental plans for European union 1939–45*, 2 vols. (Berlin: Walter de Guyter, 1984).

24. See Gilbert, *Surpassing Realism*.

similar to, but more ambitious than, Germany's *Zollverein* of the nineteenth century.[25] Powers necessary for the regulation of a European market free of trade barriers and with a common external customs union would be given to supranational regulation by the European Commission in Brussels. All other powers would remain in the domain of the member states.

Phase II: The European Union

Until the 1970s the favourable circumstances of the postwar boom years allowed traditional nation-state competition within a common market area. Due to French President Charles de Gaulle's veto in 1966, the decision-making process essentially remained unanimity-based even though the Treaties had foreseen a gradual transition to qualified majority voting. During the 1970s, however, the collapse of the US-led Bretton Woods monetary system, the tripling of oil prices during the OPEC (Organization of the Petroleum Exporting Countries) crisis, and the saturation of many traditional consumer markets brought inflation, unemployment, sluggish growth, and currency instability. Common market policies were no longer sufficient, and the European modernizers began pressing for more comprehensive integration policies. Unification of Europe seems to have indeed been a process overwhelming driven by the search for economic advantage rather than external security.[26] Increasingly, this pressure came from the Commission and the policy networks it had created with government specialists and organized interests.

Increasingly also, size and number of units became an issue. By the mid-1990s, membership had grown from the original six to 15 member states. After the collapse of communism in eastern Europe, the EU had to cope with the prospects of a membership of 25 or more states. The debate about the EU's future came to be cast in terms of **widening and deepening**. Reluctant Europeans such as British Prime Minister Margaret Thatcher had always favoured membership enlargement because they believed that a wider union would also be a weaker union. Enlargement would provide the double benefit of opening up an ever larger market and thinning out the possibility of strong central governance. Committed Europeans like the Germans, on the other hand, insisted that the kind of market enlargement they favoured had to go hand in hand with a deepening of the decision-making process: more qualified majority

---

25. Unlike a mere customs union, a common market entails full mobility of labour and capital between jurisdictions. The next highest level of economic integration after that is a monetary union, where a single currency replaces separate national currencies, and after that an economic union, where a common economic policy is in operation.

26. As argued, for instance, by David McKay, *Rush to Union: Understanding the European Federal Bargain* (Oxford: Oxford University Press, 1996).

voting in more areas and more co-decision powers to the European Parliament in order to enhance legitimacy.

The *Single European Act* of 1987 and the Maastricht or European Union Treaty of 1993 then accomplished a qualitative jump towards deepening. The common market was extended to economic and monetary union (EMU) including a European Central Bank. Most economic decisions would finally be made by qualitative majority voting. Political cooperation would be intensified in areas of foreign policy and domestic security.

If the balance of power between European modernizers and nation-state traditionalists had shifted significantly in favour of the modernizers, the result still was a typical federalist compromise. The new pillar structure would continue to separate sensitive national policy areas such as foreign affairs and domestic security from the community method of qualified majority voting. As later affirmed by the treaties of Amsterdam (1997) and Nice (2003), the method of further integration and enlargement would become increasingly characterized by flexibility, asymmetry, and differentiation. Individual opt-outs from certain policy programs were allowed, and it became possible for groups of member states to go ahead with new initiatives of "enhanced cooperation" with the proviso that others could catch up later.[27] A division of powers would be based on the **principle of subsidiarity** (see Chapter 6), tied to a political process of negotiation and agreement about the scope and dimension of European policy action rather than becoming a matter of constitutional law.[28]

Distinctiveness

It must be remembered, though, that the EU represents a novel experiment in federalism. It is the first attempt to fuse a large number of established nation-states with different cultures, languages, and national identities—not to mention a shared history of conflict—as well as highly developed political systems, bureaucratic apparatuses, and comprehensive welfare states. Only the Swiss Confederation united different language communities voluntarily, and that occurred in a centuries-long process. No federation has been formed by the union of established nation-states, and none has been formed by the union of nation-states that have reached full welfare state maturity. It is not surprising, then, that the union of Europe has taken a distinctive and in many ways

---

27. See Kerstin Junge, "Differentiated Integration," in Michelle Cini, ed., *European Union Politics* (New York: Oxford University Press, 2003).
28. If eventually ratified, the European Constitution will not radically change the nature of the EU.

confederal form with its alleged "democratic deficit."[29] What is surprising is the degree of integration that has occurred—particularly given that it has occurred in the absence of external military threat.

IMITATIONS AND VARIATIONS

The general process and dynamic of federal state formation can be understood and appreciated quite well from these few basic models. It is useful, though, to canvass some of the subsequent federations more briefly to see how these dynamics played out in different settings.

Switzerland as a Paradigmatic Case

Switzerland is by far the world's oldest continuing federal system, if by federalism we include more confederal versions, but it only became a modern federal state in 1848. We do not treat Switzerland as one of our basic models because its constitution is a blend of elements borrowed from the already existing American model (e.g., construction of the upper house), traditional elements of power division shared with the German model (e.g., administrative federalism), and a genuinely Swiss commitment to direct democracy (e.g., obligatory referendums for all constitutional changes) which is not directly affiliated with federalism *per se*. Its history, however, deserves special mention because it powerfully illustrates the way federal unions are likely to emerge from a combination of strategic, economic, and cultural factors. In fact, one of the most famous political scientists of the twentieth century called Switzerland a paradigmatic case of political integration.[30]

External Threat, Economic Welfare

Situated in a handful of mountain valleys in the European Alps, the tiny Helvetic Confederation had its beginnings very early indeed: the first federal compact among the original three territories dates back over 700 years, to 1291. Divided but also protected by geography, these three communities were united by a common interest in preserving their autonomy from external domination by foreign lords, kings, and emperors. At stake was the control of the transalpine trade routes from which these communities drew their wealth. For the purpose of defending these trade routes, the ruling patriciate armed their peasants—the beginning of Switzerland's military militia system which accounts for both its military

---

29. Andrew Moravcsik, "Federalism in the European Union: Rhetoric and Reality," in Nicolaïdis and Howse, eds., *The Federal Vision*, especially pp. 176–80.

30. Karl W. Deutsch, *Die Schweiz als ein paradigmatischer Fall politischer Integration* (Bern: Paul Haupt, 1976).

successes over much more powerful invaders and the eventual formation of a more egalitarian society.

Religious and Linguistic Plurality

By the sixteenth century, the confederation had grown to 13 cantons and a number of associate communities. They were still united primarily in the common interest of securing trade routes and the surrounding agricultural land that sustained them. But the Reformation led to religious war. After the battle of Kappel (1531), the territorial principle of cantonal religious self-determination was established. By the sixteenth century also, the accession of new territories and, eventually, cantons likewise resulted in language diversity (German, the official language until 1798, as well as French, Italian, and Romansh).[31] The same principle of territoriality also became the guarantor of lasting linguistic accommodation.

While in the United States the *Articles of Confederation and Perpetual Union* proved successful over only the shortest of constitutional lives, confederal arrangements proved entirely adequate for the Swiss cantons for a constitutional eon—the Swiss Confederation was very much a perpetual union. The Confederation grew as more cantons were admitted, but until the nineteenth century the need for a 'deepening' of the union remained minimal.

This changed dramatically when the Napoleonic armies invaded the country in 1798 and a centralized republic was established. That republic lasted only until 1815 when the old Confederation was resurrected. But the Napoleonic interlude left modern ideas of social and economic liberalism which could no longer be undone. And this in turn triggered the conflict that finally forced the transformation from a confederal to modern federal statehood.

Modernizers and Traditionalists

The trigger was very much a conflict between modernizers and traditionalists. The modernizers, mainly Protestant and living in the more urban and industrializing cantons, wanted a transformation of the confederation into a modern federal state with efficient central powers. The traditionalists, mainly from the rural and Catholic cantons, wanted to preserve both their privileges and the dominant role of the Catholic church in political and cultural life.

In 1845, the Catholic cantons, feeling threatened by growing Protestant aggressiveness, joined in a separate treaty, the *Sonderbund*, in order to defend their common interests. In 1847, they left the Confederation's

---

31. See Kenneth D. McRae, *Conflict and Compromise in Multilingual Societies: Switzerland* (Waterloo, ON: Wilfrid Laurier University Press, 1983) 39–47.

common intergovernmental body, the Assembly of Delegates or *Tagsatzung*. The Protestant cantons interpreted this as an act of secession. A short civil war ensued, the *Sonderbundskrieg*. After 26 days it ended with the defeat of the secessionists and, a year later, with the adoption of a new constitution. It created a central government constituted by the people rather than by the cantons and with the power to act on the people directly rather than only through the cantons. The historic name *Eidgenossenschaft* (Sworn Brotherhood) in German, *confederation* in French, was kept, but the reality had changed. Switzerland had become a modern federal state.

Hispanic Federations

While the federations of Latin America followed American governmental design very closely, these institutional similarities tend to obscure the fact that the Latin American road to federalism was quite different.

As we saw in the case of the United States, Americans were reluctant to endorse a new form of union government that for many looked too much like the kind of European state absolutism the original settlers wanted to leave behind. Hence, it was the modernizers who sought to superimpose the vested interests of separate settler societies with the central institutions of modern governance. In Latin America, however, authoritarian rule had left a colonial heritage of centralism. Modernization therefore meant decentralization.

Mexico

This was certainly so in the first case of Latin American federalization. Independent since 1821, Mexico had already lived through three years of political turmoil when the first federal constitution was drafted in November 1823. The battle lines between modernizers and traditionalists were clearly drawn, although in reverse order and fashion. While the Spanish conservatives—clergy, army officers, and landowners—favoured a centralist regime, the modernizing liberal middle classes—mostly of mixed Spanish and Indigenous ancestry—supported federalism.[32] After the oppression of 300 years of centralist despotism and the "irresistible" example of the United States, the federalists carried the day.

The first federal republic lasted only little more than a decade. For the next 100 years, federalism was not a major concern in Mexican politics. In between military dictatorships, foreign occupation, civil war, and revolution, there was only one return to republican federalism, in 1857, and it lasted less than a decade. Under the impression of external

---

32. See Michael C. Meyer and William L. Sherman, *The Course of Mexican History* (New York: Oxford University Press, 1979) 313–16.

threat, the war with the United States and the loss of Texas, the new constitution strengthened central and executive powers. So did the third federal constitution of 1917, created amidst a decade of revolution and chaos. It turned out to be the one Mexicans would keep.

Political stability and economic modernization, however, came with a one-party regime of centralist and clientelist authoritarianism. Federalist renewal had to wait until the 1980s when opposition parties began to score electoral victories in cities and, subsequently, states. The history of the Mexican federalist compromise seemed to have come full circle as, once again, federalism challenged the traditional preference for a centralist regime with clientelist links to the periphery.[33] For the opposition victory in the 2000 federal election, federalism provided both the institutional tools and the ideological ammunition.

Brazil

The case of Brazil is different again.[34] Brazil gained independence from Portugal in 1822, and, after a military revolt in 1889, a federal republic was created in 1891. The essential institutional elements—a presidential system with a bicameral Congress—remained in place and operation, most of the time, throughout a history that saw eight constitutions and republican rule interspersed with civilian as well as military dictatorships. Although sharing borders with all but two of the 12 surrounding countries in South America, external threat never was a serious issue. And by contrast with Mexico, the conflicts of modernizers and traditionalists followed the usual pattern, as traditional regional elites opposed modernizing impulses from the centre. Indeed, one might argue that the modernizers were altogether excluded from the original federalist compromise. Colonial administrations had created a loose clientelist network across Brazil's vast territorial expanse. Federalism became not so much a tool of liberalization as a device to secure the interests of traditional regional elites in the Congress.

From the 1930s onward, the balance of power began to shift decisively towards the centre. Inevitable economic modernization required government intervention and improved social stability. The national government was given full trade and commerce powers. The self-governing rights of the states were all but suspended by a dictatorial regime of supervision. Under the pretext of putting an end to congressional paralysis, the military dictatorship after 1964 for all practical purposes transformed Brazil into a unitary presidential regime.

---

33. See Victoria E. Rodríguez and Peter M. Ward, eds., *Opposition Government in Mexico* (Albuquerque, NM: University of Mexico Press, 1995).
34. See Celina Souza, *Constitutional Engineering in Brazil: The Politics of Federalism and Decentralization* (New York: St. Martin's Press, 1997).

It can hardly be surprising that the final process of democratization, begun in 1985 with the return of civilian rule, went hand in hand with calls for decentralization. The eighth and so far last Brazilian Constitution of 1988 seems to have finally achieved a genuine federalist compromise between the traditional interests of land and region and the modernizing interests of the world's seventh or eighth largest economy.[35]

British Empire Federations

It is one of the more curious peculiarities in the history of federalism that one of the most notoriously unitary states, Britain, actively promoted federation throughout its vast colonial empire. Given the enormous diversity of that empire, the processes and outcomes were vastly different as well. In Australia, colonial societies of British settlers and immigrants scattered across a vast continent accepted the idea of union rather cautiously and without the kind of cultural necessity that had made federalism inevitable in Canada. In India, on the other hand, the task of federal state formation fell into the hands of an immensely diverse indigenous society left with a legacy of quasi-federalist administrative institutions after independence.

Commonwealth of Australia

In the case of Australia, the first federal initiative indeed came from Britain. Around the mid-nineteenth century, the Colonial Office proposed a general assembly in order to settle intercolonial Australian disputes directly; the colonies, however, were not inclined to listen. An intergovernmental Federal Council was established in 1885 for the purpose of coordinating security and immigration policies, but not all agreed to join and it remained ineffectual. The colonies had developed independently; they had achieved responsible self-government separately; they were geographically separate, with little contiguity of population;[36] and they had little economic integration, being in the main a cluster of entrepôt economies. On top of all that, they had little sense of strategic insecurity at this stage, being both geographically privileged and firmly beneath the imperial umbrella. "In any attempt to account for the lack of interest in federation, faith in the Royal Navy has to be seen as an important and persistent factor."[37]

When the Australians finally agreed upon the formation of a federal union in 1900, they did so, as in most other cases, mainly for reasons

---

35. On recent developments see "Brazil: Burden of the Past, Promise of the Future," *Daedalus* 129:2 (Spring 2000).

36. W.G. McMinn, *Nationalism and Federalism in Australia* (Melbourne: Oxford University Press, 1994) 30.

37. McMinn, *Nationalism and Federalism* 82.

of economic modernization. A rapid increase in population began to reduce the physical distance of separate settlements. The first stirrings of a nationalist sentiment in newsprint and literature contributed to a growing sense of national identity as the native-born population came to exceed the transplanted.[38] And there was the growing realization that combined forces were necessary in order to participate successfully in an emerging regime of international trade and commerce driven by the interests of powerful nation-states. If there was any single driver to the process, it was the mundane demand for a solution to cross-border issues between the two leading colonies, Victoria and New South Wales. But there were no fundamental rifts between modernizers and tradition-alists in Australia. It simply was a pragmatic case of late state formation.

This is not to say that everybody agreed. In fact, the most distinctive characteristic of the Australian case is that the federal commonwealth was constructed from a process of public deliberation. The federal option gained momentum gradually, over a period of 50 years, in polit-ical speeches and newspaper articles and at various intercolonial meet-ings and conventions. The first of these conventions, in 1891, provided a constitutional blueprint. The second one, 1897–98, produced the final draft. But even that draft had to be amended again after it was rejected at referendum in the most important state, New South Wales.[39]

Public deliberation did not necessarily mean that the outcome was any less ambiguous than the results of the Canadian federal compromise which had been crafted by the governing elites only. In a somewhat peculiar compromise, the founders opted for the combination of a fully developed American-style senate and the retention of the British parlia-mentary tradition.

India

In significant ways, the case of India differs from all others yet again, not only because independent state formation was deferred to the middle of the twentieth century. India was under British rule but was not a settler colony. In stark contrast to Hispanic America, its own societies had not been destroyed. It neither possessed the social and ideological cohesion for an early and revolutionary break from colonial rule, as in the Amer-ican case, nor could it count on benign neglect, as in the Canadian case.

---

38. McMinn, *Nationalism and Federalism* 124. On the contribution specifically of an emerging national consciousness to the federal movement, see John Hirst, *The Sentimental Nation: The Making of the Australian Commonwealth* (Melbourne: Oxford University Press, 2000).

39. See W.G. McMinn, *A Constitutional History of Australia* (Melbourne: Oxford University Press, 1979) 115–17.

While India's economic importance for the British Empire peaked during the nineteenth century, Canada's role as a resource provider declined.

An organized nationalist movement had existed since 1885 when the Indian National Congress was established, but its cohesion and driving force were constrained by two structural impediments. On the one hand, British India included two major religious groups, Hindus and Muslims. The latter had formed their own Muslim League in 1906 and were reluctant to cooperate with the Hindu-dominated Congress. On the other hand, British India not only contained directly administered provincial territories but also a multitude of autonomous states under the rule of Indian princes who had accepted British paramountcy but could effectively govern any way they wanted as long as their conduct was not deemed detrimental to British interests.

The British did make several attempts to accommodate Indian requests for self-rule. Of these, the 1935 *Government of India Act*, fashioned after the Canadian *British North America Act* of 1867, went furthest in offering a federal scheme of self-administration, self-government for elected provincial legislatures in the territories, and a bicameral national legislature. Governance in the states remained untouched, however, and the state representatives in the upper chamber of the national legislature were not elected but appointed by the princely rulers who were, in the words of Mahatma Gandhi, "British officers in Indian clothes."[40]

By the time independence had been achieved and a constitution was being drafted by the national legislature acting as a constituent assembly, one of the impediments in the way of national unity had been removed by the creation of Pakistan as a separate Muslim state. This allowed the nationalist modernizers to press for a "federation with a strong Centre."[41] Stripped of British protection, the princes were coaxed into the fold by persuasion, appeals to the local population, and, in one case, police action. The integrity of state boundaries was deliberately not constitutionally guaranteed. With two exceptions, the states also were denied their own constitutions. The setup of legislative, executive, and judicial institutions was uniformly prescribed. By means of extraordinary emergency powers the central government could effectively and unilaterally take over the administration of individual states, a provision occasioned by the anticipation of ethnic unrest as well as by external threat as the conflict with Pakistan over Kashmir was already brewing.

The traditionalists for the most part lost. They had wanted a territorial reorganization along ethno-linguistic lines. While the constitution would initially recognize 14 regional languages, the Congress nationalists wanted to avoid giving linguistic tensions a territorial basis. Therefore,

40. Quoted in K.R. Bombwall, *The Foundations of Indian Federalism* (Bombay: Asia Publishing House, 1967) 203.
41. Bombwall, *Foundations of Indian Federalism* 256.

the federalist compromise initially remained incomplete. Over the next two decades fraught with ethnic tension and violence, new linguistic state boundaries were drawn up, in part by breaking up some of the previous pluri-lingual states, in part by creating new ones.[42]

The Indian federal state was the project of the Congress Party, which, because it was the only broadly based national party, dominated and governed Indian politics unchallenged and in centralist fashion for much of the last four decades of the twentieth century. However, its semi-authoritarian governing style could not prevent the states from gaining power and status by making use of the existing structures of federalism and by appealing to linguistic and, in the case of Punjab, religious loyalties of state populations. Thus, the Indian federalist compromise consolidated into a more balanced form over time.[43]

DEVOLUTIONARY FEDERALISM

Thus far, we have dealt with cases of federal state formation that brought previously separate or independent units together in a common union. These are our main cases. However, our survey would not be complete without considering some recent cases of federalization—those of Spain, Belgium, and South Africa—that took the opposite direction, decentralizing or devolving previously unitary states into federal systems.

Spain

The case of Spain is exemplary for the use of federalism as a tool of democratization. General Franco, Spain's fascist dictator for 36 years, died in 1975. Three years later, Spain had a democratic Constitution that granted quasi-federal rights of regional self-governance and that eventually resulted in the creation of 17 "Autonomous Communities."[44] Franco had viciously suppressed all manifestations of regionalism, especially in Catalonia which had a long tradition of rebellious republicanism. Because of this rigid centralism, democratic renewal was almost universally associated with the recognition of regional rights as the non-negotiable precondition for genuine democracy.[45]

---

42. See J.C. Johari, *Indian Government and Politics* (Delhi: Vishal Publications, 1976) 157–61.

43. See the various assessments in Akhtar Majeed, ed., *Constitutional Nation Building: Half a Century of India's Success* (New Delhi: Centre for Federal Studies, 2001).

44. It is quasi-federal because the rights of the autonomous communities are not enshrined in the Constitution. To revoke them, however, would appear a political impossibility, and therefore Spain can be treated as a federation for all practical purposes.

45. See Paul Heywood, *The Politics and Government of Spain* (New York: St. Martin's Press, 1995) 49.

As is common during transitions from authoritarian rule to democracy, there could have been bloodshed or even civil war. For two main reasons, however, this was avoided. First of all, the Franco regime had been successful in modernizing Spain's economy and much of its society. This had created a stabilizing middle class. Secondly, while a monarchy was restored as Franco had wanted, the monarch, Juan Carlos, made an early and unequivocal commitment to full democracy. This further bridged the gap between conservative traditionalists who wanted to preserve the privileges they had enjoyed under the dictatorship and the modernizers who expected equal opportunity from liberalization.

Compromise Mechanisms

However, the main dividing lines that had to be addressed by the constitutional settlement ran between centralists and regionalists. The three historic regions—Catalonia, the Basque Country, and, to a lesser extent, Galícia—revived old nationalist traditions which they now expected to be recognized. A strong regionalist movement also existed in Andalucía. Some of the other regions did not even have clear boundaries.

Essentially, the solution was a federalist compromise which, apart from a bicameral national legislature with a weak senate, contained three innovative features.[46] First, the Constitution did not create regional self-government but instead left the initiative to the regions themselves. These had to form pre-autonomous assemblies which would negotiate individual statutes of autonomy with the central government before being approved by regional referendums. A "privileged" path to autonomy was provided for the historic regions, whereas the others had to follow a more cumbersome "normal" path.

Secondly, the Constitution distinguished between immediate "high" level autonomy for the historic regions following the privileged path and "low" level autonomy under the normal path. Additional provisions allowed "exceptional" applications for full autonomy (used by Andalucía) as well as individually negotiated additional power packages (used by Valencia and the Canary Islands). Thirdly, while most tax raising powers effectively remained with the central government, and a 15 per cent income tax transfer to the Autonomous Communities came into effect only in 1993, the Basque Country and Navarra were allowed to retain their mediæval *fueros* rights of fiscal autonomy by which most taxes are collected locally and a percentage is in turn passed on to Madrid.

---

46. See Michael Keating, *The Politics of Modern Europe* (Aldershot: Edward Elgar, 1993) 343–58.

Asymmetrical Arrangements

The Spanish case demonstrates a new kind of procedural as well as institutional flexibility. The provision of different paths to autonomy was meant to accommodate the immediate aspirations of the historic regions on whose support the stability of the new democratic state depended. The **asymmetrical** differentiation of power packages in turn served the needs and aspirations of economically stronger and weaker regions. How to avoid competitive regionalism and how to square the asymmetrical distribution of powers with a fair distribution of revenue has remained a particular problem. It seems, however, that external threat, or at least external necessity, is playing its part in the consolidation of federalism once again. The name of necessity is uniform compliance with European laws and regulations. It has compelled Spain to develop a cooperative mode of intergovernmental relations between the Spanish state and its 17 Autonomous Communities.[47]

Belgium

Belgium gained independence in 1830. Perched in between France, Germany, and the Netherlands, it was composed of a French-speaking part in the south, Wallonia, and a Dutch-speaking part in the north, Flanders. In addition, a bilingual region evolved around the capital region of Brussels, and a small German-speaking minority remained in eastern Wallonia, close to the German border. All communes or municipalities belong to one of these four linguistic regions and are, with the exception of Brussels, unilingual. Thus, Belgium has always been an inherently federal society. A national balance of sorts existed in so far as the Flemish constituted the more numerous part of the country whereas Walloons possessed a stronger economy. When this economy faltered, however, tensions began to mount between the two main nationalities, driving the country to the brink of a break-up and making unitary government non-viable.

Federalization

Several rounds of federalization were initiated after 1970, culminating in the federal Constitution of 1993.[48] Apart from reforming the bicameral legislature without, however, giving the senate co-equal powers, the emphasis of the new federalist compromise was entirely on the creation of a complex system of subnational self-government. To this end, the

---

47. See Tanja Börzel, "From Competitive Regionalism to Cooperative Federalism: The Europeanization of the Spanish State of the Autonomies," *Publius* 30:2 (Spring 2000).
48. See Robert Senelle, "The Reform of the Belgian State," in Hesse and Wright, eds., *Federalizing Europe?*.

new Constitution not only recognized three territorial "Regions" (Wallonia, Flanders, and Brussels) but also three autonomous cultural "Communities" (French, Flemish, and German). Both Regions and Communities have separate and exclusive powers of self-government exercised by directly elected councils.

Distinctive Features

The regional Councils of the two main language groups perform territorially bounded tasks such as infrastructural planning and economic development. Community Councils, on the other hand, comprising representatives from the two Regions as well as from the bilingual Region of Brussels-Capital, perform tasks in the fields of culture, language, and education that extend beyond regional boundaries to all members of the cultural communities. Brussels-Capital has its own government elected from separate lists of the two language groups. The autonomy of the German minority is more limited. On Community matters, their Council has powers similar to those of the others. On regional matters, on the other hand, their representatives are part of the Walloon Regional Council.[49]

Perhaps even more importantly, given the complex array of overlapping jurisdictions, the Constitution provides extensive mechanisms of cooperation, concertation, and arbitration. By creating a novel form of federalism recognizing two different manifestations of subnational autonomy, territorial and cultural, the Belgian federalist compromise appears far more procedural than institutional. It can and will work only if all participants can see rewards resulting from a perpetual and cumbersome process of deliberation and consensus-building. This in turn somewhat muddies the political waters of responsibility and accountability. But it may well give an indication of the direction federalism may take in the future when conflicting interests can no longer be identified so easily as those between modernizers and traditionalists, non-territorial identities have to be accommodated, and the old driving forces of state formation are being replaced with those of multilevel governance and interdependence.

South Africa

At first glance, the South African case should be quite similar to the Spanish one: federalization used as a means to move from centralized

---

49. The Belgian Constitution allows the collapsing together of community and regional governance. Thus, there is only one Flemish Council for both community and region, whereas separate Councils have been retained for the French-speaking community and region of Wallonia.

authoritarianism to plural democracy. A closer look, however, reveals a somewhat different picture. In Spain, decentralization and regionalism were endorsed almost universally by the forces of democratic renewal. In South Africa, this was not the case. In Spain, federalism achieved democratic consolidation and stability. In South Africa federalism remains at best a "work in progress."[50]

Federalism had disreputable connotations in South Africa for several reasons. The British Parliament created a federal regime in South Africa in 1909, but this was for whites only. The apartheid regime after 1948 subsequently used the rhetoric of federalism to justify its policies of territorial and tribal segregation and discrimination. When change finally came, the dominant African National Congress (ANC) was a Marxist party committed to centralism and universalism. Support for a federalist polity came from the previously dominant National Party, which feared unmitigated majority rule in a racially integrated South Africa, and the Inkatha Freedom Party (IFP), which sought radical autonomy for its KwaZulu-Natal province.

The dominance of the ANC and the intransigence of the IFP in particular made a federalist compromise all but inevitable. In 1993, agreement on an Interim Constitution was reached. Attached to it were "34 Constitutional Principles" which foreshadowed the future constitutional design by prescribing a division of powers between the central government and the provinces as well as a commitment to subsidiarity whereby decisions should be made at the lowest appropriate level.

The drafting and adoption of the 1996 Constitution was preceded by an extensive process of international consultation for the purpose of gaining a comparative view of various federal constitutions elsewhere. In the end, the nod went to the German model, albeit with significant variations which shall be discussed later (see Chapter 7). The reason for this was part of the compromise itself: the highly integrated nature of the German model with its concentration of legislative authority at the federal level swayed the ANC to bite the bullet of federalism for the sake of democratic unity.

In principle, even though not formally identified as such, South Africa is now a constitutionally guaranteed federal state. In practice, it remains a fragile federal polity. Centralized federalism works well in Germany because it has been sustained by a traditional commitment to federalism. It works not so well in a new federation like South Africa where the provinces in particular lack the human and fiscal resources to play their part and where an emerging democratic political culture remains suspicious about federalism more generally.

---

50. On the following, see Richard Simeon and Christina Murray, "Multi-Sphere Governance in South Africa: An Interim Assessment," *Publius* 31:4 (Fall 2001).

SUMMARY

The archetype of the modern territorial nation-state developed as a unitary state: central rule by one sovereign government over a defined territory and (often merely assumed) one national culture. By contrast, federal states emerged differently due to particular circumstances of place and history. Important variables were late state formation no longer allowing for uniform consolidation of diverse societies, the legacy of colonial territorial agglomerations across historical boundaries of culture and ethnicity, the need for combined defence efforts against external threats, and the desire for the establishment of larger market economies. Typically, but not in all instances, the federal compromise essentially was one between economic modernizers and cultural traditionalists.

- In the American model, all these circumstances combined in the revolutionary creation of the first modern federal state. It was essentially based on a double compromise that became the yardstick for all other federal state formations thereafter: a bicameral legislature as a compromise between federal and confederal visions of union and a division of powers reflecting the modernizers' ambitions for a national market economy as well as the traditionalists' desire to retain local control over social policy, culture, and education.
- The outcomes of federal state formation among British settler colonies in Canada and Australia reflected differences in geography and sociology. Canadian federalism was crafted in order to accommodate the particular interests of a conquered people, the francophones of Québec, within a continental union designed to withstand absorption into the vortex of American expansionism. Far away from such contentious border problems, Australian federation was a much simpler exercise in combining the fortunes of separately developed settler colonies for common economic welfare.
- In India, where British dominion took the form of conquest rather than settlement, the federal outcome reflected the need for post-colonial independent state formation through the unification of a diverse range of regional cultures and traditional polities.
- Modern German federalism evolved from an old tradition of joint governance among a plurality of territorial and dynastic rulers. After 1945, it was reconstructed democratically on the basis of that tradition and under supervision of the victorious Allied forces.
- The EU constitutes a novel case of federalization among previously sovereign member states. The initial driving force at its inception in 1958 was the conviction among postwar European political leaders that lasting peace could be constructed primarily upon bonds of economic integration. However, the self-propelling dynamic of ever more widening the scope and dimension of the European market

eventually and inevitably spilled over into a deepening of joint federal governance as well.

- The Swiss experience with confederal longevity can be appreciated as a paradigmatic case of multi-religious and multi-linguistic political accommodation based on common economic interest as well as the need to secure that interest externally. The transformation from confederation to federation in the nineteenth century then followed the usual pattern of a compromise between modernizers and traditionalists.
- Hispanic federations generally followed the American model but suffered from political and democratic instability occasioned in large part by a colonial tradition of authoritarian centralism which prevented the timely development of a more cooperative and democratic political culture.
- More recently, a number of formerly unitary states have been transformed into federations, either because the unitary form of government had proven unstable (Belgium) or because federalism was seen as the most promising form of government on the road from authoritarianism to democracy (Spain, South Africa).

6 Dividing Powers

We saw in Chapter 5 how differing historical processes led some states to emerge in federal rather than unitary form. One implication of taking the federal route was that the governmental framework took shape through an explicit process of negotiation and compromise. And one of the most important issues on which agreement had to be reached was the way in which powers would be divided between the two levels of government.

Those who worked out these compromises sought to design a structure that would function effectively and with reasonable efficiency, and that would preserve for posterity the kind of federal balance they valued. As a compromise between economic modernizers and cultural traditionalists, the division of powers was typically less contentious than the issue of representation (see Chapter 7). But the divergence between original intentions and eventual outcomes has often been wide. By dividing powers between two levels of government, federalism invites a struggle over jurisdiction and an ever-present tendency to translate distributional conflicts into intergovernmental ones (see Chapter 8). When such conflicts degenerate into political gamesmanship for electoral gain, citizens tend to object to the degree of inefficiency and surplus politics this seems to generate.

This chapter examines the constitutional settlement reached over the division of responsibilities in a range of major federal states. In the older federations, framers had few relevant examples to guide them in establishing a workable constitutional design and help them assess the relationship between codified frameworks and actual outcomes. They also set about their task in an era when government played an almost unrecognizably smaller role in economy and society, a role that could be conceptualized and divided with much greater ease. More recent federations have been in the position to learn from their predecessors and, with varying degrees of effort and success, have tried to do so.

APPROACHES

Constitutional framers had to resolve at least three sorts of issues in the process of establishing the boundaries between the two levels of government. First, they had to settle on the way they were going to slice the functions of government. Second, they had to decide which level of government to assign each of the resulting pieces. And, third, they had to decide how best to give those decisions constitutional expression and permanence. The combined effect of these three sets of decisions we can call the approach they took.

Division of Powers or Division of Roles?

There are two ways in which the functions of government have been sliced: substantively or procedurally. Either the two levels of government can be assigned different substantive tasks or powers, or they can be assigned different procedural roles or functions. In Chapter 2 we labelled these **legislative** federalism and **administrative** federalism respectively.

Legislative Federalism

In the American model, discrete policy areas are assigned to the respective levels of government with each level then being sovereign within its own policy fields. Thus, foreign affairs might be placed entirely within the jurisdiction of the national government, education entirely within the jurisdiction of the subnational governments. Each government takes full responsibility for policy making, implementation, and administration within its respective areas of policy jurisdiction. In its classic application this has been termed "coordinate" federalism.[1] Theoretically, legislative federalism should result in a system of separate spheres, where the respective levels of government operate in splendid isolation, accountable to their citizens for their assigned tasks.

Since each level of government is thus self-contained, there is diminished need for the subnational governments to be represented in the national government. Legislative federalism, then, typically takes a **divided** rather than **integrated** form. In general terms, this is the model characteristic of the British settler federations—Australia, Canada, and the United States—as they were designed and originally envisaged to operate.

Administrative Federalism

This is not, though, the only ways things can be done. The alternative is for the bulk of policy responsibilities to be *shared* between the two

---

1. K.C. Wheare, *Federal Government*, 4th ed. (Oxford: Oxford University Press, 1963).

levels of government rather than divided. Joint responsibility is accompanied by divided roles. The national government is assigned the general law-making role of providing overarching policy guidance for the federation, while the subnational governments are assigned the implementation and administration roles of putting the framework into local effect. This administrative federalism[2] almost necessarily entails input from the subnational governments into the process of national policy-making. As pioneered in Germany, this integrated form of federalism means that subnational governments are represented directly in federal upper houses (see Chapter 7).

FIGURE 6.1
Typological Distinction of Legislative and Administrative Federalism

	National Government	Subnational Governments
Legislative federalism	powers to legislate, implement, administer within its domain	powers to legislate, implement, administer within their domain
Administrative federalism	powers to legislate mostly in the form of framework legislation	powers to implement and administer under national framework legislation

From Ideal Types to Empirical Reality

Of course, legislative and administrative federalism are to some extent ideal types with pure examples hard to find. There is no reason why elements of the two cannot be combined, and indeed we find some division of policy powers in the German system and some sharing of responsibilities in the British settler systems.

Patterns of Assignment

Having decided to divide the roles and responsibilities of government substantively and assign different policy responsibilities to different levels of government, countries taking that approach then had to decide which policy fields should go where. What tasks are appropriately carried out at the national level and what at the subnational level? As summed up by nineteenth-century British constitutional doyen A.V. Dicey, there was little disagreement about the general principle: "Whatever concerns the nation as a whole should be placed under the control of the national government. All matters which are not primarily of common interest

---

2.   *Verwaltungsföderalismus* is an old expression common in Germany, Austria and Switzerland, although in the latter country the expression "executive federalism" (*Vollzugsföderalismus*) is more common.

should remain in the hands of the several states."[3] Or, in more contemporary language, those activities of government whose costs and benefits can readily be contained within one set of borders should remain with the constituent units, while those activities whose costs and benefits will inevitably spill across internal borders ought to be transferred to the national government (see Chapter 11). Defence is the classic example of an activity whose benefits spill over, while public services typically have locally contained benefits.

Modernizers and Traditionalists

This coincided with the historical intentions of modernizers and traditionalists. The modernizers sought to remove from local particularisms those policy fields concerned with the functioning of a market economy—customs tariffs, currency, patents, weights and measures, trade. These were also the policy fields with extensive spillover effects. The policy fields jealously guarded by the traditionalists were those with very limited externalities at the time—education, social policy, religion, culture, and, in multilingual societies, language. Federations have typically, then, assigned responsibility for external affairs and the national market to the national government and responsibility for social affairs to the subnational governments. It was a viable compromise that allowed parochialisms and cultural diversity to co-exist with economic modernization.

Federal Finance

One policy field stands out from all the rest, and that is tax. The role and status of any particular government depends at least as much on how abundant its revenue sources are as on how extensive a field of jurisdiction it can claim. The federal compromise usually reflected both the traditional tax capabilities governments in the constituent units had at the time and a modest transfer of taxing powers to the new national government according to what was deemed necessary for an effective common market to be sustained. Later, however, the balance of taxing powers tilted towards the central government—especially with the eventual introduction of national income tax. This in turn almost inevitably resulted in a mismatch of policy responsibility and revenue-raising capacity at the subnational level.

Patterns of Enumeration

Once these issues were settled, there remained only the task of giving their decisions textual form. Setting down an agreement to federate

---

3.   A.V. Dicey, *An Introduction to the Study of the Law of the Constitution*, 8th ed. (London: Macmillan, 1915) 139.

presumes an intention to give those terms lasting effect, to create a document that binds. Here a number of options have presented themselves over the years. Variation revolves around two sorts of distinctions: that between **enumerated** and **residual** powers and that between **exclusive** and **concurrent** powers.

Enumerated and Residual Powers

Federal constitutions might choose to articulate the division of powers in terms of one, two, or three lists. The earliest and simplest approach is to enumerate the powers assigned to one of the levels of government in a single list and leave the powers of the other level(s) of government implicit. Thus, for instance, a list of specified powers will be assigned to the national government that is being created while the constituent units of the federation will retain—explicitly or implicitly—the residue of powers they traditionally exercised. These residual powers will not be enumerated because to do so would be to limit or confine them— and residual power is an open-ended, plenary, power. "We may assume that the assignment of the residual power to one or the other level of government indicates a preference ... for maximizing the power of that level...."[4] Residual powers were a grant of privileged status of some form. So, in the United States, Switzerland, and Australia, for instance, where the constituent units pre-existed and created the federation, they gave themselves the residual power; in Canada and India, on the other hand, where the federation created the constituent units as much as they created the union, it was the central government that was thus privileged.[5]

An alternative approach that is at least as intuitively appealing is to acknowledge the powers of both levels of government by drafting two separate lists. That way the two levels are granted an equality of presence in the constitution, each having concretely identified jurisdiction. Finally, the powers of both levels, plus those responsibilities to be borne conjointly or concurrently, might be enumerated in three lists.

An important point for some of the earlier federations as designs became more sophisticated in the nineteenth century was whether the lists were **exhaustive** or merely **indicative** in nature. An exhaustive list gave a specific and limited grant to powers to the government in question, intended to constrain as much as to empower. Anything not on the list is out of bounds (*ultra vires*). An indicative list, by contrast, gave

---

4. Garth Stevenson, "The Division of Powers," in Richard Simeon, ed., *The Division of Powers and Public Policy* (Toronto, ON: University of Toronto Press, 1985) 81.
5. As pointed out in Stevenson, "The Division of Powers" 81; also Ronald L. Watts, *Comparing Federal Systems*, 2nd ed. (Kingston, ON: Institute of Intergovernmental Relations, 1999) 39.

an open-ended grant of powers that intended to strengthen by enumeration of specific examples. The difference was typically signalled by a covering clause indicating restrictiveness or, alternatively, indicating a plenary grant of power.

Exclusive and Concurrent Powers

Powers assigned to one particular level of government in a federation may be exclusive, under the control of that level of government alone. However, to grant a power to one level of government is not necessarily to take it away from another. A normal feature of federal constitution-making has been the granting of implicitly or explicitly concurrent powers, exercisable by both or either level of government. Logically of course this entails some procedure or rule for resolving the clashes that will inevitably arise when two levels of government have jurisdiction over the same policy fields—a **paramountcy** provision. Other powers will be made, in explicit terms, the sole or exclusive jurisdiction of one level of government alone.

Developments

Surveying approaches taken to the division of powers from the United States to the EU reveals some clear developments. In part, these reflected a learning process. Newer federations tried to learn from the experience of older ones. At the same time, however, changes to the classic division of powers were the inevitable consequence of industrial modernization and socio-economic change, with the modern welfare state as the most important manifestation of that change.

The Reduction of the Residuum

A number of general trends can be identified over time. One of the most notable is the consistent failure of what the architects of early federations thought would be an effective device, the allocation of residual power. As we shall see in Chapter 10, judicial interpretation has not been kind to the concept of residual powers, precisely because they are unspecified. In the black-and-white text of a codified constitution, an implication does not carry the weight of an explicit grant of power. So, where residual powers had been given to the subnational units with the intent of limiting central authority, as in the United States, Australia, and Germany, we find that judicial interpretation soon opened the door to centralizing forces. Where residual power had been assigned to the central government, on the other hand, as in Canada and India, judicial interpretation has worked in the opposite direction.

From Coordinacy to Integration

With the growing complexity of modern politics and economics, the enumeration of exclusive powers gave way to concurrency and even **institutionalized power sharing**. Both the United States and Germany in particular have gone this way. There has been a general shift away from dividing policy jurisdiction (legislative federalism) to dividing policy roles (administrative federalism). Even under the American model of divided federalism, the states have in large measure become the executors of programs based on national policies. In other federal systems such as Germany, Switzerland, and India, the constitutional design from the very beginning concentrated legislative responsibilities at the national level while assigning the tasks of policy implementation and administration to the subnational units. Essentially following the German model, the EU has gone this route as well. The EU is constructed on the basis of a common supranational policy framework the implementation and administration of which is almost entirely left to the constituent member states. Enumeration of divided powers is avoided altogether, and the system relies instead on the **principle of subsidiarity** as a political guideline for negotiated task assignment.[6]

THE AMERICAN EXPERIMENT

In the Constitution of 1789, the Americans pioneered a balance between national and subnational powers that has come to be thought of as constituting true federalism. However, the minimalist American design is rather exceptional. The framers assembled at the Philadelphia Convention were far more concerned about principles of representation (see Chapter 7) than about the way powers should be distributed between the two levels of government. There was little disagreement as to what the new "general government" should be empowered to do and what the states would no longer be permitted to do. At the end of the eighteenth century, the modern age was just beginning, and the demands of government were limited. The result was a very short constitutional text difficult to change (see Chapter 9). As an inevitable consequence, modernization required increasingly stretched judicial interpretations of the constitutional text. And, quite contrary to what the original designers, those interpretations overwhelmingly strengthened the powers of Congress over the states.

---

6. This will change if and when the European constitutional treaty is ratified; however, most powers will be listed as concurrent, and the principle of subsidiarity will continue to provide the tool for sorting out who gets to do what.

Context

Being first, the Americans had little to work with or to learn from. The existing confederation, while a novel attempt at creating union in its own right, was proving increasingly inadequate. In the Old World, there were a number of confederations—notably Switzerland and the Netherlands—but these were rejected by the Americans for exhibiting the same fatal weakness as their own confederal structure.[7] For the same reason, they would not follow the native Indian practice of treaty federalism, although it doubtlessly inspired at least some of them in a more general sense (see Chapter 4). And all they could draw in these regards from their main source of intellectual inspiration in this regard, Montesquieu, was the idea that some sort of federal arrangement was the expedient means of sustaining republicanism over a large area.

The constitutional power compromise, then, as it took shape at the Philadelphia Convention, had far more to do with contemporary realities than with lofty principles or historical precedent. While all agreed on the need for an adequately resourced central government, views among the gathered delegates differed greatly, ranging from those of unabashed centralists such as Alexander Hamilton who would have been happy to abolish the states altogether to those of unrepentant confederalists.[8] While all agreed that the Congress would need the power to tax, the southern states in particular were opposed to taxes levied on their export of tobacco and other staples. For the same economic reasons, they also insisted that the idea of a ban on the slave trade would be shelved for at least 20 years. In the end, both sides agreed upon a simple division of powers that delineated the scope of the new general government and identified a few areas where the states would have to forfeit jurisdiction.

Dividing Powers or Roles?

There was no doubt that the division of powers in the new republic would assume a legislative rather than an administrative form. Prior to modern means of transportation and communication, in a union of already considerable geographical expanse with some basic unreconcilable policy differences, a division of roles whereby the states had to implement and administer national legislation would have been entirely unworkable. The issue never arose. The only precedent the framers could draw upon was substantive government as it had existed in the colonies and elsewhere. The question was which of these substantive powers should be granted to the new central government they were creating.

---

7.   See Hamilton *et al.*, *Federalist* 19, 20, 37.
8.   McDonald, *Novus Ordo Seclorum* 214.

Assigning Powers

When the delegates met in Philadelphia in 1787 to revise the *Articles of Confederation* it was very clear that something with stronger legislative and executive powers would be required for a lasting United States of America to be established. Nonetheless, a new constitution involving a massive shift of power to the central government would not have won the support of the Convention, nor would it have been ratified in the states. The Convention opened by endorsing the Virginia Plan for a more unified system, but that proposal was soon sidelined. In the end, what was accepted was a division of powers that would endow the new government with sufficient capacity to carry out its essential tasks but no more.

Essential National Powers

It only takes a cursory look at the specific powers granted to Congress to appreciate what was envisaged to be the appropriate role of the new general government. The powers listed in Section 8 of Article I are overwhelmingly concerned with either national defence or the common market. As Alexander Hamilton put it:

> The principal purposes to be answered by the union, are these: the common defence of the members; the preservation of the public peace, as well against internal convulsions as external attacks; the regulation of commerce with other nations, and between the states; the superintendence of our intercourse, political and commercial, with foreign countries.[9]

Thus, contentious differences could be quarantined and traditionalists assuaged with all other functions of government left to the states. The list concludes with a general power to make laws "necessary and proper" to the fulfilment of those functions, but there is little doubt that Congress was being limited to what was effectively the minimal range of powers that would be necessary to make the federation work as a coherent military and economic force. We might note some of the responsibilities of government absent from this list and thus beyond the jurisdiction of Congress: civil and criminal law; public services; water and land use regulation; health, education, and social welfare.

Not only was this a very limited range of powers being granted to Congress, but they were not even being granted exclusively. The listing in Section 10 of a handful of powers being withdrawn from the states— notably the power to impose import tariffs and the power to enter into treaties—implies quite clearly that the grant of a power to Congress is

---

9.   Hamilton, *et al.*, Federalist 23.

not a withdrawal of power from the states; the enumerated powers are concurrent.

At the time, dispute did not arise primarily over the assignment of powers itself but instead over the way in which the Congress would be able to exercise them. Fearing that their trade concerns would be swamped, southern delegates insisted that foreign treaties and commercial regulations would have to be approved by a two-thirds majority in the Senate. In the end, they prevailed on the issue of foreign treaties but not on that of commerce.

Enumerating Powers: The Single List

Without a great deal of debate, the delegates to the Philadelphia Convention settled on a 'less is best' approach to setting the division of powers down on paper. Although there are three sections dealing with the assignment of powers in the US Constitution—sections 8, 9, and 10 of Article I—the approach chosen was that of a minimalist single list. The specific national responsibilities indicated in Figure 6.2 were enumerated. The US Constitution has little more to say about the division of powers than this. Nothing whatsoever was said about the powers of the states. This simplicity accounts in part for the US Constitution's great ambiguity, which opened the door to the increasing judicialization of the American federal system (see Chapter 10).

FIGURE 6.2
The Main Powers of Congress in the American Single List Approach

Article I, section 8:

- "The Congress shall have Power to lay and collect tax ... to ... provide for the common defence and general welfare of the United States."
- "To coin money."
- "To regulate Commerce with foreign Nations and among the several States."
- "To establish Post Offices and post Roads."
- "To sign treaties, raise a military force, and declare war."

The Residual Power

The single list approach of enumeration signalled that the list of congressional powers was to be exhaustive and limiting. The silence on state powers indicated that it was they who should retain the plenary power. The states were thus granted an implicit and open-ended residual power of everything that was not explicitly taken away from them. As Madison put it, the powers granted to Congress "are few and defined. Those that remain to the state governments, are numerous and indefinite."[10]

The *Articles of Confederation* had given residual powers to the states explicitly, as their right of sovereignty over every power not expressly "delegated" to Congress.[11] However, the new constitution omitted any such guarantee. This was apparently rectified by the passage and ratification of the first ten amendments immediately after the Constitution came into effect. The **Tenth Amendment** containing the residual power clause was what Thomas Jefferson regarded as "the foundation of the Constitution."[12] However, it did so in more moderate language, and the Constitution no longer affirmed the sovereignty of the States, as must be expected with the transition from confederal to federal union.

Potentialities

Nobody at the time would seriously quarrel with this general approach, but those whose primary concern was the creation of a strong central government did manage to slip in two additional provisions that would later empower Congress to assume just about any power it wanted or considered essential in the national interest. One was the **necessary-and-proper** clause of section 8, which the Anti-Federalists argued in campaigning against ratification "amounted to an unlimited grant of power to Congress."[13] Congress, it finally said, shall have the power "To make all Laws which shall be necessary and proper for carrying into Execution the foregoing Powers, and all other Powers vested by this Constitution in the Government of the United States, or in any Department or Officer thereof." While to the Anti-Federalists this represented a gutting of the Constitution's federal principles, to Madison is was merely a statement of the obvious: the enumerated powers entail various component and related powers if they are to be meaningful. Either a futile attempt could be made to enumerate all those possible subordinate powers or an equally futile attempt could be made to pretend that Congress would not call upon them.[14]

---

10. In Hamilton *et al.*, *Federalist* 45.
11. Contrary to what the choice of words might suggest, these are not 'delegated' powers—that is powers granted on a revocable basis to a constitutionally subordinate body or individual—but rather assigned powers.
12. McDonald, *States' Rights and the Union* 24.
13. McDonald, *Novus Ordo Seclorum* 267.
14. Hamilton *et al.*, *Federalist* 44. In trying to evade this problem, Madison wanted to have things both ways. By arguing that Congress would act on the assumption of those necessary and proper auxiliary powers anyway—"wherever the end is required, the means are authorized"—he was providing good reason for *not* including the clause. Separately he also had to deal with the objection that it was too open-ended a grant of power. The framers had decided to omit the restrictive modifier "expressly" when referring to powers vested in Congress by the Constitution—as most notably is employed in Article II of the confederal constitution.

The other centralizing feature was the **supremacy** clause of Article 6 which established the paramountcy of national over state laws. "This Constitution, and the Laws of the United States which shall be made in Pursuance thereof; and all Treaties made, or which shall be made, under the Authority of the United States, shall be the supreme Law of the Land...." In combination with the general welfare clause and the commerce clause, the restrictive intentions of limiting the general government to a few clearly enumerated powers proved ineffective. As we shall see later, judicial interpretation played havoc with the original design. On the basis of a small range of enumerated powers, Congress could reign supreme by means of the **implied** or **incidental powers** flowing from these clauses.

Fiscal Capacity

When it came to financial resources, Congress did not need the help of judicial interpretation. With the subsequently significant exception of an income tax, obscure objections to which were removed by constitutional amendment in 1913, Congress was given broad power to tax (see Chapter 11). The states in turn were deprived of what constituted the most common and lucrative form of revenue at the time—the power to impose customs duties. However, that was the only limitation on state taxing powers included in the division of powers. Essentially, the constitutional design of taxing powers was concurrent, with all levels of government having right of access to all revenues sources except tariffs. Within their borders, the states could tax their citizens as much as they liked.

CANADA: CENTRALIST INTENTIONS

After Switzerland (discussed below), the next democratic federation was the Dominion of Canada. The charter document of the Canadian federation was the *British North America Act* of 1867 *(BNA Act)*. Like other charter documents written under British rule, it was conceived locally but vetted and enacted Imperially. Until "patriation" in 1982, when it was renamed the *Constitution Act 1867*, it remained formally an Act of the British Parliament. Although termed "Confederation," the union of 1867 was intended to be anything but.

Context

Even more than their American predecessors, the Canadians who set out to unite Britain's remaining North American colonies had to accommodate strong regional differences within the federal structure they were designing. By contrast they did so while being driven by a concern with the danger of a large and sometimes threatening neighbour. And also by contrast they were moving down a track already marked by the Americans. However, it is not difficult to imagine how Canadians in the 1860s might have looked upon the bloody civil war raging to their south and come to the conclusion that any constitution that allowed decentralization to become secession was ill-designed.

Given the deep divisions between English and French as well as between political conservatives and radicals in either camp—not to mention the worries of the Maritime provinces whose plans for a separate union were hijacked by the Canadians—there is something almost astonishing about the relative ease with which all agreed in the end to a rather centralized formula of power allocation. There was of course no long-standing tradition of autonomy and self-government comparable to the New England colonies.

The main protagonists were John A. Macdonald and Georges-Étienne Cartier, conservative leaders in English and French Canada respectively. Macdonald preferred a unitary regime but had to settle for what he saw as a powerfully centralist federation. Cartier saw federalism as the best possible compromise guaranteeing the survival of French language and culture in North America. In the end, both the modernizer and the traditionalist got what they bargained for—at least on paper.[15]

Centralist Provisions

Macdonald was satisfied with the constitutional scheme because it included a number of overtly centralist elements—elements that were indeed so overtly centralist that some commentators doubted whether Canada quite qualified as a federation at all. One of these was the status of the vice-regal provincial heads of state as deputies of the Canadian head of state (the governor-general) rather than agents of the British Crown. Another was provision for disallowance of provincial legislation by the governor-general—and hence by the prime minister, on whose advice he acted. As might have been expected, though, any impact these features may have had has been overwhelmed by the design and interpretation of the division of powers.

Assigning Powers

At its core, the result was not much different from the assignment of powers in the US Constitution.[16] The Dominion government was in charge of external security and the common market. As in the US Constitution, no public services or land use powers were included. There

---

15. See Vipond, *Liberty and Community* 15–45.
16. See Simeon and Robinson, *State, Society, and the Development of Canadian Federalism* 19–30.

were some divergences, with Parliament being granted power to legislate in the areas of criminal law and marriage, both subnational powers in the United States. The provinces retained power over traditionally local matters such as health, social welfare, and education. This was a legislative federation in that each level of government carried out its respective tasks all the way from legislation to implementation and administration. One partial exception to this was the plan for the judicial system: the law would be national, but its administration would be provincial.

In contrast to the American design, the *BNA Act* made the bulk of assigned powers exclusive to the level of government concerned, and when it made them concurrent, it did so explicitly. It was silent, however, on the question of which level of government would exercise paramountcy in cases of overlap or dispute—a curious omission given the strong desire to forge a highly centralized union. A number of rather idiosyncratic provisions also found their way into the *BNA Act* that would obscure original intentions and open the door to judicial redirection almost from the beginning.

Latent Provincial Powers, Neutralized National Powers

The provinces were given control over public lands belonging to them. In particular, they could manage and sell the timber on these lands, one of the most valuable resources at the time. The provinces also owned the rights to all other natural resources, although this was hidden in the *Act*'s provisions about revenues, assets, taxation, and debts and moved only in 1982 into the section dealing with the division of powers. On the face of it, these provisions were contradicted by the Dominion government's broad empowerment regarding the "regulation of trade and commerce." Whereas the US Constitution qualified this grant of power by restricting its application to international and interstate commerce, the *BNA Act* made no such concession to provincial autonomy. Judicial interpretation later rectified the situation.

Even more problematic was the juxtaposition of a general clause that empowered Parliament to make all laws deemed necessary for **peace, order, and good government** (POGG), with the stipulation that the provinces would retain power over **property and civil rights**. The POGG clause was meant to reinforce the superiority of the central government by giving it residual powers. The property and civil rights clause in turn was a relic from the 1791 *Constitution Act* that had created Upper and Lower Canada. Its original purpose was to allow the growing numbers of post-revolutionary loyalists streaming into Canada from the United States to set up their own British model colony instead of having to adopt French civil law and the peculiarities of seigneurial land tenure. It now took on a reverse dynamic, protecting the differences of French civil law in Québec. But its broad stipulation could be and would be construed as an empowerment for all provinces to regulate all matters falling under criminal law, including all aspects of economic policy and regulation within provincial boundaries.

Enumerating Powers

The Canadians clearly wanted to do the exact opposite of what the Americans had done. Instead of enumerating central government powers and leaving the broad residue to the provinces, they wrote a lengthy list of provincial tasks and left residual powers to Parliament. The premise underlying this was exactly that of the Americans: the government with the residual powers is the government with the whip hand.

Multiple Lists

However, the Canadians had second thoughts about this reverse single list approach and decided to add a lengthy list of enumerated national powers just in case. This second list was meant to illustrate national powers in some kind of indicative or "declaratory" fashion, and in its opening and closing paragraphs the clause is quite unambiguous in this respect. As we shall discuss in Chapter 10, though, there was no guarantee that this is how the situation would be interpreted by the courts. The dual list approach then became an exercise in drafting **multiple lists**. Not only was education put into a different section than the other provincial powers, another section specified concurrent or shared powers which at the time included only agriculture and immigration. And finally, there were hidden clauses pertaining to the division of powers in some other sections as well.

All in all, the Canadian attempt to enumerate powers in a way that would bring clarity to the exercise of divided powers was not very successful. Given its bicultural nature, the intention of making Canada a strongly centralized federal system was probably doomed under any

FIGURE 6.3
The Original Division of Powers in the Canadian Constitution

- Section 91 was drafted with a powerful POGG covering clause and then the declaratory list of the original 29 exclusive powers of Parliament. The most important of these pertain to national defence and the common market, including "any mode" of taxation and regulation of trade and commerce. It also contains responsibility for "Indians" and their reserved lands.

- Section 92 listed 16 exclusive provincial powers including those pertaining to provincial lands, property and civil rights, and "direct" taxation.

- Section 93 specified the provincial power over education.

- Section 95 listed agriculture and immigration as concurrent powers.

- Section 109 assigned to the provinces the ownership of lands, resources, and royalties.

scheme of dividing powers. Moreover, fixed on the idea of forging a national market economy, the framers did not foresee the importance of natural resources as a main source of provincial might.

Fiscal Capacities

Like the US Constitution, the *BNA Act* also gave plenary taxation power to the central government, though it went one step further and did so without any qualification. The obvious intention was to create a highly centralized system of fiscal federalism whereby the central government would raise most of the revenue and then redistribute the surplus to the provinces. Part of the original formula was that the provinces would be given 80 cents per capita for purposes of financing their government operations.

Right from the outset, though, the enumeration of tax powers was self-contradictory. On the one hand, the national power to raise revenue "by any mode or system of taxation" was, under the covering clause of section 90, an exclusive power. On the other hand, section 91 also granted the provinces an "exclusive" power to levy direct taxation. The provinces had also been given the ownership of natural resources and the royalties thereof (which, moreover, Parliament was not allowed to tax). For those fortunate provinces with strong resource endowments, these royalties turned out to be more important sources of revenue than taxation or transfers and a springboard for regional economic development, or "province building."

GERMANY: THE ADMINISTRATIVE MODEL

As we have noted in earlier chapters, Germany is an interesting case in which dramatic historical discontinuities mask a powerful underlying set of continuities. Bismarck's Constitution of 1871 was replaced by the republican Weimar Constitution in 1919, and, after the unconstitutional dictatorship of the Nazis, yet another constitution was drafted in 1949, the West German "Basic Law."[17] Yet in its essential design with regard to both dual representation (see Chapter 7) and the division of powers, German federalism did not change fundamentally through all those upheavals.

---

17. *Grundgesetz*: literally "foundational law" but commonly translated as Basic Law. This term, rather than its synonym *Verfassung* ("constitution"), was chosen to indicate the provisional character of the Constitution of West Germany, with final constitutional settlement to await reunification. When reunification came in 1989, however, the East German *Länder* were incorporated under the existing constitution and the name was kept.

A comparison with Canada may provide an explanatory clue to this continuity of the German federal design. In Canada, the dominant political tradition was a parliamentary one, and federalism was added, reluctantly, as a necessary compromise in order to achieve modern statehood. For Germany, one can make the exact reverse argument. Federalism, understood as a form of negotiated political accommodation among a plurality of territorial powers, had been a constant tradition since the Middle Ages. The forces of change, on the other hand, came from the gradual and reluctant adoption of parliamentary democracy.

In order to understand the pattern of the division of powers in German federalism, we need to take a contextual look at both the Bismarck Constitution and its peculiar accommodation of dynastic powers and at the reconstruction of German federalism in the Constitution of 1949. The Weimar Constitution of 1919–33 can largely be disregarded. While many of its formulations foreshadowed those of the current Constitution, its main emphasis was on parliamentary democracy at the expense of the legislative and financial autonomy of the *Länder*.

The corner stones of the German federal model, in essence maintained throughout its various reincarnations, have always remained the same. In order to bring about a quasi-unitary system of public services and administration, legislative powers were concentrated at the centre. As a compensation for this loss of autonomous legislative powers, the *Länder* governments not only gained a right to codetermine national legislation through their membership in the second legislative chamber, they were also assigned responsibility for implementing and administering most of those laws and policies.

Context

As we saw in Chapter 5, the North German Confederation and then the Second Reich of 1871 restored German unity under Prussian hegemony. Bismarck's 1871 Constitution, however, had to accommodate the interests of the dynastic rulers in the smaller territories. This was accomplished by leaving to them their traditional role as providers of public services. With a few exceptions such as railway and post, there was no threatening build-up of a new Imperial bureaucracy. "No centralized governmental and administrative structure for the Reich was established...."[18] Most laws were now made in Berlin; the territorial princes had a say in Reich legislation, but were free to implement and administer these laws as they saw fit. Thus, cultural identities in the *Länder* were preserved along with the loyalty of grateful subjects.

When the federal system was reconstructed in 1949, the princes were long gone, and so was Prussian hegemony. Parts of the old Prussia were

---

18. Johnson, "Territory and Power" 27.

now absorbed into Poland or the Soviet Union; another part had been under Soviet occupation and now formed the heartland of the new East German communist state; and the remaining part, in the Western zone of occupation, subdivided into several new *Länder*. This artificial redrawing of borders for the new West German federal state has often been criticized as arbitrary and lacking historical legitimacy. But it did bring about, for the first time in German history, a pattern of relative territorial equality, with regard to size as well as population and economic strength, and therefore did much to ensure the success of the new federal system.

The architects of the postwar constitution were 65 deputies elected by the newly established *Länder* legislatures. They already had before them a draft with general guidelines submitted by a constitutional convention of experts called together by the prime ministers of the *Länder*. The division of powers resulting from these two rounds of deliberations was guided by a general consensus, notwithstanding opposition from the occupying powers, in favour of centralization.[19] The new national government should have the necessary legislative powers to provide equal if not uniform living conditions for all citizens. At the same time, however, it should never again be allowed to follow the Nazi path of unbridled centralization of power. For instance, there would not be a national police force. For the same reason, if not by default, the federal system would restore the traditional pattern of dividing powers whereby the *Länder* retained the powers of policy implementation and administration.

Assigning and Enumerating Powers

There are great limits to the extent to which German federalism can be categorized according to the framework we have applied to the division of powers in the American and Canadian constitutions. Under Articles 30 and 70, residual power lies with the *Länder*. In that sense the German Constitution is like the American (and Australian). Article 73 then enumerates the powers assigned to the national government. By contrast with the American and Australian approach, though, these are exclusive powers. Article 74 then lists a number of concurrent powers. As in all other federations, a qualifying provision gives the national government paramountcy in areas of concurrent jurisdiction.

Concurrency and Joint Tasks

Article 72 has been a point of contention and amendment in this respect. Paragraph 2 stipulates the conditions under which pre-emptive national legislation is valid. These originally included:
• when individual *Länder* legislation is not sufficient;

---

19. John Ford Golay, *The Founding of the Federal Republic of Germany* (Chicago, IL: University of Chicago Press, 1958) 58–60.

- when individual *Länder* legislation might interfere with the interests of other *Länder* or those of the federation as a whole; or
- when it is needed to preserve both economic and legal unity and equitable living conditions across the country.

It was this general necessity clause which hollowed out the originally intended legislative balance of the federal system. Time and again, national legislators justified their pre-emptive legislative strikes in the name of unity and equity. As the list of concurrent powers was progressively extended to encompass a wide range of major policy fields, and the national government became active in virtually all of them, the *Länder* were systematically reduced to the status of administrative adjuncts. In essence, the only policy fields in the *Länder* domain were culture, education, and police—and even there encroachment was facilitated by the Constitution's emphasis on concurrency and framework legislation. Even though Article 75 established authority to pass such framework legislation for a specific number of fields, one can see the same principle at work with regard to the much larger catalogue of concurrent powers in Article 74. The idea of concurrency is really one of complementary legislation. National legislation establishes the general policy and program objectives, and the executive details are left to *Länder* legislation. Discontent led to a constitutional amendment in 1994 that sharpened the language of Paragraph 2 (see Chapter 9).

As if these strongly centralizing provisions were not enough, there are also so-called **joint tasks.** They were the result of constitutional reforms in 1969 when it was deemed necessary to create joint responsibilities in areas such as post-secondary education, economic and agricultural restructuring, and coastal protection. Joint tasks go beyond the complementary nature of concurrent powers in that they require negotiated program agreements including a fixed formula of cost-sharing.

Division of Roles

Shoe-horning German federalism into the conventional framework is fundamentally misleading. As we have noted, the German approach represents a major departure from the British settler tradition of legislative federalism. The key division is not between policy *fields* but between policy *roles*. With a few exceptions, policies are made nationally but implemented locally. This basic approach is laid down in Article 83: "The *Länder* shall execute federal law as a matter of their own concern in so far as this constitution does not otherwise provide or permit." The Swiss went a similar way by stipulating how specific national powers would be delegated to cantonal implementation and administration. However, it is the categorical constitutional stipulation of this principle as a general rule which makes German federalism the archetypal model of administrative federalism.

FIGURE 6.4

Division of Powers in the German Constitution

- Article 30: Similarly to Article 83, the execution of public service tasks is assigned to the *Länder*.

- Article 31: The paramountcy provision: national laws override *Länder* laws.

- Article 70: Residual powers to the *Länder*.

- Article 71: Exclusive national powers defined; delegation to the *Länder* possible by federal law.

- Article 72: Concurrent powers defined; *Länder* can legislate until pre-empted by national legislation; general necessity clause for such pre-emption.

- Article 73: List of 11 exclusive national powers, including the usual fields concerning security and market, as well as legislation concerning the cooperation of both levels of government in matters of criminal investigation and internal security.

- Article 74: List of 27 concurrent powers, including communication, transportation, social security, and hospitals.

- Article 75: National framework legislation in areas such as infrastructural planning and environmental protection.

- Articles 81 and 83: *Länder* administration of national legislation.

- Article 91a: Joint tasks regarding university construction, improvement of regional economic restructuring, agricultural restructuring, and coastal protection.

- Article 91b: Cooperation in the field of educational planning and scientific research.

Federalism Within Federalism

The division of powers in the German federation has also been affected by the process of European integration.[20] In principle, foreign affairs are an exclusive responsibility of the national government. However, Article 32 had already modified this, allowing the *Länder* to enter into international treaties in matters of their own jurisdiction and with the approval of Parliament. The same rationale led the *Länder* to demand a more direct participation in European policy-making with its direct regulatory impact upon member-state citizens. In conjunction with the Maastricht Treaty, which established the EU in 1993, therefore, a new Article 23 was inserted into the Constitution. Its gist is the increased influence of the *Länder* upon the European policy-making process when their jurisdiction is affected by such policy-making.

Fiscal Partnership

The Bismarck federation had been somewhat of an oddity in terms of the distribution of fiscal powers as well. It left to the *Länder* most of their

---

20. See Hans J. Michelmann, "Germany and European Integration," in Matthias Zimmer, ed., *Germany: Phoenix in Trouble?* (Edmonton, AB: University of Alberta Press, 1997).

own tax sources and effectively made the *Reich* dependent on negotiated transfers. After an episode of financial centralization during the Weimar Republic and its abuse during the Nazi dictatorship, the Allied supervisors of the constitutional drafting process in 1948–49 insisted that each level of government be given its own autonomous revenue sources as in the American model. Rejecting this and being unpersuaded of the relevance of the American approach to their situation,[21] the Germans reverted to the Bismarck tradition yet again. If the central government's own tax resources were not sufficient to cover necessary expenditures, it would be allowed to draw upon *Länder* resources. This obviously was a formula prone to generate perpetual intergovernmental conflict. Two rounds of constitutional reforms, in 1955 and 1969, then established the current **grand tax partnership**. Article 106 stipulates with constitutional finality that the three levels of government will receive a set share of the main revenue bases (see Chapter 11).

IMITATIONS AND VARIATIONS

With regard to the division of powers, the federations examined so far more or less exhaust the traditional patterns of approaches and designs. Nevertheless, there is considerable variability in other federal systems. We therefore explore the extent to which some of these systems imitated the established patterns, sometimes by stretching them to the limits, or tried to break the mould by attempting something new.

Imitation in Australia and South Africa

Perhaps the most acute case of imitation is the Australian Constitution, patterned closely on the American model. It grants a single limiting list of powers to the Commonwealth government and relies on a simple assertion of residual power to protect the state governments. This represents a double irony, since the approach was intended to keep the central government within a set of jurisdictional confines, but manifestly failed to do so, and was chosen despite evidence from a century of American constitutional interpretation that this might be the case (see Chapter 10). There is no doubt that the framers of the Australian Constitution were looking for a limited transfer of powers to the new Commonwealth government and the maintenance of state primacy in domestic fields. And there is no doubt they got it wildly wrong. "The Australian draftsmen took from their two precedents precisely the two features calculated

---

21. Golay, *Founding of the Federal Republic of Germany* 77.

to lead to an expansion of central power...."[22] Compounding their choice of the American single list approach was their decision to expand that list.

The federal division of powers in the South African Constitution, on the other hand, essentially followed the German model by establishing a cooperative pattern of administrative federalism. While concurrency predominates, and the provinces have been assigned only a very limited range of powers over parochial matters (abattoirs, liquor licences, etc.), the national government has been given sweeping powers to set national standards and norms. The Constitution also follows the German pattern of tax sharing although there is no fixed tax partnership over extended periods of time. Instead, revenue is apportioned annually at the recommendation of an independent commission (comprising representatives of the national, provincial, and local levels) and from a single national pool of revenue.[23] As a consequence, the South African federal system appears highly centralized and leaves to the provinces little room for autonomous development. Obviously, this was so intended, as it was in the German case. Only time will tell whether the far more diverse South African provinces can find ways of breaking out of the straightjacket of central supervision, and whether this will threaten the viability of the South African federal experiment.

Flexible Adaptation in Switzerland

The division of powers in the Swiss Constitution deserves a closer look because it provides an instructive case of how far the traditional patterns can be stretched by continuous efforts at amending the original provisions according to changing time and circumstance.

The modern Swiss Constitution dates from 1848. It was thoroughly revised in 1874 and again in 1999. Each time, a long list of previous amendments had to be incorporated into the text. Not all of these amendments pertained to a change in the division of powers, but in general three trends are discernible:
• from a single list of enumerated central government powers as pioneered by the Americans to three lists of federal, cantonal and concurrent powers;
• from the principle of legislative federalism to the practice of German-style administrative federalism; and

---

22. See, for example, James Crawford, "The Legislative Power of the Commonwealth," in Gregory Craven, ed., *The Convention Debates 1891–1898: Commentaries, Indices and Guide* (Sydney: Legal Books, 1986) 114. Delegates to the constitutional conventions—especially those from the smaller colonies—were horrified by the Canadian approach, failing to see the accumulating evidence that centralist intentions had not translated into a particularly centralist design.
23. See Simeon and Murray, "Multi-Sphere Governance in South Africa."

- from the jealous preservation of cantonal autonomy to the central allocation of the essential powers necessary for the management of a modern polity.

The 23 gentlemen who wrote the original draft—mostly cantonal government chiefs and lawyers complemented by a few merchants, doctors, and army officers—were not masters of brevity like their American colleagues. Their Constitution turned out to be a rather rambling document of 114 articles, a workhorse rather than a sacred charter. The detailed character of the provisions required frequent updating and amendment. The most recent revision, that of 1999–2000, contains 196 articles, and had to incorporate some 150 amendments adopted since the previous revision in 1874.

Assigning Powers

The original document can be read as a stock-take of the problems and aspirations with which Switzerland was confronted. Matters of military organization commanded a lot of space; there was the usual modernizers' agenda of national monetary and economic union; there was also the regulation of religious peace and language. Those assembled at the drafting table were not worried about writing history as had been the case with their American counterparts. They were concerned with who would maintain roads and bridges and how to combat epidemics. Most of all, they had no intention of abrogating the cherished tradition of cantonal autonomy. The Swiss Constitution does not begin with "we the people" but instead refers to the "peoples of the sovereign cantons."[24]

The central government gained explicit and exclusive powers over national security, the establishment of a common economic system and market, the postal system, and the establishment of a university and a polytechnic school—not to mention a monopoly on gunpowder. Cantonal powers were explicitly mentioned only sparingly. A limited right to enter into direct treaty relations with neighbouring states was mentioned, as was a right to impose consumer taxes on imported spirits. Finally, the assignment to the central government of a supervisory role in the maintenance of roads and bridges was an indication of a generally cooperative predisposition whereby the details of implementation and administration were left to the cantons. Clauses opening the door to implied or incidental powers were scrupulously avoided.

The Accommodation of Cultural Diversity

One particularly important issue was language. Almost as an afterthought, Article 109 of the 1848 Constitution declared German, French,

---

24. The 2000 version now speaks of the "Swiss people and cantons."

and Italian as the three national languages (Romansh was added as a fourth in 1938). Since the Constitution was otherwise silent about language, however, it fell to the cantons to regulate linguistic matters within their boundaries. The 1999 Constitution has moved this provision to the top, as Article 4; since the Swiss obviously do not like to leave anything to the vagaries of implication, Article 70 declares that while all four are official languages at the national level,[25] the cantons determine which to use as their own official language(s). Effectively, this has given final constitutional expression to a long-standing tradition of linguistic territoriality. With four exceptions, the cantons are officially unilingual.

Enumerating Powers

While the explicit recognition of residual powers in favour of the states found its way into the US Constitution by means of the Tenth Amendment, the Swiss continued with the confederal practice of stating it boldly up front. Article 3 of the 1848 Constitution (unchanged through all revisions) declares in no uncertain terms that the "cantons are sovereign so far as their sovereignty is not limited by the federal Constitution, and, as such, they exercise all the rights that are not delegated to the federal power." The national government, by contrast, was granted a very modest general empowerment to "advance mutual welfare," and, as reformulated in the revision adopted in 1999, it was to do so by respecting "cultural diversity" (Article 2).

Instead of creating a single list explicitly enumerating central government powers, the constitutional framers pragmatically went from task to task, each time stipulating what the national parliament was allowed to do. This approach is even more evident in the 1999 Constitution. Its second chapter, on responsibilities, is subdivided into sections on foreign affairs, national security, education, environment, public works and transportation, energy and communication, the economy, social security, and health. Individual articles under these subheadings then spell out the extent of central government responsibility.

The central government has never been authorized to create its own police force; primary schooling, culture, and religion are now explicitly mentioned as in the cantonal domain. The enumeration of responsibilities has successively increased the powers of the central government, and it has done so generally by circumscribing a growing number of precise tasks. Included, for instance, are matters such as a national school of sports, protection of forests, and the general regulation of hiking paths. Moreover, in many instances such as energy policy, for example, the new Constitution stipulates that the two levels of government are jointly

---

25. Romansh is used expressly only when dealing with persons for whom this is the native language.

responsible. In other cases, concurrency results from the cantons' residual powers.

Thus, the Swiss constitutional evolution has evolved from a single list approach to the adoption of three lists—even though these are not neatly packaged in three sections, as in the Canadian case. While the cantons have retained exclusive control over few of their traditional powers, the list of national powers has expanded considerably. Concurrency or power sharing is almost the norm.

From Division of Powers to Division of Roles

One particularly European way in which the cantons have retained their practical importance within the federation has been through their role in administering national laws and delivering local services within the national framework. Various articles of the Constitution stipulate that while the laws are to be made nationally, their implementation is to be a cantonal responsibility. The Swiss approach is one of *Vollzugsföderalismus*, "executive" or "implementation federalism." In this respect, Switzerland departed significantly from the American model of legislative federalism and has practised German-style administrative federalism. "In the last 25 years, the federal government has increasingly confined itself to the issuing of framework laws.... One of the most impressive examples of this is the implementation of federal environmental legislation ... Health is another example...."[26] Article 46 of the Constitution now states unequivocally that the cantons are in charge of implementing and administering national law and that they must be provided with sufficient fiscal resources for these tasks.

This has been supported by the uniquely Swiss practice of **public office cumulation**. Occasioned in part by the limits to human resources in a small country and society, and by the need, nevertheless, to keep in motion the modern machinery of a three-tier government, there has never been a strict division of powers in the personnel sphere. This means that at any given time dozens of members of cantonal and municipal governments occupy seats in the two legislative chambers at the national level as well. This power collusion ensures a strong presence of cantonal and local interests at the national level. In addition, there are strict principles of cantonal and linguistic proportionality in operation for all national public offices, including the governing executive Federal Council. Since the 1930s the latter has been routinely formed as a grand coalition of the four major parties. Voters can rest assured

---

26. Bernard Dafflon, "Fiscal Federalism in Switzerland: A Survey of Constitutional Issues, Budget Responsibility and Equalisation," in Amedeo Fossati and Giorgio Panella, eds., *Fiscal Federalism in the European Union* (New York: Routledge, 1999) 269.

that their particular interests will not be swept aside by any configuration of majority interests.[27]

Fiscal Arrangements

The arrangements of Swiss fiscal federalism point to a particularly noteworthy departure from the American model. We have seen in the US case how the states were deprived of their powers to impose customs duties. The Swiss Constitution of 1848 went that route as well: the creation of a customs union is one of the primary requisites for a national economy. But at the same time it established a scheme of fiscal redistribution whereby the cantons were given back a fixed amount of the customs revenue proportional to their populations.

The national government's power to tax has been limited as well. In the 1999 Constitution, income tax is limited to 11.5 per cent, corporate tax to 9.8 per cent, and a value added tax to 6.5 per cent. In addition, the central government is admonished to take into consideration the existing tax load imposed by cantons and communes (municipalities). With their traditional rights of autonomy now formally recognized in the Constitution, the communes also have authority to impose taxes, including a personal income tax.

Direct Democracy

This continuous evolution of Swiss constitutionalism must be evaluated in the context of Switzerland's most original contribution to modern governance, the constitutional referendum. As the 1848 Constitution stipulated, constitutional changes can be made at any time by means of ordinary legislative acts, but they need to be approved by an overall majority and a majority of voters in a majority of cantons. Moreover, since 1891, constitutional changes can also be initiated by the people (see Chapter 9). Put before a people steeped in the pride of tradition, sweeping constitutional amendments generally were more often unsuccessful than successful, but gradual change obviously came about nevertheless.

The question is why the people, and the cantons, did not object to this gradual increase of central government power. There are several answers. The satisfactory regulation of culture, religion, and language removed the most incendiary issues from intergovernmental conflict. The small and condensed nature of the country may account for a relatively high consensus about the need for common regulations in such policy domains as environmental protection, forests, agriculture, social security, and even hiking paths. And, finally, the administrative division

---

27. The other side of the coin is the lack of an efficient opposition. Minority interests outside the grand coalition are for the most part ignored.

of roles allows the cantons to remain the main service providers for their citizens.

Time for a New Approach?

The Swiss case more generally exemplifies the difficulties faced over time by federations who adopted the traditional division of powers model. What began as a simple compromise between modernizers and traditionalists in the first American experiment escalated into ever more complicated constructions of power assignments and enumerations occasioned by the requirements of modern governance. There is good reason, then, to give final consideration to the alternative approaches followed in two of the most recent cases of federalization, Spain and the EU. In these cases, no attempt has even been made to create a fixed scheme of divided powers; instead, much greater constitutional emphasis has been placed on mechanisms of negotiated and flexible power sharing agreements.[28]

Asymmetrical Flexibility in Spain

In order to make possible the transition to stable democracy in 1978 (see Chapter 5), both the traditional forces of the Spanish state and the newly legitimized forces demanding regional autonomy had to be satisfied. The result was what has been called an exercise in "artful ambiguity."[29] Article 2 of the Constitution, for instance, asserts that Spain is an indivisible nation made up of autonomous nationalities.

The Open List

The division of powers between the central government in Madrid and the 17 Autonomous Communities clearly illustrates this ambiguity. It needs to be remembered, here, that the Spanish Constitution was written when the process of establishing the Autonomous Communities was not yet completed. Thus Article 148 begins by listing 22 powers that the they *may* take over, and it ends with a statement that they *may* acquire further powers later on and within the framework of Article 149.

Exclusive and Framework Powers

At first glance this appears surprising because Article 149 declares itself to be a list of exclusive national competencies. However, closer inspection reveals that among the 32 items listed, there are not only the usual exclusive powers such as international relations, defence, customs, and

---

28. Again, regarding the European constitutional treaty, there would essentially be a concurrent list only.

29. Heywood, *The Government and Politics of Spain* 5.

the monetary system, but also a much longer enumeration of powers where the national government has responsibility only for developing framework legislation. Examples of the latter are: "basic legislation on environmental protection without prejudice to the faculties of the Autonomous Communities" and "basic legislation and economic system of social security, without prejudice to the execution of its services by the Autonomous Communities."

The Residual Power

At the end of Article 149, in Section 3, there is another particularly ambiguous formulation that gives residual powers to the Autonomous Communities—but only if and when such powers are assumed explicitly by the respective autonomy statutes. Until that point, the powers reside with the national government, which is immediately given some sort of paramountcy because its norms will prevail over those of the Autonomous Communities in case of conflict.

A Negotiated Division of Powers

In practice, all this meant that the Autonomous Communities had gained a right to negotiate individual packages of autonomy powers with the central government. These were meant in the end to establish equality among the Autonomous Communities—although the historic regions of Navarra and the Basque Country retained their ancient *fueros* rights of taxation dating back to concessions made to different peoples and regions in the medieval period.[30] More importantly, the ambiguous and almost "deliberately indeterminate" constitutional provisions regarding what each level of government is actually licensed to do allow for a considerable degree of asymmetrical flexibility. Albeit within constitutional limits, it has been left to the Autonomous Communities to determine individually how far they want to drive the process of taking over responsibilities. The interest for such expanded responsibilities is greater among the economically more advanced and richer areas than among the poorer ones. A Constitutional Tribunal (Court) has the last word, and, significantly, its decisions over conflicts of jurisdiction are binding and final. Its workload has been daunting, and its contribution to Spanish federalization is significant.[31]

---

30. On this and the following, see again Heywood, *The Government and Politics of Spain* 145–54. Also see Luis Moreno, *The Federalization of Spain* (London: Frank Cass, 2001) 38.
31. See Juan José Solozábal, "Spain: A Federation in the Making?," in Hesse and Wright, eds., *Federalizing Europe?* 253.

Spain's deliberately indeterminate division of powers was a response to an extraordinary situation: the transition from dictatorship to democracy, with the forces of the old regime firmly clinging to central authority and the new democratic voices for the most part being raised in the regions. It was unclear how far each side was prepared to go in support of a real federal compromise before resorting to violence. The authors of the Constitution prudently chose to create a work-in-progress. However, it seems that the open-ended construction of the Spanish Constitution and its assignment of powers also offers an interesting model more generally. At least implicitly, it acknowledges that time and circumstance will change what at any given moment may appear as the most reasonable and effective distribution of powers. And, by avoiding the enumerated finality of the classical list approach, it suggests that the role of constitutions in federal systems of divided governance is not so much to provide juridical finality but political guidance in search of mutually acceptable solutions.

Subsidiarity in the EU

A comparative assessment of the division of powers in the EU is difficult because, instead of there being a constitutional document specifying powers, a series of **treaties** containing commitments to certain policy goals has accumulated. On the basis of these treaties, the EU has been active in a growing number of policy areas such as agriculture, environmental protection, and the entire field of market integration.

Federal Evolution

How, then, is it decided who does what? Until the mid-1980s this was not so much of a problem because most important policy decisions could be vetoed by individual member states and therefore remained in the domain of international (or intergovernmental) relations. Since the *Single European Act* of 1987 and the Maastricht Treaty (Treaty of the European Union) of 1993, however, most decisions concerning the European Community (nearly all policy areas except foreign policy, defence, and domestic security) have been made by qualified majority voting. This means that now, at least, the EU has reached the status of a supranational legislator, much like the central government of a federal rather than a confederal system.

Eurosceptics and the Subsidiarity Solution

This abandonment of the unanimity rule was precisely the problem for some of the member states, notably the UK and Denmark.[32] Looking

---

32. See Desmond Dinan, *Ever Closer Union* (Boulder, CO: Lynne Rienner, 1999) 136–58.

at the United States as the most familiar model, these 'Eurosceptics' feared that European federalism would eventually mean European supremacy and that the member nation-states were in danger of losing their sovereignty to the bureaucracy in Brussels. In order to assuage these fears, the designers of the Maastricht Treaty had to come up with something that would spell out limits to legislative and regulatory centralization. The result was the principle of **subsidiarity**, originally laid down in Article 3b of the Maastricht Treaty and now incorporated as Article 5 in the amended European Union Treaty. At first glance, subsidiarity in the Althusian tradition implies only that governance should generally be carried out at the lowest practical level (see Chapter 4). Obviously, however, European governments expect it to provide much more precise instruction as to the limits of Brussels supranationalism.

What, Exactly, is Subsidiarity?

As first enshrined in the Maastricht Treaty, the subsidiarity principle consists of two different sets of formulations.[33] The Preamble of the Treaty contains the general affirmation that the EU should be governed in such a way as to ensure that "decisions are taken as closely as possible to the citizen."

Article 3b then begins with an affirmative injunction: "the Community *shall* take action wherever it has the powers to promote the treaty objectives." These include the promotion of economic and social progress, the strengthening of economic and social cohesion, and the establishment of economic and monetary union. The first sentence, in other words, affirms the member states' commitment to the ongoing process of integration.

The second sentence introduces the principle of subsidiarity, and it contains a number of limiting stipulations. First of all, it refers to Community powers that are not exclusive. This is not a situation readily comparable to concurrent or shared powers in the case of the American model. The situation is open-ended and political. The Community is not tied to a specific set of policy fields. It can in principle assume any powers it wants as long as they serve the agreed-upon objectives of integration. In order to control this potentially open-ended invitation to centralization, Article 3b then specifies that before adopting any new laws or regulations, the Community has to demonstrate, or reach an agreement, that they serve the Community objectives better than individual member state policies and regulations could. In fact, it needs to be shown that such individual policies would fall short of achieving

---

33. See Thomas O. Hueglin, "From Constitutional to Treaty Federalism," *Publius* 30:4 (Fall 2000): 143–45.

FIGURE 6.5
The Principle of Subsidiarity

Article 3b of the Treaty of Maastricht states:

The Community shall act within the limits of the powers conferred upon it by this Treaty and the objectives assigned to it therein.

In areas which do not fall within its exclusive competence, the Community shall take action, in accordance with the principle of subsidiarity, only if and in so far as the objectives of the proposed action cannot be sufficiently achieved by the Member States and can therefore, by reason of the scale or the effects of the proposed action, be better achieved by the Community.

Any action by the Community shall not go beyond what is necessary to achieve the objectives of this Treaty.

these objectives by reason of the transnational scale or effects of both objectives and proposed Community action.

The last sentence emphasizing necessity as a framing condition for all Community action can be understood as a further qualifier imposing a principle of proportionality on the scope of such action. Even when there may be agreement that the achievement of European Community objectives in a particular policy field requires action according to the scale or effects, it is still an open question as to how far that action should go—only as far as is necessary, according to Article 3b. But how far is necessary and enough?

Subsidiarity and Administrative Federalism

This question has haunted the European Community since Denmark first rejected the Union Treaty in June 1992. At the Edinburgh summit in December of the same year, a protocol on subsidiarity, later incorporated into the Amsterdam Treaty of 1997, provided further assurances that EU regulation would respect and even support member-state autonomy and flexibility of individual choices. To that end, the Community should "employ directives which stipulate results, while leaving choice of means to member states, rather than adopting detailed regulations which are directly applicable to member states, firms and individuals."[34]

Necessity, in other words, appears to guide Community action towards the provision of a common understanding of ends, not means, and it does so by following the German model of framework legislation, by which the Community provides general rules and standards, and of administrative federalism, by which it leaves the implementation and administration to the member states.

---

34. Andreas Føllesdal, "Survey Article: Subsidiarity," *The Journal of Political Philosophy* 6:2 (June 1998): 194.

Subsidiarity as Work in Progress

As with the EU itself, the construction and understanding of subsidiarity very much remain a work in progress. In a "Protocol on the application of the principles of subsidiarity and proportionality" appended to the 1997 Amsterdam Treaty, the scope of Community action was further reined in by the stipulation that it should be "as simple as possible" and that "framework" legislation should be preferred to "detailed measures." And a likewise labelled protocol appended to the European constitutional treaty spells out operational principles for the way in which the European Commission is expected to demonstrate "reason of scale" and "effects" for any new legislative proposal: it must be substantiated by "qualitative and, wherever possible, quantitative indicators" and "take account of the need for any burden, whether financial or administrative, falling upon the Union, national governments, regional or local authorities, economic operators and citizens." Not just expected: adherence to the principle of subsidiarity also falls into the domain of judicial interpretation by the European Court of Justice (see Chapter 10).

Constitutional Certitude or Federal Mutuality and Mutability?

The principle of subsidiarity as employed by the European Union has been dismissed as mere rhetoric in some quarters. In particular, those with a more legally minded belief in constitutional certitude have doubted the efficacy of stipulations that are not justiciable, that cannot be defined and enforced through the judicial process. This has been proven too rigid a view.[35] The fact is, though, that the principle of subsidiarity is primarily a principle of political guidance and not of legal adjudication. It compels the participant member states to come to a mutual understanding about necessary and unnecessary steps of integration and supranationality. Its open-endedness also does not preclude the reversion of earlier trends and decisions about the allocation of powers if and when circumstances change. For rapidly changing times, subsidiarity might turn out to be a more flexible instrument of multilevel governance than the constitutionally heavy-handed divisions of power typical of more orthodox federations.

SUMMARY

The centrepiece of any federal system is the division of powers. If federalism is about the sharing of sovereignty between levels of government

---

35. See Karen J. Alter, *Establishing the Supremacy of European Law* (Oxford: Oxford University Press, 2001) 205–06.

within one polity or union, then those governments must each have meaningful roles, responsibilities, and powers, and those competencies must have a robust constitutional basis. The architects of today's federal systems indeed sought to endow the governments they were defining with such status and in a lasting way. The federal vision differed from country to country, reflecting differing circumstances, histories, and lessons drawn from forerunners. This chapter has drawn attention to some patterns visible in these variations.

- There is a clear division between the British settler federation model of divided powers, which we have called legislative federalism, and the German or European model of divided roles, or what we have called administrative federalism. In the former, each level of government is theoretically sovereign in its own sphere, responsible for policy-making and policy implementation within its assigned areas of jurisdiction and using its own fiscal resources. In the latter, the central government has much broader policy-making powers but leaves implementation and administration to the subnational levels of government.

- Assignment of powers under the legislative model has followed a very regular pattern, with external affairs and common market responsibility being shifted up to the national government and cultural, social, and infrastructural responsibilities staying with the constituent units. This corresponds to the schism between modernizers and traditionalists and provides a *modus vivendi* for the two. Assumptions about the practicality of coordinate federalism reflects the much more limited role played by governments of the eighteenth and nineteenth centuries in economic and social life, and the much greater scope for values and cultural norms diversity before the modern era of universal individual rights.

- Writing the intended approach and assignment into constitutional documents, the designers had different options of enumeration. They could settle for a single list of central government powers; they could have two lists with enumerated powers for each level of government; they could also opt for a third list with shared or concurrent powers. The single list approach was premised on the notion of an exhaustive, limiting enumeration that would keep a central government in its place and an open-ended grant of residual power that would guarantee the constituent units of the federation the exercise of their traditional powers.

- More recently, there has been a trend of abandoning the idea of firm lists of divided powers. Instead, there are mechanisms for negotiated agreements among different level of government. In Spain, one of the innovative features is a list of powers that the autonomous communities *may* take over. In the EU, the principle of subsidiarity provides political guidance for the distribution and allocation of policy responsibilities under the treaties.

7 Federalism as a System of Dual Representation

The division of powers was a relatively easy task for designers of the early federal systems—modernizers and traditionalists knew what they wanted, and their realms were quite distinct. The way in which the constituent units would be represented at the national level turned out to be a far more contentious question. How would the federal principle be incorporated into the design of the central government—how would it be a truly 'federal' government? In order to appreciate the importance of this question, we need to take another look at the historical situation leading to federation in the first place.

In most cases, the member units had achieved the status of self-governing colonies, provinces, cantons, or states prior to federation— often as the result of hard-fought political battles. Without some form of direct representation, political leaders and elites did not want to give these achievements away to a distant central government. At the same time, however, there had been political battles for responsible government and popular representation. It seemed paramount that national governments should be controlled by a general assembly of popularly elected representatives. This in turn aroused fear, especially in the smaller member units, that their particular interests would be overridden by majority decisions in such a general assembly.

This is why a **bicameral** compromise of **dual representation** was struck. Constitute the lower house, or first chamber, on the **majoritarian** principle of representation by population but add an upper house, or second chamber, constituted on the federal principle of representation by region. Legislation would have to be passed by both chambers. In this chapter, we explore the options that constitutional framers had in organizing second chamber representation, the eventual solutions that were adopted in the major federal systems, and the degree to which dual representation has actually functioned in a federal manner. In doing so, we keep in mind that bicameralism is neither peculiar nor essential to federalism. It was an existing practice that was taken up, revived, and remodelled to varying degrees and in varying ways in different federations.

DESIGN OPTIONS

Again, as in the case of the division of powers, constitutional framers had to settle at least three basic design questions, questions that were often politically charged. First, they had to decide *in what proportion* the subnational units were to be represented. Second, they had to decide *in what way* the constituent units were to be represented. And third, they had to decide *what powers* to give the federal chamber. The combined effect of the solutions eventually adopted has determined the status and role second chambers play in each federation.

Accounting for Unequal Size

It is highly unlikely that a group of states contemplating federal union, or the regions in a state moving toward federal devolution, would be conveniently of similar population size. Indeed, as we noted in Chapter 3, the typical federation comprises constituent units with great discrepancies in population. In confederal unions, this is in principle irrelevant: each member participates as a member state, not as a group of people within a state. With the transition to federalism, however, the lines are not so clearly drawn, and those involved in thrashing out the necessary compromises had a choice that ran from the confederal principle of equal representation regardless of population at one extreme to the majoritarian principle of representation by population at the other.

Weighing the Difference

Both of these solutions at either end of the continuum violate important principles of fairness. Equal representation regardless of size makes no concession to the democratic principle of representation by population.[1] And, given the propensity for federations to comprise units of greatly differing population, equal representation will produce pronounced malapportionment. At the opposite extreme, straightforward majoritarianism only duplicates the allocation of seats and votes in the first chamber and makes no concession to the federal principle of regional representation. This deprives smaller units of protection from majority interests and violates the very foundations of federalism as a system of guaranteed group protection.

---

1.   Because representation by region rather than population violates the democratic rule of 'one person, one vote, one value'—the principle that in a democracy each person's vote should carry equal weight regardless of area of residence—it has often been seen as undemocratic or even as anti-democratic. The fact that democratic federations have instituted representation by region as a complement to representation by population rather than an alternative defuses most of that concern.

Patterns and Practices

The path of equal representation was taken by the Americans, conforming naturally to their original confederal approach under the *Articles* and carried over to the final Constitution. This results in "massive overrepresentation" of the small states; modern-day California is awarded only the same number of Senate seats as Wyoming despite having 66 times the population.[2] Among the classical federations, only Australia and, with a minor variation, Switzerland have followed this example—and in Australia malapportionment at its most extreme is only 14 to one (New South Wales versus Tasmania).

No cases of a strictly majoritarian second chamber exist. Instead, most other federal systems have adopted a **weighted** system of representation. Small member units are given more weight than they would command on the basis of their populations. Larger units still receive more seats and votes than smaller ones, but they cannot automatically dominate the decision-making process. Typically, seats and votes are adjusted on a narrow scale. In the German system, for instance, each *Land* is accorded between three and six votes according to population. In the Indian upper house, state representation varies in a range between one and 34 seats. As we shall see, one particular problem that arises from weighted representation is the need for adjustment when the regional distribution of the population changes, or, as in the case of German reunification, additional units are added.

In either case—equal or weighted representation—the intended effect of providing a second chamber buffer of regional group protection against the will of the popular majority very much depends on numbers and on socio-economic symmetry or asymmetry. If, for instance, a federation comprises several English-speaking provinces and only one French-speaking province, as is the case in Canada, neither form of minority protection will be sufficient. If, on the other hand, economic and popular strength is concentrated in a minority of large units, as has been the case in Germany after reunification, any form of equal or weighted representation that allows a majority of smaller and weaker units to gang up against the larger ones will be found unacceptable. However, it may be possible to find a balanced formula of weighted representation that allows neither side to entirely dominate the other. As we shall see in the next chapter, in matters of fundamental importance—such as constitutional changes affecting the distribution of powers—a super majority of more than 50 per cent is usually required in addition to such measures as ratification by a significant number of member units to compensate for this problem.

---

2.   Stepan, "Toward a New Comparative Politics of Federalism, (Multi)Nationalism, and Democracy" 341.

Representation of People or Governments?

The second question about federal bicameralism is who or what should be represented in the first place. Even from a democratic perspective, it is by no means an easy question to answer.

Principles of Representation

Representation is about people and their interests. As direct democracy is not feasible in larger territorial settings, the people have little choice but to delegate responsibility for their government to elected representatives. As the principle of federalism recognizes that regional populations may have interests that are different from the majority will of an entire country, it seems logical that second chambers should represent regional populations.

In federal systems, however, regional populations have their own governments, and these governments are constrained in pursuing what may be in the best interest of these regional populations by the powers that have been assigned to the central government. Quite logically again, it would follow that it is these regional governments that should have a seat and vote in national second chambers so that they can codetermine national policies on behalf of their electorates.

Senate or Council?

As we have noted in earlier chapters, there are two possible options or models for second chamber representation. In one, the **senate** model, the regional *populations* are represented. In the other, the **council** model, regional *governments* are represented. Senators generally do not act as delegates—as instructed agents of their regions—but as trustees—as individuals or party members. Council members, on the other hand, vote as instructed delegates of their governments and deliver their votes as a bloc. The council approach is more consistent with the federal principle; however, it may be seen as less consistent with the democratic one.

The Hybrid Approach

According to a somewhat hybrid third option, the representatives of second chambers can also be chosen by regional legislatures rather than by regional populations or governments. In this case, representatives may be free to vote as they choose, but how they vote may depend on the power configurations in the regional assemblies that elect them. As we shall see below, the American framers chose this third option for the US Senate, and popular election was only adopted when the Seventeenth

Amendment was ratified in 1913. While this approach of indirect election was phased out in the United States, it remains in use elsewhere, notably in Austria and India.

Significance of the Council Model

The members of second chambers in most federations are either directly elected, indirectly chosen by regional legislatures, or come into office by a mixture of direct and indirect election. Among the classical federal states, only Germany adopted the council model. It is an important model beyond its significance for German federalism, though, for a number of reasons: first, because council governance in the EU has followed a similar pattern; secondly, because it has been chosen for the new federation of South Africa; and thirdly, because in practice it is the one model that functions in a truly federal fashion. The South African case is particularly interesting in this regard, because having initially opted for a senate-style upper house, the Constituent Assembly made the very deliberate decision to reject that approach in favour of a National Council of Provinces and to adopt a much more German-style administrative federalism instead.[3]

Second Chamber Powers

Neither the type of representation nor the balance of representation matter much if the federal chamber does not have a significant role to play. The third and final question that has to be answered, then, is what powers that second chamber should be given. The upper house could be made equal in power to the lower house; it could be made weaker; it could be made stronger; or it could be made stronger in some respects and weaker in others. But since there is good political reason for any one of these options, constitutional designers have had to make difficult choices in practice. In making those decisions, they had to confront issues of democratic control and, in parliamentary systems, of responsible government.

Equal or Weaker?

The argument for **equal** powers is this: the very essence of federal bicameralism centres upon the idea that the popular or majority will needs to be balanced by the compounded will of self-governing regional populations or their governments. If this idea is to be taken seriously, it seems out of the question that second chambers should be overruled by parliamentary majorities in the first chamber.

---

3.   Haysom, "Federal Features of the Final Constitution" 513.

However, there are some serious arguments in favour of a **weaker** second chamber, particularly in parliamentary systems. One of these has to do with the very essence of representative democracy: the chamber that is most truly democratic should have the last word on at least the touchstone matters of governance. Another has to do with the parliamentary conventions of responsible government according to which the executive is accountable to the people via their elected representatives. Since the executive government—prime ministers and cabinets—cannot be accountable to two legislative chambers which might vote differently on a particular issue, second chambers cannot have equal powers. A stand-off between the two houses creates a considerably more awkward situation in parliamentary systems than it does in presidential ones.

In practice, the relative powers of federal upper houses have been curbed in either of three ways. One is to give second chambers only a suspensive veto, by which legislation can be delayed for a constitutionally determined period of time but not vetoed altogether. Another is to provide a last-resort mechanism for resolving disagreements. And the last is to limit the policy fields in which second chambers have equal powers.

Equal or Stronger?

The case for a *stronger* second chamber is more difficult to make. This was particularly the case in an era when second chambers or upper houses were often based on a limited suffrage franchise or hereditary entitlement. However, from a federalist point of view, there is a case to be made for second chamber having special powers, giving it a superior role in matters of an inherently federal nature. The US Senate was given special powers in regard to the ratification of treaties and executive appointments, notably appointment to the Supreme Court. The EU in turn constitutes a novel case of second chamber governance, which underscores the fact that its members are not yet prepared to let go entirely of its confederal origins.

Developments: Towards Council Governance?

Until recently, conventional wisdom would have it that the American senate model established the norm and the German council model was the exception. In terms of numbers, this is still the case. Yet there are signs of change. Based on the German model, the EU has developed a distinctive form of council governance that still relegates a reluctantly upgraded European Parliament to second place. As one of the world's leading experts on comparative federalism has remarked, since the EU might provide the model of federalism for the twenty-first century,[4] similar patterns of council governance might indeed develop in other cases of regional integration such as the North American Free Trade Area (NAFTA), the Asean Free Trade Area (AFTA), and Mercosur (the South American free trade association). More generally, it might eventually infuse a more democratic set of representative rules to intergovernmental organizations that are already governed by boards resembling intergovernmental councils.

A trend towards council governance can also be detected within a growing number of particular countries and regions. Among recent cases of federalization, South Africa has chosen the council model. Belgium and Spain have senates, but the political process essentially relies on intergovernmental bargaining and arbitration rather than bicameral majoritarianism, however compounded. In Northern Ireland, the Good Friday Agreement settled on a unique form of overlapping intergovernmentalism that involves not only the main internal factions but the governments of the Republic of Ireland and Britain, as well. This could become a model for conflict resolution in other parts of the world, particularly in the Middle East.

THE AMERICAN SENATE MODEL

As in the previous chapter, we begin our discussion of individual cases with the American experiment. The decision of who should be represented, and how, emerged from a tangled debate that pitted different interests and different visions against one other. The eventual outcome had great influence on federations that were to follow. There had been second chambers before—the ancient Roman Senate, the British House of Lords, and other European upper-class chambers—but these represented class interests and not territorial ones. Thus, even if the original design of the American Senate shared with these older bicameral systems an effort at constructing a "conservative brake" on the popular will,[5] it differed dramatically from them in its recognition of two different spatial manifestations of citizenship. There is no doubt, though, that the emergence of bicameralism as a key element of the federal compromise was greatly facilitated in the United States by a resurgent interest in bicameralism on traditional conservative grounds. The experience of unicameral popular rule in the various states after 1776 generated a strong desire to have an upper house, on whatever design, that would

4.   See Elazar, "The United States and the Eurpean Union" and also Daniel J. Elazar, *Constitutionalizing Globalization: The Postmodern Revival of Confederal Arrangements* (Lanham, MD: Rowman and Littlefield, 1998).

5.   Arend Lijphart, *Patterns of Democracy: Government Forms and Performance in Thirty-Six Countries* (New Haven, CT: Yale University Press, 1999) 203.

curb the democratic excesses of the people's representatives. Out of this emerged the original US American Senate, a chamber that was envisaged by its creators as a counterpart to the British House of Lords.[6] In the highly influential words of John Adams at the time, "a people cannot be long free, nor ever happy, whose government is in one assembly."[7] In the United States, constitutionalism and federalism converged to provide a powerful impetus for bicameralism and dual representation.

Big States Versus Small States?

In working their way towards a resolution of the representation issue, the framers settled on bicameralism as the way to reconcile two opposed demands. The issue was about what weight states of greatly varying size would carry in the new Congress.

Experience

As early as 1754, the so-called Albany Plan had proposed a union among the American colonies—albeit with a President-General appointed by the Crown. It also provided for a Grand Council whose members would be chosen by the colonial assemblies. Representation in the Council would be weighted according to population, with the largest colony (Virginia) receiving seven seats and the smallest (New Hampshire) two. While the British government was supportive, the colonial legislatures rejected the very idea as an infringement upon their prerogatives.[8] Some 30 years and a revolution later, the *Articles of Confederation* created the first American union. It functioned through a single-chambered Congress in which each state had one vote.

Putting Bicameralism on the Agenda

Most delegates came to Philadelphia in 1787 with the general intent of making the Confederation more effective without, however, seriously eroding the sovereignty of the states. When the Virginia delegation pressed ahead with a proposal for a radically new form of union government, the convention came alive in a whole new way. The Virginia Plan presented the delegates with the idea of two legislative houses. The first of these would be elected directly by the people on a majoritarian basis. The members of the second house would be nominated by the

6.   McDonald, *Novus Ordo Seclorum* 215. Also see Elaine K. Swift, *The Making of an American Senate: Reconstitutive Change in Congress, 1787–1841* (Ann Arbor, MI: University of Michigan Press, 1996).

7.   Gordon S. Wood, *The Creation of the American Republic 1776–1787* (Chapel Hill, NC: University of North Carolina Press, 1969) 208–09.

8.   Lister, *The Later Security Confederations* 44.

state legislatures but chosen by the first house. At this stage, then, bicameralism was put on the agenda, but it was still the conventional conservative form of bicameralism.

Having it Both Ways: The "Great Compromise"

Since the distribution of seats in the lower house would be proportional to state populations, the *Virginia Plan* would have left the larger states with the upper hand in both houses—or so delegates from the smaller states feared. After two weeks of debate, therefore, the smaller states countered with the New Jersey Plan. It proposed to retain the representative formula of the Confederation: one vote for each state in the Congress. The smaller states were in the majority, and the demographic differences were significant. With about 450,000 white inhabitants, Virginia was about ten times more populous than Delaware.[9] Giving one vote to each state as under the *Articles of Confederation* was patently unfair to the populations in the larger states. However, since the smaller ones were a majority, equality might have to be the price to pay if union was to be achieved at all.

Eventually, when deadlock threatened to shut down the Convention, a new committee finally delivered the Connecticut Compromise. This gave to each side an essential part of what it wanted: a directly-elected House of Representatives representing the people by population, *and* a Senate representing the states *qua* states. Thus, federal bicameralism was born out of the need to resolve this conflict between two conflicting considerations. And resolve the conflict it did: bicameralism would allow the two forms of representation to balance each other out.

Did it Matter?

As it turned out, the numbers game about large and small that so dominated the proceedings would not become the defining issue in the new Congress. At the Philadelphia Convention itself, the numbers game was overshadowed by the socio-economic differences between north and south, free states and slave states; there were large and small states on either side of that divide. Later again, the large number of states of greatly varying populations diffused it further. Partisanship and, more importantly, ideology, cut across it. Almost by default, it seems, equal state representation became the undisputed hallmark of American federalism—without serving any clear purpose. It also became the yardstick for other federations, although not all of them followed the example.

---

9.   Lister, *The Later Security Confederations* 25.

Indirect Election

There was never much doubt that the framers would settle on indirect election for the Senate. On the one hand, direct election was inconsistent with both the restraining role envisaged for the upper house and the federal role familiar from existing practice. The Virginia Plan had already proposed a Senate elected by the lower house—a system of indirect election regarded at the time as an effective way of refining the popular will and cleansing it of some of its baser elements. The existing Congress and Convention were also constituted in this fashion. On the other hand, the creation of a council-style upper house in the German pattern was out of the question because the post-revolutionary state constitutions had all but abolished their executive governments altogether and centred government power on their legislatures.[10]

Even though they were elected representatives of their legislatures rather than delegates of their executive governments, senators were expected from the outset to act in a delegate fashion. It was assumed that legislatures would instruct their representatives to the US Senate, and they attempted to do so.[11] However, the nature of the Senate was inherently ambiguous in this respect. State legislatures had in practice very little leverage over the senators once chosen. The Constitution included no provision for recall, and the six-year terms placed members of the Senate in a much more permanent position than the typical member of a state legislature. It was not an arrangement that would make the Senate a thoroughgoing states' house.[12]

Equal Powers

In order to appreciate the relative ease, by comparison, with which the Americans established two legislative chambers with equal powers, we need to remember that they were transforming a confederation of republican governments. Their major concern in terms of establishing an effective union government was not how the popular will should be represented in that government. Because that popular will *would* be represented, their primary preoccupation was with the representation of state interests. And if state representation in the Senate was to provide an effective check upon the majority powers in the House of Representatives, anything less than equality to the legislative powers of the House was simply out of the question.

---

10. Wood, *The Creation of the American Republic* 135–37.
11. Ralph A. Rossum, *Federalism, the Supreme Court, and the Seventeenth Amendment: The Irony of Constitutional Democracy* (Lanham, MD: Lexington Books, 2001) 96–98.
12. William H. Riker, "The Senate and American Federalism," *American Political Science Review* 49:2 (1955).

Check and Balances

The idea of equal powers between the two chambers was never challenged. In fact, as Hamilton, Jay, and Madison explain in a number of essays (*Federalist* 62–66), it constituted the core of an emerging doctrine of **checks and balances** in which the Senate was seen as the most important player. Its concurrence in legislation would allow it to serve as a 'check' on the uncontrolled passions—and "factions"—of the popular assembly. Meanwhile, its smaller number of members would ensure cohesion and authority, while the **extended duration** of senatorial mandates—six years as compared to two years for the House—and the **staggered mode of election**—renewing the mandate of one-third of senators every two years—would provide both continuity and a crucial 'balancing' effect, ensuring that the legislature was made up of groups that were 'out of sync' with each other and with public passions.

Special Powers

According to this doctrine of checks and balances, the two congressional chambers would restrain one another by a mutual veto. More importantly still, such a mutual veto would also determine the relationship between the Congress and the executive. The president would have to govern on the basis of congressional legislation, but would also have the right to veto such legislation. Two additional measures of control were given exclusively to the Senate, however. It would have the power of **ratifying** key appointments and international treaties. It has been these powers of ratification that have established the Senate as the weightier of the two congressional chambers, particularly so in public perception.

A final issue was **impeachment,** the forced removal of the president, or other "civil officers" such as federal judges, from office. Here, the House would lay the charges, and the Senate would conduct the trial and convict by a two-thirds majority.

Completing the Senate Model

The introduction of direct senate elections by the Seventeenth Amendment in 1913 was occasioned by a different kind of debate. By 1866, Congress had passed legislation regulating procedures by which the state legislatures elected senators. These procedures encouraged deadlock and corruption which brought the entire system into disrepute. Against this collusion of public and private power the "progressive movement" had formed, demanding the direct popular election of senators. The Senate resisted but eventually relented when several states threatened to push for a new constitutional convention that might have generated more far-reaching reforms.[13]

In several ways nothing much changed with the introduction of direct senatorial elections, and for the time being, the Senate remained a "Millionaires' Club."[14] However, it has been argued that this downgrading of the Senate from an albeit imperfect house of the states to a popularly elected chamber removed the keystone from the arch of the American federal system, and without that keystone, the arch soon collapsed: "...the main peripheralizing feature of American federalism was excised from the Constitution."[15] The Senate, not the Supreme Court, was the institution the founders expected to be the guarantor of the federal balance. "Following ratification of the Seventeenth Amendment, there was a rapid growth of the power of the national government, with the Congress enacting measures that adversely affected the states as states—measures that, quite simply, the Senate previously would never have approved."[16]

CANADA: A CASE OF PSEUDO-BICAMERALISM

While the Americans negotiated their way to a novel form of representative government, the Canadians generally aimed at changing as little as possible. With responsible government having recently been achieved, neither the primacy of parliamentarianism nor the appropriateness of popular democratic rule through the lower house was much disputed. In tandem with the fact that the two main provinces, Ontario and Québec, were created by devolution from an existing legislative union, it is hardly surprising that Canada did not end up with the powerful and confederal-style upper house that the Americans had given themselves. In Canada there was neither the conservative thrust for a restraint on democracy nor the confederal thrust for a restraint on majoritarianism. The consequence was creation of the only effectively unicameral federal government among the true federations.

Regional Weighting

The idea of a second and regional chamber of representation no longer had to be invented. At the first meeting of colonial delegates, the Charlottetown Conference of September 1864, there was discussion and agreement on a Federal Legislative Council with 20 members from each

---

13. Rossum, *Federalism, the Supreme Court, and the Seventeenth Amendment* 186–87.
14. See James Q. Wilson and John J. DiIulio, *American Government* (Boston, MA: Houghton Mifflin, 1998) 306–07.
15. Riker, "The Senate and American Federalism" 469.
16. Rossum, *Federalism, the Supreme Court, and the Seventeenth Amendment* 2.

of the three participant regions—Canada West, Canada East,[17] and the Maritime provinces. A month later, at the follow-up conference in Québec City, John A. Macdonald moved that the three sections of British North America should be equally represented in the upper house, with 24 members each.[18]

This time, the Maritime provinces resisted such regional equality. At Charlottetown, there were only three—Nova Scotia, New Brunswick, and Prince Edward Island. At Québec City, Newfoundland had joined the conference, and it was this increase from three to four provinces that now compelled the Maritimers to demand 32 members as compared to the 24 for the other two sections. Serious dispute occurred and eventually was settled when it was agreed to retain the original formula of regional equality, with 24 members in what was now called a senate, with four additional senators accorded to the newcomer, Newfoundland.

Still, two years later, at the final meeting in London, the issue of second chamber representation came up again. The formula ultimately prevailed, despite the fact that the Maritime region would now, after the withdrawal of Prince Edward Island and Newfoundland, consist of New Brunswick and Nova Scotia only. In 1873, when Prince Edward Island joined, it was allocated four senators with the respective contingents for the other two Maritime provinces reduced from 12 to ten.

On one level, it is easy to see why the numbers game about second chamber representation dominated the proceedings. The Maritime Provinces originally harboured plans of establishing a union of their own, and they remained reluctant participants. Adequate regional representation in a federal government was the core of what they could expect in return for joining the two larger and more populous Canadas. The French in Canada East, on the other hand, feared that any move beyond basic equality would weaken their position. After all, in a parliament elected on the principle of representation by population, Canada West with its large and growing majority of people would enjoy a superior position.

It apparently also did not matter that senate representation would be based on regions, not provinces. The two Canadas were obviously regions as well as provinces, and the Maritimes had a sense of common interest strong enough to override equality concerns. Moreover, on the basis of population, 24 senators still amounted to a substantive corrective. At the time, the Maritimes comprised only one-fifth of the British North American population, roughly 800,000 (including Prince Edward Island) as compared to 1.5 million in Ontario and 1 million in Québec. That latter differential, between Ontario and Québec, was the root

17. In 1840, Upper and Lower Canada (Ontario and Québec) were joined as Canada West and Canada East in a single legislative union.

18. See P.B. Waite, *The Life and Times of Confederation 1864–1867* (Toronto, ON: University of Toronto Press, 1965) 82, 89–94, 111.

cause for persistent parliamentary "rep by pop" demands in the one case and for the insistence on regional senate equality in the other.

In essence, the Canadians and Maritimers found a solution of weighted regional representation. Given the profound differences between the regions in terms of size, culture, language, and economic status, this was an important achievement. It became problematic, however, when the regional equality formula was extended when six senators each were given to the four western provinces in 1915. This not only means that the western provinces, with their larger populations, have fewer senators than New Brunswick and Nova Scotia, it also means that western Canada overall has fewer senators than Atlantic Canada because six additional seats were given to Newfoundland when it joined Confederation in 1949.

Today, there are 105 senators: 24 from the four principal regions; six from Newfoundland; and one each from the three territories—the Yukon, the Northwest Territories, and the recently created Nunavut.

Undemocratic Means to Democratic Ends

On another level, though, it is difficult to understand what the fuss over numbers was all about, since the members of the new Canadian Senate were to be neither elected directly by regional populations nor chosen indirectly by regional governments. These options were discussed, but in the end it was agreed that the senators would be appointed by the governor-general (and hence in reality by the prime minister). This might seem surprising, particularly in light of the conventional understanding that bicameralism is an intrinsic component of federalism. However, the Canadians did not want an upper house that would challenge the lower house. As the designers of the first parliamentary system to 'go federal,' the Canadians were acutely aware of the problems that strong bicameralism posed for the basic functioning of the system. By contrast with the presidential system, a difference or deadlock between the two houses would threaten the executive government itself. Thus, even the leading conservative, John A. Macdonald, extolled the virtues of a weak upper house: "There is an infinitely greater chance of a deadlock between the two branches of the legislature, should the elective principle be adopted, than with a nominated chamber."[19]

To create a powerful upper house in the name of federalism would also be to adopt the anti-democratic principle of checks and balances that so inspired the Americans. Canadians showed little interest in compromising on the newly won right to popular local rule by creating a second chamber that would potentially contradict the first. This was a particularly forceful consideration for the strongly democratic "Reformers" who were prominent in the negotiations. Reform leader George

---

19. Ajzenstat, *et al.*, eds., *Canada's Founding Debates* 82.

Brown spoke for many of them when he declared that "I have always been opposed to a second elective chamber, and I am so still, from the conviction that the two elective houses are inconsistent with the right working of the British parliamentary system."[20] Other Reform participants were even more explicit about the attractiveness of the appointment basis: a "stubborn" upper house could be brought back into line "quickly and sharply," thanks to this power of the government.[21]

The fact that there were no confederal-style states' rights demands for a strongly federal chamber made it possible to satisfy these preferences for parliamentary majoritarianism. Canada had neither the conservative drive to protect the rights of property holders nor the confederalist drive to protect the rights of the provinces that had led to the creation of the US Senate. The appointed Canadian Senate represented the use of undemocratic means to achieve democratic ends.

Far From Equal

Formally, the Senate was given equal powers. In reality, its unelected status has reduced its role to that of a provider of 'sober second thought.' Rarely have senators used their powers to defeat a bill that had found approval by the elected majority in the House of Commons. Although its professionalism may have increased over the years, the overall image of the Senate has not. Senatorial appointments are widely and not incorrectly seen as plum job rewards for party faithfuls heading for semi-retirement.

Senators are caught between a rock and a hard place, exemplifying the Abbé Sieyès'[22] dictum that if an upper house agrees with the lower it is superfluous and if it disagrees it is mischievous—an obstacle to democracy and responsible government. Senators do provide useful legislative services in their deliberations and fine-tuning of parliamentary bills, spending most of their time in parliamentary committees discussing key issues and making recommendations for policy initiatives. But ultimately they have little choice but to exercise self-restraint in opposing a government whose legitimacy is firmly remained grounded in parliamentary majority rule.

Exercising its Paper Powers

A more immediate reason for this self-restraint is partisanship. More often than not, parliamentary majorities have been mirrored in the composition of the Senate, providing for the assured smooth sailing of bills

---

20. Ajzenstat, *et al.*, eds., *Canada's Founding Debates* 83.
21. Walter McCrae in Ajzenstat, *et al.*, eds., *Canada's Founding Debates* 90.
22. French statesman during the period of the French Revolution.

through both chambers. Only on occasion did different Senate majorities make use of their formal powers. One such instance, and by far the most significant one, came in 1988 when a Liberal Party Senate majority was poised to oppose the Progressive Conservative (PC) government's free trade legislation. Prime Minister Brian Mulroney had to call an election over the issue, which he won. After that election, when the same Senate majority threatened to block a new goods and services tax, Mulroney resorted to a constitutional provision by which the government could "at any time" appoint four or eight additional senators—provided it did so from the four regions equally. Thus he gained a PC majority in the Senate, and the bill was passed.[23]

Although perfectly legal, both the provocative engagement of the Senate in government legislation and the prime minister's tactical appointment of additional senators further diminished the legitimacy of the Canadian Senate in the public eye or, more precisely, in the partisan public eye on either side. The fact that Canada's Senate was supposed to provide regional representation hardly played a role, even though the regions were divided over the free trade issue. Calls for Senate reform could be heard yet again, but, as in all previous instances, nothing came of it in the end.

Developments: Senate Reform Forever

The Canadian Senate has remained an oddity and not only so within the family of federations. Its members are all appointed, it has equal powers, and its historically based formula of regional representation is patently unbalanced. Not surprisingly, calls for Senate reform in Canada have come from all quarters—from prime ministers faced with rare bouts of hostile Senate opposition, from concerned democrats, and from western regions resenting their under-representation and their powerlessness in the face of central Canada's demographic dominance in the lower house.[24] However, nothing has ever come of such calls. Over the past 30 years alone, "no less than twenty-eight government and political party proposals on Senate reform have failed."[25] Ordinary Canadians, it seems, did not care enough, and the various proposals typically were embedded in package deals too complex for substantive political agreement.

---

23. See C.E.S. Franks, "The Canadian Senate in Modern Times," in Serge Joyal, ed., *Protecting Canadian Democracy: The Senate You Never Knew* (Montreal, QC and Kingston, ON: McGill-Queen's University Press, 2003) 162.

24. The four western provinces of Manitoba, Saskatchewan, Alberta, and British Columbia have together just under 30 per cent of Canada's population. Ontario has over 37 per cent alone.

25. Serge Joyal, "Introduction," in Joyal, ed., *Protecting Canadian Democracy* xix.

The "Triple-E Senate"

In particular, Senate reform became a western bargaining chip in exchange for recognition of Québec's distinct society status during various failed rounds of attempted constitutional reconciliation. These grievances were formalized by the Province of Alberta as demands for a "triple-E Senate"— a Senate that is "elected, effective and equal."[26] Alberta's proposal called for conversion of the existing Canadian Senate to essentially the American version. Seats would be allocated on the confederal principle of equal representation for each province (in this case six each); popular election rather than delegation would replace appointment; and the checks and balances device of staggered cohorts would be introduced. Senators would be ineligible for cabinet positions. The triple-E Senate would have veto rights over legislation affecting the provinces and over all treaties and Supreme Court appointments.

The decision of a strongly confederalist province to advance the senate rather than the council model is in some ways surprising.[27] General experience with elected federal upper houses has thoroughly demonstrated that modern party discipline negates any role they might play as a states' house. As sympathetic critics have argued, the proposition is poorly aimed to achieve the desired goals.[28] In a strongly populist context, though, the senate model of direct elections is a predictable choice. Outside of Alberta, the proposal has received understandably limited support. The dominant provinces of Ontario and Québec do not feel the same regionalist grievance, and other regional provinces do not feel the same desire as the rich province of Alberta for an upper house that would constrain nation-building policies.

From Demand to Virtual Reality

However, the triple-E Senate proposal was included in the Charlottetown Accord of 1992.[29] That agreement proposed a Senate with six members from each province, directly elected except in Québec where the provincial legislature would choose them. In exchange for more legitimate

---

26. Legislature of Alberta, *Strengthening Canada: Reform of Canada's Senate* (Edmonton, AB: Plains Publishing, 1985).

27. The government of Alberta had in fact made a "house of provinces" proposal analogous to the *Bundesrat* earlier, in 1982. But the triple-e slogan proved to be more attractive.

28. For example, Michael Lusztig, "Federalism and Institutional Design: The Perils and Politics of a Triple-E Senate in Canada," *Publius* 25:1 (1995).

29. See Martin Westmacott, "The Charlottetown Accord: A Retrospective Overview," in Martin Westmacott and Hugh Mellon, eds., *Challenges to Canadian Federalism* (Scarborough, ON: Prentice Hall, 1998).

political clout, some of the Senate's veto powers regarding revenue and tax bills would be converted into a merely suspensive veto.

At least for the time being, the defeat of the Charlottetown Accord in a national referendum has ended the quest for Senate reform. The prevalent explanation for its defeat is that the agreement came too late and the people trusted neither the content nor the process. While this may be so, another explanation points to the durability of constitutional arrangements once in place. Because they are the result of negotiated compromise, federal constitutions are like puzzles: taking one piece out of its familiar place is likely to affect too many others. Canadians have become used to intergovernmental relations as a means of making up for the lack of adequate regional representation (see Chapter 8). The prospects of wholesale constitutional change proved too upsetting for their political imagination.

GERMANY: THE FEDERAL SOLUTION

The German road to democratic federalism has been distinctive in many ways and so have been some of its solutions, including the construction of an upper or second chamber of regional representation. Bismarck's 1866 chamber of regional representation was a council of ruling kings and princes that also found its way into the Imperial Constitution of 1871. The Weimar Constitution replaced princes and kings with representatives of the *Länder* government but left the chamber with only limited powers and influence. The third version, reconstructed democratically at the end of World War II, followed the same pattern, regained a more powerful role, and set a precedent for council governance in the EU. Like the United States, Germany has had a tradition of strong federal upper houses as a result of the convergence of two complementary forces: anti-democratic conservatism and confederalism. The form those upper houses have taken, though, has differed significantly from the American.

Context: Evolution of the Council Model

Germany's council model of a federal upper house has roots that can be traced back to the seventeenth and eighteenth centuries,[30] and today's *Bundesrat* has been described as "the successor" to the Perpetual

---

30. Werner J. Patzelt, "The Very Federal House: The German Bundesrat," in Samuel C. Patterson and Anthony Mughan, eds., *Senates: Bicameralism in the Contemporary World* (Columbus, OH: Ohio State University Press, 1999). In fact, it can be traced back even further, all the way to the imperial assemblies of the Middle Ages even though these were convoked only periodically and therefore were not *immerwährend*.

Imperial Assembly (*Immerwährender Reichstag*) of 1663.[31] The modern version arose more directly out of the nineteenth-century process of unification under Prussian hegemony. As a first step, the German Confederation (1815–66) was quite similar to the American confederation in that its only governing organ, the *Bundestag* (Federal Assembly), was an assembly of instructed low-level delegates. It had complex voting procedures which were entirely unrealistic because the two dominant powers, Austria and Prussia, would not tolerate being outvoted.

The Imperial Bundesrat

After the Austro-Prussian war of 1866 and the exclusion of Austria from German politics, Bismarck forged ahead with a North German Confederation (1867–71) for which he developed a constitution that for the first time included a directly elected assembly. But he also retained the *Bundestag*, now renamed *Bundesrat* (Federal Council), as a chamber of continued **governmental representation** under Prussian hegemony. This established the nucleus of the *Reichsverfassung*, or Imperial Constitution, of 1871 when the states of southern Germany were persuaded to join the Confederation at the end of the Franco-Prussian war.

The lower house was the *Reichstag*, directly elected but endowed with only limited powers, and the upper house was the *Bundesrat*, effectively the Empire's supreme legislative *and* executive organ. Prussia held only 17 of the 58 *Bundesrat* seats, but in cases of conflict with the so-called medium States (such as Bavaria, which also held 17 seats), Prussia could easily pressure the smaller states and cities into majority support. The delegates did not have a free mandate but had to deliver bloc votes as instructed by their governments. Thus, the impression of Prussian hegemony was avoided yet *de facto* secured at the same time. This was smoothed over by Bismarck's skilful leadership which avoided coercive techniques. Instead, negotiations in this "princely insurance company against democracy"[32] typically went on until consensual agreement was reached.

Weighted Representation

When the West German state was reconstructed after World War II, the new federal system incorporated a federal second chamber that reflected these historic practices. As we have seen already, the idea of weighted representation has its own tradition from Montesquieu's endorsement

31. Uwe Leonardy, "The Institutional Structures of German Federalism," in Charlie Jeffrey, ed., *Recasting German Federalism: The Legacies of Unification* (London: Pinter, 1999) 4.

32. Thus, the German social democrat Wilhelm Liebknecht as quoted in Ernst Engelberg, *Bismarck: das Reich in der Mitte Europas* (Berlin: Siedler, 1990) 51.

of the Lycian confederacy, to the Albany Plan of Union among the early American colonies, to Bismarck's Imperial constitution. Its incorporation into the West German Constitution of 1949 was by no means surprising. Under strict supervision by the three Western occupying powers, the Germans drafted this constitution as an attempt to combine the best elements of German political tradition with the institutional requirements of a modern democracy.

The second chamber, again called the *Bundesrat*, was to represent democratically elected *Länder* governments as a counterweight against creeping centralization. There was no strong argument in favour of equal *Länder* representation. With most of their boundaries redrawn arbitrarily after the war, there were few historical sensibilities to defend. A formula of representation recognizing population size yet giving the smaller units additional weight appeared as a fair compromise.

The original formula accorded five votes to those *Länder* with more than six million people (at the time, North Rhine Westphalia, Bavaria, Baden-Württemberg, and Lower Saxony), four votes to those with more than two million (Hesse, Rhineland-Pfalz, and Schleswig-Holstein), and three to those with less than two million inhabitants (Hamburg, Bremen, and Saarland). The total of seats and votes was 41. West Berlin had four additional non-voting seats due to its status as a city under Allied command. With reunification in 1990, five additional *Länder* were added, and Berlin became a sixteenth *Land* with full voting rights. The formula of weighted governmental representation was adjusted because most of the new *Länder* in the east were smaller and poorer, and the four largest *Länder* in the west feared to be put into a permanent minority situation. Hence they were now given six votes in a reconstituted *Bundesrat* with 68 votes in all.

A House of the States

Like its forerunners, the new *Bundesrat* was designed to give the *Länder* direct representation in the national parliament as states rather than as populations. The *Bundesrat* is made up of delegates sent by the state governments. The *Länder* governments can send as many delegates as they have votes, but their votes have to be delivered as a uniform bloc vote as instructed by the *Land* government, and by a vote leader designated before each session. Because there are no elections, the *Bundesrat* is a permanent chamber that is called into session whenever it is required to vote on pending legislation. Its composition changes only as *Länder* governments change.

The *Bundesrat* has generally served its constitutional role constructively, even though partisanship often proved more important than the representation of regional interests. In one respect, though, the *Bundesrat* did not fulfill the role its designers had foreseen. It has not prevented

German federalism from becoming overly centralized, even becoming a case of "unitary federalism."[33] Indeed, it has facilitated that centralization by lessening local resistance to central authority. However, it remains unique in the degree to which it retains a genuinely federal character. By contrast, not even the Swiss second chamber delivers that federal representation. As Linder and Vatter have noted,

> ... empirical research has sometimes found that the [Swiss] Council of the States is not at all a federalist institution because it defends mostly the same group interests as can be identified in the National Council. Indeed, there is a strong theoretical argument for this second opinion: the Council of States, unlike the German Bundesrat, is not a representative of the executive of the member states and therefore is responsive to the cantonal constituencies rather than to government interests.[34]

As Good as Equal

While the *Bundesrat* does not qualify as a second chamber with formally equal powers, it is in reality one of the most powerful second chambers to be found in any federal system. The Constitution distinguishes two types of legislation. The first requires approval in both chambers. With regard to the second, *Bundesrat* objections (by absolute majority) can be overridden by (a likewise absolute majority) in the lower house, the *Bundestag*.

Legislation requiring bicameral approval pertains to constitutional change (two-thirds majorities in both chambers) and to all ordinary bills affecting the legislative powers and administrative duties of the *Länder* including, in particular, all money bills. About 60 per cent of all bills fall under this type of approval legislation, which thus encompasses virtually all important acts of legislation. The constitutional designers did not expect or anticipate this.

The reason for the heavy and near-equal weight that the *Bundesrat* acquired over time has more to do with the administrative division of powers in Germany's system of federalism than with the stipulations about bicameralism in the Constitution. Since the *Länder* have the constitutionally assigned task of implementing and administering most national framework legislation, their powers and duties are routinely

---

33. This argument was made quite early on; see Konrad Hesse, *Der unitarische Bundesstaat* (Karlsruhe: C.F. Müller, 1962). Hesse's argument essentially focussed on the peculiar construction of the *Bundesraat*, the role of a centralized party system in the federal system, and on the societal demands for uniform social policy goals.

34. Wolf Linder and Adrian Vatter, "Institutions and Outcomes of Swiss Federalism: The Role of the Cantons in Swiss Politics," *West European Politics* 24:2 (2001): 99.

and automatically affected, and judicial consensus developed that the *Bundesrat* would therefore have to approve such legislation.

This makes the *Bundesrat* such a powerful second chamber for a combination of reasons. Its members are prominent regional politicians who typically also play important roles in the national party system. In most important decisions, the *Bundesrat* votes are delivered by the prime ministers of the *Länder*. Via the *Bundesrat*, the *Länder* governments have the right to initiate legislation; they play a crucial role in policy formulation; and they finally bear exclusive responsibility for implementation and administration. The German chancellor and his cabinet, while accountable only to the *Bundestag*, can do little without giving serious consideration to the interests of the *Länder* governments. On the occasion of the Maastricht Treaty, the *Bundesrat* even managed to bring about a constitutional change that secured a participatory role in European affairs—until then seen as the central government's exclusive power in the foreign policy domain (Articles 23 and 50 of the Constitution as revised in 1992).

Development: Squaring Federalism with Party Governance

Not surprisingly, with the Americans and the British looking over their shoulders, the designers of the post-war Constitution sought to reconcile federalism with parliamentary democracy. They also had to weigh the British tradition of majoritarian electoral systems against the German tradition of proportional representation. The outcome was a new hybrid: the "mixed-member proportional" system (MMP).

Under this system, German voters are given two votes—one for a directly elected candidate and one for their preferred party. Half of the parliamentary seats in the *Bundestag* are filled with directly elected members, the other half from regional party lists and in such a way that the final seat distribution is proportional to the result of the national vote. In order to avoid the multiparty disaster of the Weimar Republic, access to the *Bundestag* was limited to parties that garnered at least 5 per cent of the national vote. The German chancellor was fully responsible to the *Bundestag*, but not to the *Bundesrat*.

As intended, the effect was a strong national party system with two major and a very few third parties. Partisanship soon began to overshadow federalism. Given the co-decision powers of the *Länder* governments in the *Bundesrat*, *Land* elections became dominated by national issues. The electorate understood very well that the majority powers of the national government could be constrained by opposing majorities in the *Bundesrat*, a situation that often signalled imminent government change in the next federal election. Contrary to the political traditions of parliamentary federalism in some of the British settler colonies, this role of the second federal chamber as a countervailing force in national politics has not generally been seen as a violation of political legitimacy and responsible government.

On the contrary, it has even been praised as an important element of checks and balances in a parliamentary democracy characterized by the interplay of government and opposition. The opposition in parliamentary systems has little control over the political agenda as long as the governing majority prevails. The German *Bundesrat* provides the governing majority with an effective tool for control.

Another question is, of course, whether this predominance of second chamber partisanship vitiates a more genuinely federal role for the *Bundesrat*.[35] Obviously, this depends on the degree to which partisan preferences and electoral outcomes in the *Länder* reflect regional differences of policy choice as well. While such differences may not have been very pronounced during the earlier years of the West German Republic, they have become more substantial now, after reunification, as differences between west and east, large and small, rich and poor. This in turn has strengthened the federal character of the *Bundesrat*, but it has also on occasion allowed the government in power to strike policy alliances across partisan lines.

Disagreement and Deadlock Procedures

The constitutional designers may not have considered this potential structural breach between party system and bicameral federalism, but they did provide in Article 77 of the Constitution for creation of a **Mediation Committee** comprising members of both chambers. As we saw in the Canadian case, constitution makers were acutely aware that the combination of strong bicameralism with parliamentarianism creates the potential for destabilizing the entire system. The Canadian solution was to avoid the risk; the German solution was to anticipate it. Significantly, the *Bundesrat* members on the committee are not bound by government instructions.[36] The organizational details were left to procedural rules to be established by mutual agreement between both chambers. According to these rules, the Mediation Committee is currently (after reunification) composed of 16 members from each chamber. In cases of disagreement over bills requiring *Bundesrat* approval, the Mediation Committee tries to work out a compromise which then has to be voted on again in both chambers. The Mediation Committee therefore must be seen as the linchpin of the German federal system, and it has

---

35. Thus, Gerhard Lehmbruch, *Parteienwettbewerb im Bundesstaat* (Stuttgart: Kohlhammer, 1976). For critical assessment, see Roland Sturm, "Party Competition and the Federal System: The Lehmbruch Hypothesis Revisited," in Charlie Jeffrey, ed., *Recasting German Federalism: The Legacies of Unification* (London: Pinter, 1999).

36. As they are when voting in the *Bundesrat* itself.

by and large performed its function of avoiding deadlock between the two chambers very successfully.

THE EUROPEAN UNION: A CASE OF SECOND CHAMBER GOVERNANCE

As we have emphasized, the normal way of designing federal institutions has been by way of bicameralism—complementing popular representation in one chamber with regional representation in the other chamber. In the case of the Bismarckian constitutions of 1866 and 1871 we have seen how the German princes went the opposite way. Their primary interest was mutual accommodation in the *Bundesrat*. Parliamentary representation in the *Reichstag* was to play second fiddle. European institution-building followed a similar rationale and path. The member states sought to establish a common market on the basis of intergovernmental agreement. Next to the governing Council of Ministers, the European Parliament has limited powers and serves primarily as a forum of public debate. As the EU increasingly acquires the status of a supranational polity, this lack of full parliamentary accountability has come to be seen as a serious democratic deficit.

Context: Treaty Federalism

The process of European integration was set in motion at the Messina Conference of 1955, which resulted in the founding Treaties of Rome in 1958. From the very beginning, the idea was to move beyond a system of mere intergovernmental cooperation. Jean Monnet, the driving force behind the process and its institutional outcome, had been Deputy Secretary-General of the interwar League of Nations, and he was well aware of the inherent weaknesses of confederal intergovernmentalism. Driven by the same concerns as led the Philadelphia Convention to construct a more "energetic" central government, Monnet sought to construct an effective union. Following the pattern of the High Authority in the already established European Coal and Steel Community (ECSC), he was convinced that successful market integration depended on a strong central executive. At the same time he was persuaded that the legitimacy of a community among democratic nation-states required at least the semblance of a full set of democratic institutions including a parliament and an independent court of justice (on the latter, see Chapter 10).[37]

---

37.   See John Pinder, *The European Union* (Oxford: Oxford University Press, 2001) 9–10.

The Proto-Federal Model

And indeed, the institutions created by the Treaties of Rome at first glance very much looked like those of a federal state: policy initiatives would be the prerogative of the executive European Commission. The Treaties set out the equivalent of two legislative chambers: a parliament representing the European populations and a council representing the member states. A European Court of Justice would uphold the letter and spirit of the treaties. According to that letter and spirit, the European Community (European Union since 1993) would be a hybrid system of intergovernmental politics and supranational policy integration.

Sovereign Realities

The initial postwar euphoria about a truly transnational European peace project quickly gave way to a reassertion of nation-state interests, perhaps best expressed by French President Charles de Gaulle's later formula of a Europe of fatherlands (*Europe des patries*). For this reason, the balance of powers within the European institutional setup unfolded in marked difference from what one might have expected in an emerging European federal state.

In essence, the Council of Ministers became the most powerful organ of legislative and regulatory decision-making.[38] At the outset, it appeared intergovernmental in its procedural loyalty to mutual agreement under the treaties, but even then supranational in its commitment to the adoption of a truly European body of secondary law. With the adoption of qualified majority voting in an ever growing number of policy areas, the Council increasingly has taken on the characteristics of a supranational policy-maker, leaving the treaty changing decisions to the summit meetings of the European Council where unanimity prevails.

From a federalist perspective, the roles of Council and Parliament appear reversed. While the Council performs the role of a first chamber, setting the legislative agenda on the basis of European Commission initiatives, the European Parliament clearly was designed as a weaker chamber—and has remained so even though every treaty change since the mid-1980s has upgraded its powers.[39] Directly elected only since 1979, it does not initiate legislation, and it has limited budgetary powers. Over time it has gained extensive **co-decision** powers for most policy areas, which means that legislative acts in these areas require approval of both Council and Parliament. Under the constitutional treaty, the co-decision procedure will be renamed "legislative procedure" and, extending to

---

38. Elizabeth Bomberg, Laura Cram, and David Martin, "The EU's Institutions," in Bomberg and Stubb, eds., *The European Union* 49.
39. See Bomberg, Cram, and Martin, "The EU's Institutions" 56–59.

some 95 per cent of all European laws, will become the ordinary way in which the EU passes legislation.

Another Formula of Weighted Representation

Council proceedings were designed to move from intergovernmentalism to supranationalism in two stages. For a transition period, the Council was to function like a diplomatic conference, requiring unanimous agreement among member states for most decisions. After a transition period, the Treaties foresaw the increased use of weighted or **qualified majority voting** (QMV) similar to the German *Bundesrat*. Towards the end of the transition period, however, French President Charles de Gaulle strongly objected to QMV, even withdrawing from further participation in Council proceedings in protest. The so-called Luxembourg Compromise of 1966 then effectively suspended the adoption of QMV. The member states agreed that unanimity should prevail despite treaty stipulations whenever a member state declared a decision to be of paramount national interest. Since 1985 and the adoption of the Single European Act (SEA), QMV has been reestablished as the prevalent mode of decision-making for most matters relating to the single market.

The Stress of Enlargement

While the adoption of QMV was contested because it constituted a qualitative jump from confederalism to federalism, the adoption of a weighted formula of representation was never in doubt. All participants agreed that a compromise had to be found between intergovernmental unanimity and majority rule on the basis of member-state equality. As in the German model, the formula reflected differences in size and population but gave additional weight to the smaller member states. The idea was to find a balanced scheme by which the larger states could not entirely dominate the smaller ones, and the smaller ones could not gang up on the larger ones. This would require, though, adjustments for each successive round of enlargement. And with each round, the numbers game would become more complicated:

> In the original Community of six, the three largest member states—Germany, France, and Italy—each had 4, the Netherlands and Belgium 2, and Luxembourg 1 vote. A qualified majority decision was carried by 12 out of 17 votes.[40]

By the time the EU reached a membership of 15, decisions required 62 out of 87 votes (large states—the original three plus Britain—now had 10 votes each, Luxembourg 2, and the others somewhere in between).

---

40. See Bomberg, Cram, and Martin, "The EU's Institutions" 52–53.

Contrary to the way votes are counted in the German *Bundesrat*, a decision could be adopted only if the absolute majority number of 62 was actually reached, with abstentions counted as negative votes. In terms of a balanced weight this meant that even two of the larger states (say Germany and France) could not block a decision and that the smaller ones needed the support of at least two of the five larger ones in order to carry a decision. In addition, there was a side-agreement to delay and avoid narrow decisions.

In anticipation of further massive enlargement,[41] the 2003 Nice Treaty then changed the formula yet again. As of November 2004, voting weights for the currently existing 25 member states range from 29 to three, and a decision requires 232 votes out of 321 cast by a majority of member states. In addition to this qualified majority, Council decisions also require support from at least a majority of member states, and the votes cast in favour must represent at least 62 per cent of the European population (this latter count will only be undertaken if any one member state demands it).

The constitutional draft made an effort at cutting through this ever changing number game by reducing what is effectively a triple majority requirement to a completely **new double majority voting system**: a decision would be carried by a majority of member states representing at least 60 per cent of the population. Because this was deemed insufficient protection for mid-sized member states such as Poland and Spain, the adoption of the draft failed in December 2003. A year later, a compromise was reached by raising the threshold for adoption. Article I-25 (1.) of the Constitution as signed by the heads of state or government of the 25 member states and three candidate countries on 29 October 2004[42] now reads: "A qualified majority shall be defined as at least 55% of the members of the Council, comprising at least fifteen of them and representing Member States comprising at least 65% of the population of the Union."

Consensus Politics

This preoccupation with numbers and qualified majority provisions conceals to a considerable extent the real nature of decision-making in the EU. All decisions are carefully prepared by a Committee of Permanent Representatives (COREPER), composed of senior civil servants from the national governments, before they reach the Council table. Once there, further efforts are made at avoiding a display of majority

---

41. Ten new member states have meanwhile joined in 2004; two more are expected to join in 2007; a third one is pending; a fourth one, Turkey, has been invited to begin entry negotiations.

42. But still awaiting a difficult process of ratification.

power. In marked contrast to the German *Bundesrat* again, but not unlike Bismarck's old Federal Council, the Council of Ministers has remained a "consensus-seeking machine."[43] There are many different blocs of interest—industrial, agricultural, Mediterranean, Nordic, large and small—and nobody likes to be isolated. Qualified majority votes are taken routinely, but they are usually negotiated to the point of near-unanimity, often in the form of package deals satisfying the diversity of interests in different policy fields. Weighted representation in the Council of Ministers has proven to be a flexible and sufficiently efficient method of European decision-making. Treaty changes—or, in the future, amendments to the consolidated constitutional treaty—will continue to require unanimity among the heads of state or government in the European Council.

Second Chamber Governance: More than Equal

As we noted earlier, the question for the designers in most of the classical federations had been whether to make the second chamber stronger, weaker, or equal. We have also seen that the American and Australian cases provided the clearest examples of a strong second chamber senate because of the high level of autonomy and responsible governance the constituent member units already possessed at the time of federation. In the case of the EU, composed of fully sovereign member states, the question was asked in reverse: should the European Parliament as the first chamber be stronger, equal, or weaker than the Council of Ministers. And the answer was: weaker.

Historically, this is understandable because the EU grew out of inter-governmental treaty agreement, and the member states had no intention of giving up their position as "masters of the treaties." In order to combat the widely criticized "democratic deficit," the powers of the European Parliament have been upgraded over time from non-binding consultation, to a formal cooperation procedure where parliamentary decisions could still be overridden by the Council, to an ever more inclusive co-decision right (enshrined as "legislative procedure" in the constitutional treaty).

Despite these upgrades, the European Parliament remains a weak first chamber. In the main, this is so because there is no genuinely European party system. Instead, nationally elected parties form political groups along ideological lines. The two strongest ones are social democratic and Christian democratic. By contrast with the members of the Council

---

43. Werner Weidenfeld and Wolfgang Wessels, *Europe from A to Z: Guide to European Integration* (Luxembourg: Office for Official Publications of the European Communities, 1997) 57.

who are well known nationally as government leaders and ministers, European parliamentarians usually remain outside the political limelight.

Moreover, even where it has full co-decision rights, the status of the European Parliament in the legislative process is more reactive than agenda-setting. It can block a Council decision, but it cannot override the Council with a proposal of its own. Important policy areas such as taxation and agricultural price-setting, remain outside the co-decision provision.[44] And the rejection of Council proposals requires a majority of all European Parliament members, not just a majority of votes cast. The Council remains the more-than-equal partner in European governance. In comparison to conventional federal systems—especially those with a strong parliamentary tradition—the EU can be characterized as a system of second chamber governance.

Development: A Model of Council Governance?

In a traditional context of comparative federalism, the European system of council governance constitutes an oddity that seems explainable only by the background of its intergovernmental historical genesis and in light of the EU's continued hybrid status as a political system that is both intergovernmental and supranational. However, there are good reasons to consider EU council governance as an important model of federalism nevertheless. Two issues stand out in particular: the further institutional development of the EU itself and its model character for a globalizing world.

With the latest round of enlargement, the EU finds itself at a crossroads. Even the weighted input of a single member state will prove less meaningful in a community of 25. States will be routinely out-voted, and the cry for more democracy will become louder. In order to combat its democratic deficit, the EU can upgrade democracy by bestowing full powers on the European Parliament. However, as long as the historical, cultural, and political loyalties of European citizens appear primarily tied to their nation-states, council representation remains an essential part of political legitimacy. Indeed, it may remain the only acceptable option for some time to come.

Council governance is also the prevalent mode of governance in a globalizing world. Typically, decision-making in international governmental organizations (IGOs) is the result of negotiations among delegates receiving instructions from their home governments. In today's age of high-speed communications and transportation, this no longer poses problems of time and distance as it did, say, in the American Confederation. Even more so than in the EU, however, it poses a problem of democratic accountability. Citizens are confronted with far-reaching

---

44. See Bomberg, Cram, and Martin, "The EU's Institutions" 58.

decisions over which they have no immediate control and the consequences of which they cannot gauge.

Nevertheless, as long as parliamentary democracy on a world scale remains a utopian solution, council governance will be an inevitable part of globalizing politics. In order to make it more legitimate and acceptable, new institutional means will have to be explored for enhancing the transparency of the decision-making process; for balancing, by means of weighted representation, the needs and interests of rich and poor countries; and for including the voices of large civic organizations enjoying widespread and transnational membership support.

IMITATIONS AND VARIATIONS

The unelected Canadian Senate and the hybrid form of European council governance are unique cases of dual representation in federal systems. Apart from its impact upon the design of the European Council of Ministers, the German model of governmental second chamber representation also has not found widespread imitation, although it has been adopted by the designers of the new South African federal constitution. Most other federal systems have more or less replicated the American senate model. This is also so in the case of Switzerland, even though the Swiss second chamber is called a Council of States (*Ständerat*), and there are six so-called half cantons with only one instead of two representatives in it. In Brazil and Mexico, on the other hand, there are three senators for each state, and in Mexico, one-quarter of the seats are assigned in proportion to each party's popular vote.

But there are more significant variations. In a number of federations such as Austria and India, second chamber representatives are indirectly elected by the regional legislatures following the original American practice. India's upper house also reserves a number of **special seats** for cultural minorities. In other federal systems again, upper chambers have only a suspensive veto which can be overridden by the parliamentary chamber. And finally, some federations (notably Australia) have adopted a procedure providing for a dissolution of both houses and ultimately a **joint sitting** in the case of unresolved deadlock, as discussed below.

All these variations, and combinations thereof, have to do with the historical compromises that were necessary in order to reach agreement on a constitutional document. We shall end this chapter by briefly describing three cases—Australia, Spain and Belgium—as examples of imitation and variation.

Parliamentary Bicameralism in Australia

Strong upper houses were an established part of the system of government prevailing in the Australian colonies in the late nineteenth century, and it would not have been surprising had strong bicameralism been adopted for the new national government on those grounds alone. As in the United States, this predisposition coincided with a confederal emphasis on the integrity of the states and led to the creation of a powerful Senate notwithstanding Australia's Westminster parliamentary inheritance.[45] The strongly democratic basis of Australian politics reinforced the inclination for a popularly elected version of the American model some years before the Americans themselves made that transition; however, it was not sufficiently strong to overcome the insistence of the smaller states that equal representation in at least one chamber was a prerequisite of union.[46]

Big States, Small States

The two populous colonies, New South Wales and Victoria, were opposed to the very idea that a majority of the states representing a minority of the people should be able to reject a bill approved by the majority of the people. If there was to be an American-type senate with equal representation in the new federation, it was deemed entirely inappropriate that it should have equal powers, least of all with regard to the classical budgetary prerogative of parliaments, money bills pertaining to taxation and supply.

The compromise thrashed out through several rounds of bargaining and a few referendums was this: there would be equal representation, and there would be equal powers, except that the Senate would not be allowed to initiate or amend money bills. Such a degree of equality poses potential problems for a parliamentary system, and thus another problem haunting the constitutional designers was how disagreement and deadlock between the two houses would be resolved. In the American system this was not a problem because the executive was directly elected and not directly responsible to the Congress. In a parliamentary federation, however, the government depends on majority support, and deadlock between the two chambers would paralyze the system. The Australians were the first to fuse strong federal bicameralism with parliamentarism.

Disagreement and Deadlock Procedures

This was an area in which the Australians had accumulated decades worth of sometimes "bitter" experience within the strongly bicameral

---

45. L.F. Crisp, *Australian National Government*, 5th ed. (Melbourne: Longman Cheshire, 1983) 19.

46. Despite the fact that some of the most prominent framers not only argued that small state/large state conflicts would be rare, but that party discipline would come to render the notion of a house of state representatives nugatory. Crisp, *Australian National Government* 21.

parliaments of the self-governing colonies.[47] It is here that the Australian designers found their most innovative solution. Section 57 of the Commonwealth Constitution stipulates that should a piece of legislation be twice rejected by the Senate, the governor-general may dissolve both chambers—including the whole of the normally staggered Senate—and allow the government of the day to put the issue to the people. Should that "double dissolution" election fail to resolve the matter, a joint sitting of both houses would be called. Given the larger size of the lower house and its single-member electoral system, a joint sitting would likely overwhelm the Senate negative. Only India has subsequently adopted a similar procedure, albeit without prior dissolution. Whether these two-stage procedures function optimally is another question. Some would argue that the infrequency of double dissolution elections (only five in over a century) and the extreme rarity of joint sittings (only ever held once), is indicative of inadequate design.[48]

The Dismissal of 1975

Being innovative does not necessarily mean putting tensions to rest. The question of whether the Australian Senate could or should legitimately challenge parliamentary majority governance remained a divisive issue and produced a political crisis in 1975 when the Senate refused to pass the government's annual appropriations bill.[49] The danger of such a crisis occurring was created by two facts. The first is that while denying the Senate power to initiate or amend money bills, the Constitution says nothing about simply failing to pass them. The second is that while a government can normally accumulate a swag of rejected bills to use as a 'trigger' for a double dissolution election when the time appears right, it does not have that luxury when the Senate's inaction is withholding the money needed to govern. In October 1975, the Opposition leader declared that his coalition parties' majority in the Senate would defer consideration of the appropriations bills until the prime minister agreed to request that the governor-general grant a dissolution of the lower house. The prime minister refused to comply. On 11 November 1975,

---

47. McMinn, *A Constitutional History of Australia* 65–78.
48. Indeed, experience suggests that it "has been all but unworkable," according to Department of the Prime Minister and Cabinet, *Resolving Deadlocks: A Discussion Paper on Section 57 of the Australian Constitution* (Canberra: Commonwealth of Australia, 2003) 26. The only joint sitting was the one convoked by the Labor government of Gough Whitlam in 1974. See also Jack Richardson, *Resolving Deadlocks in the Australian Parliament* (Canberra: Department of the Parliamentary Library, Parliament of Australia, 2000).
49. A bill constitutionally required to authorize government spending.

the governor-general exercised his "reserve" powers under the Constitution, dismissed the prime minister, called upon the leader of the opposition to form a new government, and then promptly dissolved Parliament upon the advice of that newly commissioned prime minister.

While some saw this as a gross violation of the conventions of responsible government, others insisted that the Senate had legitimately exercised its constitutional role of constraining majoritarian executive governance and that the governor-general had legitimately exercised his reserve powers to ensure that the Constitution was respected. One thing was clear: the Senate had been driven by partisan, not federal, considerations throughout. In the 1980s and 1990s, the major parties lost their hold on the Senate as proportional representation (introduced in 1949) underpinned a drift to a more multi-party politics. This has given the Senate a dynamic new role but not a federal one. If the Australian Senate was intended to be a federal 'House of the States' this may well be described as the "great failure of the constitution."[50]

Ambivalent Bicameralism in Spain

The Spanish case is significant for its ingenuity in linking the process of democratization after the Franco dictatorship to the regionalization of the Spanish state. A delicate balance had to be struck between the need to stabilize Spain as a democratic nation-state and the need to accommodate the quest for regional autonomy. As a result, the 17 Autonomous Communities were created with individually negotiated packages of self-governing powers. Following established federal practice, the national parliament, the *Cortes*, was made bicameral. However, the role of the upper house, the *Senado*, has remained limited.

Representation in the Second Chamber

The subregional provinces were made the electoral districts for both chambers in the national *Cortes*. Four senators are directly elected from each province. The various islands and North African cities belonging to Spain elect fewer senators—three, two, or one, according to their size. This means that these senators represent the same provincial constituencies as the deputies in the lower chamber and not the Communities. These were in turn accorded the right to appoint one senator each upon nomination by their legislatures, plus additional ones for every one million of inhabitants.

---

50. Crisp, *Australian National Government* 330.

Powers of the Second Chamber

However, the specific powers of the *Senado* are unclear, and it has only a suspensive veto. It can delay legislation and/or suggest amendments, by absolute majority; it can also initiate legislation; but it cannot overrule the Congress of Deputies. Perhaps as a compensation for their relative weakness in the central decision-making process, the Autonomous Communities have been given the right to initiate legislation in the *Cortes*, and such initiatives have been successful on occasion. "During the constituent debates, the lack of a coherent vision of the form the Senate should take explains to a large extent why the Constitution does not include a coherent and precise enumeration of its powers and, consequently, why the upper chamber has not been given a relevant and intelligible role in the new democracy."[51] As the negotiated result of what was possible at a difficult time of transition, the Spanish Senate nevertheless is an interesting and innovative case of territorial representation.

Belgium: The Recognition of Cultural Community

The transformation of Belgium into a formally constituted federal state in 1993 marked the end of a long series of conflicts between the two main cultural communities—the French-speaking Walloons and the Dutch-speaking Flemish—that had brought the Belgian state to the brink of a breakup. Belgium deserves special mentioning for two reasons. As in the Canadian case, it shows the particular problems of bicommunal federalism. Finding mutually acceptable solutions to the quest for regional autonomy is much more difficult when there are only two participants because one of them will always fear being on the losing side. Except for a generally unmanageable regime of strict proportionality and a requirement of unanimity for all issues, a balanced formula of second chamber representation is not available.

In order to address this problem, the constitutional designers had to take recourse to a number of innovative solutions. Apart from the three territorially defined regions—French-speaking Wallonia, Dutch/Flemish-speaking Flanders, and the bilingual Brussels-Capital—the Constitution also recognizes three cultural communities: Walloon, Flemish, and German.[52] Each has its own representative assembly (called council) and executive government, although, in the case of the Flemish, the governing institutions for the region of Flanders and the Flemish community have been fused. Inhabitants of the bilingual Brussels region can choose

---

51. Carlos Flores Juberías, "A House in Search of a Role: The Senado of Spain," in Samuel C. Patterson and Anthony Mughan, eds., *Senates: Bicameralism in the Contemporary World* (Columbus, OH: Ohio State University Press, 1999) 282.

52. A small minority lives within Wallonia and close to the German border.

whether they want to register as voters for the Flemish or French Community council.

A Multiple-Representative Senate

The senate has equal powers in all matters that affect the institutional order and other culturally sensitive matters.[53] Forty senators are directly and proportionally elected. In addition, 21 senators are indirectly elected, ten each from the Flemish and French Community councils, and one from the German Community council. Together, these two groups of senators can appoint ten further senators, six Dutch-speaking and four French-speaking. Finally, as a particular oddity, the children of the Belgian king also are senators, even though they do not as a rule participate in the proceedings.

Decision-making is complex as well. In some instances, majorities in both houses carry a bill. In other instances, two-thirds majorities are required as well as the absolute majority of votes from either linguistic group. In addition, the Constitution provides for various mechanisms of arbitration and concertation in cases of political and judicial conflict.[54]

Thus far, Belgian federalism has not exactly been a success. Tensions persist because even the most complex institutional arrangements have not been able to overcome bicultural polarization, which is particularly evidenced by the fact that there are only regional and no national parties. The Belgian federal experiment is noteworthy nevertheless. It departs from usual patterns of strict territoriality by recognizing cultural community as a criterion for second chamber representation. And by placing so much emphasis on deliberation and arbitration, it all but acknowledges that rights-based institutional solutions are impossible.

SUMMARY

- Establishment of a system where sovereignty is shared between two orders of government is widely seen as involving both a division of real powers and the inclusion of mechanisms for regional representation within the central government. Bicameralism emerged as the way to reconcile the democratic requirement for majoritarian representation by population and the federal requirement for representation by region.
- However, bicameralism is neither original nor intrinsic to federalism. Bicameralism was a pre-existing phenomenon much more closely

---

53. In other matters the lower House of Representatives has overriding powers.
54. See the overview in André Lecours, "Belgium," in Forum of Federations, *Handbook of Federal Countries 2002* (Montreal, QC and Kingston, ON: McGill-Queen's University Press, 2002).

connected to protection of class interests and, in the emerging checks and balances doctrine, restraint on democracy. When the conservative and the federal rationale converged, strong bicameralism resulted. This was the case in several federations, with the notable exception of Canada where both the conservative impulse and the federal impulse were weak.

- While beginning from an ambiguous position, the Seventeenth Amendment confirmed the nature of the American senate model as a popularly elected upper house that was only federal insofar as the states were accorded equal representation regardless of population.
- By contrast, the German council model, established in the nineteenth century, has maintained its character as a truly federal upper house where the governments of the constituent units are represented by their delegates. As a federal rather than a confederal chamber, though, the constituent units are represented on the basis of weighted rather than equal proportions.
- The EU has established a novel form of second chamber council governance. Voting rights in the Council of Ministers are weighted according to member-state size, and decisions are taken on the basis of qualified majority voting. In turn, it is the European Parliament that has more limited powers.
- Perhaps the most contradictory upper house in this context is the Australian one. The American senate model of an elected second chamber with strong powers operates within the context of a Westminster-based parliamentary system. Once party discipline established its iron grip on the political system, the federal quality of the Senate was eliminated while the potential for confrontational deadlock was increased.

8 Intergovernmental Relations

Searching for stable solutions, the designers of federal systems focussed on formal constitutional rules. Second chamber representation provided the member units with a formal voice in national legislation. The division of powers prescribed what each level of government could do on its own. Little attention was given to the need for subconstitutional and informal arrangements of intergovernmental coordination and cooperation. Moreover, the provisions for constitutional change or amendment (see Chapter 9) made periodic adjustment difficult.

Intergovernmental relations as an ongoing and mostly informal practice in federal systems developed as a response to this constitutional inflexibility. The divisions of power were never as clear or watertight as they had been intended, and areas of concurrent or shared jurisdiction existed from the outset. While these realities have been present from the earliest days, they became qualitatively more significant in the twentieth century and in particular since the emergence of the active state from the 1930s onwards. The rising need for welfare and social policies spawned a new practice of shared programs and joint financing schemes. Social policy, which were generally in the domain of subnational governments, increasingly depended on fiscal transfers. Fiscal federalism (see Chapter 11) became a main preoccupation of federal systems.

More than in most of the two preceding chapters, comparative caution is required. Because intergovernmental relations are for the most part the result of subconstitutional and often informal arrangements, it is not so easy to distinguish country-specific models. While we focus on those aspects that appear particularly important in each case examined, this does not mean that similar features cannot be found in other cases as well.

PATTERNS OF COOPERATION

Intergovernmental relations generally oscillate between conflict and cooperation. There is a competitive predisposition in all federal systems, both between the two levels of government and among the member units. Such competitiveness is often played up for electoral purposes, and it is sometimes reinforced by differences about policy priorities, divergent economic interests, or even more serious differences about national identity and the role of federalism in addressing these questions. At the same time, however, federal systems cannot survive without considerable levels of cooperation, and indeed such cooperation occurs.

Presidential Versus Parliamentary Federalism

For various reasons, the American model takes more of a back seat in this chapter. While there are probably more intergovernmental meetings in the United States than in any other of the classical federal states, they do not constitute as important a part of the politics of federalism as is the case elsewhere, particularly in parliamentary federations. In parliamentary federations, power is concentrated in the executive branch—in the hands of prime ministers, premiers, and their cabinets. Moreover, there is a built-in tension between parliamentary accountability and the federal division of powers. Intergovernmental relations therefore tend to become enmeshed in political power play. In federal systems based on the presidential model, by comparison, powers are more diffused, and intergovernmental relations generally follow a pragmatic path of functional coordination at the policy level.

Executive Federalism

A common characteristic of intergovernmental relations in all federal systems is their executive nature.[1] While the constitutional division of powers focusses on law-making and the roles legislatures play at different levels of government, intergovernmentalism is driven by the executive branch of government. Departmental policy specialists from both levels of government meet for the purpose of regulatory fine-tuning in areas of overlapping jurisdiction. Senior public officials meet in order to discuss the administration of joint programs. Ministers or senior civil servants meet in order to discuss how to set up such programs. In some federal systems such as the United States, for instance, there are more than 500 such meetings every year, mostly at an operational level of public administration and mostly carried out in a pragmatic spirit of cooperation under the umbrella of congressional supremacy.

When conflicting visions of federalism exist and the allocation of powers is contested, intergovernmental relations tend to become politicized. Policy spills over into politics. Functional needs of policy coordination become transformed into intergovernmental disputes about the existing condition and future direction of the federal system. Summit

---

1.   See Watts, *Executive Federalism.*

meetings of political leaders replace those among policy specialists. According to Canadian parlance, this is when **executive federalism** takes over the political process.

Dissatisfaction

In parliamentary federations such as Canada or Australia, the participants of this intergovernmental summitry are elected politicians, the prime ministers and premiers of provinces or states. They have a mandate to engage in such intergovernmental activities. However, because negotiations are typically conducted behind closed doors, and legislatures as well as the general public are informed about the results only afterwards, this type of executive federalism has come under attack from several quarters.

From the perspective of democracy and accountability, the secretive nature of executive federalism is criticized as a form of governance that emphasizes regulatory efficiency over democratic legitimacy. From a public administration perspective comes the opposite critique: the negotiated deals among different levels of government blur responsibilities and typically result in compromises constituting decidedly suboptimal solutions. And finally, there are those who are more fundamentally opposed to executive federalism because it violates the constitutional principle of divided powers.

Here to Stay

While all this is at least partially true, the necessity for some form of intergovernmental relations cannot be denied. Even the most formidable effort of constitutional designers at dividing powers cleanly between different levels of government have proven futile. Indeed, in a globalizing age of growing interdependence not only within states but also among them, there are indications that the practice of executive federalism will grow and not diminish. It is even possible to speak of a new kind of intergovernmental treaty federalism that may replace the traditional model and practice of constitutional federalism.

Informal and Formal Arrangements

As intergovernmental relations are not typically part of the constitutional setup, they had to evolve informally according to the needs of cooperation and policy coordination. In most federations, however, they have also become regularized as periodic events even though there is no constitutional or statutory requirement for such commitments. This is particularly so in the case of meetings at the executive level involving cabinet ministers or even heads of government. Apart from meetings

and conferences, intergovernmental relations can also be institutionalized in committees, boards, and councils for specific policy purposes
such as infrastructure planning, regional development, or matters of
fiscal management. Usually, such arrangements are more permanent in
nature and exist on the basis of intergovernmental agreement and convention. In some instances, however, they are the result of constitutional
amendment and therefore formalized as part of the federal system.

Intergovernmental relations are predominantly a consequence of legislative or divided federalism. The need for intensive cooperation arises
from the fact that the different levels of government operate independently from one another. The situation is quite different in cases of
administrative or integrated federalism such as Germany or the EU.
With their council form of bicameralism, subnational governments have
direct input into the national legislative process through their representation in the upper house. It is therefore not quite appropriate to classify
this kind of institutionalized legislative cooperation as intergovernmental
relations. However, the legislative process in these instances is usually
prepared and accompanied by intensive rounds of intergovernmental
bargaining, be it in a bicameral legislative mediation committee as in
the German case or among senior civil servants as in the EU.

Vertical and Horizontal Connexions

Because constitutional divisions of power require coordination, intergovernmental relations primarily take place vertically between different
levels of government. Moreover, most federal systems have developed
growing areas of shared jurisdiction and joint program financing. When
the establishment of such programs brings about a perceived or real
shift in the original distribution of powers, intergovernmentalism can
quickly become politicized and create the possibility of confrontation
between governments.

However, intergovernmental relations have also developed horizontally, among the governments of the member units of a federal system.
In part, this has been occasioned by the need for policy coordination
across the boundaries of regional jurisdiction. A typical example would
be the regular conferences among the cultural ministers of the *Länder*
in Germany. One of their purposes, for example, is to align *Land* school
curricula in order to ensure personal mobility across the country.

Horizontal intergovernmentalism has also become an important strategic tool for negotiations with the national government, especially so
in cases of conflict over the distribution of powers and finances. Intergovernmental summit meetings are often preceded by conferences or
strategy sessions among regional government leaders or cabinet ministers.
These will try to agree on a common position before confronting the
national government. The success of such efforts depends, of course, on

the level of unity among regional governments, itself in turn dependent on the degree of underlying common interest.

Again, all this is more typical for parliamentary federations than for presidential ones. In the United States, there are regular meetings of the National Governors' Association, for instance, but in Washington, state governments constitute only one lobby group among many.

Developments: A Trend Towards Treaty Federalism

Federal systems were designed to achieve a reliable and stable division of powers among different levels of government. In an increasingly complex world of trans-territorial interdependence, it seems that such constitutional power divisions are increasingly inadequate for accomplishing the desired results. Consequently, federal systems are increasingly turning to subconstitutional intergovernmental bargaining as an inevitable tool of efficient governing. Changing political, economic, and social realities are less likely to be addressed by formal constitutional amendments. Instead, there is a growing reliance on intergovernmental treaties or accords.

The EU in particular has become the prototype of a new kind of **treaty federalism**.[2] Its primary source of law is not a constitution *per se* but a set of negotiated and unanimously adopted treaties. And even though most matters of economic and monetary union under the treaties are now decided by qualified majority rule in the Council of Ministers, the final allocation of powers remains negotiable and open-ended as prescribed by the principle of subsidiarity. This will not change under the constitutional treaty, which is in many ways not much more than a consolidation of all previous treaties. Changes to this constitutional treaty would have to be made unanimously by the European Council of heads of state or government.

"FEDERAL-PROVINCIAL DIPLOMACY" IN CANADA

In all federal systems, the executives of different governments are engaged in necessary tasks of negotiating intergovernmental policy coordination. In most federations, the relationship is somewhat lopsided, though, because the national government ultimately call the shots. In the United States, for example, the states have to comply with conditions attached to fiscal transfers, and the German *Länder* have to comply with national framework legislation.

What is unique about the Canadian case is the **quasi-diplomatic** character of intergovernmental relations, which resemble the relations between sovereign nation-states. The suggestion has even been made

---

2.   See Hueglin, "From Constitutional to Treaty Federalism" 137–53.

that the Canadian federal system is in many ways more similar to the European Common Market than to other federal systems.[3]

In order to understand what is meant by quasi-diplomatic, we need to need to refer to the distinction between the *organization* of power in modern states and the *exercise* of power in international relations. Within states, there is one ultimate source of authority: the sovereignty of the people exercised on their behalf by elected representatives. No one and nothing can overrule this authority. In federal systems, this authority is constitutionally divided between two or more levels of government acting on behalf of different aggregations of the popular will. Interlevel conflicts over the constitutionally legitimate exercise of these powers are typically resolved by supreme courts. In international relations, there is no such ultimate authority. All states are equally sovereign, and, at least in principle, differences and conflicts can only be resolved peacefully by mutual agreement.[4]

This is the essence of diplomacy. In the Canadian case, intergovernmental relations can be called quasi-diplomatic because, on the one hand, there is a constitution that allocates powers to different levels of government and a supreme court watching over the exercise of these powers within legitimate constitutional limits. Yet, on the other hand, the federal system routinely relies on intergovernmental agreements as if the provinces were sovereign entities alongside the national government.

Several reasons account for this intergovernmental diplomacy. The most obvious formal one is the lack of adequate regional representation at the national level. Because—as we discussed in Chapter 7—the appointed Canadian Senate is neither democratically nor regionally accountable, provinces are less willing to accept that the national government speaks for the country as a whole. Another and more material reason has to do with the regionalized nature of the Canadian economy. While most manufacturing is concentrated in central Canada, crucial energy resources are located in the West. Because the provinces were given constitutional ownership of natural resources, the federal government often cannot use its powers over trade and commerce unilaterally. Instead, it has to rely on intergovernmental agreement.

The most serious reason for the predominance of intergovernmentalism in Canada, however, is cultural asymmetry. As a permanent minority, the francophone community in Québec has never quite accepted the constitutional settlement as fair and binding. In order to stem the tide

---

3.   Richard Simeon, *Federal-Provincial Diplomacy* (Toronto, ON: University of Toronto Press, 1972) esp. 298–300.

4.   We are leaving out the possibility of states committing themselves to various forms of international conflict resolution mechanisms.

of Québec separatism, therefore, intergovernmental diplomacy gradually began to overshadow the constitutionally prescribed formula of political accommodation.

All of the above reasons congealed around the issue of constitutional patriation, causing a prolonged constitutional crisis during the 1970s and 1980s. A particular oddity of the constitutional settlement in 1867 had been that it lacked a domestic formula for constitutional amendments. Because they may affect the distribution of powers as previously agreed upon, federal constitutions typically prescribe super majorities for such amendments (see Chapter 9). In the Canadian case, the ultimate authority over constitutional change had been left with the British Parliament.

Throughout the 1970s, intergovernmental efforts at finding a domestic amendment formula, and hence at "patriating" the constitution, failed because Québec saw itself isolated in a 1:9 situation among the provinces and ultimately would not accept anything short of a veto. In 1982, Prime Minister Trudeau proposed a comprehensive package of constitutional reforms that also included a charter of individual rights and a strengthened commitment to the provinces' ownership of natural resources. Eventually he forged an agreement with the nine anglophone provinces that allowed him to proceed without Québec's consent. This was sanctioned by the Supreme Court as legally possible even though defying political convention. This was and has remained the only instance in Canadian history that an intergovernmental agreement on constitutional change has proceeded without unanimous agreement.[5]

Since 1982, there have been two intergovernmental agreements on a constitutional package acceptable to Québec. Both failed during the process of ratification. In the case of the 1987 Meech Lake Accord, the ratification process was dragged beyond the deadline, and the agreement expired. The Charlottetown Agreement of 1992 did not find popular approval in a national referendum.[6]

As a means of reaching agreement on constitutional change, federal diplomacy failed. There was now an amendment formula requiring the consent of seven provinces representing 50 per cent of the Canadian population for most matters. But against the continuing threat of Québec separatism, it is unlikely that this can become an operational tool of constitutional politics. Instead, Canadian intergovernmental relations have wisely retreated to a subconstitutional level of policy agreements. A new era of collaborative federalism may have begun with the 1999

---

5.   See Stephen Clarkson and Christina McCall, *Trudeau and Our Times, Volume 1: The Magnificent Obsession* (Toronto, ON: McClelland and Stewart, 1991).

6.   See Jennifer Smith, "The Unsolvable Constitutional Crisis," in François Rocher and Miriam Smith, eds., *New Trends in Canadian Federalism* (Peterborough, ON: Broadview Press, 1995).

Social Union Framework Agreement. Even though it achieved not much more than spelling out procedural terms for future joint efforts at reforming social policy, Québec, although a participant in the negotiations, did not sign in the end.[7]

The Canadian case is in many ways extreme. There is no other federal system with such a degree of bicommunal asymmetry.[8] The typical formula of compound or weighted majoritarianism does not work. Intergovernmental negotiation remains the inevitable basis for unity. The Canadian case is nevertheless a model case for many institutional features of intergovernmental normality.

"Interstate Federalism"

We had earlier distinguished between divided and integrated forms of federal organization (see Chapter 2). This distinction was mainly occasioned by the integrated German council model which allows the subnational government to participate directly in national legislation. In most federal systems, however, the legislative functions of the two levels are divided by design. Each level of government performs its legislative task autonomously. In the American model, for instance, the Senate does not represent the state governments. However, US senators do represent regional interests, and these contribute to the policy formation at the national level.

In the Canadian case, the government-appointed Senate does not even perform this elementary task of regional representation. The two levels of government operate in complete separation from one another. Moreover, the parliamentary form of federalism makes each level of government directly and exclusively responsible to their respective legislatures. This further precludes any notion of legislative cooperation or coordination.

For these reasons, the Canadian system has been described as a system of "interstate federalism." The coordination of national and regional interests can be achieved solely through intergovernmental relations. By comparison, the German model would be a strong case of *intra*state federalism because the *Länder* governments are directly involved in national legislation. To put it differently: intrastate federalism compels the two levels of government to create national legislation jointly, while interstate federalism requires cooperation and coordination on the basis of separate legislative processes.

---

7. See Richard Simeon and David Cameron, "Intergovernmental Relations and Democracy: An Oxymoron If There Ever Was One?" in Herman Bakvis and Grace Skogstad, eds., *Canadian Federalism: Performance, Effectiveness, and Legitimacy* (Don Mills, ON: Oxford University Press, 2002).

8. Compare, however, Czechoslovakia and Belgium as two other cases of bi-communal polarity: the former fell apart, and the latter remains mired in bi-cultural tension.

First Ministers' Conferences

Throughout the 1970s, intergovernmental relations underwent significant changes in quantity and quality.[9] Meetings increased from 151 in 1973 to 335 in 1977. The focus shifted from social policy coordination and regularly renegotiated fiscal arrangements to economic policy and the constitution. Ministries of intergovernmental relations were established at both levels of government.

Intergovernmentalism increasingly became the domain of highly politicized First Ministers' Conferences among the prime minister and the provincial premiers. Such conferences had been convened occasionally throughout Canadian history, but they have become politically significant annual or even biannual events only since the 1960s with the onset of Québec nationalism and a general trend towards provincial political muscle-flexing in its wake. When this trend was countered by the quest for a more centrally and unilaterally driven federalism under Prime Minister Trudeau, intergovernmentalism underwent a dramatic shift towards competition and conflict. The main issues were the patriation of the Constitution, containment of Québec separatism, and energy policy in the aftermath of the OPEC crisis.

A new type of "summit federalism" began to emerge, with all the paraphernalia of international conferences, flags, government limousines, rolling cameras, and press conferences after lengthy and often nightlong meetings behind closed doors. Yet all the orchestrated hype could not prevent the eventual constitutional settlement of 1982 being concluded without Québec. After Trudeau's departure in 1984, two further attempts of bringing Québec into the constitutional fold ultimately failed because the process itself had begun to lose legitimacy and because support for the recognition of Québec as a distinct society faltered in English Canada.

The 1990s saw a return to a more policy-oriented and collaborative style in Canadian intergovernmental relations, focussing on internal and international trade and the inevitable reform of the health care system. However, this does not necessarily mean that the era of First Ministers' Conferences is over. Québec's constitutional isolation can only be addressed by intergovernmental agreement in the long run. And the ultimate failure of Trudeau's national federalism from above has played into the hands of provincial governments who are pushing in turn for a newly decentralized federalism from below. At the beginning of the new millennium, there are signs of an interprovincial common front and

9. On this and the following see Simeon and Robinson, *State, Society, and the Development of Canadian Federalism* 283–95.

challenge to Parliament's role as a guarantor of equitable living conditions for all Canadians. Sooner or later, Ottawa will have to take on that challenge.

Premiers' Conferences

Since the 1960s, interprovincial Premiers' Conferences have been annual events. Their main purpose was to prepare a common provincial position for upcoming First Ministers' Conferences. While there was considerable success in forging a common front against the perceived or real centralization of power, interprovincial unity ultimately did not survive Trudeau's challenge of constitutional patriation. Only a "gang" of eight provinces signed an accord opposing unilateral action without unanimous provincial support, and when that most traumatic conference in Canada's history was over, on November 5, 1982, all provinces bar Québec had come on side.[10]

Regional Clubs

The fragmented nature of Canada's federal system is also evidenced by the existence of two other interprovincial alliances of a regional nature. In the east, the Council of Maritime Premiers was established in 1971. Originally occasioned by the idea of a union among the three Maritime provinces, and endowed with a permanent secretariat for joint policy initiatives, its quarterly meetings also became a forum for the formulation of common regional economic concerns within the federation. In the West, regular meetings of the premiers of the three prairie provinces and British Columbia have also focussed on economic policy, especially with regard to agriculture and natural resources. Prior to the constitutional showdown of 1982, the western premiers' Task Force on Constitutional Trends played an important role in opposing the "increasing tendency of the Government of Canada to legislate in subject areas which historically and constitutionally have been considered to be in the provincial sphere."[11]

The more collaborative style of intergovernmental relations since the traumatic events of the Meech and Charlottetown Accords, and after a paper-thin victory over separatism in the 1995 Québec referendum, essentially meant that Parliament would for now carefully abstain from

10. See J. Peter Meekison, ed, *Constitutional Patriation: the Lougheed-Lévesque Correspondence* (Kingston, ON: Institute of Intergovernmental Relations, Queen's University, 1999).

11. Quoted in Donald V. Smiley, *Canada in Question* (Toronto, ON: McGraw-Hill Ryerson, 1980) 107.

legislating in provincially sensitive subject areas.[12] When political attention shifted from the constitution to budget deficits, and the provinces were confronted with substantial reductions to transfers for social spending, they initiated the Social Union Framework Agreement as an insurance policy against unilateral action.[13] At the same time, the new political game of budget-cutting and tax reduction at the provincial level, notably in Ontario and Alberta, signalled an erosion of pan-Canadian social solidarity more generally.

Developments: Institutionalizing Executive Federalism

The new strategy appears sound. Since comprehensive constitutional reform has proven to be an equation with too many variables, Canadian intergovernmental relations have returned to a more pragmatic level of accommodation and agreement. A lot can be said in favour of path dependency: it is difficult to break away radically from established institutional patterns of politics and policy-making. The position of Québec has always been one of ambiguity, and there is probably no final and precise constitutional solution that will change that. Likewise, as long as the political economy of Canada remains centred on the export of natural resources, it will always be difficult if not impossible to prescribe a mutually agreeable national economic policy. With regard to both, the Canadian state will have to remain a negotiating state, and the continuation of federal diplomacy will remain its best option.

This is particularly so also in the realm of social policy where the Canadian federal state found itself on a slippery slope of rising costs and shrinking revenue. Electoral gamesmanship in some of the richer provinces has begun to woo voters with accelerating rounds of income tax reduction. In the Social Union Framework Agreement, the provinces wrested from Ottawa a concession, at least in principle, to abstain from taking a unilateral lead in prescribing national standards of social equity and solidarity. It remains to be seen whether negotiated agreements among executive elites can take the place of a firm constitutional commitment without eventually eroding one of the cornerstones of the federalist compromise.

The institutionalization of executive federalism in the recent establishment of a Council of the Federation among provincial premiers and territorial leaders is an indication that Canada's federal system will continue to go down the road of negotiation.[14] The founding agreement

---

12. An exception was the *Clarity Act* of 2000 in which some general conditions for the legitimacy of future separatist initiatives in Québec were spelt out.

13. See Simeon and Cameron, "Intergovernmental Relations and Democracy" 280–81.

14. See Jennifer Smith, *Federalism* (Vancouver, BC: University of British Columbia Press, 2004) 145–59.

includes a commitment to the establishment of a permanent executive committee staffed from federal and provincial governments, and its mandate pertains to the continuous monitoring of all aspects of Canadian economic and social union. For now, the Council does not include the prime minister (nor Aboriginal leaders), but such inclusion may be only a matter of time. If successful, the Council would signal a profound transformation of the Canadian federal system, from a classical parliamentary federation to a new model more akin to the German and European council governance.

INTERGOVERNMENTALISM AND COUNCIL GOVERNANCE IN AUSTRALIA

The compromise lying at the heart of designing federal systems never allows as clean a disentanglement of jurisdictions as the founding constitutional minds might have wished. This is clearly evident in the Australian case with its long list of concurrent Commonwealth powers, its few exclusive powers, and its assignment of residual powers to the States (see Chapter 6).

The much more limited role of government in the early years allowed the clearer division of coordinate federalism to prevail and encouraged the view among commentators that Australia it was a system of coordinacy rather than concurrency.[15] Since the mid-1970s Australian intergovernmental relations have commanded more attention. Initially following the American lead of proclaiming various rounds of "new federalism," and later taking important cues from the EU, Australian government leaders have turned toward intergovernmental reform as a precondition for economic modernization and more efficient governance.

In doing so, they reopened old questions and grievances, ranging from vertical fiscal imbalance and the heavy-handed conditionality of the Commonwealth grants system (see Chapter 11), to the very question of whether federalism was compatible at all with parliamentary governance. By contrast with the Canadian case, however, both the debate and its modest results did not touch upon fundamental constitutional questions, instead gearing the intergovernmental process towards intensified collaboration and formal institutionalization. The driving force has been the growth of Commonwealth power and the unusual degree of centralization in Australian federalism, underpinned by a regionally homogeneous population, and advanced in particular by the country's original and largest political party, the Australian Labor Party (ALP), which has been strongly opposed to federalism altogether for a good part of its history.

---

15. See Brian Galligan, *A Federal Republic: Australia's Constitutional System of Government* (Cambridge: Cambridge University Press, 1995) 189–201.

Premiers' Conferences

Formal intergovernmental relations commenced with Federation itself and have been a regular focal point of Australian federalism ever since. In the so-called **premiers' conferences**, the state premiers meet with the prime minister and Commonwealth treasurer on an annual basis. In the early years, it was a reasonably equal relationship: the High Court had yet to make its decisive turn in favour of centralizing interpretation of the Constitution, and the Commonwealth had yet to consolidate and enlarge its policy dominance. The premiers used this forum to coordinate resistance to Commonwealth expansion and even attempted to establish a permanent premiers' conference secretariat and to oblige the Commonwealth government to approach the states collectively through its executive officer.[16]

Yet soon enough, circumstances began to play into the hands of the Commonwealth. Help came from the authorities in London, who preferred to deal with one government rather than six. Australia's engagement in World War I drove home a powerful message about the need to think of Australia as a unified nation. As elsewhere, the Great Depression years and another world war led the way to a greater acceptance of fiscal and social policy centralization. And, much in line with the general political mood, Australia's High Court accompanied these developments with decisions that were generally in favour of the Commonwealth.

The imminent shift in intergovernmental power relations was foreshadowed in 1919 when for the first time it was the Commonwealth that convened a Premiers' Conference to discuss postwar reconstruction.[17] Eight years later, the creation of the Australian Loan Council, transformed the Premiers' Conferences into events convened, led, and increasingly dominated by the Commonwealth. It nevertheless set in motion a process of intensified intergovernmental relations. Premiers' Conferences among the states continued, but the main event became an annual Premiers' Conference convened by the prime minister in the national capital, Canberra, immediately to be followed by the annual Loan Council meeting.

Intergovernmental Councils

The need for inter- or transgovernmental mechanisms had not been unforeseen in Australia's constitution-writing. Inspired by the American example, the framers included a requirement in the Constitution (s.101) that "There shall be an Inter-State Commission, with such powers of adjudication and administration as the Parliament deems necessary for

---

16. McMinn, *Constitutional History* 124–25.
17. McMinn, *Constitutional History* 134.

the execution and maintenance ... of the provisions of this Constitution relating to trade and commerce...." The Commonwealth eventually legislated to fulfil this ambition, and it may have gone on to provide the nucleus of a comprehensive set of federal governance arrangements. However, the Commission was promptly stripped of its adjudicatory powers by the High Court for being in violation of the Constitution's requirement for a strict separation of judicial powers, and it was allowed to lapse.

The Loan Councils

The Loan Council set a unique precedent for the evolving pattern of centralized executive federalism in Australia. The Council was established in 1923 to coordinate overseas borrowing by Australia's seven governments. Through a constitutional amendment approved in a national referendum, the Loan Council gained the exclusive right to manage public debt and borrowing of both the states and the Commonwealth. In this, it was established as an autonomous body of financial regulation. In practice, however, it became an important directive instrument for the Commonwealth. Behind closed doors, decisions were made by qualified majority vote, with the Commonwealth holding two regular votes plus a casting vote.

Ministerial Councils

More generally, council governance became an almost routinely practised form of institutionalized intergovernmentalism. In 1934, the Australian Agricultural Council was set up, followed by a Transport Advisory Council in 1946. Similar institutions at the ministerial level for immigration, education, regional development, and other policy domains followed over the years. More recent additions have included such things as the National Environment Protection Council to which Australia's first ministers gave their approval in 1994.

A Supreme Council

Consolidation of this form of council governance came in 1991–92 with the establishment of a peak intergovernmental meeting called COAG, the Council of Australian Governments, which included the prime minister, the state premiers, the chief ministers of the two self-governing territories, and the president of the Australian Local Government Association. COAG reflected both an escalated commitment to institutionalized intergovernmentalism and the dual fact that increasing numbers of policy areas were becoming thoroughly concurrent in practice and that many of the areas where the Commonwealth had policy ambitions were areas of state jurisdiction. A significant part of Australia's extensive microeconomic reform agenda was carried and coordinated through COAG in the 1990s, reflecting the fact that it was a Commonwealth initiative that concerned matters largely within state jurisdiction.[18]

COAG meets only briefly and only once a year. However, from its inception it has taken on the image of much enhanced intergovernmentalism. Among other things, it acts as the peak body to which a comprehensive range of ministerial councils report. The underlying reality, though, is not entirely consistent with this image. COAG has no statutory— let alone constitutional—foundation; it has not changed the powerful imbalance in Australian federalism; and it is an institution existing and functioning at the pleasure of the prime minister.

"COOPERATIVE" FEDERALISM IN THE UNITED STATES

American federalism is widely regarded as synonymous with cooperative federalism. According to this view, the US Constitution established a partnership between two levels of government. While each level was assigned differentiated sets of tasks, the constitutional design compelled all governments to work together for the common good.

A less common historical interpretation concludes that the American case is more in line with the Australian experience:[19] American federalism was originally designed and practised as a **dual** system of governance and only evolved into its modern **cooperative** form after 1933 when congressional regulation began to dominate intergovernmental relations under the impact of New Deal legislation and economic modernization. As we indicated in the introduction to this chapter, the truth probably lies somewhere in the middle. However, there cannot be any doubt that American intergovernmentalism has undergone a dramatic transformation during the twentieth century.

While centralizing trends of cooperation in the name of national unity probably commenced with the Civil War in the nineteenth century and further intensified when the United States began to assume the role of a world power towards the end of that century, it was the experience of the Great Depression that established the New Deal as a regime of intergovernmental cooperation under the aegis of Congress. By the end of World War II, and notwithstanding the question of civil rights, the United States had evolved into an exceptionally homogeneous national

---

18. See Martin Painter, *Collaborative Federalism: Economic Reform in Australia in the 1990s* (Melbourne: Cambridge University Press, 1998).

19. See Harry N Scheiber, "The Condition of American Federalism: An Historian's View," in Laurence J. O'Toole, ed., *American Intergovernmental Relations* (Washington, DC: Congressional Quarterly, 1985).

state, and intergovernmental relations almost entirely became subservient to the proliferation of national programs emanating from Washington.

From then on also, the fundamentals of the constitutional settlement no longer were under dispute even though its interpretation was almost continually contested before the courts. Consequently, intergovernmental relations developed pragmatically into a giant machinery of program delivery. At the core were the so-called **grants-in-aid**, which were mostly conditional federal financing programs offered to states and local governments for specific policy purposes deemed to be in the national interest (see Chapter 11). During the 1970s and 1980s most notably, American intergovernmental relations took on a top-heavy regulatory and at times even outright coercive character,[20] despite much talk about a new and more deregulatory as well as collaborative federalism. Towards the end of the century, there was talk about a "devolution revolution," but it remains an open question whether much has changed.

The Intergovernmental Maze

The United States is neither the largest nor the most populous country in the world, but it surely must have the most complex and interdependent system of government. In fact, by the 1980s there were more than 80,000 governments operating within its boundaries: one national; 50 state; and the rest local, including 3,000 counties, 18,000 municipalities, 17,000 townships, 15,000 school districts, and 28,000 special districts for particular purposes such as regional water management or metropolitan transportation and transit.[21]

Intergovernmental relations in this maze of governments have always centred on financial aid, especially since 1913 when Congress gained the power to impose a national income tax that gave it superior access to revenue. In fact, when Americans talk about intergovernmental relations, they almost exclusively have in mind the vast array of grants-in-aid upon which state and local governments increasingly have become dependent.

As in all federal systems, cash transfers initially played a modest role in American governance. They began to grow rapidly in numbers and dollar amounts during the twentieth century when Congress assumed supremacy over such policy fields as welfare, health, and highway construction. But it was not until the 1960s that they began to overshadow the entire system of governance. In 1964, there were 51 such programs amounting to $10 billion. Ten years later, there were 550 programs costing $43 billion. After 1980, the Reagan presidency proclaimed a

---

20. See Kincaid, "From Cooperative to Coercive Federalism."
21. See Laurence J. O'Toole, "Overview," in O'Toole, ed., *American Intergovernmental Relations* 34.

new federalism based on deregulation and budget-cutting. The result was a consolidation into approximately 400 grants programs to the tune of $100 billion dollars, which amounted to a 13 per cent cut in federal transfers.[22]

American intergovernmental relations primarily focus on specific program delivery and not on fundamental issues concerning the constitutional division of powers. Their proliferation since the 1960s had a lot to do with a new federal focus on local government that deliberately bypassed state authorities. And last but not least, American intergovernmentalism more than anywhere else appears to be characterized by administrative redundancy. For a long time, the assumption was that the richest country on earth could afford that in the name of democracy.

Regulatory Federalism

Driven by the grants-in-aid regime of fiscal transfers to states and localities, American intergovernmental relations underwent a dramatic change of character during the 1960s. Until then, most grant programs had been developed in cooperation with the states and served state purposes such as highway construction or farm aid. The 1960s, however, ushered in a new era of heightened national consciousness and priorities. Increasingly, new grants programs were initiated and designed in Washington. Health, education, poverty, crime, and drug control became national priorities. Increasingly also, grants-in-aid programs came with strings attached.

At least initially, such programs were set up without much intergovernmental cooperation. Congress unilaterally would pass an Act specifying amounts of dollars committed, eligibility, matching requirements, and regulatory conditions. The states would decide on their participation in the program with a bill of their own and register their intention with Washington. The states' applications would then be examined for eligibility and compliance with regulatory conditions. Finally, the specifics of implementation and administration would be laid down in a bilateral agreement.

By the late 1970s, state and local governments had to comply with over 1,000 conditions if they wanted to receive grant money from the various programs (see Chapter 11). And, given their increasing fiscal dependency on this money, they had little choice in the matter. In addition, there was a proliferation of so-called **mandates**, or general regulations, mostly concerning civil rights and environmental protection, and

---

22. O'Toole, "Overview" 7; much of the information in this and the following sections is owed to the competent overview in Wilson and DiIulio, *American Government* 50–83.

comprising thousands of requirements with which the states had to comply regardless of whether they received grants or not.

Beginning with the Reagan presidency during the 1980s, various proclamations of a new "new federalism" aiming at program simplification and the reduction of mandates and conditions have resulted in little change. In fact, mandated regulations in particular continued to grow almost exponentially during these years. American intergovernmental relations remained caught in a web of regulatory federal control. To the extent that there was change, it was not so much occasioned by a commitment to a more balanced federalism in which the states would become more significant intergovernmental partners as it was driven by a neo-conservative agenda of reduced public spending and the downloading of fiscal responsibilities to lower levels of governments. As one observer noted at the time, the ultimate purpose of this new "new federalism" was to abandon the earlier and more liberal notion that the federal government was responsible for nationally equitable standards of public services for all citizens.[23] Without the necessary financial commitment in the form of grant money, the continuing regulation of whatever Congress considered to be in the national interest put additional political and administrative strains on state and local governments.

Only in part can this regulatory nature of American intergovernmental relations be explained by congressional supremacy or presidential ambition. Other explanations point to the ideology of checks and balances that sees one government as a legitimate constraint upon another. In comparison to Australia and Canada, the wisdom of the constitutional division of powers itself is seldom questioned. Intergovernmental relations therefore are more centred on policy than politics. National policy regulation does not immediately become a fundamental issue of power encroachment.

The Intergovernmental Lobby

When Americans talk about intergovernmental relations, they usually have in mind the administrative dimension of fiscal federalism: the myriad meetings among government officials and policy specialists trying to sort out and make the best possible use of the grant system. What is missing, at least from a Canadian or Australian comparative perspective, is intergovernmentalism from the input side, the participation of the lower levels of government in national policy formation. Canada has its First Ministers' Conferences, and Australia has both the Premiers' Conferences and permanent intergovernmental councils. The prevalent view of American federalism as a system of divided federalism does not

---

23. George E. Peterson, "Federalism and the States," in John L. Palmer and Isabel V. Sawhill, eds., *The Reagan Record* (Cambridge, MA: Ballinger, 1984) 259.

accord to the state or local governments a similarly institutionalized place at the federal bargaining table.

Instead, state and local governments have to rely on lobbying like everyone else. Coinciding with the expansion of the grant system, a so-called intergovernmental lobby established itself permanently in Washington. The five largest lobby groups are the National Governors' Association, the National Conference of State Legislatures, the National League of Cities, the US Conference of Mayors, and the National Association of Counties. These organizations have permanent offices in Washington, employing over 400 people, and spending some $45 million annually—all with the overriding purpose of influencing congressional grant legislation in their favour.

The governors have set up an annual conference organized by their Washington office, and since 1970 they expect this conference to be attended by the president, cabinet officers, and congressional leaders.[24] Its purpose is to convince national policy-makers of the need to align the grant programs with state goals and objectives. Given that a large percentage of these grants is directly aimed at the local level and there-fore by-passes state control altogether, state lobbying often amounts to little more than an exercise in futility.

The role of the states in the intergovernmental system is further weakened by the functionally disjointed practice of congressional policy-making. Specific funding programs are the result of bargaining within and across a plethora of special congressional subcommittees, and the process of lobbying is left in the hands of policy specialists. A general position towards the states is often not discernible.

Development: Towards Devolution?

In comparison to Canada or Australia, it is difficult to find the big picture in American intergovernmental relations. The separation of legislative and executive powers in the presidential system has resulted in a greater dispersal of powers and agencies than is the case in parliamentary federations. In the latter, the insistence on responsible govern-ment and parliamentary accountability at each level tends to bundle intergovernmental issues into larger political packages, and the functional nature of intergovernmental relations tends to spill over into a more fundamentally political arena of competition, cooperation, and conflict. The emphasis on checks and balances between different branches and levels of government in the American system, on the other hand, leaves less room for grand political gestures. The diffusion of power within

---

24. On this and the following, see Sarah McCally Morehouse, "The Governor in the Intergovernmental System," in O'Toole, ed., *American Intergovernmental Relations*.

the congressional system—across partisan lines as well as among a variety of special issue caucuses and committees—results in a piecemeal approach to policy-making, program by program, issue by issue, regulation by regulation. The intergovernmental players then have to live with the outcome.

The cumulative and expansive nature of the intergovernmental grants system as well as the financial centralism that came with it have been singled out as in need of reform by nearly every American president since the late 1960s. Most efforts were only modestly successful in halting or at least slowing down new program commitments to federal spending. The Republican Congress of 1994 proclaimed what has become known as a **devolution revolution**. Its main thrust again was not so much real power decentralization as it was an attack on national deficit spending and the redistributive nature of welfare spending in general. However, signed into law by Democratic president Bill Clinton and accompanied by both spending cuts and the usual slew of regulatory impositions, the *Personal Responsibility and Work Opportunity Reconciliation Act* of 1996 did effectively hand the responsibility for welfare back to the states (see Chapter 11).

If early assessments are not mistaken, the devolution revolution has done little to change the scope and dimension of American intergovernmental relations.[25] What has changed instead is the ideology of central control and the way this control is exercised. Previously, grants money came with delivery-related conditional strings attached. In order to get money, the states had to design welfare programs in very specific ways. Now, they can design them any way they want, but in order to keep the funds flowing, or to receive bonus payments, they must produce results such as significant reductions of welfare recipients and out-of-wedlock births among welfare mothers. One consequence of this new result-oriented flexibility has been that the states in turn have begun to download welfare tasks to local government levels.

Welfare devolution only affects a small portion of the grants machinery, and most observers remain sceptical about a more substantive devolution revolution sweeping across the entire spectrum of American politics. However, as localities in particular are engaged in a new experimental process of putting people back to work and keeping teenagers out of trouble, a more substantive drive towards devolution may yet see the light of day. It would be supported by a generally prevailing ideology of less and smaller government(s), and it would be seconded by a trend change in the Supreme Court's interpretation of states' rights (see Chapter 9).

---

25. See Richard P. Nathan and Thomas L. Gais, "Early Findings About the Newest New Federalism for Welfare," *Publius* 28:3 (Summer 1998).

A DIFFERENT APPROACH: INTEGRATED FEDERALISM

Intergovernmental relations are practical responses to the need for cooperative policy management among divided powers within a federal system. The more these powers operate independently from one another, as in the United States in particular, the more such cooperation becomes necessary. A related yet different question is whether this cooperation is based on balanced partnership, as increasingly so in Canada, or whether it is centrally dominated, as in Australia and the United States.

In Chapter 2 and elsewhere, we noted that there are two basic ways of structuring a federation. In **divided** systems of federalism, each level of government operates independently. Intergovernmental relations for the most part focus on the output side of policy-making, program implementation, and delivery. In **integrated** systems of federalism such as Germany, on the other hand, lower level governments have an institutionalized role of participating in federal policy-making because their representatives sit in second chambers with equal or near equal voting power. Compromises focus on the input side of policy formation.

The dividing lines are not quite as clear-cut in practice. All three federal systems discussed so far—Canada, Australia, and the United States—are cases of divided federalism. States and provinces have no direct formal role in federal legislation. But in Canada, the institutionalized practice of First Ministers' Conferences acknowledges that, at least in a number of crucial policy areas touching upon sensitive provincial interests, national decision-making without provincial government input is no longer acceptable.

What is fundamentally different in integrated systems of federalism, then, is the formalized co-deciding role lower level governments play in national legislation. In fact, and contrary to prevailing views,[26] it may not even be appropriate to speak of intergovernmental relations here, because both levels of government are integrated into one unit of governance. Exploring further the two most prominent cases of integrated federalism, Germany and the EU, we find that there remains a need for informal intergovernmental cooperation nevertheless.

Cooperative Interlocking in Germany

In most federations intergovernmental relations play a bridge-building role that is meant to bring to these systems of divided jurisdiction and governance a complementary measure of coordination and cooperation. In the German system, on the other hand, the construction of the *Bundesrat* as a governmental council already constitutes the strongest

---

26. See Watts, *Comparing Federal Systems* 58.

possible measure of institutionalized coordination and cooperation. Intergovernmental relations are meant to enhance this relationship even further and to provide an additional measure of informal mediation in cases of conflict.

The German intergovernmental machinery is probably the most intertwined or, as the German jargon goes, **interlocked**, of all major federations. There are several explanations for this. Because of its *Bundesrat* construction (see Chapter 7), German governance is dominated by the national legislative process. In addition, Germans have a historical predisposition for planned uniformity. The Constitution compels all governments to cooperate towards equitable living conditions for all Germans, and it also stipulates that they have to do so by respecting the federal nature of the political system. At the same time, major cooperative endeavours are not left to intergovernmental agreement but are enshrined in national or even constitutional law.

In a largely homogeneous society, there has been little room for the idea, often cited as one of the driving forces in American federalism, that the *Länder* should be laboratories for social experimentation (see Chapter 11). Hence even in policy fields where the *Länder* have exclusive jurisdiction—notably education and culture—coordination has been paramount. The "permanent" conference of the cultural ministers, for instance, harmonizes education curricula in order to create equitable living conditions and to facilitate the mobility of families with children. It is complemented by various educational planning councils in which the central government participates as well. Similar councils exist for financial and macroeconomic planning. While the original idea of *Länder* coordination was to avoid encroachments by national regulation, the end result has been quite the opposite. It is difficult to deny the national government a leading role when the goal is harmonization rather than differentiation.

A particular case of institutionalized intergovernmentalism are the so-called **joint tasks** that were established by a far-reaching constitutional reform in 1969.[27] In three policy fields—post-secondary education, regional development, and agriculture—a regime of joint financing was created. In addition, the central government gained a formal role in educational planning as well as in research and development. Other than in the case of conventional intergovernmental agreements which require unanimity, joint decision-making in these policy fields fell to planning committees endowed with a qualified majority rule procedure by which the national government has as many votes as the *Länder* taken together.

---

27. On this and the following, see Frank Pilz and Heike Ortwein, *Das politische System Deutschlands* (München: Oldenbourg, 1995) 45–64.

As the heart and centre of German intergovernmentalism, the joint tasks have been criticized as an inefficient form of vertical executive power collusion that undermines the autonomy of the *Länder* parliaments in particular. Moreover, it has been called a **joint-decision trap**[28] whereby necessary policy decisions are frustrated by the vested interests of too many participants (see Chapter 11). These concerns must of course be balanced against the experience with intergovernmentalism in other federations. It would be difficult, for instance, to accord to the American grants system a higher level of efficiency or to argue that Canadian executive federalism is more democratic.

German intergovernmental relations have also gone the more orthodox informal route. While the division of powers under Germany's distinctive system of administrative federalism allows the *Länder* to implement and administer most legislation in their own right, this administration remains under federal supervision. In addition, the *Länder* also act directly on behalf of the national government in specific matters such as the German highway system. As a consequence of both, a fine-tuned informal relationship has developed among the key civil servants at both levels of government.

As early as 1951, the standing orders of the Bonn government established that the chancellor could invite the *Land* prime ministers for informal talks about pressing political, economic, or social problems. Soon thereafter, the practice of prime ministerial conferences was established, originally serving purposes of coordination, but increasingly in preparation of the meetings with the chancellor. While the conference of the prime ministers has become a regular event several times a year, summit meetings with the chancellor have been more irregular. A particularly noteworthy meeting was the intergovernmental summit meeting of 1993 during which Chancellor Kohl and the prime ministers agreed upon the so-called "solidarity pact"—joint transfer payments to the new and poorer eastern German *Länder*.[29]

Another issue that sets German intergovernmental relations apart from most other federal systems is the role and influence of party politics. Germany has a strongly centralized national party system. The dynamic of the bicameral legislative process is driven by the question as to whether the government has command of a supportive majority in the *Bundesrat* which in turn depends on the outcome of intermittent *Länder* elections and the government majorities, or coalition governments, resulting from them. Particularly in situations when the passage of important bills may be blocked by an opposing party majority in the *Bundesrat*, therefore, intergovernmental contacts are important tools for

---

28. Fritz W. Scharpf, "The Joint-Decision Trap: Lessons from German Federalism and European Integration," *Public Administration* 66 (1988).
29. The pact was renewed under Chancellor Schröder in 2002.

necessary compromise. The solidarity pact of 1993, for instance, was as much a compromise among the two levels of government as it was one between the governing conservatives under Chancellor Kohl and the Social Democrats who at the time had the deciding edge in the *Bundesrat*.

Thus carried by the main two political parties on the right and left, the cooperative nature of intergovernmental relations coincided with the legendary German model of social partnership between capital and labour that had developed during the early decades after World War II as a safeguard for democratic stability. It also was facilitated by the truncated West German state with its smaller number of relatively homogeneous *Länder*. There were fears that the inclusion of five much poorer *Länder* of East German would lead to both social destabilization and a deterioration of the spirit of intergovernmental solidarity. And, indeed, some of the richer and more conservative *Länder* in the west, together with those who had always opposed the integrated nature of the German federal system, tried to press for a more fiscally disentangled and competitive brand of federalism (see Chapter 11).

However, as evidenced by the 1993 solidarity pact and its renewal in 2002, it soon became clear to all participants that the socio-economic woes of reunification needed more intergovernmental solidarity, not less. Another reason why the access of the new *Länder* to the intergovernmental system did not challenge established patterns of cooperation has to do with the way in which reunification was brought about: by annexation rather than integration. West German parties took over, and most eastern *Länder* have been governed by western politicians. For these reasons it seems unlikely, at least for the foreseeable future, that the nature of German federalism and its interlocked regime of intergovernmental cooperation will change.

Council and Comitology in the EU

So far we have seen that intergovernmental relations generally operate at two levels: agenda-setting executive summit meetings among political leaders and the ingoing business of intergovernmental policy cooperation at a lower functional level. The one exception to this is the United States, where the high level of organized executive federalism is missing. In the EU, we find both levels of intergovernmentalism again: summit meetings among the member states' government leaders and the president of the European Commission as well as a fine-tuned network of ongoing intergovernmental cooperation at the policy level. In both instances, however, European intergovernmentalism goes well beyond the conventional picture.

As in other federal systems, summit meetings were not an original part of the design. The EU[30] came into existence on the basis of the Treaties of Rome in 1958, as an intergovernmental agreement analogous to other international treaties. The Treaties of Rome, however, set up a far-reaching institutional framework of European governance, with the European Commission as the main policy-making executive, the European Council of Ministers as the main legislative body, and the European Parliament as a secondary body of democratic representation and legitimacy. These institutions were to function on their own and as stipulated under the Treaties. Since the Council of Ministers was constructed like the German *Bundesrat*, it was here that negotiation and cooperation among the member-state governments would take place.

When French President Charles de Gaulle boycotted Council of Minister meetings in 1965 because they were about to revert from unanimity to qualified majority voting as foreseen by the Treaties, it became clear that there was a need for some sort of intergovernmental summitry. Summits were needed to determine the further path of integration and in preparation for far-reaching decisions to be taken by the Council of Ministers. In 1974, regular meetings of the **European Council** were established.[31] They soon became the most important agenda-setter for the EU even though they did not have any formal basis in the original treaties. In the Maastricht Treaty of 1993, however, the European Council was at least recognized as a political body above the Community that would give guidance and direction to the further process of integration. It was also established that it should meet twice a year, in accordance with the Council presidency that rotates every six months among the member states, and that there could be extraordinary meetings on specific issues. Under the yet to be ratified constitutional treaty, the European Council will be recognized as one of the EU institutions, with its own appointed president for two and a half years and a newly established capacity to make certain decisions regarding EU governance by qualified majority.

Over time, then, the European Council emerged as the "constitutional architect"[32] of European integration. Both the Single European Act of 1987, which prepared the grounds for the completion of the internal market, and the 1993 Maastricht Treaty, which established the EU in its current institutional form, were the result of European Council agreements. In both instances, the European Council initially established a so-called Intergovernmental Conference (IGC) for the preparation and

---

30. Formerly: European Communities or European Community.
31. See Philippe de Schoutheete, "The European Council," in John Peterson and Michael Shackleton, eds., *The Institutions of the European Union* (Oxford: Oxford University Press, 2002).
32. Weidenfeld and Wessels, *Europe from A to Z* 115.

drafting of the treaty revisions eventually adopted. These IGCs consist of an ongoing series of intergovernmental meetings involving government leaders, ministers, and the civil service. In the case of the IGC leading up to the conclusion of the *Single European Act*, the foreign ministers met seven times between September 1985 and January 1986. A European Council meeting in December 1985 exclusively dealt with the single market, and in between these meetings two "working parties" of high-ranking officials thrashed out most of the details. European Commission representatives were present at all meetings as well.[33]

Since the EU can be best understood as a hybrid form of federalism, combining elements of supranational majority rule with confederal or intergovernmental[34] agreement, it would seem logical to see the European Council as the confederal part of the institutional setup. However, the reality is more complicated than that. First of all, intergovernmental agreements are normally limited to particular areas of mutual interest and benefit. Because they are based on unanimous agreement, moreover, their purpose is precisely to preserve the autonomy or sovereignty of the participants. And, indeed, when the practice of European Councils was first regularized, at least some observers thought that was an indication that European integration would take a more confederal turn. In fact, however, the European Council became the main motor of supranationalism. Its first milestone agreement, the *Single European Act* of 1987, not only put the EU on a trajectory towards the single market, it also affirmed qualified majority rule in the Council of Ministers for most matters of economic and monetary union.

Secondly, while the European Council normally operates on the basis of unanimous agreement, there have been noteworthy exceptions. In 1985, when the plans for the single market and increased majority voting in the Council of Ministers were on the table, three governments—Britain, Denmark, and Greece—objected to the idea of a preparatory IGC. In a move then unprecedented, a vote was taken, and the road to the *Single European Act* was opened by a margin of 7:3.[35] Clearly, the European Council had established itself as a European institution that had become part of a supranational integration process itself. Too much was at stake for even the most powerful dissenters, Britain's then Prime Minister Margaret Thatcher in particular, to derail or obstruct the decision once it was taken.

One of the institutional anomalies of the EU in terms of federalism is that while there are two levels of government—the member-state level and the European level—and while there is extensive supranational

---

33. Dinan, *Ever Closer Union* 116.
34. In the wider sense as between sovereign nation-states.
35. The European Community only had 10 members then; see Dinan, *Ever Closer Union* 116–17.

governance on the basis of European laws and regulations, there is no fully developed European executive government. Executive governing functions are in the hands of the European Commission; however, although it operates independently from the member states and has even been given the exclusive right to initiate policy, its activities remain under the control of the Council of Ministers in several ways.[36] The Council ultimately not only makes the binding legislative decisions, it can also "impose requirements" on the way in which the law is implemented and administered by the European Commission, and it has established a large number of policy-specific committees supervising the Commission's initiatives.

This committee system of supervision and executive control, also known as **comitology** in European jargon, constitutes another form of intergovernmental relations because it is here that the informal interaction between member-state governments and European executive takes place at the policy level. There is a committee for each and every one of the Community's main activities, and its members are policy specialists from the national government administrations. According to the procedural rules laid down by the Council, even a minority of committee members can block a controversial Commission initiative until the matter comes before the Council where it can be stopped altogether. The entire process is further coordinated and overseen by COREPER, the committee of permanent representatives. These most senior officials representing member-state interests are in charge of preparing the agenda for Council meetings.[37]

It is not easy to put European intergovernmental relations into a comparative perspective with conventional federal states. In the latter, there is a constitutional division of powers that assigns political tasks to different government levels. Intergovernmentalism comes into play as a residual activity of necessary cooperation and coordination. In the EU it has remained a principal category of decision-making. Under the treaties, the member states agree on the need for certain areas of policy integration. Before European governance can come into play in its own right, an intensive intergovernmental negotiating process is necessary in order to determine its scope and dimension. The principle of subsidiarity (see Chapter 6) in particular has given expression to this reality. For each law and regulation it requires a process of intergovernmental deliberation in order to determine the appropriate level of action.

The most significant difference between the EU and most other federal states is of course that it is a federal union still in the making. The emphasis on intergovernmental decision-making and agreement has

36. On this and the following see Pinder, *The European Union* 40–41, 52, 183.
37. See Jeffrey Lewis, "National Interests: COREPER," in Peterson and Shackleton, *The Institutions of the European Union*.

been so disproportionate because the EU is not yet a finished project. Even once adopted, the constitutional treaty will not bring about finality. There will be enumerated lists of exclusive and concurrent powers, but the exercise of the latter will remain tied to the principle of subsidiarity. Accordingly, the intergovernmental component of European governance will remain high. More generally, it seems unlikely that the core member states which have to pay for most of the programs will surrender their powers to a more independently governing European Commission. For the time being, it seems, the comitology network of intergovernmental control will remain a central part of European treaty federalism.

Integrated Federalism in Spain?

Germany and the EU constitute the main variation of integrated intergovernmental relations. Yet another and perhaps surprising case of integrated variation and imitation deserves brief mentioning: Spain. This may be surprising because Spain as a federal system is essentially characterized by a dual constitutional construction: The central state and the 17 Autonomous Communities largely operate independently of one another; the Autonomous Communities are only weakly represented in the Senate (see Chapter 7); and the political dynamic primarily has been one of regional competition with one another and with the central state. This is understandable in large part because of Spain's evolution as a federal democracy, with the regions acquiring powers from Madrid in negotiated statutory settlements (see Chapter 5). As a consequence, one would assume that Spanish intergovernmental relations might more likely resemble the American case: functional policy coordination on the basis of separate legislative processes and under central government supremacy.

And indeed, this is how Spanish intergovernmental relations evolved— at least initially and with regard to domestic policy-making. However, it was the process of European integration that infused the Spanish system with an innovative approach.[38] In a 1994 agreement, the national government and the Autonomous Communities set up a general Conference on European Affairs (as well as a number of policy-specific sectoral conferences) in order to coordinate Spain's position in European affairs. With several meetings a year, these conferences have formalized Spanish intergovernmental relations by giving the Autonomous Communities a co-decision right in national decision-making. Conferences are usually preceded by self-coordinating meetings among the Autonomous Communities in which joint positions are generated on the basis of one vote per Community. These positions are then shared with the central

---

38. This section largely follows Börzel, "From Competitive Regionalism to Cooperative Federalism."

government. In European matters affecting exclusive powers of the Autonomous Communities, the position is binding. If a matter concerns shared or concurrent jurisdiction, both sides must reach an agreement in order to determine the Spanish bargaining position. In cases of exclusive central state powers, the Autonomous Communities can only make non-binding statements. As in the German case of "federalism within federalism" (see Chapter 6), the Autonomous Communities thus have gained a measure of access and influence in the foreign policy field, traditionally regarded as one of the exclusive policy domains of national governments.

As in the German case also, the rationale for this central state concession has been the prevailing regime of administrative federalism in Spain. While it is the Spanish state that ultimately bears responsibility for its part in European policy-making, the implementation and administration of European laws and regulations are for the most part left to the autonomous communities. Moreover, many European policy initiatives, particularly in the field of economic development and structural cohesion, are directly geared to regional cooperation and participation. Europe's regions also have well-established direct relations with the EU, at the Commission, and in the Committee of the Regions. The process of Europeanization therefore compels central governments to listen more carefully to regional concerns.

This is of course more so in the EU's four federal systems—Germany, Austria, Belgium, and Spain—than in the unitary member states. But it is this new relationship between the EU and the regions that at least in part also accounts for devolution in the UK as well as the ever louder regional demands for constitutional federalism in Italy.

The Spanish case of "federalism within federalism" is significant because it may provide a model for regional and even global integration and governance more generally. While international treaties and the governing policies of international organizations are based on nation-state agreement, the impact of such agreements typically is regional or local in nature. The Spanish case points to the need for strengthening regional autonomies and regional participatory access to world affairs.

SUMMARY

Intergovernmental relations are a central feature of all federal systems because the exercise of divided powers among different levels of government requires cooperation and coordination—and much more so than when the classic federations were formed. A number of common characteristics can be identified:

- Intergovernmental relations favour executive federalism; bypassing parliamentary accountability, decisions are made by government leaders and their administrations.

- Intergovernmental relations are most commonly based on informal meetings and contacts. However, in some federal systems they are recognized as part of the formal institutional setup.
- Intergovernmental relations are conducted both vertically, between different levels of government, and horizontally, among the lower level governments, and particularly so in order to take a common stand against the national government.

Thus, the organization and intensity of intergovernmental relations in different federal systems depend on whether the division of powers remains politically contested and on the extent to which regional interests are represented in the national legislative process:

- The lack of legitimate regional senate representation and the underlying regional conflicts over the division of powers in Canada has resulted in a politicized climate of interstate federalism. Intergovernmental relations are dominated by First Ministers' Conferences and national as well as regional Premiers' Conferences.
- In Australia, intergovernmental relations have been marked by a dynamic of centralizing cooperation. Premiers' Conferences and formally institutionalized intergovernmental councils are overshadowed by central control over spending powers.
- In the United States, intergovernmental relations have been driven by the system of grants-in-aid. The resulting intergovernmental maze is controlled by a top-heavy form of regulatory federalism. Because there is no equivalent to the kind of executive federal summitry typical for other federations, state and local governments have to rely on an organized intergovernmental lobby.

In these cases of divided federalism, intergovernmental relations are meant to coordinate separate legislative processes at each level of government. In other cases of integrated federalism, subnational governments directly participate in national legislation, and intergovernmental relations therefore more directly aim at organizing and coordinating the legislative process itself.

- Germany is the main model of such integrated or intrastate federalism. In the upper *Bundesrat*, the *Länder* governments directly co-decide national legislation. Direct cooperation is also required for a number of constitutionally established joint tasks. Both regular prime ministerial conferences and summit conferences with the chancellor aim at legislative cooperation and at the coordination of policy implementation which is mostly left to the *Länder*. Intergovernmental relations are overshadowed by a competitive national party system, especially when the opposition commands a majority in the *Bundesrat*.
- In the EU, intergovernmental relations are even more strongly controlled by the constituent member states. The integration process is driven by intergovernmental treaty agreements in the European

Council. In the Council of Ministers, the member states have the last word on all legislation under the treaties. Moreover, a network of intergovernmental committees, known as the European comitology, controls the executive powers of the European Commission.

- Spain has established a limited regional co-decision right in European affairs. Similar to the German case of "federalism within federalism," this points to the need for strengthening regional participation in world affairs more generally.

9 Constitutional Amendment

As we have emphasized, federalism is the expression of certain principles and compromises. It is about the acknowledgment of territorial group rights and identities alongside individual citizen rights. Consequent upon this is the need for dual representation and a legislative process in which the representatives of both citizens and territorial collectivities co-decide by means of their respective majorities and in which a division of powers ensures the constituent units meaningful levels of self-governing authority.

However, there has to be something else: a guarantee that all of the above remains in place unless there is broad agreement for change. As Dicey put it, "The law of the constitution must be either legally immutable, or else capable of being changed only by some authority above and beyond the ordinary legislative bodies...."[1] How broad must that broad agreement be? If we think of the original constitutional compromise as a kind of treaty among equal partners, only unanimity will do. If the rules of the game are changed, each and every participant has a right to veto. It is a logical feature of any constitution—but particularly a federal one—that it includes not only rules about the political system it is describing, but also rules about itself. Constitutions need to contain provisions for their own amendment, provisions that stipulate what consensus threshold must be achieved to change the rules of the game. Such rules have a dual quality. On the one hand, they 'entrench' a constitution by protecting it against opportunistic change. On the other hand, they make a constitution flexible by providing an understood and authoritative mechanism for making change.

In the context of federalism, constitutional amendment includes everything from minor adjustment to significant reconfiguration of the division of powers or of such federal institutions as the upper house, to the negotiation of outright secession. Both the amendment procedures and the experience of constitutional amendment vary significantly across the world of federal states. For older federations in particular, there has

---

1.   Dicey, *An Introduction* 142–43.

been a long process of struggling to adapt an original division of powers to the profound social and economic changes that have occurred over a century of modernization. In several of our federations, amendment procedures have proven sufficiently strict to prevent all but a few notable changes being made to the original compact, leaving necessary adaptations to be accommodated either through judicial interpretation (as we shall discuss in Chapter 10) or through administrative and political means (as we shall discuss in Chapter 11).

One contrast is that between the relatively sparse constitutions that restrict themselves to laying down the rules of the game in general terms—the procedural framework—and more practical and detailed ones that not only elaborate on those rules but have also come to include substantive rules concerning the types of policy commitments governments are required to make. At one extreme is the US Constitution, which has assumed an iconic status; at the other extreme is the Swiss Constitution, subject to frequent adjustment and embellished with a variety of substantive injunctions.

AMENDMENT PROCEDURES

Conceivably, federal constitutions could be bound by the rule of unanimous consent: change can only be made to the founding agreement if all parties to that agreement agree. Such a tough requirement, however, would not only make change exceedingly difficult, but would also fail to reflect the nature of a federal as distinct from a confederal union. The bar must be set high enough to prevent partisan change but not so high as to prevent all change. As a compromise, then, federal constitutions typically rely on special majority requirements. These may be **super majorities**, such as the two-thirds approval by both legislative chambers in Germany; or **multiple majorities**, such as passage by the two houses of Congress and ratification by the states in the United States—or, quite commonly, some combination of the two. As one might expect, amendment rules tend to mirror adoption rules: the procedure that was stipulated for ratification of the constitution in the first place is reflected in the process stipulated for subsequent amendment. In most cases, these rules force proposed constitutional changes to run a political gantlet to be accepted.

Adjusting to Changing Needs

Precisely because of the legalism inherent in the constitutional setup of federal systems, and because of the impact such a legalistic predisposition will have upon political culture all the way down to popular perceptions of right and wrong, there is a certain rigidity to constitutional federalism. The most notorious case is that of Canada, which for many years has stumbled from one political crisis to another because of the inability, on the part of both politicians and populations, to agree on a constitutional formula adequately accommodating francophone minority interests. Long overdue fiscal harmonization and tax reforms in Switzerland have been delayed because they require constitutional change in favour of central government responsibility.

In many of these instances, and others, the resistance to change cannot be blamed on federalism itself, at least not in its entirety. It is worthwhile recalling that complex or divided societies resorted to a federal compromise on the road to modern statehood because social uniformity in a unitary political system was not to be had in the first place. At the bargaining table, the original participants wanted assurances about their irrevocable powers and rights written in constitutional stone. From this perspective, the degree to which federal systems have responded nevertheless to the need for constitutional change and changing power arrangements can be seen as a success story of amicable adjustment.

Who Should Have a Say?

In principle it seems appropriate that those bodies who agreed to the original constitution also should have a say in its amendment. Such an approach helps satisfy those submitting to the new order that they are not losing control of their constitutional destiny. Depending on the circumstances and values, then, amendment procedures may grant authority primarily to national legislatures, national and subnational legislatures, or even national legislatures and the people themselves.

Assuming that the national legislature is truly bicameral, the first option at least contains a minimal double majority element, which thus includes some sort of brake on unalloyed majoritarianism. The granting of authority over the constitution to the national legislature alone is not on the face of it consistent, however, with federalism or likely to emerge from the process by which a federation was created in the first place. It suggests that one order of government possesses the power to make unilateral alterations to the relationship between the two orders of government. The exception to this is where the national legislature itself has a strongly federal character and incorporates some sort of subnational veto power into its decision-making process (as in the German *Bundesrat*). The standard pattern, however, is for national legislatures to generate proposals for constitutional change, acting as repositories of the national will, but for the constituent units of the federation to have an independent voice in the procedure. This approach incorporates a much more substantial double (or triple) majority requirement.

A separate and additional consideration is raised by the principles of constitutionalism in a democratic society: should the people's representatives, in whatever combination, have the power to alter the institutions through which they govern without the express consent of the people? Thus, a third possibility is for constitutional amendments to require some form of popular ratification through a referendum process.

How High a Threshold?

If one criterion is about who should get to participate, another is about what level of approval should be required. The default option for democratic processes is the **simple majority**—50 per cent plus one of the votes cast. This is a rather modest requirement. It is particularly vulnerable, first, to the problem of narrow partisan majorities (should 51 per cent of the population be able to rule over 49 per cent of the population?). And it is also vulnerable to manipulation of the process by the calling of votes when opposition ranks are temporarily depleted. Bumping up the requirement a notch, some federations require an *absolute majority*: 50 per cent plus one of all those *eligible* to vote. This guards against transient majorities, but not against the problem of narrow partisan majorities. Thus, more common is to require *super majorities*. India, Germany, and the United States require a two-thirds super majority in the legislature; Brazil and Spain require three-fifths; and South Africa requires three-fourths.

In Canada, there is even a **unanimity** requirement for amendments related to specific matters such as parliamentary representation and language policy. In the United States, equal Senate representation cannot be taken away from a state without its consent. In other words, in this instance it cannot be overruled by any form of majority.

Who Gets to Propose?

A question of considerable importance is who has the right to **initiate** constitutional change. While having a veto power is very important, it is not the same as having the power to initiate. Veto efforts have to be successful every time a proposal arises; initiating efforts only have to be successful once. Repeated efforts may overcome a veto under conducive conditions (notably periods of national emergency), and this puts the excluded party at a significant disadvantage. The end result may be some sort of ratchet effect whereby change occurs only in one direction, typically a centralizing one.

In most federations, the initiative lies with the national government, and bills can usually be introduced in either of the two chambers. As in the case of the American, Australian, and Indian constitutions, for instance, this deprives the states of initiating constitutional change in their favour and thus contributes to the centralist bias built into most federations. However, there are exceptions. The Canadian *Constitution*

Act 1982 allows the provinces to initiate amendment. In Brazil, a majority of the state legislatures can propose an amendment. In Spain, the Autonomous Communities can request consideration of an amendment, individually or collectively, from the central government or from the lower chamber. In the latter case, up to three members of a particular Autonomous Community can appear before that chamber to defend their initiative. And in Switzerland, finally, the people itself can initiate constitutional change.

Beyond the Bounds?

A final question is whether there should be **absolute limitations** placed on constitutional change. From the perspective of parliamentary democracy and popular sovereignty this may seem a strange proposition. With all the additional caution built into the process of constitutional amendment, why should some matters be ruled out of bounds altogether? The designers of the classical federations in the eighteenth and nineteenth centuries obviously did not think so and simply did not mention any. For the Indian constitutional designers in the mid-twentieth century this was not enough. "For the removal of doubts," they wrote into the amending formula of Article 368, "it is hereby declared that there shall be no limitation whatever on the constituent power of Parliament to amend by way of addition, variation or repeal the provisions of this Constitution under this article." Being free of imperial shackles for the Indians also meant being free of constitutional shackles. In the words of one of the framers, "One can ... safely say that the Indian Federation will not suffer from the faults of rigidity or legalism. Its distinguishing feature is that it is a flexible federation."[2]

Guarding Against Authoritarianism

But perhaps there are some fundamental principles that need to be made non-negotiable. Drafting their constitution at the same time as the Indians, but with an entirely different set of political concerns, the Germans did inscribe a number of limitations into the amending formula of their postwar constitution. Amendments regarding the division of the federation into *Länder*, the participation of the *Länder* in national legislation, and the catalogue of basic individual rights and freedoms were all declared inadmissible. Brazil has a similar list of non-amendable components that also includes democratic voting rights. And the Spanish Constitution contains a stipulation whereby amendments may not be made during periods of national emergency as declared by the absolute

---

2. Quoted in Austin, *The Indian Constitution* 255.

majority of the House of Representatives at the exclusive proposal by the government.

There were historical reasons for these absolute limitations. The Germans had just gone through a period of totalitarian dictatorship that had used popular support and formally correct procedures to suspend basic rights and abolish all forms of decentralization. Brazil and Spain had lived through similar periods of authoritarian legislative abuse. The question remains how such limitations can be justified in terms of democracy. In the case of basic individual and human rights, the justification is couched in an acknowledgement that these are natural rights of a value higher than all human legislation. It is more difficult to find a justification for the removal of the federal form of government from the agenda of potential constitutional change. The German and Brazilian designers felt that, after a period of centralized dictatorship, federalism as a system of divided governance and mutual control had to be constitutionally enshrined as indispensable for the safeguarding of democracy. Perhaps the oddest example of an attempt to set boundaries on the ability to amend was the "Corwin Amendment" proposed for the US Constitution in 1860. It sought to exclude from amendment something in the Constitution that wasn't actually there—the right to practise slavery—by prohibiting any future amendment that would interfere with that institution.[3]

CONSTITUTIONAL PERMANENCE IN THE UNITED STATES

The US Constitution is often praised as the oldest codified constitution in the world. And indeed the only country with a longer uninterrupted constitutional history would be the United Kingdom—which does not have a codified constitution. Over a span of more than 200 years, only 17 amendments have been made to the original text since the first ten amendments were added as part of the original ratification package. The Germans, by contrast, have made over 100 changes to their constitution during the first 27 years of its existence.[4] And the Americans have passed over 5,000 amendments to their state constitutions.[5]

---

3. Richard B. Bernstein with Jerome Angel, *Amending America: If We Love the Constitution So Much, Why Do We Keep Trying to Change It?* (New York: Times Books, 1993) 87.

4. Klaus von Beyme, *Das politische System der Bundesrepublik Deutschland* (München: Piper 1987) 29.

5. Kermit L. Hall, "Mostly Anchor and Little Sail: The Evolution of American State Constitutions," in Paul Finkelman and Stephen Gottlieb, eds., *Towards a Usable Past: Liberty under State Constitutions* (Athens, GA: University of Georgia Press, 1991) 395.

The Amendment Procedure

It was the problem of amendment that led to the drafting of the US Constitution in the first place. As a confederal rather than federal order, the *Articles of Confederation* had stipulated a unanimity rule for amendment; when desperately needed changes were stymied by the ability of one state alone to hold out against all the others,[6] the basis was laid for a plenary reconsideration of the existing constitutional arrangements. At the Philadelphia Convention, the creation of a federal rather than a confederal form of government involved the shift to a more federal amendment procedure, one that requires consensus not unanimity. According to Article V section 1, constitutional amendments require a two-step process of **proposal** and **ratification**. Proposals must pass by a two-thirds majorities in both houses of Congress, or be passed by a special national convention convoked by the Congress at the request of two-thirds of the state legislatures. The latter method has never been used, though the possibility of it being used may have had an impact on constitutional politics. Following passage through Congress or a constitutional convention, the proposed amendment must then be approved by the legislatures or special ratifying conventions of three-quarters of the states.

Congress may or may not impose a deadline on the process of ratification. The usual time limit is seven years. However, the Twenty-seventh Amendment of 1992—requiring that congressional pay increases take effect only after an intervening election—began its ratification process in 1789 as the second amendment along with the "bill of rights," both of which were proposed in amendments three through thirteen. Neither the first nor the second proposed amendments were ratified, and they were assumed to have lapsed. However, no deadline was stipulated, and after a long hiatus, it was taken up again in 1984. The ratification process—which by the time Michigan clinched the deal in 1992 required the approval of 38 out of 50 states—took 203 years.

With these strenuous multiple super majority requirements, the US Constitution, then, is almost invulnerable to opportunistic change. All votes require super majorities (including the very high three-quarters requirement for ratification), and three different bodies must pass it— the House of Representatives, the Senate, and the states. The framers ensured that only those changes that represent, as President Washington put it in his farewell address of 1796, "an explicit and authentic act of the whole people"[7] are made.

---

6.   By Rhode Island in 1781 and New York in 1783. McDonald, *Novus Ordo Seclorum* 171.

7.   See David E. Kyvig, *Explicit and Authentic Acts: Amending the U.S. Constitution 1776–1995* (Lawrence, KS: University Press of Kansas, 1996).

The Record of Amendment

Only 33 amendment proposals have ever cleared the two-thirds hurdle in both houses of Congress, and 27 of these have been ratified by the states.[8] As one would expect with the bicameral super majority requirement, proposals that succeed in Congress stand a good chance of being ratified. Over 10,000 proposals have been put to Congress, but the vast majority have been filtered out at that stage.

It is possible to see the proclivity for constitutional change in the United States in an even narrower light. The first ten amendments, known as the Bill of Rights, were in fact the result of promises during the constitutional ratification debates. Since these promises effectively contributed to winning acceptance of the Constitution in the larger and more sceptical states—Virginia, Massachusetts, and New York[9]—they were really part of the original compromise. "It would be misleading to think of the Bill of Rights as 'amending America,' for ideas of rights have always been vital to American national identity and to the American experiment. Demands for a national bill of rights predated, accompanied, and even … made possible the adoption of the Constitution."[10] That would leave only 17 truly subsequent amendments, a number that Germany has sometimes surpassed within one legislative period.

What has been Changed by Amendment?

More important than the actual numbers are the political changes effected by constitutional amendments. In the American case, most have had to do with civil rights or functioning of the presidency, and only a few with federalism and the division of powers. In contrast to Canada and Australia, the US Constitution has never been amended to alter the division of powers by transferring authority from one level of government to the other.

By insisting that due process requirements applied to the states, the Fourteenth Amendment of 1868, introduced three years after the Civil War and the abolition of slavery, established justiciable limitations on the states' ability to circumvent uniform civil rights standards throughout the nation. It thereby marked a significant centralization of power. The Seventeenth Amendment of 1913 introduced popular election of senators. This did not alter the division of powers in the Constitution, but as we saw in Chapter 7, it may well have influenced the division of powers in practice. By removing senatorial elections from state government control, the Seventeenth Amendment lessened the Senate's

---

8. Bernstein and Angel, *Amending America* 169 and *passim*.
9. See Bernard Bailyn, *et al.*, *The Great Republic* (Lexington, MA: D.C. Heath, 1985) 37.
10. Bernstein, *Amending America* 47.

tendency to act as a house of the states. By comparison, the Sixteenth Amendment of the same year proved to be directly intrusive upon state powers because it cleared away obstacles to Congress introducing a national income tax and thereby laid the basis for fiscal dependence of the states and hence their policy subordination (see Chapter 11). It was only necessary, though, because of a particularly controversial Supreme Court ruling.[11] That is the sum total of changes to American federalism through formal constitutional amendment over more than two centuries of operation. As we shall see in Chapter 10, Article V has been the poor sister of constitutional change by comparison with the Supreme Court's role in American federalism.

CANADA: PATRIATION GAMES

The Americans understood very well that the original federalist compromise would only stand the test of time if it was firmly anchored in a constitutional document that would be very difficult to alter without the kind of consent that was required to establish it in the first place. All the more astonishing, then, is that the importance of an amendment procedure escaped the Canadians altogether. The "fathers of Confederation" in Canada left that task to the British Parliament; the *British North America Act* of 1867 (*BNA Act*) was silent on the matter of amendment. This, though, was consistent with the fact that the *BNA Act* itself did not go through a formal ratification process among the participating colonies.

As a consequence of this reluctance to anchor ultimate legal responsibility within the new federation, amendment procedures were the subject of protracted constitutional dispute. This culminated in the "patriation" of the Constitution by the government of Prime Minister Pierre Trudeau in 1982; with that patriation, a set of revisions included for the first time an amendment procedure. As an elaborate compromise among many players with a long history of vested interests, however, the *Constitution Act 1982* involved much more than giving Canada its own power of making constitutional changes. By doing so without the consent of Québec, it left the country with an ongoing crisis caused by that province's secessionist threats. Not least as a consequence of these, it appears unlikely that the general qualified majority procedure or the unanimity procedure (see Figure 9.1) adopted in 1982 will actually be used in the foreseeable future.

From a comparative federalism perspective, one might argue that Canada is an aberrant case from which little can be learned about the normality of constitutional change and judicial review. However, this is not necessarily so. Precisely because Canadians were forced to think

---

11. Bernstein, *Amending America* 120.

about constitutional change at such a late moment in their federal history, they had to re-examine some of the fundamental principles of federalism and the federalist compromise. This in turn opens up an instructive comparative perspective with regard to the practice of constitutional change in some of the other federal systems where the validity of procedures adopted long ago is rarely questioned. It also provides a comparative vantage point for newly federalizing national and international systems where the level of complexity precludes adoption of the old formulas.

The Procedure You Have When You Don't Have a Procedure

Over its more than 130 years of existence, the Canadian constitution has been changed about as many times as its American counterpart—21 times before patriation in 1982.[12] Most of these changes were effected by the British Parliament acting on a resolution from the Parliament of Canada. The absence of a formal amending procedure might have facilitated change, since there was no procedure to constrain Canadian governments intent on change. And indeed, those hoping to create a *faux* federation that would settle into a unitary mould might have thought the less said about procedures that could tie the hand of future national governments the better.[13] On the other hand, as we suggested at the outset of this chapter, constitutions must also be seen as facilitative, and the absence of an amending procedure may alternatively have obstructed change.[14] Like much else in the constitutional framework they created, the failure to include a formal amending procedure seems to have worked against the intentions of the framers.

Amendment Substance and Process

Only three substantive amendments were made to the *BNA Act* in its 115 years of operation.[15] All involved an augmentation of Parliament's power to legislate in the area of social policy. The major amendment was the granting in 1940 to Parliament of a power to make laws with respect to unemployment insurance. This finally paved the way for resolution of a bitter conflict over public responsibility for human suffering in the Great Depression that had been channelled into jurisdictional issues when legislation was declared unconstitutional by the Judicial Committee of the Privy Council (see Chapter 10). The answer

---

12. James Ross Hurley, *Amending Canada's Constitution: History, Processes, Problems and Prospects* (Ottawa, ON: Ministry of Supply and Services, 1996) 18.
13. William S. Livingston, *Federalism and Constitutional Change* (Oxford: Oxford University Press, 1956) 20–21.
14. Livingston, *Federalism and Constitutional Change* 19.
15. Hurley, *Amending Canada's Constitution* 19.

to adverse judicial decisions was constitutional amendment. However, Prime Minister Mackenzie King moved slowly to bring about the necessary amendment. Although no firm convention of provincial endorsement for constitutional amendment existed at this point, his government delayed any action on this matter until it had unanimous—i.e., including Québec—provincial support. In doing so it created a precedent that such consultation and consent as well, perhaps, as unanimous consent was required.[16] The only other constitutional variations occurred in 1951 and 1964 when Parliament was given formal powers to provide old-age pensions.

Entrenchment Attempts

From the 1920s on there was a succession of attempts to establish an amending procedure. In each case the crucial issue was how to formalize and quantify provincial approval. Under the arrangements of 1867, such approval was required only by convention, which meant that the British Parliament might not grant an amendment in the face of substantial provincial opposition.

The Fulton-Favreau formula of 1964 proposed unanimous adoption of a constitutional change by Parliament and the provincial legislatures in matters directly affecting provincial powers. In most other matters of significance to the federal system, two-thirds of the provinces representing at least 50 per cent of the Canadian population would have to concur. The 50 per cent rule meant that affirmation from either of the two central provinces of Québec or Ontario was necessary, but it was not required from both. The Victoria Charter of 1971 contained an amending formula based on regional representation. Again, there was a unanimity requirement for some amendments, but others could pass with the approval of Ontario, Québec, and two Atlantic and two western provinces. The Victoria Charter also included a bill of rights.

With or Without Québec?

Each proposal was rejected by Québec. A decade later, after the first separatist referendum on sovereignty association in Québec, Prime Minister Trudeau forced the issue by announcing that he would seek approval unilaterally from Britain for constitutional patriation, including an amending formula and a charter of rights and freedoms, without unanimous or even substantial provincial support if necessary. In a reference case (see Chapter 10) brought before it by several provinces, the Supreme Court ruled in one of its most controversial judgements that such unilateralism was legal but in violation of constitutional convention.

---

16. Livingston, *Federalism and Constitutional Change* 60.

While convention is not legally enforceable, this authoritative ruling meant that Britain was likely to pass a constitutional package only if it was carried by substantial provincial support. Back at the intergovernmental bargaining table, Trudeau and the nine anglophone premiers eventually forged a deal that went ahead to become the *Constitution Act 1982*. In essence, it re-activated the Fulton-Favreau formula of 1964 and added a charter of rights as proposed by the Victoria Charter.

Constitutional Patriation and the Amending Formula

With regard to the unfinished business of constitutional change, however, the settlement of 1982 can be appreciated as a balanced approach to maintaining the original compromise. The inclusion of a charter of individual rights, however, constituted a deliberate attack on Québec's collective cultural identity, since Québec's traditional language policies could now be challenged before the Supreme Court as violations of individual rights. Judicial interpretation and review on that basis could interfere with Québec's political agenda in a way that had not been possible before. It is chiefly for this reason that the constitutional deal of 1982 was rejected by the government of Québec.

The Final Compromise

Reflecting the complexity of modern statehood and governance in a society divided by regional and cultural fault lines, the amending formula enshrined in Part V, sections 39–49, of the *Constitution Act 1982* contains five different procedures for constitutional change (see Figure 9.1). These include categories of amendment that require ratification by the governments of two-thirds of the provinces representing more than 50 per cent of the population and categories that require unanimous support of the governments of provinces. Notable by its absence was any introduction of a Swiss or Australian-style role for the people in this process— a decision that reflects the fact that the entire patriation exercise was carried without reference to the people.

As is readily evident, this is not anything like the concise amendment provision in the US Constitution. Instead, it is a lengthy enumeration of ifs and whens. Particularly noteworthy are the opting-out provisions under the qualified majority procedure. Seven or more provinces representing 50 per cent of the Canadian population can agree to give Parliament the power to establish a major new social program, for instance. At the same time, one or a minority of provinces can declare that they do not want to be part of that program.

The original suggestion as put forward by eight of the ten provinces, including Québec, was to compensate all provincial opt-outs. The final deal of November 1981, without Québec's consent, dropped the

FIGURE 9.1

Amendment Rules in the Canadian Constitution Act 1982

1. A general qualified majority procedure requiring approval by the federal parliament and **two-thirds** (seven) of the provincial legislatures representing at least 50 **per cent** of the Canadian population; if an amendment under this procedure reduces provincial powers or rights by creating new federal powers, Senate support is required as well; however, such an amendment will not apply to a province the legislature of which declares its dissent. Finally, if the exemption of a province from such an amendment concerns education or culture, that province will be compensated by the federal government for its own exercise of that power.

2. A **unanimity** procedure requiring approval by the federal Parliament and all provincial legislatures for specifically enumerated matters such as the monarchy, the minimum number of parliamentary seats for a province, and the general use of French and English.

3. A **bilateral** procedure for matters affecting only one or several but not all provinces such as boundary changes and language use within a province; in this instance, approval is required by the federal Parliament as well as by the provincial legislature(s) to which the amendment applies.

4. A procedure for amendments by **Parliament alone** for matters of governance that do not affect the provinces.

5. And finally, a procedure whereby **provincial legislatures** can amend their own constitutions.

In addition, there is a section that enumerates matters that require amendment by the general qualified majority procedure but are not open to a provincial opt-out. Among these are the principle of proportionate representation of the provinces in Parliament and the creation of new provinces.

compensation idea altogether. In an unsuccessful last-minute attempt at reconciliation, compensation was reinstated before final ratification of the *Constitution Act 1982*, albeit only for matters of education and culture, but not for much more costly social programs.

The Canadian provisions for constitutional change reveal an almost desperate attempt to allow asymmetrical policy and program flexibility without giving up the idea that a constitution has to apply to all constituent parts equally and symmetrically. A few years later, it was the violation of this idea of formal constitutional symmetry, by recognizing Québec as a "distinct society," that sealed the fate of the Meech Lake Accord. The die-hard champions of constitutional symmetry could not or would not see that this more symbolic than substantive gesture towards Québec was far less significant than the opting-out provisions of the amendment formula.

Attempts at Resolution

Two unsuccessful attempts were made by the Progressive Conservative Mulroney government to end Québec's constitutional isolation. The Meech Lake Accord of 1987 contained an extended list of constitutional amendments requiring unanimous approval, but its major stumbling block was Québec's recognition as a distinct society. Considerable uncertainty surrounded the legal and political implications of such a justiciable declaration. The Accord died in 1990 when two provinces failed to ratify it in time. The Charlottetown Accord of 1992 more or less contained the same provisions on constitutional amendment and, as a major concession to western provinces in particular, the so-called triple-E Senate (discussed in Chapter 7). This was put to the people—a first in Canada for constitutional amendment. It was narrowly defeated, however, in the national referendum in most provinces including Québec. Although the referendum was only consultative, the result was taken as decisive.

The difficulty of the Canadian situation is its extreme asymmetry, with nine anglophone provinces and one francophone province, a large number of whose denizens regard themselves as forming a distinct nation. As we saw before, changing the original constitutional agreement of a federation typically requires some sort of super majority. In the case of Québec, however, anything short of a veto cannot really be satisfactory. Under the Fulton-Favreau formula, it would have gained such a veto alongside with all other provinces. Ironically, Québec's dissent in this instance was based on the fear that its own desire for constitutional change could be blocked by another province. The Victoria Charter, on the other hand, was rejected because it left the door open for national social policy programs over which Québec wanted to have exclusive control.

It would be easy to view all this as intransigence. In reality, as the failures of the Meech Lake and Charlottetown Accords illustrate, making substantive changes to the original federalist compromise almost inevitably amounts to unhinging that compromise in all its component parts. To find a new one, in a much more complex world, and among a much larger number of participants with their vested interests, has proved to be an impossible task.

CONSTITUTIONAL FLEXIBILITY IN GERMANY

The Constitution of the Federal Republic of Germany is notably more flexible than either the American or the Canadian. Amendment is easier and has occurred more frequently. This is for at least four reasons. First, the procedure itself is somewhat less demanding and in particular relies much less on multiple majorities. Second, the Constitution is a more practical and detailed document than an iconic one and so is much more conducive to practical and detailed adjustment. Third, Germany's administrative federalism is much less liable to polarized conflict over such changes and adjustments. And fourth, the depth of underlying difference has simply not been there.

The German Amendment Procedure

The provisions regarding constitutional amendment in Article 79 of the Constitution are clear and simple:

1. Amendment can only be made by a law that expressly changes or supplements the constitutional text.
2. Amendments must be approved by two-thirds of the members in both legislative chambers, the Bundestag and the Bundesrat.
3. Core elements of the Constitution cannot be amended at all. These include protection of individual rights; the democratic nature of the system; and, most importantly for our purposes, the existence and role of the Länder.

One can easily see the framers' efforts at avoiding constitutional ambiguity as much as possible. Amending acts must be explicit about what they amend or supplement to avoid backdoor changes to the Constitution. Most importantly, there is no subnational ratification process; the national Parliament alone amends the Constitution. On the face of it, this contradicts the federal principle that the rules governing the relationship between the two levels of governments must not be susceptible to alteration by one level alone. The existence of the upper house as a true house of the states solves this problem. The delegates of the *Länder* governments vote in the *Bundesrat*, ensuring direct subnational participation in the amendment process. And finally, there is the exemption of certain provisions from constitutional change. Article 1 of the Constitution proclaims the inviolability of human dignity and then declares that the legislature, the executive, and the judiciary shall be bound by the subsequent catalogue of fundamental rights as directly enforceable law. Articles 20 and 79 regarding the *Länder* and the federal order more generally amount to a *constitutional guarantee of federalism*.

The Experience with Constitutional Amendment in Germany

Between 1951 and 1996, the German Parliament passed 43 laws amending the Constitution.[17] Since each of these laws can and as a rule do affect several constitutional articles, by inserting new ones and either amending or deleting existing ones, the actual number of constitutional amendments is in the hundreds. Thus, the German Constitution has proven itself readily adaptable.

Changes

Of the many changes that have been made to the German Constitution, a handful stand out for their significance. In the late 1960s, alteration

---

17. Heinz Laufer and Ursula Münch, *Das föderative System der Bundesrepublik Deutschland* (Opladen: Leske Budrich, 1998) 366–69.

was made to the division of powers by inserting the so-called "joint tasks" (see Chapter 6). In the early 1990s, the Constitution was adjusted for reunification. In the same period, new provisions were made for increased *Länder* participation in EU affairs, and the approach to the division of powers was again varied, this time by changing the treatment of concurrent powers in favour of the *Länder*.

While the alterations of the 1960s were widely criticized as a further blow to the legislative autonomy of the *Länder*, the amendments of the 1990s came in the context of calls for a new and more decentralized federalism. Following the report of the Joint Constitutional Commission of the *Bundestag* and *Bundesrat*, amendments were passed to put a brake on centralization. In particular, Article 72, which regulates the exercise of concurrent powers, was given a more precise and restrictive wording. As we have discussed in Chapter 6, Article 72 gives the national Parliament sweeping powers to pre-empt *länder* legislation in the name of national unity and equitability. The first problem with this clause for the federal balance in Germany is that it invited expansive interpretation through the so-called "clause of need" whereby assumption of national responsibility could easily be justified. "The *Constitutional Reform Act* of 27 October 1994 has now changed the 'clause of need' for the federation into a 'clause of necessity' in favour of the *Länder*...."[18] That terminological change was intended to place a much greater burden of proof upon centralization initiatives. The second problem was that the Constitutional Court refused to police the clause, preferring to categorize its application as a "political matter"—which, as we shall discuss in Chapter 10, is scarcely a plausible excuse since this is inherently the nature of all constitutional law. In response, the amendments also included a direct injunction that the Court exercise responsibility for interpretation of Article 72. The third problem was that concurrency was a one-way street: all developments flowed in a centralizing direction. In response to that, a new provision for resumption of *Länder* responsibility was written into the Constitution.

The amendments of 1994 represent an unusual and interesting case of formal attempts to counteract the centralizing tendencies common to federal systems—something we certainly have not seen in the American or Canadian cases. However, neither the degree of amendment nor the effect of that amendment matched the ambitions of the decentralists; in particular, judicial interpretation has failed to support the initiative. Whatever *Länder* hopes there may have been, they were dashed by the first post-reform decision of the Federal Constitutional Court on this matter[19] (see Chapter 10).

---

18. Leonardy, "The Institutional Structures of German Federalism" 13.
19. 24 October 2002–2 BvF 1/01.

Amendment Within a System of Integrated Federalism

The participation of the *Länder* governments in constitutional changes via the *Bundesrat* underscores most impressively the integrated rather than divided nature of the German federal system. Since no single party or coalition government has ever held two-thirds majorities in both houses, constitutional change requires the direct cooperation not only of both levels of government but also of all major political forces in the country. As the frequency of constitutional adjustment and change indicates, the *Länder* governments rarely if ever have withheld such cooperation. As in cases of regular legislation requiring approval by the *Bundesrat*, differences are worked out in the crucial Mediation Committee where the *Bundesrat* representatives work for a compromise reflecting as closely as possible the majority position of the *Länder* governments.

THE EU: MAINTAINING CONFEDERAL CONSENT

In federal systems, constitutional change requires elaborate procedures and the support of more than simple majorities because it changes the pact or covenant that all constituent members originally agreed to. At the same time, the national character of a federal system is emphasized by the fact that constitutional change can indeed be brought about without unanimity and some members can be overruled. The process of constitutional change, therefore, gives expression to the very essence of the federalist compromise.

From this perspective, the EU is not a conventional federal system because its primary body of law is a series of treaties rather than a constitution, and because changes to these treaties, or the adoption of new ones, requires the consent of all members. The EU has nevertheless moved impressively towards federalism by adopting comprehensive and innovative mechanisms of cooperation in order to facilitate and speed up necessary or desirable treaty changes.

A Constitution of Treaties?

Apart from the **accession treaties** by which the original Community of Six has been expanded to a union of 25 members, there are currently no fewer than eight treaties in effect and operation (see Figure 9.2). Effectively, the EU is governed by two fundamental treaties, the Treaty of the European Community (TEC), which comprises the primary body of Community law prior to Maastricht, and the Treaty on European Union (TEU), which expands the integration objectives to economic and monetary union, foreign policy, and internal security cooperation. The Amsterdam and Nice Treaties foreshadowed issues of governance and decision-making occasioned by the intended Eastern European enlargement of the EU (ten new members in 2004; two more members by 2007;

membership negotiations with Turkey beginning in 2005). The enormous complexity of this treaty jumble, together with the need to improve the EU's operation compelled the launch of a **European Constitutional Convention** in 2002 with the goal of generating a new and comprehensive framework for European governance. After various rounds of revising the constitutional draft treaty produced by the Convention, the Treaty Establishing a Constitution for Europe (constitutional treaty) was signed in October 2004. It is now awaiting ratification by the member states.

FIGURE 9.2
The Treaty Framework of the EU

1. 1952: The original **ECSC Treaty** (European Coal and Steel Community).

2. 1958: The **EEC Treaty** (European Economic Community).

3. 1958: The **Euratom Treaty** (European Atomic Energy Community).

4. 1967: The **Merger Treaty** brought these three original treaties under the governance of common institutions (Council, Commission, Parliament, Court) even though they continue to exist as separate treaties. At this stage, the European Communities became known as the European Community.

5. 1987: The **SEA** (*Single European Act*) required extensive economic policy harmonization for the completion of a single European market by 1992. It also contained procedural amendments and additions to all previous treaties.

6. 1993: The **TEU** (Treaty on European Union) or "**Maastricht Treaty**" established economic and monetary union and the pillar structure by adding to the supranational European Community two intergovernmental pillars on foreign policy and internal security cooperation. The EEC Treaty was restyled into the Treaty of the European Community (**TEC**).

7. 1999: The **Amsterdam Treaty** further strengthened the supranational character of the EU while also endorsing flexibility and symmetry in its future development.

8. 2003: The **Nice Treaty** anticipated changes in decision-making rules related to the impending membership accession of (mostly) eastern European countries.

"Amendment"

In terms of federalism, the mode of treaty change is intergovernmental agreement. Before 1985, such changes were prepared in committees and then formally adopted by the European heads of governments. Since 1975, these summit meetings have been formalized and regularized as European Council meetings. Since 1985, however, so-called Intergovernmental Conferences (IGCs) have become the main instrument for initiating and orchestrating change.

At the European Council meeting in Milan of that year (see Chapter 8), the European Commission under the new and activist leadership of Jacques Delors presented its White Paper calling for completion of the single market and containing in its appendix approximately 300 proposals for economic policy harmonization. The idea was to convene an intergovernmental conference to prepare for what eventually became the *Single European Act*. Opposition came mainly from Britain, Greece, and Denmark. In an unprecedented move, the Italian Council President forced the issue by calling a vote, permitted under the Treaties but never used before. The IGC was established by a 7:3 vote in favour (there were only ten members at the time), and, with the eventual full cooperation of all members the SEA was adopted two years later.

Similarly, the Maastricht Treaty was prepared by two IGCs, one on monetary union and one on political union. The treaties of Amsterdam and Nice were preceded by IGCs as well. Participation in these IGCs is normally a matter of the member-states' foreign ministers whose meetings are in turn prepared by a committees of their senior officials. However, given the importance of such fundamental treaty revisions as the SEA or the TEU, Europe's government leaders routinely take an active part.[20]

The most recent IGC dealt with the constitutional treaty. It became necessary when the first attempt at adopting the draft treaty failed in 2003. If and when ratified, the constitutional treaty will be an unprecedented milestone in the history of European treaty 'amendments,' replacing all previous treaties with one consolidated document. It will also add a number of innovative changes, such as a European charter of rights, a more specifically enumerated list of concurrent powers, and a new formula of qualified majority voting in the Council of Ministers. It also contains a complicated provision for amendment (see Figure 9.3), which in essence continues with the tradition of unanimous consent for treaty changes.

In comparison with amending procedures in conventional federal systems, this provision significantly extends further the idea that constitutional change should be difficult. In its requirement for a combination of unanimous consent and consultation, it constitutes a novel degree of participatory involvement. While hardly a model for the established federations, it may indeed provide a blueprint for new types of treaty federalism in a globalizing world.

The Constitutional Convention

In the introductory chapter, we referred to these recent developments as comparable to the Philadelphia Convention of 1787 which crafted the US Constitution. The reason for this is not so much the originality of the text that resulted from it—far more a consolidation of previous *acquis communautaire*[21] as laid down in the various previous treaties

---

20. See David Phinnemore, "Towards European Union," in Michelle Cini, ed., *European Union Politics* (Oxford: Oxford University Press, 2003).
21. The *status quo* of integration on the basis of the entire body of European law to date.

FIGURE 9.3

Amending Provisions in the European Constitutional Treaty
Article IV.443 (Official Journal of the European Union, 16 December 2004)

Ordinary Revision Procedure

1. The government of any Member State, the European Parliament or the Commission may submit to the Council of Ministers proposals for the amendment of this treaty. These proposals shall be submitted to the European Council by the Council and the national Parliaments shall be notified.

2. If the European Council, after consulting the European Parliament and the Commission, adopts by a simple majority a decision in favour of examining the proposed amendments, the President of the European Council shall convene a Convention composed of representatives of the national Parliaments of the Member States, of the Heads of State or Government of the Member States, of the European Parliament and of the Commission. The European Central Bank shall also be consulted in the case of institutional changes in the monetary area. The Convention shall examine the proposals for amendments and shall adopt by consensus a recommendation to a conference of representatives of the governments of the Member States as provided for in paragraph 3.

3. The European Council may decide by a simple majority, after obtaining the consent of the European Parliament, not to convene the Convention should this not be justified by the extent of the proposed amendments. In the latter case, the European Council shall define the terms of reference for the conference of representatives of the governments of the Member States.

4. The conference of representatives of the governments of the Member States shall be convened by the President of the Council of Ministers for the purpose of determining by common accord the amendments to be made to the Treaty establishing the Constitution.

5. The amendments shall enter into force after being ratified by all the Member States in accordance with their respective constitutional requirements.

6. If, two years after the signature of the treaty amending the Treaty establishing the Constitution, four-fifths of the Member States have ratified it and one or more Member States have encountered difficulties in proceeding with ratification, the matter shall be referred to the European Council.

than a bold new beginning—but the process which generated it. Indeed, the European Convention was radically different from all previous inter-governmental activities in that it was composed of:

- one member each from the 15 member-state governments;
- one member each from the 13 candidate states with pending membership applications;
- two members each from the 15 member-state parliaments;
- two members each from the parliaments in the 13 candidate states;
- 16 members of the European Parliament; and
- two representatives of the European Commission.

In addition, representatives from various EU committees and organizations were admitted as observers, an Internet-based forum invited participation from European civil society, and European youth were involved in a special youth forum.

The plenary of the Convention met once a month. Working groups on particular issues and policies met even more frequently. This was a broad-based attempt at assuaging widespread criticism that the process of integration and enlargement was driven by a narrow coalition of transnational business interests, governments, and EU bureaucrats.

In this, it can be compared to the efforts at public involvement preceding the 1992 Charlottetown Accord in Canada which were occasioned by similar criticisms of excluding the public. In the case of the Philadelphia Convention of 1787, public involvement was generated afterwards through the ratification process to which the *Federalist* papers contributed. The European Convention shared with both of these events a concern among its participants that the existing constitutional arrangement has proven insufficient and in need of substantive reform if not transformation in order to meet new challenges. Ratification of the final document as signed in October 2004 will be difficult because referendums are required in various member states where the outcome is uncertain due to considerable opposition.

VARIATIONS: BACK TO THE PEOPLE

In all the cases we have examined so far, as well as in a range of other federations, whatever procedures are employed to safeguard the original federal compact, power is exercised by representative bodies on behalf of the people. In some countries, this is not enough. They require that the people themselves control constitutional change. In both Switzerland and Australia, all amendments must be ratified by the people in a national referendum, with that referendum itself containing a double majority requirement: a national majority and a majority in a majority of cantons or states. With its uniquely strong tradition of direct democracy, Switzerland goes one step further and includes provision for its citizens to *initiate* a constitutional referendum. In Switzerland, any citizen, or group of citizens, can propose a specific constitutional amendment. If this initiative is supported by 100,000 signatures, Parliament has two options. It can either put the question to a constitutional referendum as is, or it can make a counter proposal in which case the voters have a choice. The Swiss Constitution is the epitome of the type we described in the introduction to this chapter as including sundry substantive matters of government responsibility in addition to stipulating the basic procedural rules through which the system should function. Many amendments insert into the Swiss Constitution policy demands that in other systems would be satisfied or at least sought through the legislative process, a direct consequence of the fact that the ability to initiative referendums applies only to constitutional matters and thus the constitution gets used for subconstitutional purposes.

Numbers Game

In the case of Switzerland, the double majority requirement means that a constitutional amendment needs approval in at least 12 cantons. Given the discrepancy in size between cantons, this creates the potential for a considerable tension between the democratic principle of majoritarianism and the federal principle of regional representation. Switzerland's division into a large number of small and mostly rural cantons on the one hand and a few large and urban cantons on the other means that a constitutional amendment can be approved by a large popular majority country-wide but ultimately be rejected by negative votes in a majority of cantons representing not more than some 20 per cent of the population.[22] In the case of Australia, this federalization of the constitutional referendum appears similarly problematic because, in a federation of only six states, approval in a majority of four states would not be successful when these states represent less than half of the Australian electorate, as neither would approval in three of the most populated states representing more than half of the electorate.[23] In addition, the numbers create a *de facto* super-majority requirement: the minimum margin in a group of six is a two-thirds majority.

A Brake on Change?

In both systems, constitutional referendums may have a conservative effect; they may retard political change. The most notorious example for this was the delayed introduction of universal suffrage in Switzerland. Extension of the franchise to women was repeatedly rejected in referendums, and only in 1971 were women finally given the vote in national elections. Another and more general problem is plebiscitarian manipulation. Typically in Switzerland again, large and powerful interest organizations will concentrate their campaigning efforts on those cantons most likely to constitute a blocking minority. In the view of one critic, "the double-majority rule in direct democracy is an effective veto device."[24] Nonetheless, Parliament-initiated referendums have enjoyed a two-thirds success rate, although citizen-initiated ones almost always fail.[25]

---

22. There are 20 full and six half cantons in Switzerland. Half cantons only have half a vote in referendum outcomes. A constitutional amendment can be blocked technically by a negative vote in 11.5 cantons. See Wolf Linder, *Swiss Democracy* (New York: St. Martin's Press, 1994) 74–75.

23. P.H. Lane, *Introduction to the Australian Constitution* (Melbourne: The Law Book Company, 1990) 4.

24. Linder and Vatter, "Institutions and Outcomes" 98.

25. Linder and Vatter, "Institutions and Outcomes" 97. Ninety per cent of CIR fail.

In Australia, where only eight of 44 referendum questions have succeeded in a century since Federation, popular consultation is often associated with constitutional conservatism. On a number of occasions, Australian governments have been rebuffed by the people in their attempt to effect change to the operation of the Senate or the division of powers. However, the people have supported important changes on some occasions (notably to endorse a national welfare state in 1946 and to grant the Commonwealth power to legislate for Aborigines in 1967), and it could be argued that the high failure rate merely reflects that fact that the voters were wise and the proposals ill-considered.[26] Comparing the Australian experience with the American, we might also note that the very high success rate for referendums in the United States reflects the impact of a bicameral super-majority legislative process for generating amendments while the very low success rate in Australia reflects the impact of an executive-driven simple-majority process for generating amendments. To get through both houses of Congress with a two-thirds vote, any proposal has achieved a breadth of support far beyond that required in the Australian process.

Consulting the People for a Change

On the other hand, critics argue that in general the referendum is a poor technique for resolving constitutional issues since it presents an artificially polarized yes/no choice with no opportunity for negotiation, compromise, and the practice of deliberative democracy.[27] A case in point is the 1992 Charlottetown Accord referendum in Canada. Canada does not use constitutional referendums, but, as in any other country, the government may decide to link the passage of a particular bill to direct popular approval. The constitutional package of the Charlottetown Accord was negotiated as an exercise in executive federalism in a last attempt at bringing Québec into the constitutional fold. It included various compromises with the other provinces in return for their support. Despite extensive public hearings, the people rejected the Accord. The referendum procedure obviously was not able to accomplish what conventional intergovernmentalism had failed to achieve previously: trust in the legitimacy of the political process.

26. Brian Galligan, "The Republic Referendum: A Defence of Popular Sense," *Quadrant* (October 1999); and Brian Galligan, "Amending Constitutions Through the Referendum Device," in Matthew Mendelsohn and Andrew Parkin, eds., *Referendum Democracy: Citizens, Elites and Deliberation in Referendum Campaigns* (Basingstoke: Palgrave, 2001).

27. Simone Chambers, "Constitutional Referendums and Democratic Deliberation," in Matthew Mendelsohn and Andrew Parkin, eds., *Referendum Democracy: Citizens, Elites and Deliberation in Referendum Campaigns* (Basingstoke: Palgrave, 2001).

QUÉBEC AND CANADA:
SECESSION AS CONSTITUTIONAL AMENDMENT

An ultimate form of constitutional change is secession. As we discussed in Chapter 2, secession poses a cruel challenge to democratic federal states, which tend to be predicated on the assumption that the original compact was a one-way street. In an age, though, where legitimacy is based on the democratic right to self-determination, this is difficult to enforce. How can constitutional federations think the unthinkable?

Canada provides the most interesting case of separatism and secession. This is so because unlike quite a number of other cases of federal failure, including, more recently, Pakistan (1971), Czechoslovakia (2002), and Yugoslavia (1991–95), the break-up has been avoided to date.[28] Canada shares with these and other cases a number of characteristics that have been identified as generally problematic for the stability of federal systems (see Chapter 3). One is the bicommunal nature of federalism, which essentially divides the country into an English- and a French-speaking part. The other and related characteristic is asymmetry, an uneven distribution of population and allocation of resources and opportunity structures across the federation.

The Secession Referendums

Twice—in 1980 and in 1995—the francophone province of Québec held a referendum on separation. In each case the question asked was widely considered (at least in English Canada) to be deliberately imprecise for the strategic reason of garnering as much support as possible. Both times the referendum failed, though very narrowly so the second time around. The imprecision was twofold. First, Québecers were not asked directly if they wanted to separate from the rest of Canada; instead, they were asked if they wanted to give their provincial government a mandate to move towards such a separation. Secondly, the exact nature of the relationship with the rest of Canada after the act of separation was left unclear. An expectation was fostered that some form of economic union, including the continuation of a shared currency, would soften the blow.

In addition to its opposition to these deliberate ambiguities, the Canadian government argued that separation could not be imposed unilaterally and that the conditions of an eventual secession had to be negotiated with the country as a whole. It also denied that Québec could secede legitimately as an act of national self-determination under international law.

---

28. Equally interesting is the case of Belgium which, however, moved from a unitary to a federal constitution in 1993 in order to avoid break-up.

Constitutionalizing secession

Under the uncompromising and goal-oriented leadership of Intergovernmental Affairs Minister Stéphane Dion, himself a francophone and political science professor in the federalist tradition of former Prime Minister Pierre Trudeau, the federal government initiated a process of legal and legislative clarification of the conditions for legitimate secession. To this end, it first asked the Supreme Court of Canada for a constitutional reference decision (see Chapter 10) and, then, on the basis of the ruling, introduced and passed a Clarity Bill outlining the conditions under which it was willing to negotiate a legitimate separation of Québec.

The Clarity Bill was itself criticized as vague, because it outlined operational principles rather than hard and precise conditions. But, together with the constitutional reference, it was recognized internationally as a major contribution to the formulation of a general framework for legitimate secession. Because of this significance in a globalizing world with a growing number of volatile minority situation and secessionist threats, both the constitutional reference and the Clarity Bill deserve some concluding thoughts in this chapter.

Judicial Interpretation

The Supreme Court of Canada was asked, first, whether the unilateral secession of Québec was constitutionally possible; second, whether such a right of unilateral secession could be invoked under the international law of self-determination; and third, whether international law would take precedence over domestic law.

In its decision of 20 August 1998, the Supreme Court held that secession of a province "under the Constitution" could not be achieved unilaterally and without negotiation with the rest of the country; that Québec could not invoke an international right of self-determination because this was only possible when a nation or people was denied a meaningful exercise of its political rights; and that the issue of the precedence of international over domestic law therefore did not have to be considered. Federalists (as opposed to separatists) welcomed this rejection of "a legal theory that confuses self-determination with the right of secession."[29]

In the context of federalism, it is the Court's answer to the first question in particular that warrants closer examination. It held that the quest for separation was legitimate in a democracy if it was based on a

---

29. Stéphane Dion, "The Supreme Court's Reference on Unilateral Secession: A Turning Point in Canadian History," in Ronald Beiner and Wayne Norman, eds., *Canadian Political Philosophy: Contemporary Reflections* (Don Mills, ON: Oxford University Press, 2001) 312.

clear majority in favour of a clear proposition. As we noted in Chapter 2, it is difficult to reconcile an absolute prohibition on secession with the principles of liberal democratic self-determination—but, by the same token, if it must be taken seriously in a democracy, it must be indubitably democratic. The Court went on to state that democracy means more than simple majority rule because it exists in the larger context of other constitutional values. In a federal system, these include respect for historical ties of interdependence and an obligation to engage in discussions about constitutional change. As a consequence, therefore, the Court concluded that legitimate secession required "principled negotiation with other participants in Confederation within the existing constitutional framework."[30]

The remarkable character of the Court's decision lies in its affirmation of federalism as a process of negotiation rather than merely as a legal framework of rights and obligations. Furthermore, there is a clear recognition of federalism as a system with shared sovereignty and governance that outweighs the democratic principle of majority rule.

The Clarity Bill

As intended all along, the government responded with its Clarity Bill in December 1999 (Bill C-20).[31] Reiterating the Supreme Court's opinion that a fully democratic expression of the will to secede could only be the result of a referendum "free of ambiguity both in terms of the question asked and in terms of the support it achieves,"[32] the Clarity Bill set out the conditions under which the Canadian government would enter into negotiations about secession with a province.

To begin, Parliament would consider, within a specified period of time, both whether the question was clear and whether the result of the referendum was clear. To this effect, the Clarity Bill specified a number of conditions. The question must allow clear expression of a popular will to secede in order to become an independent state. Neither questions asking merely for a mandate to negotiate secession nor questions envisaging a range of options other than outright secession will be accepted as clear. With regard to the clarity of outcome, Parliament is to take into consideration both the actual result of votes cast and the rate of participation among eligible voters.

The Clarity Bill further specified that secession may only be accomplished legitimately by means of a constitutional amendment—which

---

30. Supreme Court of Canada, *Reference re Secession of Quebec* [1998] 2 S.C.R. 217.

31. Passed as the Clarity Act—*An Act to give effect to the requirement for clarity as set out in the opinion of the Supreme Court of Canada in the Quebec Secession Reference*—29 June 2000.

32. *Reference re Secession of Quebec.*

would entail meeting the requirements established by the *Constitution Act 1982*. And it firmly stated that such a constitutional amendment will not be introduced unless such negotiations had settled a number of issues including the division of assets and liabilities, territorial boundary changes, and Aboriginal and other minority rights.

As it turned out, the government also followed the lead of the Court and abstained from making numerically explicit what would be considered a "clear majority." This omission in particular drew some criticism because it certainly would appear in line with federalist practice to specify qualified or compounded majority rules. It allowed speculation as to whether the Clarity Bill's real objective was simply to raise the procedural threshold to whatever level would be just beyond the reach of Québec's separatist aspirations. Implicitly it would seem that the requirement for a "clear majority" is a requirement for an absolute rather than a simple majority, that is, a majority of all those eligible to vote. Even without pressing for something higher than 50 per cent plus one, this raises the bar considerably.

SUMMARY

- Constitutions must strike a balance that gives them both permanence and flexibility. In addition, federal constitutions must preserve the condition of shared sovereignty, preventing one order of government unilaterally downgrading the other.
- Amendment provisions do this by establishing procedures and thresholds that seek to make change contingent on the appropriate degree of consensus across the appropriate range of institutions and players. The procedure chosen for any particular federation will tend to reflect the procedure through which the constitution was adopted in the first place.
- Multiple majorities and super majorities are the main devices used to confirm that required degree of consensus. However this might be achieved, amendment of federal constitutions requires the consent of both orders of government.
- While in the United States the *Articles of Confederation* were almost immune to change by virtue of the unanimity requirement typical of confederal systems, the federal constitution that replaced the *Articles* was made very difficult to change. Super majorities and multiple majorities ensure that only those proposals with a very high degree of support get through, while at the same time the ability of any one state to veto change is abolished. In over 200 years of operation, only a very few changes have been made to the federal system in the United States.
- In Canada, The *BNA Act* neglected to include an amending procedure at all, relying on its status as an imperial statute both for its superiority and for its amendment via ordinary legislation of the

British Parliament. Contested conventions of amendment grew up over the years, creating the circumstances for the highly contested "patriation" initiative in 1982. Patriation included substantial changes through the insertion of the Charter of Rights and Freedoms and entrenched a long-discussed amending formula.

- The existence of a truly federal upper house in Germany makes possible a federal amendment procedure that does not involve the *Länder* directly. Instead, the representatives of the *Länder* governments in the *Bundesrat* have a direct co-decision right.
- The most anomalous case is the EU. It has a more confederal-style treaty basis but has now moved away from a strict unanimity requirement under the constitutional treaty in a way that is more consistent with federalism.
- The Swiss and Australian constitutions go a step further than the others and require popular endorsement of amendment proposals. In Switzerland, where this includes popular initiation and where direct democracy is an established practice, the referendum procedure has been consistent with change to a degree not experienced in Australia.
- Secession is a radical form of constitutional amendment that Canada has acknowledged is a legitimate and appropriate consideration in a democratic federation. Acknowledging that possibility allows for its constitutionalization: for the establishment of a set of procedures that both open and constrain the opportunity for separation.

10 Judicial Review

As we noted in the previous chapter, federal systems require codified constitutions—constitutions superior to the normal processes of politics and law-making and able to demarcate the relationship between two contending levels of government. Without such a set of guarantees the idea of shared sovereignty would not be viable. Constitutions, in turn, require interpretation; there must not only be a set of rules binding the players, but an umpire to interpret and apply those rules. In the absence of a suitable alternative, that umpire has been a judicial one: a final court providing authoritative determination of constitutional meaning and constitutionality. The development of federalism has thus simultaneously meant the development of **judicial review**. Judicial review in turn has had a significant impact on the development of some of the most important federal systems. And thus, as Dicey saw it in a much-quoted assertion, "Federalism ... means legalism—the predominance of the judiciary in the constitution—the prevalence of a spirit of legality among the people."[1]

The fact that arm's-length constitutional interpretation is such an important component of federal systems raises a number of analytical questions.

- *The political nature of constitutional law.* First of all, how did judicial review arise, and how do we deal with the fact that although they have become thoroughly "judicialized," constitutions are fundamentally different from other forms of law? As political agreements, their interpretation is inescapably a political matter, and thus for many commentators judicial review is not a necessary—and not a necessarily desirable—component of federalism.[2]
- *Varying reliance on the courts.* Second, why do some federations rely so much more on judicial resolution of jurisdictional issues than others? Dicey's legalism has not been universal: judicial review has always

---

1. Dicey, *An Introduction* 170.
2. For example, Paul Weiler, *In the Last Resort: A Critical Study of the Supreme Court of Canada* (Toronto, ON: Carswell/Methuen, 1974) 165–74.

been a far more prominent feature of English-speaking federalism than of European.

- *The significance of judicial review.* Third, to what extent should the courts be credited with (or blamed for) determining the way federal systems have evolved over the years? There have been many instances where commentators—usually critics—have explicitly or implicitly attributed decisive importance to judicial decisions in shaping federations. Others adopt a more sociological approach and argue that while paths sometimes diverge, the courts over time respond to underlying social and economic realities and play no shaping role over the medium to longer term. The strongest expression of this latter view is to be found in the commentaries of one of the best-known theorists of federalism, William Riker, who dismissed the "importance of utterances by judges" as "vastly overestimated" and argued that societies get the outcomes they demand.[3]
- *Judicial review and the erosion of federalism.* And fourth, if the courts have played an important role in shaping federal systems, have they done so in any particular direction? For some commentators, the answer is no, courts have dexterously and fairly balanced national and subnational interests, either in individual decisions or in the longer term effect of a series of decisions. For others the answer is yes, judicial interpretation has been a more insidiously centralizing force in the history of federal systems.

THE COURTS AND THE CONSTITUTION

Early federal constitutions made little provision for the problem of interpretation. Unless they made explicit provision to the contrary, though, it is a role that has been inevitably (but not automatically) assumed by the courts. While the term judicial review can have a broader meaning, for our purposes here it is taken to mean specifically *the practice by which an independent judiciary invalidates disputed legislative acts whenever it considers those acts to be in conflict with the constitution.* While a weak form of judicial review merely assesses whether legislative acts are being properly applied or administered, the term in this sense entails the much stronger role of judging whether those acts are themselves valid.[4] Judicial review occurs when the courts are given—or establish for themselves—a mandate to be the authoritative source of

---

3. Riker, "Federalism" 110.
4. Although presumably only in formal (i.e., legal or constitutional) terms, not in terms of their wisdom or justice. The latter might be called "strong" judicial review, the former "moderate." See Christopher Wolf, *The Rise of Modern Judicial Review: From Constitutional Interpretation to Judge-made Law,* rev. ed. (Lanham, MD: Rowman and Littlefield, 1994) 101.

constitutional interpretation. It makes the courts the 'guardians of the constitution.' The problem with this is that the courts purport to declare what the 'law' is when a constitution is much more than law. Under the guise of legalism, the courts are making what are unavoidably political judgements. Mindful of this, the South African Constitutional Assembly of 1994 deliberately assigned responsibility for jurisdictional matters to the upper house of Parliament, the National Council of the Provinces (NCOP), rather than to the Constitutional Court. In a move that underscored the nature of the conundrum involved, this choice was vetoed by the Court itself. "The Court seems to have accepted the proposition that it was a better guardian of provincial power than the NCOP would be. Yet there is good reason and comparative jurisprudence to believe that the opposite could be the case."[5] Monopolization of the authority of constitutional interpretation by the courts raises a number of hard questions about the methods and make-up of the judiciary.

Judicial Systems

Supreme Courts or Constitutional Courts?

The Americans pioneered a particular approach to judicial review. That approach was to embed constitutional responsibility in the normal judicial system. At the apex of that system, the US Constitution created a **supreme court**. The Supreme Court of the United States is the final appeal court of the American judicial system, with jurisdiction over the full range of federal law (though not over matters of state law). Cases work their way up as trial court decisions are appealed to higher courts until they reach the point where either their appeal is rejected or they are considered in the final court of appeal. This is the approach that was also taken in Canada, Australia, and India. In such a system, courts at all levels participate in the review function.

The European approach has been quite different: rather than embed constitutional responsibility in the normal legal system, specific **constitutional courts** were established to deal solely with issues directly related to constitutional matters. This approach, the Renner-Kelsen model, was pioneered for the Austrian Constitution of 1920 and has been widely followed in Europe (e.g., in Germany, Spain, Belgium, and the EU). It arose to fill a need created by the absence of a norm of judicial review within the existing judicial system as Austria was remade in federal form after defeat in World War I[6] and its adoption in the Federal Republic

---

5.   Haysom, "Final Features of the Federal Constitution" 517.
6.   Theo Öhlinger, "The Genesis of the Austrian Model of Constitutional Review of Legislation," and Georg Schmitz, "The Constitutional Court of the Republic of Austria 1918–1920," both in *Ratio Juris* 16:2 (June 2003). It is closely associated with the contribution of Austrian legal theorist and constitutional architect Hans Kelsen.

of Germany reflected the desire to escape from a system where courts merely administered laws—including vicious ones. In the new South Africa, the most recent federation to adopt this approach, the Constitutional Court model was insisted upon by the African National Congress (ANC) out of a desire to ensure that the power of constitutional interpretation was not monopolized by a narrow legal fraternity whose experience was with parliamentary supremacy rather than separation of powers and "that the old apartheid judges should not be custodians of the new democracy"[7]—concerns remarkably like those driving judicialization in postwar Germany. An additionally interesting aspect of the South African journey was the role of the Court in vetting the document by which it was constituted (see Figure 10.1).[8]

FIGURE 10.1

The South African Constitutional Court and the Constitution

South Africa's new post-apartheid Constitutional Court was given an unusual reflexive role in constituting the Constitution under which it was itself constituted. The interim Constitution of 1994 stipulated that the final Constitution had to be certified by the Court before it could come into effect. This has been seen as not only working to ensuring a greater adherence to principles of constitutionalism, but also as helping to break deadlocks arising out of the negotiations in the Constitutional Assembly. In 1996 a draft Constitution was submitted to the Court and subjected to the normal judicial process of legal representation and argument. In its judgement, the Court declined to certify the draft, citing a number of deficiencies ranging from insufficient entrenchment of rights to an insufficiently strong amendment procedure. A revised second draft was certified by the Court that same year.

Judicial Process

In federal systems, there are essentially two ways in which the behaviour of governments can be challenged before the courts. Either it is alleged that a law or other government action violates the constitutional division of powers, or it is argued that a law, while within the constitutional range of powers, violates other constitutional provisions such as individual rights and freedoms in particular. Cases of this latter kind do not affect the intergovernmental power balance directly, of course, but by finding for or against a government in question, supreme courts exercise considerable political power because they are actually telling a government how far it can go within its assigned constitutional rights.

In cases of conflict between two levels of government, most supreme or constitutional courts have direct or **original jurisdiction**—they do not

---

7. Patric Mzolisi Mtshaulana, "The History and Role of the Constitutional Court of South Africa," in Andrews and Ellman, eds., *The Post-Apartheid Constitutions* 535.

8. Christina Murray, "Negotiating Beyond Deadlock: From the Constitutional Assembly to the Court," and Carmel Rickard, "The Certification of the Constitution of South Africa," in Andrews and Ellman, *The Post-Apartheid Constitutions*.

wait for the case to reach them through the appeal process. In other cases, they exercise indirect jurisdiction as courts of **final appeal**. The process of admitting appellate cases is very selective. Typically, such a case will be heard when particularly important constitutional principles have been raised and when these principles have found two different interpretations at the lower courts.

Opinions and Judgements

All final courts of judicial review are composed of several judges, ranging in number from the handful who sat as the Judicial Committee of the Privy Council (JCPC), to the currently nine members of the US and Canadian Supreme Courts, to the 25 of the European Court of Justice. This means that the judgement in any case is the outcome of several opinions, opinions that may well be quite diverse. It is quite possible, then, that judicial decisions are carried on the basis of a narrow majority, with strong and substantial dissent from other members of the bench. And indeed, while decisions are sometimes unanimous, a number of landmark cases have been decided by single vote majorities. To confuse the issue further, individual judges may well give differing reasons for supporting the same general conclusion. And if that were not enough, opinions may well include not only the *ratio decidendi*, or the reasons for the decision, but also *obiter dicta*, or further—gratuitous—observations on the matter. Both *ratio* and *obiter* may be drawn upon in later judgements.

This diversity of views, this ambiguous message that courts may send, is entirely consistent with the intractably political nature of the task they face. The practice of releasing dissenting opinions has been an important element of judicial review in a number of countries, contributing to a broader and more open jurisprudence. Dissenting views may provide important reasoning for revised interpretations down the track.[9] Given, though, that the power of judicial review derives in no small part from the cogency with which it is executed, there is a natural tendency to suppress dissent on the bench. Courts speaking with one voice will have a greater impact than those speaking with many voices. Some final courts, therefore, conceal their diversity of views by issuing only a single, anonymous collective decision—as do the main constitutional courts in Europe today. It is no coincidence that during two of the most formative

---

9.   In the words of one US Supreme Court Chief Justice, "A dissent in a court of last resort is an appeal to the brooding spirit of the law, to the intelligence of a future day, when a later decision may possibly correct the error into which the dissenting judge believes the court to have been betrayed." C. Evans Hughes, quoted in Henry J. Abraham, *The Judicial Process*, 5th ed. (New York: Oxford University Press, 1998) 213.

periods of judicial review we shall examine below—the period when John Marshall was chief justice of the US Supreme Court and the period when the JCPC ruled on the Canadian Constitution—the single rather than the multiple voice ruling prevailed.

The Power of Judicial Review

Montesquieu characterized the power of the judiciary as "null," and Alexander Hamilton expressed a commonly-held assumption when he wrote in *Federalist* 78 that the judiciary would be the "least dangerous" of the three branches of government. The courts have neither will nor force, Hamilton argued. Unlike the legislature, they do not *make* laws or hold the power of the purse, and unlike the executive, they do not hold the power of the sword. Early constitutional thinkers, in other words, did not foresee the power that supreme courts would wield by assuming the inevitable task of interpreting often ambiguous constitutional meanings in societies where the rule of law had become firmly established. As one American justice famously said, "We are under a constitution, but the Constitution is what the judges say it is."[10] Later constitutional designers, such as those putting together the German Constitution of 1949, anticipated this reality by specifying the court's tasks in far more extensive detail. Supreme courts have not overshadowed the political process in all federations.

The powerful impact of judicial review on the trajectory of federal systems is reinforced by two particular features of these highest courts. First, supreme or constitutional courts have a unique ability to reverse previous judgements and introduce a new line or direction of interpretation—not infrequently using reasoning drawn from dissenting opinions in earlier cases. While strongly influenced by previous decisions, final courts are not bound by them; they respect *stare decisis*, or 'precedent,' but they are not captive to it. This is for the simple reason that there is no higher authority to overrule them for having wandered off the straight and narrow as there is for lower courts. In consequence, judicial review in federal systems tends to occur in quite identifiable phases as the court changes its complexion with new appointments and switches from one prevailing view to another over time.

This brings us to the second reason for the power of judicial review: there is little further recourse. What has been said with respect to the Canadian case well applies further afield. "There is an awful finality about judicial decisions, for there is no easy legislative override and constitutional amendments are almost impossible."[11] From time to time,

---

10. Chief Justice Hughes, quoted in Merlo John Pusey, *Charles Evan Hughes* (New York: Macmillan, 1951) 204.
11. Saywell, *The Lawmakers* 308.

judges do wash their hands of responsibility for altering the operation of federal constitutions by declaring that politicians and the public are welcome to correct the situation through the amendment process. Occasionally—but only very occasionally—corrective amendment has occurred.[12]

Decisions and Advice

In most instances, the courts render decisions on the basis of litigation that appears before them. That is to say, they pass judgement on a specific constitutional question arising from the application of an existing law to a specific situation. Courts are entirely reactive; they cannot initiate consideration of matters. Nor, generally, can their opinions be canvassed in advance of actions. Quite deliberately, courts typically do not dispense advice. The US Supreme Court declared early on that it would not do so, for fear of compromising its ability to make binding judgements should the matter appear before it. Significant exceptions to this exist, however—such as Canada, where the Supreme Court is required by statute to hear **reference cases,** or Germany where, under the constitutional provision for **abstract law control,** the Court will issue opinions on general constitutional questions.

If the line between formal judgements and advisory judgements represents one of the boundaries of judicial review, another is represented by the line between interpreting the law and interpreting convention. The nature of constitutions as more than law is reflected in the importance of the practices and understandings that inevitably constitute a crucial component of the framework of rules under which a political system operates. Courts may occasionally provide their interpretation of what those conventions might be; however, convention lies outside the boundaries of justiciability.

Establishment and Appointment: A 'Federal' Court?

Given this wide and far-reaching range of activities, often bordering on **activist** policy-making rather than a narrow and **strict** reading of the constitution, an important question is: who has the right to appoint the judges sitting on supreme or constitutional court benches? In principle, one would imagine that a court sitting in judgement on the division of powers between two co-sovereign orders of government ought to be

---

12. As it did early on in American constitutional history when the Eleventh Amendment was ratified in 1795, restricting the scope of the Supreme Court, in response to the Court's decision in *Chisholm v. Georgia* (1793) 2 U.S. 419. The Thirteenth and Fourteenth Amendments abolishing slavery may be seen as overturning *Dred Scott*; and the Sixteenth Amendment granting full powers of income tax to Congress was a direct response to the Supreme Court's adverse ruling in *Pollock* 1895 (see Chapter 11).

constituted in such a way as to ensure the necessary impartiality. This is not, however, typically the case. More often than not federal constitutions allocate this crucial judicial power to the national government, with the national government alone exercising the power of appointment. This is the case for the supreme courts of the United States, Canada, and Australia. The design of the US Supreme Court has been described in this respect as "careless." It was made subordinate to Congress in both its composition and its jurisdiction and given only indirect federal character.[13]

The one way in which the US Supreme Court was given some federal character was in the requirement that appointments be approved by the Senate, the states' house—a requirement that does not exist in the parliamentary federations of Australia and Canada. However, given the rather limited way that the US Senate functions as a states' house (see Chapter 7), this represents but a minor concession to the federal principle and is hardly sufficient to make the Court an impartial umpire. In Germany, where the upper house has a genuinely federal character, parliamentary appointment does act to give the Constitutional Court a truly federal basis. Finally, the most truly federal constitutional court would seem to be the European Court of Justice, which is composed of one member chosen by each EU member state for a fixed term.

The Effect of Judicial Review

Given that the judiciary have developed a far more important role than was originally envisaged, it is not surprising that a great deal has come to hinge on how the courts go about the task of construing the wording of constitutions, what methods and assumptions they use in sorting out ambiguities and applying general precepts to concrete cases, and whether there have been identifiable tendencies or biases in judicial review.

How should a Constitution be Interpreted?

There is no self-evidently correct or appropriate way to interpret a constitution, and there is certainly no agreed-upon way. One can identify a number of quite different approaches courts take to constitutional interpretation,[14] some with radically different implications. The first is the **original intent** or historical approach: interpret the constitution as meaning what its authors intended it to mean. This approach has the virtue of staying—or at least attempting to stay—true to the constitution

---

13. McDonald, *Novus Ordo Seclorum* 255–57. This carelessness was more understandable given that the practice of judicial review did not exist and was not accepted at the time.

14. See Philip Bobbit, *Constitutional Fate: Theory of the Constitution* (New York: Oxford University Press, 1982).

as a founding agreement. However, it has a number of drawbacks. These include disputes about what that original intent was, questions about the extent to which current generations should be bound by the decisions of previous generations, and practical concerns about anachronistic constraints limiting the ability of governments to cope with new circumstances.[15]

Similar in implication is the approach that seeks to interpret any particular section of the constitution in line with the spirit or structure of the overall document. If the document means to create a balanced federation, then the court must be mindful of that in defining the limits of any particular grant of power.

Diametrically opposed to these intentionalist philosophies of interpretation are what we might call the textual and the practical approaches. The textual or **literalist** approach argues that the constitution must be expected to speak for itself. Meaning cannot be imputed, and it was up to the founders to give their intentions clear and effective expression. This approach is well summarized by the insistence of an Australian chief justice that "There is no other safe guide to judicial decisions in great conflicts than a strict and complete legalism."[16] If this results in undesired outcomes, then it is up the people and their legislatures to make the desired corrections, not the courts.[17] The strength of this approach is that it sidesteps difficult questions about intention; its weakness is that it is not clear that there is any such thing as a purely 'legal' interpretation of a constitution.

Like the first approach, the last one looks outside the constitution for guidance. However, instead of looking backward to original intentions, it looks forward to current needs. In the practical or **progressive** approach, the constitution must be regarded as a "living tree" adapting and branching out to fit its changing circumstances.[18] This belief in consciously adapting the constitution to current needs through liberal interpretation, finally, places the judiciary at the edge of moderate judicial review and on the edge of usurping the legislative function.

---

15. On the elusiveness of intent and the importance of distinguishing between constitutional "meaning, intention, and understanding" in the American founding, see Jack N. Rakove, *Original Meanings: Politics and Ideas in the Making of the Constitution* (New York: Knopf, 1996).

16. Sir Owen Dixon at his swearing in, in the *Commonwealth Law Reports* 85 (1952): xiv.

17. As Justice Isaacs asserted, writing for the majority in the High Court of Australia judgement in the Engineers' case, *Amalgamated Society of Engineers v. Adelaide Steamship* (1920) 28 CLR 129.

18. The "living tree" metaphor was used by Lord Sankey of the Judicial Committee of the Privy Council in *Edwards v. Attorney-General of Canada* (1930) AC 124.

Perverse Outcomes?

One of the recurrent themes of judicial review is the way that constitutional interpretation has run counter to the original intentions of constitutional design. In the United States and Australia, where the intention was to limit central power by means of strict enumeration, the courts have supported centralization by giving broad interpretations to implied powers contained in general clauses. In Canada and India, on the other hand, where the original intention was to limit subnational powers, these have been interpreted more generously and at the expense of central power.

Insidious Centralization?

In a good range of cases, it is possible to detect a general trend of judicial centralization, whereby the courts have sanctioned a long-term drift of power toward the national government. This is consistent with the view that "constitutional review by the highest courts in federal systems has been a principal device of centralized policymaking."[19] One analysis argues that "There appear to be no exceptions to the centralist theory of the judicial function."[20] According to this argument, the centralizing impact of supreme courts is institutionally determined. Established, appointed, and even possibly coerced by central governments, they will either voluntarily subscribe to a nationally oriented vision or, when they deviate from that, be intimidated into conforming.

The obvious counter-example is Canada, where as we just noted, judicial interpretation implemented a substantial correction to the centralist design of the federation in its formative years. However, there is an exceptional feature to judicial review in Canada that resolves this apparent contradiction. In Canada's formative years, the JCPC in London exercised the judicial review function, and its institutional allegiance was to the British Empire, not to the Government of Canada.[21] In both its brief period of early independence, and in the period since the imperial tie was cut, the Supreme Court of Canada has been much more centralist in its jurisprudence.[22] Significantly, both the Australians and

---

19. Martin Shapiro, *Courts: A Comparative Political Analysis* (Chicago, IL: University of Chicago Press, 1981) 55.
20. André Bzdera, "Comparative Analysis of Federal High Courts: A Political Theory of Judicial Review." *Canadian Journal of Political Science* 26:1 (1993): 29.
21. A reality made particularly clear in the case of *Nadan v. The King* (1926) AC 482, where the decision was deliberately made to conform to perceived British interests *vis-à-vis* Ireland. See Jacqueline D. Krikorian, "British Imperial Politics and Judicial Independence: The Judicial Committee's Decision in the Canadian Case *Nadan v. The King*," *Canadian Journal of Political Science* 33:2 (2000).
22. Saywell, *The Lawmakers* 34 and 274–75.

the Indians rejected the idea that the JCPC would be the arbiter of their federal systems and chose to keep constitutional interpretation at home. In the Indian case, this was "because of the experience that other Dominions, particularly Canada, had had with judgements of the Privy Council going against the wishes of the framers."[23]

THE UNITED STATES: INVENTION AND LIMITS OF JUDICIAL REVIEW

As the pioneer of both modern state federalism and judicial review, the United States represents a particularly instructive case. Exploring some of the watershed decisions in Supreme Court jurisprudence provides insights of more general value both into the relationship between those making the law and those applying, interpreting, and judging the law and into the enormous scope for interpretation that a division of powers creates. For some time now, the role of the US Supreme Court in adjudicating the division of powers between Congress and the states has been overshadowed by its role in judging the constitutional power of American governments over their citizens. However, recent changes in the orientation of the Court have led to a reconsideration of prevailing interpretations of the federal system.

Judicial interpretation of the US Constitution has revolved around a small number of key clauses in the list of powers assigned to Congress. We recall from Chapter 6 that the US division of powers followed the single exhaustive list approach, with plenary residual power left to the states as was made explicit in the Tenth Amendment. The sweeping centralization of American federalism sanctioned by the Court has been justified in large part on the basis of Congress's power to regulate commerce among the states and to provide for the general welfare. In addition, the necessary-and-proper clause has been used to sanction a wide interpretation of the enumerated powers, while the supremacy clause has been used to elbow state laws aside when Congress has decided to legislate ("pre-emption").

Among the questions at issue have been how widely the "commerce" net can be cast, where the line between commerce *among* the states and commerce *within* a state should be drawn, and what constitutes necessary and proper. Interpretation has been key to national policy-making in areas already a province of government but left to the states when the Constitution was composed—such as policing. And it has also been crucial to extending national jurisdiction over issues—such as environmental protection—scarcely imagined in the 1780s.

---

23. Austin, *The Indian Constitution* 171n.

Origins of Judicial Review

In pioneering the codified constitution and inventing modern federalism, the Americans also pioneered judicial review. Judicial review did not develop automatically, though; nor was it uncontested. After a decade of constitutional experimentation and learning at the state level, the Americans drafted and ratified their second constitution in a context where judicial review was quite novel, if not still alien—alien both to the influential concept of separation of powers as articulated by Montesquieu (since it meant that the judicial branch intruded upon the legislative branch) and alien to their native ideas of the paramount status of the legislature as the voice of the people.[24] Its gradual acceptance reflected a growing sense that the courts might act as a proxy for the people as against their governors, whoever those governors might be.[25] Despite this hesitant start, judicial review became one of the most prominent and defining features of the American system.

The Reticence of the Constitution

Article III, Section 1 of the US Constitution stipulates that "The judicial Power of the United States, shall be vested in one supreme Court, and in such inferior Courts as Congress may from time to time ordain and establish." Section 2 lists the various areas within which the Supreme Court exercises jurisdiction. Notable by its absence from that list is interpretation of the Constitution or the assessment of the constitutionality of congressional, presidential or state government acts. In other words, the US Constitution created a separate judicial power but did not assign responsibility for constitutional interpretation to that body. For those who advocated a vigorous central government—the "Federalists"—this was self-evidently a function that should be exercised by the Supreme Court. For those defending states' rights—the "Antifederalists"—this was a function that should be exercised in a more popular and dispersed manner where the three branches have an equal role and quite possibly the state governments do too.

---

24. The 1784 New York case of *Rutgers v. Washington* is frequently cited as a turning point where a state judiciary expressly denied the rightfulness of judicial review while edging closer to such an action in its decision. Wood cites the 1787 North Carolina case of *Bayard v. Singleton* as the first instance of an American court invalidating an Act as unconstitutional. Wood, *The Creation of the American Republic* 460–61. On the latter, see Sylvia Snowiss, *Judicial Review and the Law of the Constitution* (New Haven, CT: Yale University Press, 1990).
25. Wood, *Creation of the American Republic* 453–54.

The Willingness of the Court: Marbury v. Madison

The Federalists not only carried the Constitution over the state-by-state ratification hurdle, but also captured office in the new American government they had created. They used this position to appoint fellow travellers to such important institutions as the Supreme Court, and by far the most significant of those appointments was John Marshall.

In 1803, the US Supreme Court under newly appointed Chief Justice John Marshall was confronted with a very delicate dilemma. The Antifederalist administration of Thomas Jefferson had recently taken office and refused to carry through with several judicial appointments that had been hurriedly signed and sealed in the last hours of the outgoing administration. In seeking a judicial order that his position be confirmed (a "writ of *Mandamus*"), one of these frustrated appointees, William Marbury, placed the Court in a difficult spot indeed. If it ruled in favour of Marbury, the Court faced the humiliation of being ignored by the administration. If to avoid that humiliation it ruled in favour of the new secretary of state, James Madison, the Court faced the humiliation of appearing spineless.

Marshall's resolution of that conundrum was a turning point in the development of federalism because it established irrefutably the essence of judicial review. He declared that under the *Judiciary Act*, Marbury had every right to a Court order in his favour. In the next breath, though, Marshall also declared that Congress had gone beyond its constitutional authority in granting the Court powers to issue such an order in the first place. The relevant sections of the *Judiciary Act* were unconstitutional. Where did the Supreme Court derive its authority to make such decisions of unconstitutionality? To answer that question, Marshall repeated the simple but compelling argument made by Alexander Hamilton in *Federalist 78*.[26]

First, he asserted that "an act of the legislature, repugnant to the Constitution, is void. This theory is essentially attached to a written constitution, and is consequently to be considered, by this Court, as one of the fundamental principles of our society."[27] Secondly, he asserted that "It is emphatically the province and duty of the judicial department to say what the law is." Finally, he completed the circle by asserting that the Constitution was law, and that "If two laws conflict with each other, the courts must decide on the operation of each." Marbury did not get his writ of *Mandamus*, but the US Constitution got its guardian. Justice Marshall had chosen his ground carefully, since the matter was

---

26. A view, importantly, that had been given judicial expression a few years earlier in a dissenting opinion by Justice James Iredell of the Supreme Court in *Calder v. Bull* (1798) 3 US 386.
27. *Marbury v. Madison* (1803) 5 US 137.

limited to the functioning of the Court itself,[28] but nonetheless he made the decisive breakthrough establishing implicitly that the Court would rule on questions of constitutionality in general.

Constitutional Intent, Constitutional Reality: The Enumerated Powers

For Marshall there were two steps to establishing a centralist reading of the potentially quite confederal US Constitution. The first was to establish the authority of the Supreme Court. This he had done with *Marbury*. The second was to use that authority to put his stamp on the way the grant of powers of Congress was construed. This he did with *McCulloch v. Maryland*.

The Facts

In 1816 Congress legislated to revive an earlier experiment by chartering the Second Bank of the United States (BUS). This national bank quickly established branches across the country, but in doing so, provoked the ire of various state-licensed banks. Prompted by one of those aggrieved competitors, the State of Maryland imposed a punitive tax on the BUS. Such a tax was unconstitutional, but the state argued that the BUS itself was unconstitutional. Who was right?

The Issues

Fundamental to the issue was the decision to divide powers by means of a single list that contained an exhaustive, or limiting, list of national powers and left everything else to the states. As Chief Justice Marshall himself noted in his decision, "This government is acknowledged by all to be one of enumerated powers. The principle, that it can exercise only the powers granted to it, [is] now universally admitted.... Among the enumerated powers, we do not find that of establishing a bank or creating a corporation."[29] On the face of it, the State of Maryland was correct: banks could only be chartered by the states, and thus the BUS was unconstitutional and in no position to challenge taxes imposed on it.

The Decision

This, however, was not the way Marshall saw things. His 1819 decision in the *McCulloch v. Maryland* case completely rewrote the way the relationship between enumerated and residual powers would work. The *intent* may have been for Congress's enumerated powers to be specific

---

28. See McDonald, *States' Rights and Union* 56–57.
29. *McCulloch v. Maryland* (1819) 17 US 316.

and limiting and for the states' residual power to be plenary, but what in the Constitution said this was to be so? Legally speaking, intent only matters in so far as it is translated into justiciable text. Article I, Section 8, concludes with the provision that Congress has the power "to make all laws necessary and proper for carrying into execution the foregoing powers." The creation of a national bank was interpreted as an **implied power** arising from such enumerated powers as coining money and regulating its value. This immediately begged the question of *how* "necessary and proper" was such an action. Marshall's response was that the clause does not require Congress to limit itself to legislation that is "*absolutely* necessary"; rather, it establishes a much lower hurdle.

But what about those boundaries protecting the residual powers of the states from such encroachment? Under the old *Articles of Confederation*, centralization was sternly checked by the opening clause that asserted in emphatic and unequivocal terms the sovereign superiority of the states. The BUS would not have stood a chance under that constitution. The Court had to deal with the fact that this clause had been transposed onto the new constitution as the Tenth Amendment. Marshall responded to this point again with a close textual analysis. Whereas the *Articles of Confederation* had reserved for the states all those powers "not expressly delegated to the United States," the Tenth Amendment merely says "not delegated." *Expressly* is a powerful modifier, and without it the Tenth Amendment is much less categorical than Article II of the old US confederacy. These may be lawyers' quibbles, perhaps, but they are of great consequence when lawyers are making the decisions— particularly when they are seeking a convenient peg on which to hang their own views.

Limits of Judicial Review

The subtlety of Marshall's approach to judicial review in *Marbury v. Madison* helped the Court avoid a showdown with the political arm of government. When judicial review became more controversial or more ambitious, it soon confronted its limitations. Its next major invalidation of an Act of Congress—the notorious *Dred Scott* slavery decision of 1857—so discredited the Court and was so decisively erased by the Union victory in the Civil War that Congress was not subject to judicial challenge again for some time.[30]

---

30. In its *Dred Scott* decision, the Supreme Court handed down an inflammatory endorsement of slavery, declaring not only that slaves and their descendants could never be citizens of the United States, but that the legislation which maintained the fragile accord between free states and slave states (the Missouri Compromise) was invalid since it stipulated that certain of the states being newly admitted to the Union were to be free states and thereby denied rights of property. *Dred Scott v. Sandford* (1857) 60 U.S. 393.

Roosevelt's Recourse

The climactic attempt by the Supreme Court to curtail congressional power and maintain a balance in American federalism came in the 1930s, and in that clash the Court was also powerfully rebuffed. When they captured Congress and the White House, the Roosevelt Democrats used their position to launch an ambitious range of measures to combat the Great Depression. The Supreme Court, however, declared much of this New Deal legislation to be beyond Congress's authority under the Constitution, since it assumed wide-ranging powers to regulate work conditions and the operation of business. Whereas the Jefferson administration might simply have ignored an adverse decision in the *Marbury v. Madison* case, that was no longer an option now that the Supreme Court had stamped its authority on the US Constitution; instead, President Franklin Roosevelt opted for direct confrontation.

In taking on the recalcitrant justices, Roosevelt had a silence of the Constitution working in his favour—that "careless" drafting. The section on the judiciary says nothing about how many positions are to be on the bench of the Supreme Court. By threatening to use his power of appointment to "pack the Court" (which, however, would have had to clear the Senate hurdle) and render the obstructive justices a minority on the bench, the president made it clear there was a limit to the power of judicial review. The prudent justices quickly managed to come up with a much more expansive interpretation of the commerce power[31] and by 1941 signalled their full retreat from judicial review of congressional Acts.[32]

A One-sided Umpire?

The nature of judicial appointment being what it is, Roosevelt was able to stack the Supreme Court with more sympathetic justices in the fullness of time. This helped perpetuate an expansive interpretation of Congress's enumerated powers while also opening the way for the Court to play a much more active role in protecting individual rights. Further Democratic Party appointments in the 1960s created the strongly

---

31. Chief Justice Marshall had first indicated the scope and significance of the commerce power in his decision overturning state regulation of transport across state boundaries in the important 1824 case *Gibbons v. Ogden* 22 US 1. Beginning with the 1895 case *United States v. E.C. Knight* (156 US 1) and continuing up to the 1935 *Schecter Poultry* (295 US 495) decision, the Court sought to draw a line between the production of a good (state matter) and its actual trade across state boundaries.

32. In *United States v. Darby* (1941) 312 US 100, where the Court upheld the *Fair Labor Standards Act* of 1938. See also *Wickard v. Filburn* (1942) 317 US 111, which was such a complete reversal of the previous interpretation of the commerce clause as to be almost a caricature.

rights-oriented Warren Court, reinforcing these trends. Abandoning any attempt to adjudicate the relationship between Congress and the states, the Court took the position that the commerce clause embraced largely whatever Congress said it embraced.[33] This could only represent a hollowing-out of federalism, since it effectively made one set of players also the umpire. Meanwhile, the Court turned its attention to the recalcitrant states, using the weight of the Fourteenth Amendment to force a range of political and legal reforms on them. The impact of this was, in an interesting way, double-edged. On the one hand, it represented a radical blow against state autonomy and federal diversity. On the other hand, though, the "Court did as much as any force in the land to rehabilitate the states and their localities" by forcing them to update their practices, thus laying the basis for a revival of their position in the federal system.[34]

New Federalism?

This approach lasted into the 1980s until eventually a string of conservative appointments changed the ideological orientation of the bench and brought federalism back into contention. Justice William Rehnquist, who had been writing dissenting opinions as a conservative in the minority, found himself writing Court judgements as the Chief Justice of a much more conservative bench in the 1990s. The new direction began with a case in 1991 when the Court articulated a clear manifesto of federal balance and in 1992 when it struck down parts of a congressional Act on the grounds that they "commandeered" the states and thus violated the Tenth Amendment.[35] While regarded by Jefferson as the cornerstone of the Constitution, the Tenth Amendment had been fatally weakened by *McCulloch* as we saw above, and since the 1930s it has largely been a dead letter. In its controversial *United States v. Lopez* decision of 1995,[36] the Court struck down an Act of Congress on the grounds that it exceeded Congress's enumerated powers in the Constitution. The story was this. A student brought a handgun to Edison High School in San Antonio, Texas, with the intent of selling it

33. See the decision in the Ollie's Barbecue case, *Katzenbach v. McClung* (1964) 379 US 294, where application of the *Civil Rights Act* was upheld under the commerce clause. The Court declared that "where we find that the legislators, in light of the facts and testimony before them, have a rational basis for finding a chosen regulatory scheme necessary to the protection of commerce, our investigation is at an end." This approach underpinned the Court's decision in the 1985 case *Garcia v. San Antonio Metropolitan Transit Authority* (469 US 528) to reject arguments that state authorities were constitutionally immune from national regulatory legislation.
34. David B. Walker, *The Rebirth of Federalism: Slouching toward Washington*, 2nd ed. (New York: Chatham House, 2000) 178.
35. *Gregory v. Ashcroft* (1991) 501 US 452; *New York v. United States* (1992) 505 US 144.
36. See Kenneth T. Palmer and Edward B. Laverty, "The Impact of United States v. Lopez on Intergovernmental Relations: A Preliminary Assessment," *Publius* 26:3 (1996).

to another student involved in a gang war. He was arrested, charged, and convicted for violating the national *Gun-Free School Zones Act* of 1990, an action that superseded equivalent charges made under state law. The conviction was finally overturned by a 5:4 decision of the Supreme Court. Writing for the majority, Chief Justice Rehnquist found that the *Act* was unconstitutional in that it did not constitute a matter relating to Congress's authority under the commerce clause.

Why was the *Gun-Free School Zones Act* justified under the commerce clause in the first place? The answer is expediency. Congress had decided to assume responsibility for regulating the presence of firearms on school properties across the country. However, Congress was aware that it did not have the constitutional authority to do that. Such regulation amounts to an act of policing which is, at least within the boundaries of one state, entirely a residual power of the states. So the *Gun-Free School Zones Act* was passed as part of Congress's power to regulate economic activities. While the task of differentiating between those commercial acts that are local in nature and those that are interstate is inevitably arbitrary, differentiating between commercial acts and those that really are not commercial in nature at all is much easier.[37] Congress had put the Court in a strong position to revive judicial review and perhaps American federalism.[38]

CANADA: IMPERIAL VERSUS HOME-GROWN JUDICIAL REVIEW

As we saw in Chapter 9, Canada is another case of a federation where formal constitutional amendment has played little role in its evolution. It is also another case of a federation where that role has been played much more vigorously by the courts. Particularly in its early years, judicial interpretation accomplished a radical reinterpretation of the original design. More recently, judicial interpretation has played a reinvigorated role with the inclusion of the Charter of Rights and Freedoms in the *Constitution Act 1982*.

Judicial Review in the Constitution

The *BNA Act* of 1867 was notably incomplete as a constitution in several respects. Not only did it fail to lay down any amending rules—

37. As the Court noted in its ruling, "the possession of a gun in a local school zone is in no sense an economic activity that might, through repetition elsewhere, have such a substantial effect on interstate commerce. Section 922(q) is a criminal statute that by its terms has nothing to do with 'commerce' or any sort of economic enterprise, however broadly those terms are defined."

38. Though for a different view, see Robert F. Nagel, *The Implosion of American Federalism* (New York: Oxford University Press, 2001).

as we noted in Chapter 9—it also made no provision for judicial review. Nor did it insist upon a separation of powers between the judicial branch and the rest of government or even assert its own supremacy. Section 101 did say that the Parliament *could* establish a "General Court of Appeal for Canada," but the Supreme Court of Canada was not created until 1875. Moreover, the Supreme Court has not, for much of its life, actually been supreme. At British insistence, the final authority on Canadian constitutional matters until 1949 was the JCPC in London, a legal board that acted as the source of judgement for the Crown on empire matters. At least, though, there was no obstacle to judicial review even though the practice was completely alien to British conventions of parliamentary supremacy. As a statute, the *BNA Act* would automatically be interpreted and applied by the courts; as an Imperial statute, the *BNA Act* would override local laws and thus be superior to the ordinary legislation of Canadian governments.[39]

We recall from Chapter 6 that by sharp contrast with the United States, the Canadian Constitution was designed with a powerfully centralist bias, particularly as embodied in the granting to Parliament of general and residual powers but also in granting broad powers over economic matters and criminal law.[40] The challenge faced by those sitting in judgement on constitutional issues in Canada was how in particular to reconcile Parliament's broad grant of residual authority and economic powers with federalism. The list of Parliament's powers in Section 91 establishes a general authority "to make laws for the Peace, Order, and good Government of Canada" (the POGG clause). Among the enumerated powers is Parliament's potentially sweeping authority to legislate for "The Regulation of Trade and Commerce." It is worth contrasting the unqualified grant of power over trade and commerce given to the Canadian Parliament with the much more cautious and 'federal' grant of power given to Congress to regulate international and interstate commerce and hence by implication *not* commerce within any one state.

Imperial Responsibility for Judicial Review

As soon as the *BNA Act* came into force, it fell to the provincial superior courts to undertake judicial review of provincial and national legislation

---

39. Its superiority as an Imperial statute was made explicit by passage in the same year of the *Colonial Laws Validity Act* which made any colonial legislation repugnant to British law invalid. Weiler, *In the Last Resort* 165. A supremacy clause was eventually inserted into the Canadian Constitution as s.52(1) of the *Constitution Act 1982*.

40. Also see Frederick Vaughan, *The Canadian Federalist Experiment: From Defiant Monarchy to Reluctant Republic* (Montreal, QC and Kingston, ON: McGill-Queen's University Press, 2003) 67.

in light of the new Constitution. For a brief period after its establishment in 1875, the Supreme Court of Canada acted as the supreme court of Canada. However, it was soon superseded in that role once the process of appeals to the JCPC got underway. Until the JCPC heard its final appeal in 1954 it was in Britain, not in Canada, that the meaning of the Canadian Constitution was determined. Throughout the formative years of Canadian federalism, the JCPC substantially reversed the intended meaning of the division of powers and the pattern of interpretation initiated by Canadian courts,[41] minimizing the plenary power of Parliament and carving out clear jurisdiction for the provinces. The British law lords, it seems, had no intention of allowing the creation of a strong and sovereign central government for what they still regarded as part of their colonial empire.

Breathing Life into Canadian Federalism

In a series of decisions between 1883 and 1925, the JCPC declared that the provinces were to be sovereign, not subordinate, entities and provided a reinterpretation of the division of powers consistent with such a premise.[42] This was accomplished by two means. One was to insist that POGG could not be interpreted as a plenary grant of power, because to do so would be to nullify Canadian federalism.[43] Instead, the JCPC ruled, the POGG clause would have force only in exceptional circumstances: either when a national emergency existed or when the matter at hand had a truly national dimension.[44] That this might be an exercise in creative jurisprudence departing from both the intentions and the letter of the Constitution was of little concern to the British law lords, who saw their task as being to "breath life into Canadian federalism."[45]

The Hard Rock of Provincial Powers

The other interpretive means used by the JCPC to breathe constitutional life into Canadian federalism was to consider the scope of such important Dominion powers as trade and commerce in light of the granting to the provinces jurisdiction over "property and civil rights." The conflict between judicial review and national policy-making came to a head in Canada—just as it had in the United States—over ambitious legislative programs to tackle the Great Depression. As far as the JCPC was concerned, these regulatory and social measures trespassed upon provincial

---

41. Saywell, *The Lawmakers* 34.
42. Beginning with *Hodge v. The Queen* (1883) 9 App. Cas. (P.C.) 117 and culminating in *Toronto Electricity Commissioners v. Snider* (1925) AC 396 40.
43. Lord Watson in the Local Prohibition case, *AG for Ontario v. AG for Canada, 1896.*
44. Lord Haldane in the 1922 *Board of Commerce* case.
45. Lord Watson's phrase, quoted by Saywell, *The Lawmakers* 121.

jurisdiction over property and civil rights, jurisdiction that in their view took priority over any of Parliament's powers to legislate for the peace, order and good government of Canada or to regulate trade and commerce. Furthermore, the JCPC rejected attempts to follow the American lead and use the spending power as a way of circumventing the division of powers.[46] One could be excused for wondering if it was the Canadian and not the US Constitution that had the Tenth Amendment guaranteeing the rights of the states.[47]

Finally, the JCPC rejected any idea that the Dominion's treaty power, Section 132, allowed it to legislate in areas of provincial competence by virtue of having undertaken international obligations dealing with those matters.[48] Here, though, the parallel with the United States ends. The Canadian government was in no position to 'pack' the JCPC in the way that Roosevelt could with the US Supreme Court. The Macdonald vision of a *faux* federation drifting happily toward unitary government was not to be.

Patriation of the Review Function

Judicial review was patriated in 1949 when the Parliament of Canada passed legislation abolishing appeals to the JCPC. This move was driven in considerable part by perceptions of the JCPC's decentralist bias, perceptions that had been strongly reinforced by its invalidation of the New Deal program. Abolition of appeals to the JCPC was contested by several provinces but upheld on appeal to the JCPC itself.[49] The Supreme Court of Canada was set up as a court functioning under central government aegis and with very limited concessions to federalism (see Figure 10.2), and thus the rupture was a radical one, with considerable potential for

---

46. In ruling that the *Employment and Social Insurance Act* was *ultra vires*, the JCPC made clear that in its view such use of the spending power was a constitutional means to an unconstitutional end. "If on the true view of the legislation it is found that in reality and in pith and substance the legislation invades civil rights within the Province, or in respect of other classes of subjects otherwise encroaches upon the provincial field, the legislation will be invalid." *Attorney-General of Canada v. Attorney-General of Ontario* 1937.

47. Saywell, *The Lawmakers* 183.

48. The Labour Conventions case, *Attorney-General of Canada v. Attorney-General of Ontario* 1937.

49. Ontario, British Columbia, and New Brunswick, supported by Québec, went to the JCPC with an appeal against the decision of the Supreme Court agreeing to the legislation to abolish such appeals. Manitoba and Saskatchewan supported the legislation. The JCPC ruled that with the passage of the *Statute of Westminster* in 1931, the Government of Canada was free to disassociate itself from Britain in this way and thus gracefully removed itself from the scene. See *Attorney-General of Ontario v. Attorney-General of Canada* 1947.

altering the orientation of Canadian federalism. While it was not accompanied by a sudden break in the pattern of constitutional interpretation, it did open the way for a succession of decisions that added up to an unmistakable return to a more centralist orientation.

The Weight of Precedent?

Change was unlikely to come rapidly. A particular interpretation of the division of powers and a formidable body of precedent had become established under the rule of the JCPC. In 1952, aeronautics was accepted as a national responsibility under the "national dimensions" test of the POGG clause.[50] In 1959, interpretation of the Trade and Commerce clause was significantly broadened to encompass intraprovincial matters.[51] In 1967, Parliament's jurisdiction over offshore minerals was upheld under the POGG clause.[52] In 1975, sweeping wage-and-price control legislation was upheld under the national emergency test of the POGG— though the government refrained from making a substantial claim for national powers in this area.[53] In 1978 and 1979, provincial jurisdiction over natural resources was made subject to the Trade and Commerce power insofar as those products were destined for outside markets.[54] In 1997 and 2002 respectively, environmental protection and gun control regulation were sustained as valid exercises of Parliament's criminal law

FIGURE 10.2
How 'Federal' is the Supreme Court of Canada?

As prescribed by the *Supreme Court Act*, there are nine judges on the bench of the Supreme Court of Canada; they are appointed by the governor-general "in Council" (hence by the prime minister); and their tenure is limited to 75 years of age. The *Supreme Court Act* requires that three of the nine judges come from Québec with its distinctive civil law system, and the provision of a quorum of five judges allows that Québec civil law cases can be heard by a panel with a majority of judges from that system.

Beyond that, however, there are no constitutional or statutory requirements to give the Court a federal character, and the exclusion of Parliament and the provincial governments from the appointment process has been a source of criticism. However, by convention, the other six judges are appointed according to a regional formula—three from Ontario, two from the west, and one from Atlantic Canada. In addition, functional bilingualism is expected from all judges, and the position of Chief Justice normally alternates between anglophone and francophone judges.

---

50. *Johanneson v. West St. Paul* 1952.
51. The Court refused leave to appeal the Manitoba decision in *Regina v. Klassen* that the power could extend to trade that was entirely within a province.
52. In *Reference re Offshore Mineral Rights of British Columbia*.
53. In *Reference re Anti-Inflation Act*.
54. In the *Canadian Industrial Gas and Oil v. Government of Saskatchewan* (1978) and *Central Canada Potash Co. Ltd. and Attorney-General of Canada v. Government of Saskatchewan* (1979) cases.

power notwithstanding the absence of explicit jurisdiction in those substantive fields.[55]

The Charter

Entrenchment of the Charter of Rights and Freedoms in the Canadian Constitution via the *Constitution Act 1982* has been of far-reaching consequence for the legal fabric of the Canadian federal system. Judicial interpretation and review in the American case slowly but steadily shifted from the adjudication of the proper exercise of powers to the protection of individual rights. The late adoption of such a bill of rights in the Canadian case changed the main thrust of judicial interpretation and review with a bang.

Balancing Rights

In scope and dimension, the Charter goes far beyond a conventional bill of rights in that it contains sections on fundamental freedoms as well as democratic, legal, mobility, and language rights. Its most peculiar feature from a comparative perspective is Section 33, the notwithstanding clause, by which Parliament or a provincial legislature can override three parts of the Charter—fundamental freedoms, legal rights, and equality rights—for a renewable five-year term.[56]

The main intention of these provisions became immediately clear as did the reasons for Québec's objection. The Supreme Court struck down that part of a Québec language law forcing anglophone parents moving into the province to have their children educated in French as a violation of the Charter's minority language provisions. It also struck down a sign law forcing anglophone businesses in the province to display their shop signs in French only. In this latter instance, however, the Court saw this as a violation of freedom of expression, and the Québec government therefore could invoke the notwithstanding clause, pass a different language bill, and continue the sign requirement in modified form. The notwithstanding clause seeks to balance individual and collective rights, constitutional and legislative supremacy.

According to one observer, there is something intrinsically democratic about "declining to give judges the last word on fundamental rights." Moreover, the periodic review requirement "imposes an obligation of deep deliberation over political choices that may conflict with Charter rights."[57] Such deliberation, aiming at "getting along" rather than "getting

---

55. In the cases of *Regina v. Hydro-Quebec 1997* and *Reference re: Firearms Act 2000*.

56. Thus democratic, mobility, or language rights are excluded.

57. Melissa Williams, "Toleration, Canadian-Style: Reflections of a Yankee-Canadian," in Ronald Beiner and Wayne Norman, eds., *Canadian Political Philosophy* (Don Mills, ON: Oxford University Press, 2001) 217.

it right," in turn appears as intrinsically federalist in the sense that it designates as the essence of politics an ongoing commitment to negotiated compromise rather than to the final adjudication of rights.[58] In this view, instead of regarding the notwithstanding clause as a flaw in constitutional design, it can be appreciated as expression of a level of political maturity beyond conventional federal systems. Whether it will actually be used in any regular or widespread fashion or will prove to be something of a "paper tiger" remains to be seen.[59]

Impact

The Charter has not turned Canada into an American-type litigation society, at least not yet. While minority groups have welcomed the opportunity to have their quests for substantive equality affirmed, governments have for the most part exercised litigious restraint. The main reason may be found in the continuing strong tradition of parliamentary sovereignty.

Prior to 1982, constitutional reference cases were prime instruments of constitutional interpretation and review. With the insertion of the Charter in the 1982 constitutional package, they have lost much of their exclusivity because constitutional issues now became routinely interpreted, albeit indirectly, in rights-based cases coming before the Supreme Court. On the basis of charter rights, the Supreme Court invalidated 23 national and 18 provincial statutes during the first ten years of their operation. While most of the national invalidations concerned matters of legal procedure, the provincial ones were "more substantive in nature, eight of them involving minority language rights, and most frequently in Québec."[60]

There is no doubt that the Charter has led to a certain degree of "Americanization" in Canadian constitutional jurisprudence.[61] It was intended to curb provincialist aspirations, and it did that because, as in the American case, individual rights protection typically affects the traditional catalogue of subnational powers more strongly than it affects national powers.

GERMANY: PRAGMATIC LEGALISM

If the United States is the prime example of a litigation society, Germany definitely qualifies as the almost opposite extreme of a regulation society.

---

58. Williams, "Toleration" 218.
59. See Howard Leeson, "Section 33, The Notwithstanding Clause: A Paper Tiger?," in Peter Russell and Paul Howe, eds., Choices 6:4 (2000) Institute for Research in Public Policy.
60. Rand Dyck, Canadian Politics: Critical Approaches, 2nd ed. (Scarborough, ON: Thompson Nelson, 1996) 115.
61. Dyck, Canadian Politics 113–15.

We have encountered the difference already in the Chapter 6 discussion of the division of powers. The Americans drafted a short document with general contours and left most of the details in the hands of politicians, citizens, and, increasingly, judges. By comparison, the designers of the much more extensive West German Constitution intended to create a document that would leave open to chance as little as possible. We have also encountered the difference in the Chapter 7 discussion of different patterns of dual representation.

German political culture evolved from a tradition of statist legalism rather than individual liberalism. This preference for intergovernmental accommodation rather than competition goes back to the Imperial federation in the late nineteenth century, as do the social policies that are regulatory and corporatist rather than driven by the market and by industrial conflict. After the disastrous experience with unfamiliar and unrehearsed party competition in the Weimar Republic, and emerging from the abyss of Nazi totalitarianism, the postwar constitution was intended to provide Germans with a detailed and unambiguous set of rules.

Legal Positivism and Beyond

Germany shares with other continental European societies a tradition of codified rather than common law.[62] This means that the legal system does not evolve as 'judge-made' law—through case law and precedent—but instead remains tied to a firm set of codes and statutes that can be changed only politically by the legislative power. There has always been, in other words, significantly less room for judicial interpretation than in Anglo-American common law systems. Law is considered to be 'state-made,' and the role of the courts is only to apply this law to cases and issues before them. Indeed, judicial review was not only foreign, it was forbidden. "From 1780 in Germanic states and from 1791 in France, judicial interpretation of statutes was explicitly prohibited by constitutions, and penalties were prescribed in the penal codes for any transgression."[63] This tradition was reinforced by the delayed establishment of democratic rule; only a constitution based on the consent of the people can assume a position superior to government.[64]

Legal Positivism

From this conception of law stems an historical predisposition for **legal positivism** in Germany. This means that the law is taken at face value

---

62. See David P. Conradt, *The German Polity* (New York: Longman, 2001) 228–29.

63. Alec Stone, "The Birth and Development of Abstract Review: Constitutional Courts and Policymaking in Western Europe," *Policy Studies Review* 19:1 (1990): 82.

64. Snowiss, *Judicial Review* 2–3.

and its meaning not questioned. And since it is state-made alone, and therefore not supposed to contain metaphysical elements of legal justice beyond the state, be they natural law or fundamental human rights, the loyal administration of such law cannot challenge state authority. This allowed German courts to adjudicate monstrous Nazi laws with the same level of conscientious diligence as they had administered the laws of the previous democratic Weimar Republic—they were following a broad European tradition of conceiving a strict separation of powers between the legislative and judicial functions of government. Legislatures make law; courts declare the law; and for courts to alter or question the law would be to usurp the legislative function.[65]

Constitutional Adjudication and Judicial Review

Within these limits, there was some scope for courts to play a role in constitutional adjudication between governments within a federation or between government agencies within any jurisdiction. Thus, Germany has a long tradition, going well back into the confederal period of the Holy Roman Empire, of using a special high court to settle intergovernmental disputes.[66] The stillborn liberal constitution of 1849—the Frankfurt Constitution—expanded on this tradition to move in the direction of judicial review. However, the autocratic Imperial federation of 1871 put a stop to these developments and left constitutional interpretation entirely in the hands of the upper house of Parliament. Neither the requisite constitutional supremacy, nor the requisite separation of judicial power, nor the requisite democratic foundation were present.[67] Under the democratic Weimar Constitution, judicial adjudication was reintroduced, and it was then for the first time that German courts moved to expand their role and assert a judicial review power in the spirit of *Marbury v. Madison* by striking down parliamentary acts as unconstitutional. Unlike *Marbury v. Madison*, though, this was done with a deeply conservative spirit hostile to the entire regime,[68] and thus—perhaps like *Dred Scott*—served not to strengthen but to discredit judicial review.

The Coming of the Constitutional Court

When the West German state was reconstituted in 1949 as a democratic polity, therefore, the constitutional designers were very much concerned

---

65. Donald P. Kommers, *Judicial Politics in West Germany: A Study of the Federal Constitutional Court* (Beverly Hills, CA: Sage, 1976) 35–36.
66. Kommers, *Judicial Politics* 30.
67. Werner Heun, "Supremacy of the Constitution, Separation of Powers, and Judicial Review in Nineteenth-Century German Constitutionalism," *Ratio Juris* 16:2 (2003).
68. Kommers, *Judicial Politics* 40.

with establishing a legal order tied to principles of democracy that could no longer be changed politically and at the same time would find judicial support before the courts.[69] Judicial review was embraced, but a scepticism about the reliability and aptitude of the regular judiciary reinforced the broader sense that judicial review ought to be conducted by a special court established for that purpose. Thus, following the Austrian model, a federal constitutional court, the *Bundesverfassungsgericht*, was newly established as the final authority on German democratic constitutionality and given a clear mandate to assert the supremacy of the Constitution.

The Federal Constitutional Court

Contrary to the appointment practice in most other federal systems, Germany's constitutional guardians are elected by a complex procedure requiring substantial degrees of interparty cooperation and compromise. Half of the 16 judges are elected by a committee proportionally composed of members of the *Bundestag*. The election of the other half requires a two-thirds majority in the *Bundesrat*. All judges are firmly appointed to one of two "senates" (or benches). The first senate deals mainly with basic rights issues, the second with jurisdictional conflicts— hence their election by the house of the states. Judges are elected for a 12-year term, which may be cut short by mandatory retirement at age 68. They cannot be re-elected.

The Adoption of Judicial Review

The propensity for legal positivism in the German juridical tradition left little room for judicial interpretation and review. The grotesque administration of legalized injustice by German courts during the Nazi years was very much on the minds of postwar (West) Germany's constitutional framers. And, indeed, they proceeded with the creation of a Constitutional Court whose powers would not only be unprecedented in the context of German political and legal history but would moreover go beyond those of constitutional courts in any other federal system— a supreme watchdog over the political system's adherence to the constitutional principles of *democracy, federalism,* and *social solidarity* which even the legislative sovereign was not allowed to touch.

The Process

Over the years, the Constitutional Court has commented and rendered decisions on more than half of the 151 articles contained in the

---

69. See Martin Borowski, "The Beginnings of Germany's Federal Constitutional Court," *Ratio Juris* 16:2 (2003).

Constitution.[70] As in other systems, most of these had to do with individual complaints about basic rights violations, complaints which are seldom successful but reach the court more frequently than elsewhere because it is the only court engaged in constitutional adjudication. Second in line and one of the more distinctive procedures of German constitutional adjudication is the **concrete law control**: if a lower court comes to the opinion that a law under consideration in a particular case might be unconstitutional, it has to halt its proceedings and refer that law to the Federal Constitutional Court for adjudication.

More relevant to the federal system but far less frequently invoked has been the **abstract law control** procedure that can be initiated upon request of the national government, a *Land* government, or by one-third of the members of the *Bundestag*. This referral procedure operates independently from any concrete case. A decision on the constitutionality of any national or *Land* law or regulation can be requested as well as ratification of laws pertaining to international treaties. This abstract law control has been used by both levels of government, but one of its main consequences has been careful constitutionality checks of all legislation at the drafting stage. Similarly relevant is the Court's adjudication of disputes between or within the branches of government. The *Bundesrat*, for example, may ask the Court to rule on the constitutionality of a law made by the *Bundestag* alone when it thinks that such a law requires its approval. Similarly, the *Bundestag* may call upon the Court when the government makes an executive decision which in the opinion of the Parliament (or, more likely the parliamentary opposition) requires its involvement and approval.

The Experience with Judicial Review

More than anything else the "eternity clause," which determined that the new Germany had to be a democracy, a federal state, and a social state, opened the gate to judicial review. In addition to policing the federal character of Germany, the Court has sought to enforce the Constitution's insistence that Germany also be a democratic and a social state.[71] The Court has consistently admonished both levels of government to be loyal to the federal order.

---

70. Conradt, *The German Polity* 236.
71. In 1956 the Court ruled that a political party intending to damage or overthrow the **democratic order** was unconstitutional and on that basis declared the Communist Party of West Germany dissolved; *BVerfGE* 5, 85 (1956). In 2000, the Court affirmed that it was in the constitutional spirit of a **social state** to compensate property losses of lower value (in the former Communist east) at a higher rate than those of higher value because the less wealthy could expect a higher level of social solidarity from such a state; *BVerfGE* 102, 254 (2000).

The first time the Court struck down an Act of the German Parliament was in the *Southwest* case of 1951. Affirming its mandate under the Constitution to exercise a judicial review function, the ruling of the Court was notable for declaring not only that a governmental action was unconstitutional, but that the section of the Constitution under which that action had been carried out was itself unconstitutional, since it conflicted with more fundamental assertions elsewhere in the Constitution.[72] When it struck down legislation creating a national broadcaster in the *Television* case of 1961, the Court declared that the enumerated national powers are exhaustive and limiting. Broadcasting is a cultural matter, and the Constitution assigns jurisdiction over cultural matters to the *Länder*. Moreover, the Court admonished German governments to conduct themselves in a federal manner, articulating the "comity" doctrine that:

> the unwritten constitutional principle of the reciprocal obligation of the federation and the states to behave in a pro-federal manner governs all constitutional relationships....[73]

In a number of more minor cases, the Court has attempted to guard *Länder* powers against continual encroachment. However, in some important areas it has notably failed to stem the tide of centralization. In one of those, it was called upon to assess the constitutionality of fiscal equalization measures that transfer significant funds from the more to the less affluent *Länder* (for which see Chapter 11). Although the Constitution requires equalization to be practised, it requires only a "reasonable" degree (Article 107); moreover, Article 109 grants the *Länder* budgetary autonomy. The Court acknowledged the legitimacy of the objections but judged the existing arrangements to be within the bounds of reasonableness.[74]

Eminently Political

The Federal Constitutional Court has brought German federalism into the era of judicial review and been active in policing the division of powers, typically with a view to maintaining the federal character of the state and providing some modest defence for the *Länder* against centralizing initiatives. It cannot be said, however, that the introduction

---

72. This and the following discussion is drawn from Donald P. Kommers, *The Constitutional Jurisprudence of the Federal Republic of Germany* (Durham, NC: Duke University Press, 1989) 75–78 and *passim*.
73. Quoted by Kommers, *Constitutional Jurisprudence* 82.
74. *Financial Equalization Case 1952*. Equalization should not go beyond the *Länder* average, and it should not substantially weaken a particular *Land's* financial strength.

of judicial review has significantly altered the dynamic of German federalism. Judicial review has not assumed the wildcard role it has played in the American, Canadian, or Australian systems. The potential may well have been there:

> The legalism inherent in German federalism contains the seeds of perpetual constitutional conflict... In truth, however, most federal-state conflicts never reach the Constitutional Court. They are usually resolved politically through the mechanisms of cooperative federalism....[75]

Germany's form of integrated federalism and its council-based federal chamber work to minimize the litigiousness of the system. Thus, it might be said that in at least one major federal system federalism does not mean legalism.

Perhaps the Court's biggest impact has, then, been one of omission rather than commission. In keeping with the more political rather than juridical approach to federal arbitration, the Court declined to adopt an active role in policing Article 72 under which a large amount of centralization has occurred. In response to this failure, the *Bundesrat* pressed for more legalism by sponsoring a constitutional amendment that tightened up the test for assumption of national responsibility and expressly mandated the Court to exercise a judicial review function in this regard. In the first test case under the revised Article 72, the Court disappointed German federalists yet again.[76] It rejected Bavaria's challenge and upheld national legislation in the area of aged care. Its one concession to the stronger emphasis on federal balance was to emphasize the distinction between national framework legislation and the right of the *Länder* to implement and administer the policy in their own way. The Federal Constitutional Court, it seems, is in no hurry to see Germany's model of administrative federalism altered in the direction of a more American-style division of powers.

THE EU: JUDICIAL CREATION OF SUPRANATIONALITY

Again the EU fits oddly into the comparative picture of federal systems. It is nevertheless an important case with a model character for other forms of supranational governance in a globalizing world. The issue is how intergovernmental treaty relations can become the basis for a more legally certain system of governance that is open to independent court adjudication. The European Court of Justice (ECJ) has played a crucial and sometimes unexpected role in this transformation process. Originally designed as a watchdog over the treaties, it has acquired direct

---

75. Kommers, *Constitutional Jurisprudence* 94.
76. 24 October 2002–2 BvF 1/01.

jurisdiction not only over member states but over corporations and individual citizen within these member states as well.

Towards Legal Certainty

The story of how this came about is a fascinating story of largely unintended consequences. The original designers of the European Community agreed that there had to be a court that would admonish member states to comply with treaty provisions. Much like the American case, few detailed thoughts were spent on how exactly the court would do that. And, as in the American case, it fell upon the court itself to seize the initiative and establish its authority as the ultimate arbiter and interpreter of European treaty law.

The European Court of Justice

Officially titled The Court of Justice of the European Communities, the ECJ goes back to the beginnings of the EU, having been established by the first treaty in 1952. In keeping with the confederal origins of the EU, the ECJ is composed of one judge chosen by each member country (now 25), thus making it, as we noted earlier, one of the most truly federal of such courts.[77]

The ECJ does not follow the supreme court practice elsewhere of issuing multiple or dissenting opinions; rather, it speaks with one voice and thereby increases the effect of its decisions. The ECJ, in other words, decides cases on the basis of one single judgement. It has been said that what in fact goes on during the judges' chamber deliberations behind closed doors "may be considered amongst the best-kept secrets in the Community."[78]

The bulk of cases reach the ECJ by process of referral from national courts dealing with specific issues within their country that raise questions of Community-wide application. Apart from approximately 200 preliminary rulings of this kind per year, the ECJ also adjudicates many **direct cases** brought before it by other Community institutions, member states, and natural or legal persons. Most of these have to do with violations of trade and competition law. In order to stem this tide, a lower Court of First Instance has been established (1989) for which the ECJ has become the court of appeal. And further, the Treaty of Nice (2003) has empowered the Council to create judicial panels (for which the Court of First

---

77. To keep the Court a manageable size with the enlargement of 2004, plenary sittings have now been limited to a sitting bench of 11. Often, the Court also decides in chambers of three or five judges.

78. Kieran St Clair Bradley, "The European Court of Justice," in Peterson and Shackleton, eds., *The Institutions of the European Union* 120.

Instance will be the appeal court) as gateways for the adjudication of specific areas of Community law.

What Status?

In establishing itself as the highest court of the EU, the ECJ had to go one step further than other supreme courts. When the US Supreme Court issued its first landmark rulings, it could at least start from the legally certain assumption that the United States was a sovereign country, that the Constitution was the highest law of the land, and that all other courts were to be bound by the Supreme Court's decisions (though resistance to the latter was only removed with the defeat of the South in the Civil War).

When the ECJ began its work, it was not clear that the treaties had established, or were meant to establish, a supranational political system with sovereignty in its own right. As much as the presumption prevailed that the member states had retained their sovereignty in full, the treaties were no more than international agreements. The signatories had pledged to uphold these treaties, to be sure, and they had even agreed to make joint decisions by qualified majority rule eventually, *but they had not explicitly agreed to make their national bodies of law subservient to European law.* Finally, it was far from clear that national court systems would have to look to the ECJ instead of their own high courts as the final authority of legal adjudication.

Establishing Supremacy

However, it was clear that the signatories wanted to establish something that was meant to be more lasting and of a more intensive character than a set of merely international agreements. And here the Court took its cue by issuing its early decisions with a clear intention of providing the system with the kind of legal certainty that the founding politicians had omitted or even evaded. Essentially, it did so in three logically connected steps:[79]

- In its most formative cases, the ECJ first declared that it was the manifest intention of the treaties to establish a system of shared sovereignty, a "new legal order."[80] The treaties, then, had to be regarded as the source of primary law comparable to a constitution. All laws and regulations made under the treaties would constitute a body of secondary law. Within this context, the ECJ could begin to

---

79. On the following see Dinan, *Ever Closer Union* 301–04.
80. *Van Gend en Loos v. Nederlandse Administratie der Belastingen* (1963) and *Costa v. ENEL* (1964).

interpret the validity of Community law as if the treaties had constitutional character.

- Secondly, the ECJ established on this basis what is known as the **direct effect** of primary or treaty law.[81] It held that the Community constituted a new legal order under which individual citizens or corporations could claim protection from contravening national laws and actions. Such individuals, in other words, could claim that a particular domestic law or regulation violated their rights as members of the Community, and the ECJ would in fact invalidate that domestic law or regulation.

- And thirdly, the ECJ established the **supremacy** of Community law as following logically from the above. In a 1978 decision that summed up all previous developments, the ECJ held that "every national court must ... apply Community law in its entirety ... and must accordingly set aside any provisions of national law which may conflict with it."[82] This was taken one step further in a 1987 decision that despite what the treaty might say, the courts of member countries do not have the authority to invalidate Community acts, since to do so would be to make Community law different from country to country.[83]

Mutual Recognition

The main work of the ECJ has been in enforcing the common market. In doing so, it elevated the status of the European Community by cementing the quasi-constitutional character of the treaties. One of its innovations was the principle of **mutual recognition**, designed to accommodate the fact that, under the circumstances, harmonizing standards across jurisdictions would be impossible or undesirable. Instead, the ECJ decided in the *Cassis de Dijon* case of 1979 that differing national standards could continue provided that each country recognized the standards of the others as valid.

Contested Terrain

Member states have routinely complained about the ECJ and its supranationalist interpretations of treaty law, and they have often delayed compliance with its rulings. Not surprisingly, the most vigorous opposition has come from the UK. Britain joined the Community after the ECJ had already established Europe's basic legal judicial framework.

---

81. See Lisa Conant, *Justice Contained: Law and Politics in the European Union* (Ithaca, NY: Cornell University Press, 2002) 53.
82. *Simmenthal v. Commission* (1978).
83. Court of Justice of the European Communities, "Judgment of 22 October 1987, *Foto-Frost v Hauptzollamt Lüübeck-Ost*, Case 314/85," *Reports of Cases before the Court.*

Moreover, the very existence of a constitutional high court was alien to Britain's tradition of common law and parliamentary supremacy. In 1991 there was a "national furor" when the ECJ for the first time overruled an Act of the British Parliament.[84] The British government even tried to negotiate a treaty revision that would have weakened the ECJ's position and role. However, the overwhelming view prevailed that the legal system of the Community was in everyone's best interest and therefore should be left unchanged.

Accounting for Success

The big question is why this view should prevail when the ECJ assumed powers of adjudication that were unforeseen and when governments would routinely be exposed to rulings criticizing or even invalidating their behaviour. As some commentators have noted, despite beginning from a far weaker constitutional base, judicial review has encountered far less resistance in the EU to date than it did for decades after the ratification of the US Constitution.[85] In serving as a surprisingly powerful agent of centralization, the ECJ also stands out as the one exception to the centralizing rule: it is one of the most truly federal of such courts. Notwithstanding its impeccably federal credentials, the ECJ has, in the view of some critics, been lax in enforcing the subsidiarity principle.[86]

A first answer to why this has occurred may be found in a certain degree of deference to legalistic solutions more prevalent on the European continent with its statutory and Roman law tradition than, say, in Britain. Secondly, legal certainty was one of the fundamental objectives of European integration in the first place. Most of the early decisions of the ECJ had to do with trade and competition policy. Market harmonization required certainty of the law. This was in the interest of the powerful transnational business interests driving the integration process.[87] Thirdly, it may also be significant that the EU incorporates many of the confederal assurances for member states that antifederalists feared they had lost with the US Constitution.[88] Finally, one can discern in the universal acceptance of the ECJ and its rulings a genuine desire for and commitment to a European order of peace and stability that overrides nationalist sentiments. It is this commitment more than anything else that distinguishes the EU from trade and other international agreements elsewhere.

---

84. Dinan, *Ever Closer Union* 311–12.
85. Leslie Friedman Goldstein, *Constituting Federal Sovereignty: The European Union in Comparative Context* (Baltimore, MD: Johns Hopkins University Press, 2001).
86. George A. Bermann, "The Role of Law in the Functioning of Federal Systems," in NicolaVdis and Howse, eds., *The Federal Vision* 202.
87. See Conant, *Justice Contained*.
88. Goldstein, *Constituting Federal Sovereignty* 43.

This commitment has also contributed to the ECJ's acceptance by national courts which routinely ask it for preliminary rulings on the compatibility of national laws with Community law. This "complicity" is particularly remarkable for the fact that such requests do not come only from supreme courts which are obliged to seek "authoritative guidance" from the ECJ but also from lower level courts which may or may not do so.[89] Given that the entire system of European jurisprudence—like the rest of the EU—still finds itself in a state of evolutionary flux, the current acceptance and practice of European law supremacy can be best understood itself as a form of "negotiated compromise."[90]

VARIATIONS AND EXCEPTIONS

Variant experiences range from the case of Australia, where patterns of both federal design and judicial interpretation show strong parallels with the United States, to Switzerland, an entirely anomalous federation in tackling the challenge of jurisdictional clarification without a supreme judicial umpire at all. The supreme court model of constitutional guardianship that we have examined in the American and Canadian experiences is also found in Australia, India, and Brazil—the two other federations emerging out of the British tradition and one strongly influenced by the American system. Otherwise, the discrete constitutional court approach has prevailed. Newly federalizing states in Spain, Belgium, and South Africa have all established a court with exclusively constitutional concerns and invested those courts with clear authority to practise judicial review.

Constitutional Undoing in Australia

The Australian case is worth noting for the way, as with the American and Canadian cases, the realities of constitutional interpretation and political practice diverged so sharply from constitutional intentions. As we noted in Chapter 6, the framers of the Australian Constitution deliberately opted for the American constitutional design because they wanted nothing to do with the kind of centrally dominated approach adopted in Canada. Partly as a consequence of choosing the American approach they ended up with something closer to what Sir John A. Macdonald had intended but manifestly failed in practice to achieve for Canada. Unlike the *BNA Act*, the Commonwealth Constitution quite clearly established a judicial separation of powers and by reasonably strong implication assigned a judicial review function to the High

---

89. Dinan, *Ever Closer Union* 305.
90. Alter, *Establishing the Supremacy of European Law* 38.

Court.[91] It also signalled its supremacy.[92] Unlike the Canadian case, the High Court rather than the JCPC controlled the process of constitutional interpretation.

Centralizing Decisions

Once the framers lost their grip on the High Court, judicial interpretation shifted from an intentionalist to a literalist philosophy, and the weakness of the single list design and the "asymmetrical" allocation of powers it created became apparent.[93] Particularly damaging to the position of the states has been the blanket grants of authority under the Section 96 'spending power,' whereby the Commonwealth may grant money to the states "on such terms and conditions as the Parliament thinks fit," and the Section 51 "External affairs" power.

With the spending power, the High Court has licensed not only broadly intrusive use of conditional grants,[94] but also the more coercive reduction of state power through punitive use of that spending power. In 1942, the Commonwealth took full control of the income tax by making eligibility for receipt of grant moneys conditional upon the states vacating the field.[95] With the external affairs power, the High Court has refused to draw any limits on the extent to which the Commonwealth may legislate in areas of state jurisdiction pursuant to an international treaty or covenant (though it did so by narrow majorities with strong dissenting opinions).[96] This contrasts with the extremely restrictive interpretation

---

91. In sections 71 and 74 respectively. Though see James Thomson, "Constitutional Authority for Judicial Review: A Contribution from the Framers of the Australian Constitution," in Gregory Craven, ed., *The Convention Debates 1891–1898: Commentaries, Indices and Guide* (Sydney: Legal Books, 1986).

92. In a weaker version of the US Constitution's supremacy clause. Clause 5 of the preamble says: "This Act, and all laws made by the Parliament of the Commonwealth under the Constitution, shall be binding on the courts, judges, and people of every State...."

93. Michael Crommelin, "The Federal Model," in Gregory Craven, ed., *Australian Federation: Towards the Second Century* (Carlton: Melbourne University Press, 1992) 43. The watershed decision was the Engineers' case, *Amalgamated Society of Engineers v. Adelaide Steamship Company* 1920. For a general survey, see Brian Galligan, *Politics of the High Court: A Study of the Judicial branch of Government in Australia* (St. Lucia: University of Queensland Press, 1987).

94. See the Court's dismissive one-sentence judgement in the "Roads Case," *The State of Victoria v. The Commonwealth* (1926) 38 CLR 399.

95. This was upheld by the High Court as a legitimate use of the spending power under s.96. See *South Australia v. the Commonwealth* (1942) 65 CLR 373.

96. The landmark cases have concerned imposition of racial discrimination legislation implementing principles of the United Nations Covenant on Human Rights and protection of "world heritage" wilderness sites listed with UNESCO: *Koowarta v. Bjelke-Petersen* (1982) 153 CLR 168 and *The Commonwealth of Australia v. Tasmania* (1983) 158 CLR 1 (the Franklin or Tasmanian Dam case).

applied by the JCPC to the equivalent clause in the *BNA Act*. As in the United States, the existence of a clause in the Australian Constitution guaranteeing protection of residual state powers (Section 106) has proven of little support to a jurisprudence of states rights.

People's Federalism in Switzerland

We suggested at the outset of this chapter that judicial review is almost unavoidably part of the functioning of a federation. How else can the inevitable constitutional ambiguities and jurisdictional disputes be resolved? Constitutional or supreme courts play that crucial umpiring role and in the process may well have a considerable impact on the evolution of a federation. But there is an exception to this otherwise firm generalization: Switzerland. While following the American lead in several respects when designing their restructured federation in 1848, the Swiss did anything but follow the US Supreme Court model.

The Judicial Role in the Swiss Constitution

As a loose confederation for most of its history, Switzerland, like other confederations, did not develop a practice of judicial review. With the transition from confederation to federation in 1848, a federal court, the *Bundesgericht*, was given constitutional status and assigned the task of adjudicating disputes that "do not pertain to public law" between the cantons or between the national government and the cantons, of enforcing the rights protected in the constitution, and of deciding on any other matter over which national legislation should give it jurisdiction.[97] In the absence of the latter, the Court could not rule on constitutional challenges arising from contested legislation. When a complete revision of the Constitution was effected in 1874, this implicit restriction on the Court's role was more forcefully articulated:

> the Federal Court shall apply the laws and generally binding decrees adopted by the Federal Assembly, as well as the international treaties approved by this Assembly. (Article 113.3)

While the failure of the US Constitution to establish who should exercise the constitutional review function created a vacuum into which the Supreme Court could readily slide, no such convenient ambiguity existed in the Swiss Constitution. This explicit prohibition foreclosed the opportunity for a Swiss version of *Marbury v. Madison*. Aided by international developments, the Court has in recent years become a little

---

97. Articles 101, 105, and 106 respectively.

more adventurous in the field of rights protection;[98] however, it has never intruded into the sphere of the division of powers. When Parliament was drafting the complete revision of the Constitution in 1999, it rejected a proposal from the Federal Council (the executive branch) that this prohibition be abandoned, and it remains as Article 189.4 of the Constitution ratified by the people that year and taking effect in 2000.

Speaking for the People

We recall from our discussion of the United States that judicial review only became a viable proposition for courts to assert once the idea took hold that the judiciary could serve as a proxy for the people. When all popular sovereignty was channelled through the legislative branch in the revolutionary period, judicial review could only be seen as a usurpation of the power of the people. Thus, it is no surprise to find that the only federation to practise participatory democracy—referendum democracy—is the only federation without judicial review. In Switzerland, the absence of judicial review and the continuing rejection of such a role for the Federal Court is to be explained by the continuing vitality of direct democracy.

SUMMARY

This chapter has explored the development and experience of judicial review in a number of federations, giving attention to the way courts have established themselves as authoritative sources of constitutional interpretation and umpires of the federal system and used that position to declare what a constitution means in any given setting. While this assumes that the courts play an important role in determining the evolution of the division of powers, it is not intended to imply that it is a uniquely important role. As numerous commentators have reminded us, economic, social, and more broadly political forces have been important sources of change and development in federal systems. Among the points made in this chapter are the following.

- The power of courts to invalidate acts of a legislature on the basis that they violate the constitution emerged with federalism itself. As the country that pioneered federalism, the United States, then, also pioneered the practice of judicial review. Judicial review involves the reduction of inherently political questions to matters of legal judgement. Not surprisingly, the assumption of this role by the Supreme Court, beginning with *Marbury v. Madison,* did not go uncontested.

---

98. Christine Rothmayr, "Towards the Judicialisation of Swiss Politics?," *West European Politics* 24:2 (2001).

- In the English-speaking federations, judicial review has emerged as a function of the regular judicial process and system—albeit one that culminates in a final court that is superior to the legislature. In the European world, judicial review is a more recent function that only became accepted with twentieth-century democratization and was formalized via the creation of separate constitutional courts rather than through the regular judicial system.
- Beginning with its decision in *McCulloch v. Maryland*, the US Supreme Court has facilitated a fundamental centralization of powers in American federalism. It has permitted a broad interpretation of some of the enumerated powers (notably the commerce power), and it has permitted a broadening of the range of areas on which Congress may legislate well beyond the enumerated powers via such devices as the necessary-and-proper clause and the general welfare clause. The characterization of state jurisdiction in terms of residual powers as protected by the Tenth Amendment proved a weak bulwark against this expansion. When the Supreme Court baulked at such demands, clear indication of its limits has been provided.
- Likewise, judicial review steered the Canadian constitutional law in a direction contrary to original intentions. By contrast with the American case, however, judicial review in the formative JCPC era went in a decidedly decentralist direction. Again, though, residual powers proved of little use. In accordance with the prediction of national supreme courts patterning a nationalizing jurisprudence, judicial review has moved away from the JCPC orientation since the last appeal was heard in 1954 and the Supreme Court of Canada became indeed the supreme court of Canada.
- Judicial review came late to Germany, being a major departure from the positive law tradition. It has also had a much more moderate impact on the evolution of German federalism. With its uniquely federal upper house and its administrative rather than legislative division of powers, German federalism is much less in need of judicial arbitration. Dicey was wrong: federalism does not necessarily mean legalism.
- The ECJ, by contrast, has played a noticeable role in pushing the EU away from confederalism and towards federalism. In the fashion of *Marbury v. Madison*, it has used its position to assert a superiority over member-state laws—although the supremacy of European law remains embedded for the time in a negotiated compromise among member states, national courts, and the ECJ.
- Having followed the American design model, Australia also shared the American experience with judicial review: enumerated powers meant to be exhaustive and limiting gained expansive interpretation

while guarantees of residual powers for the states proved to be hollow. Meanwhile, Switzerland stands out as the exception: the one federal state without judicial review of central government powers. Such a deviation from what often seems an essential component of federalism has been made possible by a reliance on mechanisms of direct democracy.

11 Federal Governance

For most citizens and many academic observers, the real question about federalism is how well it works: does it improve or does it complicate the policy outputs of government? In what ways is federalism part of 'good governance'?

The classic legislative federations were established in an altogether different era when the size and scope of government were limited, and it was relatively easy both to divide responsibilities and to imagine two levels of government operating in their own spheres with little clash or overlap. As we have seen, the division of powers followed a simple pattern of assigning responsibility for national security and the common market to the national government and leaving service delivery and the making of cultural and social policy to the subnational units. This was what we described as the federalist compromise between modernizers and traditionalists. Industrialization and the growth of government have done away with such conducive conditions and loaded federalism with great challenges. The 'mixed economy,' the welfare state, the rise of environmental policy, and the enormous increase in taxation have all greatly complicated policy-making in a system of divided jurisdiction— as have the vastly greater mobility of labour, geographical scope of economic activity, and quality of communications and transportation. Massive adjustment has been required. To what extent did federalism hinder that adjustment, and to what extent does it complicate and burden the making and implementation of policy today?

HOW SHOULD FEDERATIONS MANAGE POLICY RESPONSIBILITIES?

The reference point for discussion of public policy in federal systems is a set of propositions about how the division of policy responsibilities *ought* to be structured between the respective levels of government. Dicey stated in general terms how that structuring ought to be guided; however, his formulation begged some important questions. "The details of this division [of powers] vary under every different federal constitution, but the general principle on which it rests is obvious. Whatever concerns the nation as a whole should be placed under the control of the national government. All matters which are not primarily of common interest should remain in the hands of the several states."[1] Using the important concepts of **public goods** and **externalities**, public finance economics has provided an analytic framework for reflecting on the optimal division of powers and responsibilities between levels of government in a federal system. It has developed, in other words, a **logic of assignment.**

The two concepts of public goods and externalities have been widely applied to explaining and justifying the tasks of government in general, and only a small elaboration is required to extend the analysis to a comment about what different levels of government should do. Externalities exist when the consequences of a transaction (its costs and benefits) 'spillover' to affect third parties. Economic logic says that positive externalities will be undersupplied by the market, since those providing the benefit cannot keep it all to themselves, while negative externalities will be oversupplied since individuals will have an incentive to push their cost burden onto others. Now turning to federalism, we can see that costs and benefits can analogously spill over from one jurisdiction to the other.

The Logic of Assignment

Assuming that society has decided the extent and way in which government should address the various forms of market failure and modify market outcomes, the next question in a federal system is how those tasks should be split between the different levels of government. As we saw in Chapter 6, the founders of federal systems typically sought to differentiate between those roles most appropriately executed at the subnational level and those most appropriately executed at the national level. Public finance economics seeks to put that on a more rigorous footing by applying the concept of externalities. Each function of government should be executed by that level of government whose territory most closely conforms to the spread of costs and benefits. Negative or positive externalities need to be avoided. Any function whose costs or benefits spill over significantly onto other jurisdictions should be executed by a higher level of government.

This applies to both the revenue-raising and service provision sides of government activity. At one extreme, the provision of local roads, basic utility services, or recreation facilities has little or no spillover effects beyond a local area, and thus there is no need for such tasks to

---

1.   Dicey, *An Introduction* 139.

be assigned to a higher order of government. At the other extreme, the provision of military defence has enormous spillover effects and thus should be assigned to the national level of government.

Taxes and the Exit Threat

On the revenue side, the logic of this approach says that each level of government should use the type of taxes that are not vulnerable to exit effects. We can illustrate this in simplified terms. Individuals can easily drive to another municipality to shop, or move out of a neighbourhood altogether, so it makes little sense for local government to rely on either sales taxes or income taxes. Similarly, corporations can easily relocate from one state or province to another, so there is a limit to the extent that corporate income taxes can be levied at the subnational level.

According to this logic, then, property taxes are most appropriately assigned to local government and take the form of a 'benefit tax'—that is to say, one where the connection between the tax paid and the concrete benefits gained is quite evident. Retail sales taxes may be assigned to state and provincial governments, particularly in federations where the jurisdictions are sufficiently large to discourage trans-border shopping. The more sophisticated value-added type of sales tax (the VAT in Europe; the GST in Canada and Australia), however, is more suited to national implementation because of its chain-of-supply nature. Finally, personal and corporate income taxes function best at the national level, though some sharing with subnational jurisdictions is quite feasible.

The Redistributive-developmental Divide

Because it is closely linked to taxation, redistributive expenditure is also seen by public finance economists as being affected by this logic. National governments are the most appropriate level to have responsibility for the welfare state since subnational jurisdictions are too subject to exit pressures from business and higher income taxpayers. By contrast, it has been argued, developmental policy and expenditure is best undertaken by lower order governments.[2] This follows the logic that since developmental policy is oriented towards economic not social needs, it is appropriate that it be delivered by the level of government most disciplined by market forces and most attuned to local needs. A conflicting perspective, however, finds strong evidence that the capacity of subnational governments to exercise economic policy powers effectively is also negated by their dependence on the wider system.[3]

---

2. Paul E. Peterson, *The Price of Federalism* (Washington, DC: Brookings Institution, 1995) 18.
3. Paul Brace, *State Government and Economic Performance* (Baltimore, MD: Johns Hopkins University Press, 1993).

Implications and Complications

The externalities argument for assignment of responsibilities and powers in a federal system raises a number of issues, including the question of how many levels of government there should be and the refusal of the real world of policy to fit neatly into logic of assignment categories.

Dualistic, Tripartite, or Multilayered Federalism?

One question is how many orders of government there should be. Federalism is classically a simple dualism between two sovereign levels of government. All federations, though, also include a third, lower tier of government—though typically with much weaker constitutional status. It is this threefold division of responsibilities that most public finance theory takes as given. Local government assumes those limited taxing powers that are minimally affected by mobility and those limited service roles whose costs and benefits are contained within a very small geographic area with limited spillovers or externalities. The state, cantonal, or provincial governments assume a variety of important functions that have only modest spillover effects. And the national government taxes mobile sources, provides national public goods, and addresses spillover problems. However, are all these functions of a scale that corresponds with the three orders? Taking the logic to its conclusion, one would have to argue for several orders in a multilayered federal system.[4] And, indeed, we find in some federal systems something equivalent to this. For instance, in the United States a plenitude of jurisdictions for the governance of specific functions whose scale lies somewhere between state and local government have been created.

Ambiguities and Anachronisms

However elegant the externalities theory of assignment may be in principle, it proves slightly less useful in practice. Reality is a good deal messier than such neat divisions suggest, and many policy areas fall somewhere in between or change over time. To find a significant policy area of primarily regional scope but yet is without interjurisdictional spillovers is hard indeed. Modernization has contributed enormously to this, with many concerns that were once genuinely local becoming if not fully at least significantly national. Whether it be transportation, policing, or environmental protection, modernization has substantially widened their geographical scope. Older federations may thus have

---

4.   As for example do Bruno S. Frey and Reiner Eichenberger, *The New Democratic Federalism for Europe: Functional, Overlapping and Competing Jurisdictions* (Cheltenham: Edward Elgar, 1999) in the proposal for "functional, overlapping and competing jurisdictions."

begun with a division of powers that was logical at one time but which have become anachronistic later on.

Prescriptive and Explanatory Dimensions

The theory of externalities and public goods, then, provides a prescriptive framework for determining how powers and responsibilities ought to be divided between levels of government. Each function should be exercised by the lowest level of government possible without creation of serious spillover or exit problems. In addition to being prescriptive, this approach may also yield explanatory or empirical insights. The actual division of powers and responsibilities in federal systems reflects this logic.[5]

Maximizing Subnational Autonomy

Complementary to this analytic framework is the advocacy of a maximally workable degree of subnational autonomy within federal systems. As the subsidiarity rule expresses, powers and responsibilities should be allocated to the lowest practical order of government. This applies both on the taxing and spending sides. It is generally held from this point of view that governments should have their own fiscal resources roughly equal to their spending responsibilities. That way, the government providing the benefits to voters also inflicts the pain, and thus a measure of fiscal accountability is in operation. Maintaining high levels of subnational autonomy should, according to this view, ensure that federalism will deliver what are perceived to be some of its main benefits. There are, however, somewhat different ways of developing this argument.

A Framework for Policy Optimization

Federalism offers the potential for local communities to choose the mix of policies they find most amenable and thus for geographically distributed diversity of taste and interests to be accommodated. Such accommodation of diversity can only occur if the subnational governments have sufficient fiscal and policy autonomy. In the classic public finance formulation, the presumption of local responsibility in federal systems produces more optimal mixes of public goods.[6] Prevailing norms in

---

5. As, for instance, argued by Peterson, *Price of Federalism*.
6. Charles M. Tiebout, "A Pure Theory of Local Expenditures," *Journal of Political Economy* LXIV (1956); and Wallace E. Oates, *Fiscal Federalism* (New York: Harcourt Brace Jovanovich, 1972). See also, James Buchanan, "Federalism as an Ideal Political Order and an Objective for Constitutional Reform," *Publius* 25 (1995).

some jurisdictions may favour stronger or weaker environmental protection; local communities will vary in the mix of public/private provision they favour; and so on. At least in theory, then, federalism allows citizens to choose to a much greater degree the kind of community they wish to live in than they would be able to in a unitary state.

Market-preserving Federalism

Another argument for maximizing local autonomy reflects a more specific political preference. For those championing the free market, a major benefit of divided jurisdiction is the constraint it imposes on government. One dimension of this is **competitive federalism**: the view that a system of multiple jurisdictions creates the potential for individuals and firms to defect from a particular regime whose policies they dislike. Only in federal systems can citizens employ what Hirschman called the "exit" option: they can indicate discontent by defecting rather than engaging in a process of change ("voice") or simply resigning themselves to the status quo ("loyalty").[7] In unitary states, exit involves leaving the country altogether—a possible option but one with all sorts of costs involved. Proponents of this devolutionary form of federalism do not argue, though, that subnational units should be given *carte blanche* to follow their own paths. As Ferejohn and Weingast have stated, "the long history of legal discrimination against African Americans demonstrates that states cannot be trusted on all dimensions of public policy. Competition among states is unlikely to prevent particular states from abrogating certain citizen rights...."[8] However, they do argue that policy autonomy and competitive federalism will produce desirable outcomes across a range of policy domains.

In a somewhat different version, the vertical division of powers plays an important role in constraining governments to operate according to market rules.[9] If subnational governments are assigned substantial spending powers, while only the national government has the power to print money and set the bank rate, then profligate spending will be curtailed. Both of these propositions assume (and endorse) the American model of dual or legislative federalism rather than the European model of integrated or administrative federalism, which promotes the idea of separate jurisdictions as autonomous players.

---

7.   Albert O. Hirschman, *Exit, Voice and Loyalty: Responses to Decline in Firms, Organizations, and States* (Cambridge, MA: Harvard University Press, 1970).

8.   John A. Ferejohn and Barry A. Weingast, "Introduction," in *The New Federalism: Can the States Be Trusted?* (Stanford, CA: Hoover Institution, 1998) ix. Also see John Kincaid, "Extinguishing the Twin Relics of Barbaric Multiculturalism—Slavery and Polygamy—From American Federalism," *Publius* 33:1 (2003).

9.   Barry Weingast, "The Economic Role of Political Institutions: Market-preserving Federalism and Economic Development," *Journal of Law and Economics* 11 (1995).

A Race to the Bottom?

Sceptics point out that conditions for market-like federalism where citizens can enjoy consumer sovereignty do not exist in the real world. The 'commodity' offered by any particular regime is too multifaceted and heterogeneous to imagine many individuals determining their location by any one particular suite of policy preferences. More importantly, some factors of production are enormously more mobile than others; notably, both capital and particular highly skilled workers are more mobile than labour in general. Thus, for many critics, competitive federalism is in reality about encouraging a **race to the bottom**, where jurisdictions compete against each other to make themselves more attractive to footloose capital and the affluent and less attractive to the indigent.[10] Less generous and more punitive social welfare programs, lower tax levels, more permissive environmental regimes, tougher labour laws—these are the sort of policies that governments might be impelled toward under circumstances where they have to survive in a competitive market for investment.

Devolution Debates in the United States

The United States has always been the federal system with the most internally competitive features. Critics argued that its race-to-the-bottom characteristics have been intensified by the so-called "devolution revolution," most dramatically so when President Clinton signed the *Personal Responsibility and Work Opportunity Reconciliation Act* of 1996.[11] That *Act* ended the entitlement basis of one of America's original national welfare programs—Aid to Families with Dependent Children (AFDC)—and did so in a way that devolved greater authority onto the states. Potentially, states face a dual reinforcing pressure: the pressure to avoid becoming a "welfare magnet," attracting unwanted migrants from states with less generous programs, and the pressure to remain attractive to business in the face of competition from jurisdictions who might be lowering their taxes by lowering their expenditures. Competitive federalism and local control may be undesirable for a range of reasons.[12]

---

10. John D. Donahue, *Disunited States: What's at Stake as Washington Fades and the States Take the Lead?* (New York: Basic Books, 1997); Sandford Schramm and Samuel H. Beer, eds., *Welfare Reform: A Race to the Bottom?* (Washington, DC: Woodrow Wilson Center Press, 1999).

11. How devolutionary and how revolutionary it really was is another question. See John Kincaid, "Devolution in the United States: Rhetoric and Reality," in Nicolaïdis and Howse, eds., *The Federal Vision*.

12. See for example the position taken by Robert Howse, "Federalism, Democracy, and Regulatory Reform: A Sceptical View of the Case for Decentralization," in Knop, *et al.*, eds., *Rethinking Federalism*.

Devolution of social programs and services runs against the recommendations of public finance theory, given the extensive spillover issues in that major policy domain. Thus,

> the recent fiscal reforms in welfare policy appear to be a significant institutional experiment with an alternate [*sic*] paradigm of federalism, one which emphasizes the ability of states, not the central government, to handle cross-jurisdiction spillovers. If the experiment proves successful, then other central government policies like Medicaid ... environmental and business regulation, infrastructure spending, and perhaps even Social Security and Medicare may become candidates for fiscal decentralization also.[13]

Proponents of devolution find little evidence that a destructive race to the bottom is likely to occur. The United States has always had a devolved model of national social programs that allowed considerable differences in generosity from state to state, which was a condition of their initial acceptance by southern Democrats. This flexibility did not spark a downward spiral then, however, and there is no reason to think that the current devolutionary model will either. Policy choices are more powerfully determined by "local preferences" and tend to be well entrenched. Instead, what has occurred, proponents argue, is a beneficial opportunity for states to experiment with alternative delivery styles.[14]

THE POWER TO TAX

Given the fundamental importance of financial resources to government, it is not surprising that the functioning of federal systems is highly affected by the relative financial strength of the different levels of government. The advantaged fiscal position of most national governments has been a major factor in driving the centralization of federations over the past century. It has arisen as a consequence of two parallel developments: the capturing of powerful revenue bases by the central government and the enormous growth in the expensive public services provided traditionally by subnational governments. When Alexander Hamilton confidently remarked in *Federalist* 34 that the states would not need a great taxing power since they "will naturally reduce themselves within *a very narrow compass*," he could not have foreseen the transformation of the role of government a century later. The result has been **vertical**

---

13. Robert P. Inman and Daniel L. Rubinfeld, "Rethinking Federalism," *Journal of Economic Perspectives* 11:4 (1997): 60.

14. Craig Volden, "Entrusting the States with Welfare Reform," in Ferejohn and Weingast, eds., *The New Federalism*.

fiscal imbalance (VFI): the discrepancy between the spending responsibilities and revenue capacities of the two levels of government.

Questions of fiscal balance are not a recent issue in federal systems; indeed, they typically arose immediately federal union was contemplated. The creation of a customs union is an intrinsic component of such a union and that in turn generally means the transfer to a national government of the power to levy customs duties, historically one of the most important revenue sources.[15] But in this story the most important development has been the rise over the twentieth century of direct taxation—the personal and corporate income tax—as the most prolific source of government revenue and its capture by central governments. Even within the classic federations, though, there is considerable variation in the degree to which national governments monopolize tax revenue. At one extreme lies Australia, where a high degree of fiscal centralization has funded a high degree of policy centralization. At the other extreme lie Switzerland and Canada, where revenues are more evenly balanced between national and subnational levels of government. The outlier is the EU, which, as we noted in Chapter 5, has taken a quite different direction, one reflecting its quite different circumstances.

The American Model of Pluralistic Fiscal Federalism

The Americans adopted the simplest approach to tax assignment. In its enumerated powers, Congress was granted a plenary power to tax; in their residual powers, the states were also left with a plenary power to tax. There are exceptions in each case, but they are relatively minor. The states were prohibited from levying import or export duties, typically one of the minimum conditions of a federal union since it is necessary to maintain the internal common market. Congress, meanwhile, was constrained by a clause in the Constitution that required direct taxes to be levied "in proportion to the number of inhabitants," a concession to the slave states.

Uncertain Beginnings

Just as the first modern income tax was introduced by the British Parliament to fund the war against Napoleon (1799), so Congress introduced the first American income tax to keep the Union forces in the field during the Civil War (1862). Once victory had been secured and the great revenue need subsided, the federal income tax was allowed to

---

15. Distinctly anomalous in this respect is India, where the states raise a good part of their revenue from imposts of inter-state trade with the result that "the prevailing sub-central tax system has created a host of tariff and non-tariff barriers." M. Govinda Rao, "Indian Fiscal Federalism from a Comparative Perspective," in Arora and Verney, eds., *Multiple Identities in a Single* 293.

lapse. Under pressure from agrarian populists who wished to ease the reliance on tariffs, it was later reintroduced. This time, however, it was challenged in the courts, and the Supreme Court decided to interpret the direct proportion clause in such a way as to make a federal income tax unconstitutional.[16] Furor over this decision paved the way for the Sixteenth Amendment in 1913, which removed any possible constitutional obstacles[17] and allowed the rise of the federal income tax over the twentieth century.

Lopsided Concurrency

Jurisdiction has remained concurrent, however, and the national income tax has not displaced state claims to that important revenue source. Indeed, Congress has accommodated the states by allowing deductibility of state imposts. It thereby subsidizes those states who choose to levy their own tax in parallel—if in a rather inefficient and inequitable way.[18] As a consequence of this, the Untied States has a decidedly pluralistic or truly federal tax structure. Those states who have chosen to do so— 43 out of the 50—levy their own sales tax and their own corporate and personal income tax.

Notwithstanding this basic equality of access to major tax bases, the system fails to generate a balanced share of revenues. Over the twentieth century, a massive reversal of fiscal fortunes occurred. As recently as 1932, fully half of all tax revenue was raised by local government, with national and state governments taking a quarter each. Forty years later the local government share had been halved and the national share more than doubled.[19] In 2002, just under 60 per cent of all American tax revenue was raised nationally. With the increase in the national share came the increasing dependence of state and local governments, whose reliance on transfers reached a high point of 27.6 per cent of their total expenditures in the late 1970s, levelling off at 17 per cent by 1990.[20]

Balanced Federalism in Canada

When they made their decisions about tax assignment, Canadians adopted a slightly more complicated approach. In its list of exclusive

---

16. *Pollock v. Farmers' Loan & Trust Co* (1895) 157 US 429.
17. Bernstein, *Amending America* 120.
18. Janet G. Stotsky and Emil M. Sunley, "United States," in Teresa Ter-Minassian, ed., *Fiscal Federalism in Theory and Practice* (Washington, DC: IMF, 1997) 373. Inequitable because it allows higher income earners to reduce their marginal tax rate and thereby reduces the progressivity of the system.
19. Bruce A. Wallin, *From Revenue Sharing to Deficit Sharing: General Revenue Sharing and Cities* (Washington, DC: Georgetown University Press, 1998) 2.
20. Stotsky and Sunley, "United States" 369.

national powers, Parliament was given a plenary authority to tax. In their list of exclusive powers, the provinces were given authority to levy "direct" taxes and to collect royalties from the exploitation of natural resources. This raised two rather awkward questions: first, how could the two jurisdictions each exercise an exclusive power over the same subject; second, what exactly is a "direct" tax? In the standard definition, direct taxes are imposts on income and wealth—by contrast with indirect taxes, which are imposts on transactions, notably the sale of goods and services. However, peculiarities of Canadian interpretation have led to provinces being allowed to levy *both* sales and income taxes under this heading. Thus, "with minor exceptions, both levels of government have full access to all current major revenue sources."[21] In practice, then, the Canadian situation approximates to the American.[22]

In outcome terms, the result is that primary tax revenues are split almost evenly between the two levels of government in Canada, and a modest amount is redistributed in the form of intergovernmental transfers.[23] While in the immediate postwar years the provinces were relegated to a more subordinate fiscal position, the repatriation of "tax points" over the years to the provinces has restored the balance. Currently, the Canadian government controls a marginally larger share of tax revenue than the provinces and territories, but once the third level of government is included, the national share of the total falls to 47 per cent.[24] Thus, Canada is one of only two federations where the subnational governments raise over half the total tax revenue. The other is Switzerland.

---

21. Kenneth Norrie and L.S. Wilson, "On Re-Balancing Canadian Fiscal Federalism," in Harvey Lazar, ed., *Toward a New Mission Statement for Canadian Fiscal Federalism* (Montreal, QC and Kingston, ON: McGill-Queen's University Press, 2000) 80–81.

22. The main differences are that with the exception of Québec, the provinces have integrated their income taxes with national income tax and there is a national VAT as well as a retail sales tax in most provinces. On Québec, see R. Lachance and F. Vaillancourt, "Quebec's Tax on Income: Evolution, Status, and Evaluation," in D.M. Brown, ed., *Tax Competition and the Fiscal Union in Canada* (Kingston, ON: Institute of Intergovernmental Relations, 2001).

23. According to the Government of Canada, its own-source tax revenue was $179 billion in 2002–03 while the provinces and territories raised a total of $161 billion. Thirty-five billion dollars was transferred to the provinces and territories, bringing their total revenue up to $196 billion. See, Canada, Department of Finance, *The Fiscal Balance in Canada: The Facts* (Ottawa, ON: Government of Canada, 2003).

24. Douglas M. Brown, "Fiscal Federalism: The New Equilibrium Between Equity and Efficiency," in Herman Bakvis and Grace Skogstad, eds., *Canadian Federalism: Performance, Effectiveness, and Legitimacy* (Don Mills, ON: Oxford University Press, 2002) 62.

Germany: The Tax Sharing Approach

While modern German federalism inherited its integrated model from the quasi-federal *Reich* of the nineteenth century, history provided less to build on when it came to designing postwar fiscal arrangements. In confederal style, the Bismarck Constitution relied on the *Länder* to transfer resources upward to the Reich from their tax revenues. Despite adopting the integrated model for the postwar constitution, the Federal Republic was structured along the conventional division of tax sources found in the systems of legislative or divided federations. This discrepancy could not last, and after a modest reform in 1955, Germany's fiscal arrangements were brought into line with the realities of administrative federalism in a major constitutional change in 1969. The keys to this system are that it involves **joint taxation** and that those joint rights are constitutionally guaranteed.

Under the 1969 arrangements some division of tax sources remains, with 30 per cent of the national tax take, 9 per cent of the *Länder* tax take, and 5 per cent of the municipal tax take coming from sources exclusive to them.[25] All the remainder, however, comes from major tax sources—notably the income tax and the VAT—to which the levels of government have joint claim. Article 106 of the Constitution insists that the three levels share in the proceeds proportional to their expenditure burdens and requires that the exact apportionment be regulated by legislation "requiring the consent of the *Bundesrat*"—currently 50/50. The resulting system still leaves an element of VFI, with the lower orders of government relying on direct grants for 15 per cent of their total needs.

Imitations and Variations: At the Extremes

Fiscal Decentralization

While Canada is notable for the fact that the subnational governments together control (just) over half the total tax revenue raised, the pronounced decentralization of Switzerland is evident in the fact that the cantons and communes control two-thirds of total tax revenue. This is supported by the fact that "tax sovereignty lies primarily in the cantons and secondarily in the confederation to such an extent that it is stated in the federal Constitution."[26] Swiss fiscal decentralization pales, though, in comparison with that of the EU.

---

25. Paul Bernd Spahn and Wolfgang Föttinger, "Germany," in Teresa Ter-Minassian, ed., *Fiscal Federalism in Theory and Practice* (Washington, DC: IMF, 1997) 231.
26. Dafflon, "Fiscal Federalism in Switzerland" 273.

Fiscal Centralization

Excluding South Africa, which remains virtually a unitary state in terms of fiscal federalism,[27] Australia represents the most acute case of VFI, with the Commonwealth controlling all major tax sources and engaging in massive annual transfers to the states. Through idiosyncratic judicial interpretation, the states have been prevented from levying their own general sales taxes and thus lack that important revenue source available to subnational governments in Canada and the United States.[28] Through the coercive spending power of the Commonwealth (see below), the states have been excluded since 1942 from the income tax. They were granted all the net revenue from the national value-added tax (the "GST," Goods and Services Tax) introduced in 2000. However, that remains a Commonwealth government tax and the revenues are effectively an intergovernmental transfer. The Australian states rely on transfers for almost half their entire budgetary needs.

Why the Prevalence of VFI?

It is easy to understand why revenues are so disproportionately controlled by the Commonwealth government in Australia—the Commonwealth monopolizes the national tax base. It is less easy to understand why VFI exists across all federations. Given that national and subnational governments both have broad access to the lucrative revenue sources in Canada, "the traditional reason for expecting a vertical fiscal gap does not apply."[29] The same can be said for the United States. While we have seen that the theory of fiscal federalism is first and foremost a prescriptive theory, it also seems to carry explanatory weight here. The major revenue sources are subject to considerable exit pressure. Endemic VFI is consistent with the prediction from this observation that subnational governments will be driven to under-tax and thus look to the national government to resolve that problem for them.[30] The massive reversal in local versus national tax take in the United States reflects the rise in importance of the income tax. As public finance theory recommends, local governments rely largely on property taxes. Some local governments in the United States do levy an income tax, but given high mobility rates, any significant reliance is simply non-viable. Only at the national level can an income tax be immune from exit pressures. Also

---

27. The provinces raise a derisory 3.8 per cent of their revenue themselves and are reliant on transfers for the remaining 96.2 per cent. Joachim Wehner, "Fiscal Federalism in South Africa," *Publius* 30:3 (2000).

28. Chris Caleo, "Section 90 and Excise Duties: A Crisis of Interpretation," *Melbourne University Law Review* 16:2 (1987).

29. Norrie and Wilson, "On Re-Balancing Canadian Fiscal Federalism" 80–81.

30. For Canada see Norrie and Wilson, "On Re-Balancing Canadian Fiscal Federalism" 95–96.

consistent with this is the absence of progressivity in the American state tax systems, where high income earners pay the same effective rate as low income earners.[31]

It must be acknowledged, though, that exit pressures will vary from federation to federation and will not always exert a significant force on local policy choices. A case in point is Switzerland where "... an individual can pay as much as two or three times the amount of tax on the same income and wealth, depending on where he lives. Even neighbouring cantons sometimes have considerable permanent differences in tax burden...."[32]

EU Exceptionalism

Reverse VFI

In a much more confederal way, the EU practices reverse VFI: the member states control almost all the tax sources and the 'central government' has to rely on transfers currently limited to a mere 1.27 per cent of European Gross National Product or GNP (under the Berlin Agreement 1999–2006). This may sound paltry, but in several ways it is not. First of all, it must be remembered that the EU is a particular case of administrative federalism: while EU law sets policy goals, policy implementation and administration are left almost entirely to the member states. Secondly, even 1.27 per cent of the GNP of the world's largest integrated market system constitutes a huge amount of money—98.6 billion Euros in 2002—and this money is spent on a very few large items: nearly half of it on agricultural policy and another third on cohesion policy (regional development).[33] And thirdly, the transfers to individual member states from these funds are substantial, at least for some— 4 per cent of the Portuguese Gross Domestic Product (GDP), for example, and 1.7 per cent of the Spanish GDP.[34] Nonetheless, it has been argued that progress towards fiscal federalism has not matched the integration that has occurred in a number of other areas, and that may be the recipe for a legitimacy crisis caused by the incapacity of the EU to provide effective economic management and redistribution.[35]

---

31. Walker, *The Rebirth of Federalism* 220–21.
32. Dafflon, "Fiscal Federalism in Switzerland" 281.
33. Alberta Sbragia, "Key Policies," in Bomberg and Stubb, eds., *The European Union* 115 and 125.
34. Brigid Laffer and Michael Shackleton, "The Budget," in Wallace and Wallace, eds., *Policy-Making in the European Union* 214.
35. Mark Bainbridge and Philip Whyman, *Fiscal Federalism and European Economic Integration* (London: Routledge, 2003); Tanja A. Börzel and Madeleine Hosli, "Brussels between Bern and Berlin: Comparative Federalism Meets the European Union," *Governance* 16:2 (2003). Also see, Loukas Tsoukalis, "Economic and Monetary Union," in Helen Wallace and William Wallace, eds., *Policy-Making in the European Union*, 4th ed. (Oxford: Oxford University Press, 2000).

Exceptions to the Exception

It also must be noted that the EU has taken on some important fiscal powers—notably in establishing a set of fiscal benchmarks with which member states are required to comply—and that its fiscal powers are not notably weaker than those of establishment federations in an equivalent stage of their development.[36] Under the 1997 Stability and Growth Pact, for example, the member states have been committed to keeping their national deficits under 3 per cent of GDP, and the Council resolution also contained the provision of punitive measures against violators.[37] And while the EU's fiscal resources may be derisory, with monetary union and the creation of the European Central Bank in 1999, its monetary policy is not.

Growth Path

The EU's fiscal minimalism reflects the fact that, as we noted in Chapter 5, it represents the first experiment in constructing a federal order through the union of established nation-states with their own developed administrative structures, regulatory regimes, and welfare systems. The chief alternative policy instrument to ownership or expenditure is regulation, and exactly as one would predict in these circumstances, the EU has gone down the regulatory path initially charted by the Americans. "Regulation is by far the most important type of policy-making in the EC, the 'first pillar' of the EU.... lacking an independent power to tax and spend, the Community had no other way to grow than as an almost pure type of regulatory state...."[38] And grow in this direction it has: "today close to 80 per cent of new economic regulation of productive activity in Western Europe comes from Brussels."[39] It is not surprising that populist anti-EU rhetoric exploits the image of Brussels as casting a suffocating regulatory web over the peoples of Europe.

---

36. McKay, *Designing Europe* 3–4.
37. However, such measures have not been taken even though France and Germany have been violating the 3 per cent ceiling over several years. The purpose of the Pact was currency stabilization. Given the relative strength of the Euro in relation to the declining US dollar, however, some observers doubt that the Pact has a chance of surviving, especially when one of the violator countries, Germany, is also the greatest net contributor to EU revenue.
38. Giandomenico Majone, "Regulatory Legitimacy in the United States and the European Union," in Nicolaïdis and Howse, *The Federal Vision* 253. See Giandomenico Majone, *Regulating Europe* (London: Routledge, 1996). For further discussion, see R. Daniel Kelemen, *The Rules of Federalism: Institutions and Regulatory Politics in the EU and Beyond* (Cambridge, MA: Harvard University Press, 2004).
39. Moravcsik, "Federalism in the European Union" 161.

THE POWER TO SPEND

If VFI is apparently an inevitable feature of federal systems, it then raises the question how the gap is to be bridged—what the central government can and should do with its surplus revenues. It may be the case that "… the strengths of a federal system are best brought forth when … annually legislated fiscal interactions between different tiers are strictly limited."[40] However, this may be unrealistic. The options are considerable, ranging—in terms of the federal principle—from the entirely benign to the highly intrusive and centralizing. In the former category is Australia's GST. In 2000, Australia belatedly introduced its first comprehensive consumption tax, the "Goods and Services Tax" (GST), a national, single-rate, value-added tax. This was legislated under the Commonwealth's plenary power to levy taxes, but automatically provides all its net revenue to the states.[41] In practice, though, it is the conditional grants that have been most prominent. Those who pay the piper call the tune in federal systems as elsewhere. The stronger fiscal position of central governments has proven a tempting and powerful lever for the extension of central government power into areas of subnational jurisdiction. This is the **spending power**: the use of intergovernmental transfers to circumvent constitutional limitations. In some federations this power has a clear constitutional status, in others it has a rather doubtful one; in general it has become well established regardless.

Conditions, Conditions, Conditions

At the neutral end of the spectrum, the immediate option for central governments is simply to bridge the fiscal gap by transferring to the subnational governments whatever surplus funds it has available. However, beginning early in the twentieth century, central governments in the United States, Canada, Australia, and other federations introduced a few, small, intergovernmental grants that had conditions attached. Typically these were requirements that the money be spent in the designated way: perhaps on roads, perhaps on swimming pools. From that small base, conditional grants expanded, and in times when zealous reform-minded governments came to power nationally, they expanded dramatically. **Conditional grants** became a powerful instrument for

---

40. Ronald McKinnon and Thomas Nechyba, "Competition in Federal Systems: The Role of Political and Financial Constraints," in Ferejohn and Weingast, eds., *The New Federalism* 3.

41. As per the 1999 *Intergovernmental Agreement on Reform of Commonwealth-State Financial Relations* between the Commonwealth and the States and Territories.

launching major national policies in areas of subnational jurisdiction. In particular, national health and social welfare programs were launched via this method.

The range of conditions attached diversified as the practice developed. To avoid the fungibility problem that specific purpose grants may simply substitute for moneys the subnational government is free to shift to other projects, grants may require **matched funding**, typically dollar for dollar. In addition to stipulating what program their money is to be spent on, central governments have stipulated how that program is to be run, thus enforcing national policy goals and standards. But why stop there? Central governments learned that conditional grants could contain stipulations that had only a peripheral relationship with the program on which the money was targeted. Funds that the subnational governments were required to devote to highway construction could also contain requirements that a particular speed or blood alcohol limit be imposed on all roads as a condition of receipt.

Is the Spending Power Constitutional?

The explicit authority to use financial superiority for policy extension varies greatly between federations. In no federation was it originally envisaged that the superior fiscal capacity of the central government would provide a legitimate basis for erosion of the division of powers. However, federal constitutions differ significantly in how much explicit licence they provide for the exercise of such power and in the impact of judicial review. Again, here, Australia and Canada mark two extremes.

The United States: Contested Interpretation

In the US Constitution, the power to influence policy within state jurisdiction by means of monetary inducements rests on the highly ambiguous opening words of Article I, Section 8: "The Congress shall have power to lay and collect taxes, duties, imposts and excises, to pay the debts and provide for the common defence and general welfare of the United States." From the Convention itself onwards, there have been those who wished to see this as applying only within the boundaries of the enumerated powers—as Madison assured his readers it did in *Federalist* 41—and those who wished to see this as a more expansive grant of power (the Hamiltonian view). Early American presidents vetoed several congressional Acts on the basis that they did not conform to the narrow interpretation.

In 1936, the Supreme Court invalidated one piece of the New Deal on the basis that Congress was using its taxing and spending power as "but means to an unconstitutional end," violating the Tenth Amendment.

Yes, in theory, states can decline the offer of funds and thereby avoid the attached conditions; in reality, though, "the asserted power of choice is illusory."[42]

In that same ruling, though, the Court also included as *obiter dicta* the momentous statement that "the power of Congress to authorize expenditure of public moneys for public purposes is not limited by the direct grants of legislative power found in the Constitution." Within two years this had become the operative line, and the Court reversed its stand on the spending power. When, more recently, the constitutionality of conditional grants was again challenged, this was declared to be a binding precedent, and the intrusion into state responsibilities was countenanced on the basis that the states were free to decline the offer of funds.[43] As we noted in Chapter 10, by the 1940s, the Supreme Court had effectively abandoned any attempt to be the guardian of the federal balance.

Canada: Stretching Interpretation

The *BNA Act* of 1867 did not provide even this degree of support for the spending power. In so far as a spending power has been claimed to exist, it has been inferred simply from Parliament's plenary power to tax. In the decentralist days when the JCPC was Canada's highest authority on the Constitution, the attempt by Parliament to exceed its enumerated powers through fiscal instruments was firmly ruled *ultra vires* on the basis that it was indeed means to an unconstitutional end.[44] In vetoing the *Employment and Social Insurance Act*, the JCPC ruled that "If on the true view of the legislation it is found that in reality and in pith and substance the legislation invades civil rights within the Province, or in respect of other classes of subjects otherwise encroaches upon the provincial field, the legislation will be invalid."

The enormous postwar expansion in the use of the spending power in Canada, however, has not been contested in the courts. Politically it has been challenged, and the abortive Meech Lake Accord promised in Section 106A to provide some constraint on exercise of the spending power. Use of the spending power seems to rest on a broad support within English Canada for the national social programs it funds.[45]

---

42. *US v. Butler* (1936) 297 US 1.
43. *South Dakota v. Dole* (1987) 483 US 203.
44. In vetoing the *Employment and Social Insurance Act*, the JCPC ruled that "If on the true view of the legislation it is found that in reality and in pith and substance the legislation invades civil rights within the Province, or in respect of other classes of subjects otherwise encroaches upon the provincial field, the legislation will be invalid."
45. Hamish Telford, "The Federal Spending Power in Canada: Nation-building or Nation-destroying?," *Publius* 33:1 (2003).

Germany: Constitutional and Institutional Limitations

As we noted above, the German system of revenue-base sharing is much less prone to generate the kind of VFI that massively strengthens the hand of the central government. Protection against heavy-handed exercise of the spending power is further provided by Article 104a, which sanctions grants of financial assistance to the *Länder* but in such a way as to leave little room for the coercive use of such moneys. Such grants are also required to be given legislative form "requiring the consent of the *Bundesrat*."

Australia: Explicit and Open-ended Authority

Australia is the federation that has not only the highest degree of VFI, but also the most explicit constitutional support for the spending power. The two, it turns out, have a strongly symbiotic relationship.

Section 96 of the Commonwealth Constitution asserts with brutal directness that "the Parliament may grant financial assistance to any State on such terms and conditions as the Parliament thinks fit." While this was drafted to ensure that the national government had a free hand to assist needy states,[46] it clearly does little to discourage broader interpretation. As we noted in Chapter 10, the High Court has interpreted this as precluding any possible limitations on the conditions that the Commonwealth imposes on state governments through the spending power. Indeed, it has endorsed the use of the spending power as a weapon to exclude the states from access to the kind of tax bases that would reduce their dependence on such grants. The spending power was used to eject the states from the income tax field, thus providing the Commonwealth with all the funds it needed to maximize the influence of the spending power. For every shilling that a state continued to raise in income tax, the Commonwealth would withhold a shilling in transfer payments.

Developments

One way or another, then, the spending power has developed into a major vehicle for centralization in systems of divided or legislative federalism. The use of conditional grants was intimately related to the great postwar growth of the welfare state in the period from the late 1950s to the early 1970s.

---

46. Saunders, "Hardest Nut to Crack" 171.

The United States: Conditionality Rules

The system of intergovernmental transfers in the United States has been dominated by conditional—or what are called in the US "categorical"—grants. An extensive range of strongly conditional programs forms part of a wider network of **mandates**—both funded and unfunded—through which Congress has come to impose its policy objectives on the states since the New Deal era.[47] A range of ambitious national policy objectives from the "Great Society"[48] on drove a doubling in grants in the 1960s and again in the 1970s.[49]

A large proportion of these grants are conditional both in the requirement that they be spent on a particular item and that state or local governments match funding. As with other federal systems, public heath care dominates—of the 593 grant programs in 1993, Medicaid alone accounted for 40 per cent of the total funds.[50] Empirical studies suggest "that grants exert a powerful influence on both the level and composition of spending by recipient governments."[51] This is in no small part due to the aggressiveness with which Congress has imposed conditions. These include "cross-cutting requirements" that impose conditions applicable to any and all grants and "crossover sanctions" whereby small grants carry large conditions enforced by connection with other larger grants.[52] Cross-cutting requirements are used to impose a wide range of political and social regulation on the states such as equal rights, environmental standards, and assistance for the handicapped.

The introduction of General Revenue Sharing (GRS) by the Nixon Administration in 1972 was intended to alter this dominant characteristic of American federalism by replacing specific purpose program payments with block grants that restored some policy autonomy to state and local governments. By the time GRS was eliminated in the name of spending restraint and competitive federalism in 1982, a total of $83 billion in general purpose payments had been made.[53] Even the GRS funds came with cross-cutting requirements, though, and their elimination only confirmed the American emphasis on conditional grants, which make over 80 per cent of all payments to the state and local governments.

---

47. Paul Posner, *The Politics of Unfunded Mandates: Whither Federalism?* (Washington, DC: Georgetown University Press, 1998).
48. The phrase used by US president Lyndon Johnson (1965–69) to promote a range of social justice and welfare policies and programs.
49. Walker, *Rebirth of Federalism* 3.
50. Stotsky and Sunley, "United States" 371.
51. Stotsky and Sunley, "United States" 372.
52. Posner, *Unfunded Mandates* 4.
53. Wallin, *Revenue Sharing to Deficit Sharing* 120.

The Rise and Fall of Conditional Grants in Canada

Notwithstanding their strong constitutional tax powers, the Canadian provinces agreed to relinquish control over revenue in return for cash transfers after World War II. In the early 1960s, they relied upon those cash transfers for almost one-quarter of their funding needs.[54] As the new national programs became established and at the same time fiscal pressures mounted on the national budget, a process of reducing transfers in favour of restoring taxing powers and reducing conditionality on remaining transfers occurred. By the late 1990s, provincial reliance on cash transfers had been almost halved to 13 per cent of their total expenditures. Almost all of that came in two packages: one entirely unconditional equalization grant and one moderately conditional broad block grant.[55] "Canada is unique among federations in having so much of its intergovernmental transfers (about 94 per cent) consolidated into block payments."[56] As a source of conflict between the two levels of government, conditionality has taken a back seat to adequacy. As in other federations, the temptation to transfer the pain of necessary budget economies to the subnational governments has been too great to resist. This has exposed another problem with VFI: the problem that what can be given can also be taken away.

The Rise and Rise of Conditional Grants in Australia

Conditional grants exploded in significance in Australia in the early 1970s as a reformist Labor government sought to circumvent the limitation of the division of powers to launch a variety of new social programs. They rapidly rose to constitute almost half of all the substantial transfers made to the states and, notwithstanding changes of government, have remained at that level ever since, being utilized for an enormous range of social, environmental, educational, and other purposes.

SHARING THE WEALTH

Before completing our discussion of the redistribution of funds from national to subnational governments, it is necessary to shift from consideration of vertical transfers to horizontal ones. As we discussed in Chapter 2, federalism is implicitly about sharing, about different regions entering into or participating in a common project with a larger community of interest and community of concern. All federations engage in some kind and some degree of **horizontal fiscal equalization** (HFE), redistributing resources from one region to another to maintain some

---

54. Lazar, *Toward a New Mission Statement* 14.
55. The Canada Health and Social Transfer.
56. Brown, "Fiscal Federalism" 63.

uniformity of services. However, this notion of HFE as sharing presumes a static relationship between donor and recipient regions. Another way to interpret equalization, though, is in dynamic terms. Equalization is a form of risk pooling, where jurisdictions accept that today's good fortune may be tomorrow's need and that what they share with others now they may receive back in the future. Canada and Australia saw major historical shifts in the twentieth century with hinterland regions going from needy to wealthy status over the course of decades. Politically, though, memories and time horizons may be short. Commitment to such sharing varies greatly between federations and in some cases has been subject to both political and academic criticism.

Basic Law or Ordinary Law?

Even though it might be regarded as inherent to federal union and thus part of the basic compact, equalization may well be an entirely subconstitutional matter. Equalization was given constitutional status in Germany with Article 107, which allowed a differential distribution of *Land* revenue shares to achieve a "reasonable equalization," and in Switzerland, where Article 135 declares that "The Federation shall promote financial equalization among the Cantons." Having been practised in Canada since 1957, a formal requirement for equalization was also written into the *Constitution Act 1982*. The American and Australian constitutions contain no such requirement, and in those federations equalization remains an entirely subconstitutional matter.

FIGURE 11.1
The Canadian Constitution Act 1982

36(2): Parliament and the government of Canada are committed to the principle of making equalization payments to ensure that provincial governments have sufficient revenues to provide reasonably comparable levels of public services at reasonably comparable levels of taxation.

Varying Commitment

The degree of equalization is, however, not necessarily determined by the degree of constitutionalization. While Germany has one of the most comprehensive systems of equalization, so does Australia where no constitutional requirement for horizontal redistribution exists at all. The other main examples of constitutional entrenchment, Switzerland and Canada, practise a more moderate degree of equalization.

Topping and Tailing

Comprehensive HFE involves redistributing funds among the subnational governments based on a "formula" that adjusts for the differences between local fiscal capacities and local expenditure needs. In Australia, VFI and HFE are integrated, with the large volume of Commonwealth transfers (including GST revenues) being divided among the states according to the equalization formula. Since 1933, an autonomous agency, the Commonwealth Grants Commission, has had statutory responsibility for those allocations; its sophisticated formula ensures that not only are weaker states brought up to the national average but that stronger states are brought down. The Canadian formula avoids such a thorough levelling by excluding the richest province (Alberta) from calculation of the national average and by bringing the poorer ones up to that adjusted average without bringing the richer ones (Ontario and Alberta) down.[57] The Swiss approach is not dissimilar. "The differences in the cantons in terms of size, geography, population and economic potential are so great that, without equalisation measures, fiscal federalism would perform under regional disparities which would be intolerable." However, "there are ... no claims from cantonal governments or the citizenry that equalization measures should compensate entirely for differences between the cantons.... The pragmatic objective is to render regional disparities politically acceptable so that remaining differences do not endanger the cohesion of the federation."[58]

Sink or Swim

While not following the German or Australian model of a ruthless equalization, Switzerland and Canada demonstrate a commitment far beyond anything practised in American federalism. The United States stands out as the one substantial exception to the rule that federalism entails sharing and means ensuring that public services are offered to citizens at a common level regardless of local economic conditions. Certain transfer programs are or have been implemented on the basis of some kind of equalization formula (for instance Medicaid); however, no systematic equalization occurs, and, indeed, there has been an overarching assumption that this is not an element of the American federal compact where an ethos of competitive federalism is predominant and where congressional representatives from the south historically insisted

---

57. In 2003 the average provincial government per capita revenue was assessed at $6,000 and the poorer provinces lifted to that level. Alberta's per capita revenue—after equalization—meanwhile remained at closer to $10,000.

58. Dafflon, "Fiscal Federalism in Switzerland" 284.

that national programs take a particularistic form. Here it may be significant that the United States has a presidential rather than parliamentary system of government; "fiscal equalization faces political obstacles in the Congress, whose members are elected to 'bring home the bacon,' not to reward other jurisdictions."[59] National programs indeed transfer wealth from one region of the country to another, but typically with no regard to local need and not infrequently in complete disregard to patterns of relative wealth. Whether this results in a redistribution from wealthier to poorer regions or vice versa is a matter of chance. In recent times, it has been vice versa, with the wealthiest states being the biggest per capita recipients.[60]

Politics Against Markets in the EU

As we noted above, the EU spends most of its budget on agricultural and cohesion policies. From the inception of the European Economic Community, the Common Agricultural Policy (CAP) has been designed as an income stabilization policy for European farmers.[61] It subsidizes prices above the world market level and places protective tariffs upon agricultural imports. Curbing this runaway expenditure has proven extremely difficult because the governments of the main recipient countries (France, Spain, Greece, Ireland, Denmark) have come to rely on the CAP as a convenient welfare institution and fear the loss of electoral support of an important and well-organized constituency. These transfers have been particularly welcome in the new member states.

Cohesion policy essentially consists of structural fund transfers to less developed regions of the EU under the heading of six objectives:[62] regions with a per capita GDP of less than 75 per cent of the EU average; regions affected by industrial decline and above EU average unemployment; long-term unemployment; occupational integration of young people and adaptation of workers to industrial change; agricultural and forestry assistance and diversification away from traditional agricultural activity; and development of sparsely populated Nordic areas.

The EU's Cohesion Illusion

Together, the CAP and the structural funds can be seen as program-specific but unconditional grants in lieu of an income-related European

---

59. John Kincaid, "American Experiences in the Theory and Practice of Fiscal Federalism," in Arora and Verney, *Multiple Identities in a Single State* 326.

60. Walker, *Rebirth of Federalism* 250.

61. See Elmar Rieger, "The Common Agricultural Policy: Politics against Markets," in Wallace and Wallace, eds., *Policy-Making in the European Union*.

62. See David Allen, "Cohesion and the Structural Funds: Transfers and Trade-offs," in Wallace and Wallace, eds., *Policy-Making in the European Union* 252.

social welfare policy and as an exercise in HFE. Both are embedded in the typical continental European view that market forces spread unevenly and that losers have to be compensated for the costs of integration. Among the two, the CAP is particularly problematic in light of such international trade agreements as the General Agreement on Tariffs and Trade (GATT) and the World Trade Organization (WTO). More problematic in principle is the fact that the gap between rich and poor countries, and particularly between rich regions in rich countries and poor regions in poor countries, has remained tremendous.[63] The accession of the eastern European member states poses almost insurmountable problems of cohesion for generations to come. It is hard to imagine that the current *acquis communautaire* of European fiscal policy will suffice to stabilize economic and monetary union in the long run. The EU will find itself at a crossroads: it will either have to go the American way and abandon a serious commitment to equalization, or, if it wants to maintain the traditional approach of European welfare capitalism, it will have to cough up serious and costly new fiscal stabilization policies.

Varying Views

Like all policies that modify market outcomes, equalization of revenues across jurisdictions within federal systems is a contested practice. Modifying market outcomes means moderating market forces. Thus, the argument is periodically made that subnational governments lose both the incentive and the imperative to improve their performance if costs and benefits are diminished and markets lose the signals the bring about their own adjustments. Regional disparities and the issue of whether equalization subsidizes development or underdevelopment in poorer regions has driven the debate in Canada.[64] However, Germany is arguably the most contentious case.

The German Conundrum

Germany's unique practice of requiring a second round of equalization transferring surplus revenues directly from the affluent to the mendicant *Länder* has an almost punitive character. The admission of several much poorer new *Länder* into the German federation placed a new strain on the equalization system by accentuating the wealth gradient that had to be flattened. Indeed, according to a chorus of commentary, it has made

---

63. See Angela Bourne, "Regional Europe," in Michelle Cini, ed., *European Union Politics* (Oxford: Oxford University Press, 2003) 283.
64. See Dan Usher, *The Uneasy Case for Equalization Payments* (Vancouver, BC: Fraser Institute, 1995); Robin W. Boadway and Paul A.R. Hobson, eds., *Equalization: Its Contribution to Canada's Economic and Fiscal Progress* (Kingston, ON: John Deutsch Institute for the Study of Economic Policy, Queen's University, 1998).

the system "unsustainable." As a consequence, equalization is now widely criticized as a practice that removes the incentives for richer *Länder* to perform, since whatever advances they make will be promptly creamed off, and removes the compulsion for the poorer ones, since they are provided with windfall funds. "There is ... little incentive for revenue-weak *Länder* to improve their performance"—and they haven't.[65] Meanwhile, there may not even be sufficient incentive for the richer *Länder* to bother collecting some of their taxes at all, since most of it will be confiscated.[66] And of course changes to either the constitutional or the legislative components of the equalization system in Germany must gain the consent of the *Bundesrat*, where the beneficiaries hold a majority.[67] Thus, criticism of the policy becomes criticism of the entire system itself. It is a criticism, however, that has come primarily from neoliberal quarters. Overall, German federalism has fared well under its regime of 'brotherly' federalism.

The American Case

At the other extreme, have the pronounced inequalities between regions in the United States been exacerbated or ameliorated by the absence of equalization policies? Proponents of competitive federalism argue that the evidence is on their side. While years of transfers to Canada's disadvantaged Atlantic provinces seems to have produced little amelioration, they argue, the American sunbelt states have been able to pull themselves up by their bootstraps:

> As late as 1950, the relative poverty of the southern American states was thought to be endemic. But by making their labour markets more flexible and by setting less generous welfare provisions, resulting in lower payroll taxes than in the northern states, southern states began to attract private corporate investment on a vast scale, and by the 1970s, much of the formerly backward region had become the prosperous Sunbelt.[68]

However, it must be acknowledged that there are too many other variables at work here to be able to draw any conclusions from such a rudimentary comparison. Among these variables are lower energy costs

---

65. Charlie Jeffrey, "German Federalism from Cooperation to Competition," in Maiken Umbach, ed., *German Federalism: Past, Present, Future* (Basingstoke: Palgrave, 2002) 178.

66. Spahn and Föttinger, "Germany" 246.

67. See the discussion in Wolfgang Renzsch, "Challenges and Perspectives for German Federalism," in Maiken Umbach, ed., *German Federalism: Past, Present, Future* (Basingstoke: Palgrave, 2002).

68. McKinnon and Nechyba, "Competition in Federalism Systems" 48.

in the south, for instance, and the fact that many of the sunbelt industries are new industries of the second (electronic) industrial divide rather than old 'rustbelt' industries such as steel making that were successfully lured away from the northeast.

HOW DO FEDERATIONS MANAGE POLICY RESPONSIBILITIES?

If much of what we know about political processes is correct, federalism should have an impact on policy processes and outcomes. Politics and policy should be characteristically different in federal and unitary states. There is no consensus though on whether this is the case or in what way it might be the case. At one extreme, federalism scholar William H. Riker dismissed the idea that federalism has a significant impact: "It is difficult to escape the conclusion that the accidents of federalism (i.e., the constitutional and administrative detail) do not make any difference at all."[69] In his view, what society wants it will achieve through one institutional avenue or another. At the other extreme, there are a number of scholars who have pointed to the federal division of powers as a major influence on particular policy outcomes or as the cause of specific policy problems. This was most famously formulated by Dicey: "Federal government means weak government." In particular, it weakens government in its attempt to control or modify markets: "Federalism, as it defines, and therefore limits, the powers of each department of the administration, is unfavourable to the interference or activity of government.... This may be a merit of the federal system; it is, however, a merit which does not commend itself to modern democrats."[70] One influential line of analysis, then, ascribes to federalism a potentially powerful role in delaying or derailing policy innovation and implementation. However, by contrast, another view sees in federalism the potential for greater policy innovation.

Federalism and Policy Constraint

In Theory

Each of these two views is based on clear and compelling logic. Federalism is associated with delay and frustration of innovation because divided jurisdiction fragments governmental power and thereby reduces policy capacity. One level of government may have the constitutional authority but not the fiscal resources or ability to contain spillovers, while the other level of government may have the resources and reach but not the requisite authority. Legislative adaptations to incorporate

---

69. Riker, "Federalism" 144
70. Dicey, *An Introduction* 167 and 169.

the federal principle in the national legislative process may impose tough concurrent majority requirements. In addition, opposed interests may exploit and amplify these disjunctures.

In systems of divided or legislative federalism, the potential to obstruct policy innovation or adaptation is going to be highest in those cases where new demands arise for action that lies outside of the scope of the level of government with the formal jurisdiction and where powerful vested interests stand to lose from the shift. The policy constraint imposed by a system of divided federalism will also vary according to the specific framework in place, with some versions more "demos-constraining" than others.[71] In systems of administrative or integrated federalism, policy-making may also be obstructed by the degree of consensus required. This possibility has been labelled the "joint-decision trap"[72] and has been regularly held up as the major institutional problem in the politics of the German Federal Republic. The problem is analogous to the one we have seen that hampered the effective operation of confederal systems: the inability to act without an elusively broad consensus or even an oppressive unanimity requirement.

In Practice

Federalism's reputation for policy obstruction arose in the largest part because of the obstacles it placed in the way of adaptation to new social and economic conditions early in the twentieth century. This included periods in the United States, Canada, and Australia when it seemed that the judiciary, backed by conservative business interests, was intent on using the division of powers to create a governmental no-go area and thereby enforce a regime of *laissez-faire*. In Canada and the United States, this disjuncture between political demands and political capacities reached a crisis point in the 1930s as the courts prevented national governments from assuming policy responsibilities which apparently could only be discharged effectively at the national level. Federalism, it seemed to a number of exasperated critics, was cruelly preventing desperately needed collective solutions to widespread personal suffering. Neither the kind of bold economic management nor the kind of great new social programs required to ameliorate the effects of the Great Depression could be supplied by the states or provinces. The scope was national, and the resource needs were national, but the jurisdiction was not.

In none of the three main systems of legislative federalism was the constitution written to grant central governments authority to engage

---

71. Alfred Stepan, "Toward a New Comparative Politics of Federalism" 333.
72. Scharpf, "The Joint-Decision Trap." For an assessment, see Stephen J. Sylvia, "Reform Gridlock and the Role of the Bundesrat in German Politics," *West European Politics* 22:2 (1999).

in hands-on microeconomic management such as that involving price controls or to establish national welfare systems. Insofar as they were considered a legitimate function of government at all, both were seen as inherently local responsibilities. The growth of modern industrial society made such presumptions obsolete and the constitutions built on them anachronistic. Adaptation was possible, but it would inevitably take time. In the United States, the impact of this disjuncture was first felt in the late nineteenth century when efforts were made at both the state and national level to provide a regulatory framework for a rapidly industrializing society increasingly operating across state boundaries. This gave rise to the first American national regulatory agency, the Interstate Commerce Commission, which functioned for over a century from its creation in 1887 until deregulation finally brought about its demise in 1995. However, federalism regularly obstructed initiatives at both levels through this period. As we saw in Chapter 10, the ability of the two political branches to intimidate the judicial branch in the United States brought about a rapid adjustment once the full impact of the Great Depression worked its way through the electoral system. Taxing and spending powers augmented the commerce power in allowing Congress to break the bonds of dual federalism and spread widely into areas of formerly state jurisdiction. This was predicated on a radical rereading of the Constitution that, while forced upon the Supreme Court, established a lasting consensus that provided abundant scope for the growth of national power.

In Canada, adjustment occurred more slowly, waiting for formal amendment. In Australia, the obstacles of federalism were confronted head-on with a comprehensive constitutional amendment passed by the required referendum in 1946. Even then, though, the division of powers managed to hinder policy innovation by allowing opponents to exploit key qualifying clauses in the context of a highly sympathetic High Court. In Switzerland, federalism seems to have contributed to delayed and reduced welfare state development, not only in slowing policy adoption but also in allowing individual cantons to frustrate national policy choices through their control over implementation. However, it must be noted that the restraining effect of federalism cannot easily be disentangled from that of referendum democracy.[73]

Breaking the Mould

The significant obstacles to the establishment of the modern welfare state and its programs of regulation and redistribution thrown up by a

---

73. See Herbert Obinger, "Federalism, Direct Democracy, and Welfare State Development in Switzerland," *Journal of Public Policy* 18:3 (1998).

system of divided jurisdiction were to a great extent a one-off phenomenon. Systems designed in a pre-industrial age adapted awkwardly to the conditions of industrial society and in particular to the enormous growth in externalities. However, the eventual breakthrough was decisive. That process of adaptation broke the original mould to large extent, facilitating a continuing growth in central government powers and absorption of new policy domains into the national policy framework. When environmental issues burst onto the political stage in the 1960s, national governments faced much less difficulty in assuming responsibilities in what had universally been a matter of local concern and control. In the United States, the treaty power proved a useful device early on, with national lawmakers able to bring local matters under their umbrella by linking them to international commitments.[74] However, once the potential of the commerce clause had been established, that provided a more powerful tool, proving supremely, even infinitely, elastic. Since the mid-1960s, Congress has "pre-empted" state law across a broad environmental field among others. This has been part of a massive centralization of power in American federalism where Congress has not only occupied a number of policy fields, but used its expanded power to impose its own agenda of social reform on the operation of the state governments themselves. Federalism does not seem to have impeded the making of national environmental policy in the United States.[75]

In Australia, the treaty power[76] has proven an effective means for assertion of national leadership, being exploited with dramatic effect in the 1980s. In Canada, where the decentralist mould was not broken in the same way it was in the United States and Australia and the treaty power has remained uniquely weak, national environmental powers have been more tenuous, relying in particular on Parliament's jurisdiction over the criminal law.[77] Even then, evidence suggests that Canadian governments have shown little environmental policy ambition and that it is the weight of economic development considerations, not the division of powers, that has constrained environmental policy.[78]

---

74. Edward A. Fitzgerald, "The Constitutional Division of Powers with Respect to the Environment in the United States," in Kenneth M. Holland, F.L. Morton. and Brian Galligan, eds., *Federalism and the Environment: Environmental Policymaking in Australia, Canada, and the United States* (Westport, CT: Greenwood Press, 1996) 25.

75. John Kincaid, "Intergovernmental Costs and Coordination in US Environmental Protection," in Holland, *et al.*, eds., *Federalism and the Environment* 82.

76. Section 51(xxix) of the Commonwealth Constitution.

77. F.L. Morton, "The Constitutional Division of Powers with Respect to the Environment in Canada," in Holland, *et al.*, eds., *Federalism and the Environment*.

78. Kathryn Harrison, *Passing the Buck: Federalism and Canadian Environmental Policy* (Vancouver, BC: University of British Columbia Press, 1996); Grace Skogstad, "Intergovernmental Relations and the Politics of Environmental Protection in Canada," in Holland, *et al.*, eds., *Federalism and the Environment*.

Policy Constraints and Opportunities in the EU

The dilemma federalizing Europe faces is exactly the opposite to the one experienced by the classic federations as they made the painful transition to modern industrial society. The EU is a union of states the core of which have their own well-established social policy regimes, regimes that have the heaviest commitment to social spending and the strongest culture of collective provision in the world. They increasingly face the pressures that helped prevent the member units of the classic federations from developing their own welfare states—particularly the pressure of downward competition. At this point there is little possibility of the various national welfare states being superceded by an EU-wide one. The EU has in that sense created a problem for its member states that only some sort of regulatory solution can address.[79]

In environmental policy, the picture is rather different. If the comparison between the United States and Canada contains a general explanatory truth, one ought to expect that environmental policy in the EU must be standing on feet of clay. As we have noted throughout this book, the EU is in many ways still more confederal than federal. The decentralist mould has not been broken, and, under the subsidiarity provision, it is even gaining strength. Nevertheless the EU provides a cautionary tale of success in terms of environmental policy. "The EU [environmental] policy process has demonstrated that it is capable of making binding decisions, which most federal systems would find extraordinarily challenging."[80]

Four main reasons account for this success story. First, living in a densely populated space and greatly alarmed by the 1986 Chernobyl nuclear catastrophe in Ukraine, Europeans were more aware of limited resources and environmental fragility early on than citizens elsewhere and more exposed to environmental externalities and the cross-border nature of environmental problems. Secondly, the European environmental policy process was led by "green-minded governments and advocacy groups" that proved capable of "pulling the 'laggards' towards accepting higher standards of environmental regulation than many could have agreed at the national level."[81] For reasons of economic competitiveness, Germany in particular pressed for the kinds of standards at the European level which its own political power configuration (the rise of the Green party) forced it to adopt domestically. Thirdly, European institutions

---

79. Fritz W. Scharpf, "Democratic Legitimacy under Conditions of Regulatory Competition: Why Europe Differs from the United States," in Nicolaïdis and Howse, eds., *The Federal Vision.*
80. See Alberta Sbragia, "Environmental Policy: Economic Constraints and External Pressures," in Wallace and Wallace, eds., *Policy-making in the European Union* 315.
81. Alberta Sbragia, "Environmental Policy" 293.

provided a congenial environment for the environment issue. The independent Commission could initiate policy on the basis of professional expertise, and a particularly "green-minded" European Parliament proved supportive—likely because its members are more removed from the mainstream of power politics than their colleagues in national parliaments. And finally, the dominant instrument of environmental policy, regulation, is, as we have noted, the "first pillar" of the EU.

Federalism and Policy Facilitation

In Theory

On the other side of the ledger, federalism has long been seen as providing unusually fertile conditions for policy innovation because it creates, at the lower level, multiple governments any one of which might take the lead in experimenting with new solutions. This was one of the virtues James Bryce famously attributed to federalism when he penned his landmark nineteenth-study of American government, *The American Commonwealth*:

> Federalism enables a people to try experiments in legislation and administration which could not be safely tried in a large centralized country. A comparatively small commonwealth like an American state easily makes and unmakes its laws; mistakes are not serious, for they are soon corrected; other States profit by the experience of a law or a method which has worked well or ill in the State that has tried it.[82]

Some years later, Justice Brandeis of the US Supreme Court restated this somewhat more pithily in a much-quoted dissenting opinion. "It is one of the happy incidents of the federal system that a single courageous state may, if its citizens choose, serve as a laboratory, and try novel and economic experiments without risk to the rest of the country."[83] Such **laboratory federalism**, then, can unleash policy innovation on a local level that would not win sufficient support on a national level and then—should it prove successful—spread by demonstration effect, allowing policy learning to infect otherwise resistant jurisdictions. In a different context, Pierre Trudeau, later to become prime minister, in turn used this logic, enlivened with a dash of Chairman Mao, to argue that "Canadian socialists must consider federalism as a positive asset...."[84]

---

82. James Bryce, *The American Commonwealth*, 3rd ed. (London: Macmillan, 1893) 353.
83. In *New State Ice Co. v. Liebmann*, 285 US 262 (1932).
84. Pierre Elliot Trudeau, "The Theory and Practice of Federalism," in Michael Oliver, ed., *Social Purpose for Canada* (Toronto, ON: University of Toronto Press, 1961).

Almost by definition, laboratory federalism is limited to systems of legislative federalism since only in such systems do the subnational governments have constitutional responsibility for both the implementation and the making of policy within a substantial range of policy areas. Thus, one recent criticism of the German model has been that the *Länder* have insufficient scope for generating their own strategies for dealing with economic and social policy challenges. However, even in the English-speaking federations with their strong element of divided jurisdiction, policy experimentation may require such conducive conditions that it would be a rather limited phenomenon. It of course presumes that the subnational governments have the relevant powers and capacities together with sufficient policy space. From a rational actor point of view, it presumes that there are sufficient jurisdictions willing to make themselves the guinea pig—or, to put it in more technical language, of being willing to internalize the costs of an experiment whose benefits will spread as positive externalities to other jurisdictions (as either something they now know to avoid or now have good grounds to try themselves). And, finally, it assumes that the different jurisdictions and levels of government encounter circumstances sufficiently similar to make specific policy responses broadly relevant.

In Practice

It should not be excessively difficult to make some sort of empirical assessment of the laboratory federalism thesis. If federalism is indeed facilitating such social learning, it will be evident in both horizontal and vertical diffusion—a spread of successful innovations across the subnational jurisdictions and an adoption by the national government of policies that have proven themselves at the subnational level. In practice, though, hard evidence of the laboratory effect at work has not been so abundant.

Accounts of American federalism identify the period 1870–1932 as a period when the states set the pace in devising ways of responding to the new pressures of modern industrial society.[85] A survey of policy learning in the United States, though, shows patterns more random than supportive of the thesis.[86] The policy challenges thrown up by the Great Depression are a good illustration of the constraints that limit the spread of laboratory federalism. Resource limitations and the problem of externalities made it very difficult for individual jurisdictions to respond effectively or to innovate in policy. Exceptions are well known— Wisconsin has a celebrated record as a pioneer in American social

---

85. Walker, *Rebirth of Federalism* 84 and *passim*.
86. Keith Boekelman, "The Influence of States on Federal Policy Adoptions," *Policy Studies Journal* 23 (1992).

policy—but they are exceedingly few. No Australian state or Canadian province implemented significant new programs in this period. While they had the constitutional room for manœuvre, fiscal constraints were overwhelming. However, the pioneering in postwar Saskatchewan of a public hospital insurance scheme (1947) and after it a public health insurance scheme (1962) provided a major impetus to Canada's adoption of the Medicare system of national public health insurance, introduced in 1966. According to one interpretation, "federalism provided the dynamic institutional levers that diffused public hospital and medical insurance across the country as a whole."[87] In a somewhat paler version, Queensland's introduction of public hospital care in 1945 pioneered public health care in Australia.[88] Some successful 'experimentation' occurred and confirmed the laboratory metaphor by then being reproduced on a larger scale.

Federal Complexities of Modern Governance

The nationalization of policy that occurred over the twentieth century by no means abolished the subnational role. To varying degrees, policy took a federal form, bridging the two levels of government and establishing the practices of what is somewhat euphemistically called **cooperative federalism**. In many instances, it is the case that, while increasingly subject to national rules and obliged to participate in national programs in a way that spoke of a more coercive reality, the subnational governments remained the vehicles through which those programs were implemented. These compromises have regularly raised questions of effectiveness, efficiency, and accountability.

Health Policy

The development and operation of complex, resource-intensive, and politically charged modern health care systems has been a particular challenge for federal systems. While the impact of federalism on health systems may well be contingent on other variables and may or may not be significant,[89] it is certainly the case that in a number of federations the complexities of health care policy have been compounded by the

---

87. Antonia Maioni, "Federalism and Health Care in Canada," in Keith G. Banting and Stan Corbett, eds., *Health Policy and Federalism: A Comparative Perspective on Multilevel Governance* (Montreal, QC and Kingston, ON: McGill-Queen's University Press, 2002) 179.

88. In general, see Gwendolyn Gray, *Federalism and Health Policy: The Development of Health Systems in Canada and Australia* (Toronto, ON: University of Toronto Press, 1991.

89. Keith G. Banting and Stan Corbett, "Health Policy and Federalism: An Introduction," in Banting and Corbett, eds., *Health Policy and Federalism* 20.

complexities of divided jurisdiction. Again, there is strong reason to presume that systems of administrative federalism would avoid many of the entanglements found in systems of legislative federalism. Under an administrative division of powers, a uniform national framework could be established at the centre and the full responsibility for management and administration delegated to the individual jurisdictions, with a relatively clean division of functions prevailing. And, indeed, for precisely these reasons we find that in Germany federalism has little impact on the health system.[90]

The historical division of powers characteristic of legislative federalism has, by contrast, given rise to entangled and potentially conflictual arrangements for the delivery of such major components of social policy as health care. As we have seen, the compromise between modernizers and traditionalists left social policy in the domain of subnational governments. Modernization, however, has placed a premium on nationwide policies and programs in many of these areas, and constitutional and subconstitutional adjustment has occurred to make those possible. In the United States, Canada, and Australia, the result is overlap and ambiguity in responsibilities. Australia and Canada are good examples of the way health care systems inevitably straddle the jurisdictional divide, with governments entangled in a high-profile and complex relationship between local responsibilities and national policy-making. The compromises reached in those two countries are quite different, but each is illustrative of the impact legislative federalism has on major areas of policy-making in the modern state.

In Canada, a national framework was imposed and has been sustained through the spending power (notwithstanding a significant downward transfer of the cost burden over time), with the provinces otherwise globally responsible for running their individual health systems. Analogous arrangements prevail in the United States where both Medicare and Medicaid run as nationally funded programs, the latter involving joint funding and a high degree of intergovernmentality.[91] In a complex and conflicted relationship, national legislation in Canada establishes the essential features of the provincially administered health care system— characterized by universality and a prohibition on private payment— while regular intergovernmental negotiations take place over how generously the provinces will be funded.[92] The arrangement has allowed a certain amount of policy experimentation and variation, notably in

90. Dietmar Wassener, "Federalism and the German Health-Care System," in Banting and Corbett, eds., *Health Policy and Federalism*.

91. David C. Colby, "Federal-State Relations in United States Health Policy," in Banting and Corbett, eds., *Health Policy and Federalism*.

92. Duane Adams, ed., *Federalism, Democracy and Health Policy in Canada* (Montreal, QC and Kingston, ON: McGill-Queen's University Press, 2002).

Québec,[93] but not in a way that has generated broad policy learning. In Australia, more fraught arrangements evolved whereby the public funding of physician services comes from a Commonwealth government program (Medicare), while hospital management and funding is the preserve of the states (subsidized by large Commonwealth grants because of the high degree of VFI). One arrangement encourages political conflicts at the level of executive federalism over the generosity of transfer payments but allows each jurisdiction the global management authority necessary for effective governance. The other encourages both political conflicts over funding formulae and administrative inefficiencies connected with blame and cost-shifting with periodic calls for a rationalization of the entire intergovernmental arrangement.[94]

SUMMARY

- Federalism, a system of government that emerged in the much governmentally simpler times of the late eighteenth and nineteenth centuries, has had to adapt to the complexities of modern industrial society. This has posed a considerable challenge, in particular to the application of the traditional division of powers.
- The theory of public finance has generated a set of prescriptive guidelines for dividing responsibilities between two or more levels of government in a federal system. This logic of assignment focusses on the extent to which any particular function can be contained within one jurisdiction. Should significant externality or spillover effects be present, then the logic says the matter ought to be the responsibility of a higher level of government. Similarly, should subnational jurisdictions be subject to significant mobility pressures, then likewise, higher level coordination or responsibility is called for.
- On this basis, it has widely been accepted that the redistributive functions of the modern Keynesian welfare state, involving progressive taxation and various needs-based social expenditures, should be carried out by the national government. National governments will not be subject to the intensity of mobility pressures that will lead subnational jurisdictions to shy away from such commitments. Subnational governments, meanwhile, can maintain a responsibility for both infrastructure provision and industry support. This logic has supplanted what we have described as the historical compromise between nationalizing modernizers and regional traditionalists whereby

---

93. Maioni, "Federalism and Health Care in Canada" 180.

94. For instance, Stephen Duckett, "Commonwealth/State Relations in Health," in Linda Hancock, ed., *Health Policy in the Market State* (St Leonards, NSW: Allen and Unwin, 1999).

economic functions were assigned to national governments while social responsibilities were left to the constituent units.

- Inherent in the idea of federalism is the principle of maximal suitable autonomy for lower-level jurisdictions, a version of which is implied in the European principle of subsidiarity. Governance will be better, and policy choices more finely tuned to local needs, the closer to the people government is. In one school of thought, this takes the form of a belief in competitive federalism—the proposition that the best in federalism is brought out by a division of powers that allows different jurisdictions maximum opportunity to vary their policy settings to satisfy residents and attract investment. This may conflict with the logic of assignment as described above, potentially encouraging a race to the bottom in social provision and environmental protection.

- The United States, Canada, and Australia were all federations established on the basis of a high level of concurrency in their tax assignment, with the subnational governments being limited in certain—but only certain—respects. In all federations, though, the national government has achieved a position of financial superiority whereby surplus revenues are available for redistribution to the subnational governments. This vertical fiscal imbalance (VFI) in turn has provided national governments with powerful leverage for influencing policy that lies formally within the jurisdiction, indeed perhaps exclusive jurisdiction, of the subnational governments. While VFI is much more acute in some federations (notably Australia), some degree is almost inevitable given the realities of public finance economics. Only at the national level can the most potent tax, the income tax, be levied free of downward pressure from mobile factors.

- Much more a matter of choice is horizontal fiscal equalization (HFE), the transfer of funds from more affluent to less affluent jurisdictions to maintain a common level of public services across the federation. Such interregional solidarity might be regarded as inherent in a federal compact, and it is the norm in modern federations. However, there remains one exception—the United States—where it has not been implemented and has never even been seriously proposed. Equalization is not consonant with competitive federalism, which in the United States is widely regarded as being the approach that maximizes the benefits that a federal order can provide. Views differ on the economic consequences of HFE, with opponents arguing that the US example demonstrates that economic adjustment is hindered by regional transfers. Even in the rest of the federal world, the degree of equalization varies, and it may be argued that compromise versions—such as that practised in Canada—are less prone to the putative disabilities of regional transfers than those rigorous schemes operational in Germany and Australia.

- Policy-making in federal systems is complicated by the division of powers, by the impact of judicial review, and potentially by federal bicameralism. One tendency of federal structures is to obstruct policy innovation; in certain contentious periods, federalism came under fire for frustrating attempts to respond to new economic and social challenges. In addition, though, a number of commentators have judged one of federalism's virtues to be the scope it provides for policy innovation and experimentation. The hypothesis of laboratory federalism is that multiple jurisdictions means a lower threshold for initial introduction of innovative policies and scope for horizontal and vertical diffusion. The two tendencies—one conservative, one progressive—are not mutually exclusive, and at varying times one or the other tendency has been more in effect. Laboratory federalism, though, requires a number of permissive or conducive conditions.

- Any clear and meaningful division of powers that may have characterized the federations of the United States, Canada, and Australia in their beginnings has been made thoroughly porous, weak, and difficult to perceive by the realities of modern government and the assumption by national governments of extensive new responsibilities. Efficiency, effectiveness, and accountability may all be reduced by the administrative complexity and political tension this creates. In many ways what has occurred is a slide away from legislative federalism to administrative federalism, from a division of powers to a division of functions. In a number of areas in the classic federations, the subnational units have been given the implementation and administration functions while the national government has extended its broad policy-making role. However, this has occurred without the central institutions of integrated federalism that ensure a direct participation of the constituent units in that umbrella policy-making.

Conclusion

We have come to the end of a lengthy journey. Even among the classical federations we found great diversity of normative intention, institutional design, and political practice. This should not have come as a surprise, however. In its most elementary sense, federalism is a very broad concept of shared sovereignty and divided governance among autonomous members in a political union. It is the historical antidote to the idea of empire as well as to modern unitary statehood. As such, it allows for as much variety in design and practice as other forms of government. Yet, as is the case with other forms of government as well, this variety can be sorted into a relatively small number of basic models.

One reason for this variety lies in the historical process by which federal systems have been constructed. They have not come about by means of conquest, a revolutionary bang, or simple evolutionary tradition. Instead, they have been the result of careful deliberation and compromise among constituent groups or founding members. And even though our comparative inquiry has shown how the designers of the later federal systems learned from earlier experiments, the eventual outcome very much reflected the diverse cultural and economic predispositions among these groups and founding members. By comparison, and obvious variety notwithstanding, modern unitary states were more likely constructed upon abstract principles of sovereignty and democratic accountability.

A common argument levied against federal states is precisely this: that they are inherently less democratic than unitary states because they are the result of conservative interests adamant about preserving their old regional privileges and powers.[1] Yet our comparative inquiry has shown the ingenuity and flexibility of federalism in designing all kinds of institutional as well as procedural mechanisms that address and satisfy the requirements of modern democratic governance in terms of public participation, representative inclusiveness, and policy responsiveness.

---

1. See Smith, *Federalism*.

Thus, it may be well so that the American founders had in mind a conservative project protecting their interests and privileges against the maelstrom of democratic majority power. However, there can be no doubt that their federal experiment reached far beyond that by being constructed upon universal principles of accountability and government restraint by means of multiple checks and balances. In the parliamentary federations, this relationship between federalism and the legitimacy of democratic majority rule has remained more tenuous. In the Althusian-European tradition, on the other hand, there is much more emphasis on negotiated agreement among autonomous collectivities than on the primacy of majority rule.

What is so democratic about majority rule anyway? When John Locke endorsed it as the "Power to Act as one Body," he assumed that the legitimacy of such power stemmed from a social contract whereby "any number of Men" had "so consented to make one Community or Government."[2] That assumption was as false then as it is now because neither the Scottish, nor the Welsh or Irish had been asked.[3] Precisely herein lies the great potential of federalism for the construction of a multicultural and multinational world of states and societies: in giving up the assumption of *one government fits all*, a more complex design of organized diversity becomes possible.

Another common argument against federalism is its often alleged inability to make timely and efficient policy decisions. There may be duplication of services and programs, and compromises required by shared multilevel governance are suspected of amounting to suboptimal solutions or worse. Federal fatigue among voters and service recipients is a fairly common phenomenon in many federal states. Such criticisms are necessary and appropriate as a reminder that federalism does not automatically provide governance closer to the people and in their best interest. However, it also tends to overlook the comparative record.

Among the world's richest countries, the so-called G7 nations, three are federations (the United States, Canada, and Germany); two are experimenting with devolution (Italy and the UK); and even the most notorious Jacobin state among them, France, has loosened the grip of centralized administration in recent years.[4] Among the federations in this club are some of the most formidable welfare states. In other words, the point to be made about federal governance is not its alleged lack of efficiency and accountability, but its spectacular success in providing citizens with political, economic, and social stability against considerable

---

2.   Locke, *Two Treatises of Government* II, 95–96.

3.   Nor, for that matter, the American colonies who broke away from Britain for exactly that reason.

4.   Even Japan was not immune, with demands for more local autonomy being voiced there as well.

odds of socio-cultural and -economic diversity and asymmetry leading to the adoption of a federal form of governance in the first place.

This in turn is the reason why federalism has become so attractive to a growing number of countries and regions such as Belgium, Spain, South Africa, and the EU. The adoption of federalism in the post-colonial societies of the developing world is quite a different story, though. The so-called federalist revolution of the twentieth century was in large measure one of post-colonial imposition. Federal structures were superimposed upon multinational or tribal societies thrown together within arbitrarily drawn boundaries. More often than not, they did not fit the societies and cultures they were supposed to serve.

The federations of South America had in fact formed in the nineteenth century but struggled all through the twentieth century in search of democratic consolidation. In Africa, while South Africa became a belated if fragile post-apartheid success story, such consolidation remains out of reach for Nigeria. The record for Asia is mixed as well. Only India has emerged as a democratic federation. It is perhaps the greatest success story among all federations because consolidation was accomplished against great odds, including size of population and extreme multi-ethnic and -lingual diversity as well as socio-economic asymmetry. It is from the Indian example that Russia, still a federation more in name than in reality, and China, the last of the great empires, will have to learn the lesson of renouncing authoritarian centralism.

We began this book by suggesting that the age of federations may only begin now, at the beginning of the twenty-first century—at least in a meaningful and democratic way. But we almost exclusively based our comparative inquiry on a small number of classical federal systems that all have in common a strong tradition in, and commitment to, Western-style liberalism and representative government. If our suggestion is to have any weight, the principles and practices of the classical models will have to undergo significant modification in order to accommodate new societies in a globalizing world. For such a world, the EU rather than the United States will provide the more likely blueprint. The federalizing experiment of the Good Friday Agreement in Northern Ireland may prove to be more significant yet.[5]

This is not to say that important lessons cannot still be learned from the established federations:

- *Dividing powers* among different levels of government will remain the principal task of federalism in its search for balance between a commitment to universal rights and freedoms and the retention of particular autonomies. While the classical models of legislative and

---

5.   Compare McGarry, "Federal Political Systems and the Accommodation of National Minorities."

administrative federalism provide the traditional alternatives, the principle of subsidiarity as employed in the EU may point to a more flexible and task-oriented mode of deciding who should do what. And the Belgian experiment with the constitutional recognition of self-governing cultural communities at least in principle points to the possibility of a novel non-territorial dimension of federalism.

- *Dual representation* likewise will continue to belong to the standard arsenal of federal governance. Whether federal systems adopt the senate or council model will likely depend on the degree to which citizens remain attached to particular communities. If institution-building in the EU is an indication, a more confederal type of weighted council governance may well emerge as the more feasible model. In a global-izing world of integration *and* fragmentation, bicameralism may have to be extended to tri- or even multi-cameral experiments that will give a representative voice to cities, for instance, or even to civic organizations. At the same time, federalism might become more com-plete by establishing bicameralism at the lower level of the two-tiered federal state.

- *Intergovernmental relations* surely will gain in importance no matter what direction federalism may take in the future. In an ever more complex and interdependent world a simple formula for the division of powers and tasks will not be found. The need for coordination among different levels of government will increase. In Canada, the practice of First Ministers' Conferences may be rolled into the newly created Council of the Federation once the prime minister and Aborig-inal leaders are participants as well. The intended constitutionaliza-tion of the European Council as the apex of EU relations points in the same direction. Again, the legitimacy of this kind of executive federalism will hinge on procedures and mechanisms of participatory inclusion and transparency.

- *Constitutional amendment* poses the most intricate problem for fed-eralism. One of the hallmarks of federal systems is their commitment to a firm set of rules enshrined in a constitutional document. More than anything else this is what makes federations different from the anarchy of international relations. Yet, there is a need of adjustment to changing times and circumstances. Here is where the limits of majority rule become most glaringly obvious. And here is also where the system of international organizations and treaties can learn the most. The various formulae of super and double majorities can serve as guidelines for the development of new forms of governance beyond the traditional unanimity requirement of diplomatic relations.

- *Judicial review* is not a phenomenon limited to federal systems, but has a particular importance. In unitary systems, nothing can challenge the will of the sovereign legislator. In federal systems of shared sovereignty, each level of government can overstep its boundaries and challenge the powers of the other. Again, there is much to be learned for the emerging international system. With the exception of Switzerland's reliance on referendums, the constituent members of federations have committed themselves to the acceptance of supreme courts as final arbiters of their constitutional relationship with one another and with the central government. Not all states, and not all federations, are as yet prepared to accept international agreements, treaties, and conventions as superior to their own bodies of law — and none have accepted the idea of binding themselves to the judicial verdicts of anything like a world supreme court. Yet the stability of the emerging world system will depend on such acceptance. The EU as a federal multi-state system provides an extraordinary precedent in this respect. The emergence of international dispute settling mechanisms and the establishment of the International Criminal Court in the Hague point in the right direction.

Much of this potential of federalism for innovative political design, however, is just that: potential. Just like with any other set of institutions and procedures, federalism is only as good as the intentions and abilities of those putting it to use. In fact, as our final chapter on federal governance argues, opinions remain divided as to whether federalism really provides this laboratory for experimentation and innovation or whether it is marred by an innate tendency to obstruct efficient policy formation and delivery. In any case, federal systems are more complicated in design and more difficult to govern than Locke's "Power to Act as One Body." For politicians serious about getting on with the business of the day as much as for citizens impatient about efficient and timely policy delivery, therefore, federalism can be a frustrating experience. But then again, who ever said that democratic governance should be easy?

Bibliography

Abraham, Henry J. *The Judicial Process.* 5th ed. New York: Oxford University Press, 1998.

Adams, Duane, ed. *Federalism, Democracy and Health Policy in Canada.* Montreal, QC and Kingston, ON: McGill-Queen's University Press, 2002.

Ajzenstat, Janet, Paul Romney, and William D. Gairdner, eds. *Canada's Founding Debates.* Toronto, ON: Stoddart, 1999.

Allen, David. "Cohesion and the Structural Funds: Transfers and Trade-offs." In Wallace and Wallace, eds., *Policy-Making in the European Union.*

Alter, Karen J. *Establishing the Supremacy of European Law.* Oxford: Oxford University Press, 2001.

Althusius, Johannes. *Politica.* Indianapolis, IN: Liberty Fund, 1995.

Andrews, Penelope, and Stephen Ellman, eds. *The Post-Apartheid Constitutions: Perspectives on South Africa's Basic Law.* Johannesburg, SA and Athens, OH: Witwatersrand University Press and Ohio University Press, 2001.

Ansell, Christopher K., and Giuseppe di Palma, eds., *Restructuring Territoriality: Europe and the United States Compared.* Cambridge: Cambridge University Press, 2004.

Arora, Balveer, and Dougles C. Verney, eds., *Multiple Identities in a Single State: Indian Federalism in Comparative Perspective.* New Delhi: Konark, 1995.

Austin, Granville. *The Indian Constitution: Cornerstone of a Nation.* Oxford: Oxford University Press, 1966.

Baack, Ben. "Forging a Nation State: The Continental Congress and the Financing of the War of American Independence." *American Economic Review,* LIV:4 (2001).

Bailyn, Bernard, *et al. The Great Republic.* Lexington, MA: D.C. Heath, 1985.

Bainbridge, Mark, and Philip Whyman. *Fiscal Federalism and European Economic Integration.* London: Routledge, 2003.

Banting, Keith G., and Stan Corbett, eds. *Health Policy and Federalism: A Comparative Perspective on Multilevel Governance.* Montreal, QC and Kingston, ON: McGill-Queen's University Press, 2002.

Bermann, George A. "The Role of Law in the Functioning of Federal Systems." In NicolaVdis and Howse, eds., *The Federal Vision* 202.

Bernstein, Richard B., with Jerome Angel. *Amending America: If We Love the Constitution So Much, Why Do We Keep Trying to Change It?* New York: Times Books, 1993.

Boadway, Robin W., and Paul A.R. Hobson, eds. *Equalization: Its Contribution to Canada's Economic and Fiscal Progress.* Kingston, ON: John Deutsch Institute for the Study of Economic Policy, Queen's University, 1998.

Bobbit, Philip. *Constitutional Fate: Theory of the Constitution.* New York: Oxford University Press, 1982.

Bodin, Jean. *The Six Bookes of Commonweale*: a facsimile reprint of the English translation of 1606, corrected and supplemented in the light of a new comparison with the French and Latin texts. 1576; Cambridge, MA: Harvard University Press, 1962. Originally published as *Les Six Livres de la République.* Cambridge, MA: Harvard University Press, 1962.

Boekelman, Keith. "The Influence of States on Federal Policy Adoptions." *Policy Studies Journal* 23 (1992).

Bomberg, Elizabeth, and Alexander Stubb, eds. *The European Union: How Does It Work?* Oxford: Oxford University Press, 2003.

Bomberg, Elizabeth, Laura Cram, and David Martin. "The EU's Institutions." In Bomberg and Stubb, eds., *The European Union.*

Bombwall, K.R. *The Foundations of Indian Federalism.* Bombay: Asia Publishing House, 1967.

Borowski, Martin. "The Beginnings of Germany's Federal Constitutional Court." *Ratio Juris* 16:2 (2003).

Börzel, Tanja. "From Competitive Regionalism to Cooperative Federalism: The Europeanization of the Spanish State of the Autonomies." *Publius* 30:2 (Spring 2000).

Börzel, Tanja A., and Madeleine Hosli. "Brussels between Bern and Berlin: Comparative Federalism Meets the European Union." *Governance* 16:2 (2003).

Bourne, Angela. "Regional Europe." In Michelle Cini, ed., *European Union Politics.* Oxford: Oxford University Press, 2003.

Brace, Paul. *State Government and Economic Performance.* Baltimore, MD: Johns Hopkins University Press, 1993.

Bradley, Kieran St Clair. "The European Court of Justice." In Peterson and Shackleton, eds, *The Institutions of the European Union.*

"Brazil: Burden of the Past, Promise of the Future," *Daedalus* 129:2 (Spring 2000).

Brown, Douglas M. "Fiscal Federalism: The New Equilibrium Between Equity and Efficiency." In Herman Bakvis and Grace Skogstad, eds., *Canadian Federalism: Performance, Effectiveness, and Legitimacy.* Don Mills, ON: Oxford University Press, 2002.

Brown, Roger H. *Redeeming the Republic: Federalists, Taxation, and the Origins of the Constitution.* Baltimore, MD: Johns Hopkins University Press, 1993.

Brownsey, Keith, and Michael Howlett, eds. *The Provincial State in Canada.* Peterborough, ON: Broadview Press, 2001.

Bryce, James. *The American Commonwealth.* 3rd ed. London: Macmillan, 1893.

Buchanan, Allen. *Secession: The Morality of Political Divorce from Fort Sumter to Lithuania and Quebec.* Boulder, CO: Westview Press, 1991.

Buchanan, James. "Federalism as an Ideal Political Order and an Objective for Constitutional Reform." *Publius* 25 (1995).

Bzdera, André. "Comparative Analysis of Federal High Courts: A Political Theory of Judicial Review." *Canadian Journal of Political Science* 26:1 (1993).

Cairns, Alan C. "The Governments and Societies of Canadian Federalism." *Canadian Journal of Political Science* 10:4 (1977).

Caleo, Chris. "Section 90 and Excise Duties: A Crisis of Interpretation." *Melbourne University Law Review* 16:2 (1987).

Calhoun, John C. *A Disquisition on Government.* 1840; Indianapolis, IN: Bobbs-Merrill Educational Publishing, 1953.

Canada, Department of Finance. *The Fiscal Balance in Canada: The Facts.* Ottawa, ON: Government of Canada, 2003.

Carey, George W. *The Federalist: Design for a Constitutional Republic.* Urbana, IL: University of Illinois Press, 1989.

Chambers, Simone. "Constitutional Referendums and Democratic Deliberation." In Matthew Mendelsohn and Andrew Parkin, eds., *Referendum Democracy: Citizens, Elites and Deliberation in Referendum Campaigns.* Basingstoke: Palgrave, 2001.

Clarkson, Stephen, and Christina McCall. *Trudeau and Our Times. Volume 1: The Magnificent Obsession.* Toronto, ON: McClelland and Stewart, 1991.

Colby, David C. "Federal-State Relations in United States Health Policy." In Banting and Corbett, eds., *Health Policy and Federalism.*

Conant, Lisa. *Justice Contained: Law and Politics in the European Union.* Ithaca, NY: Cornell University Press, 2002.

Conradt, David P. *The German Polity.* New York: Longman, 2001.

Conway, John F. *The West: The History of a Region in Confederation.* Toronto: James Lorimer, 1983.

Craven, Gregory. *Secession: The Ultimate States Right.* Carlton: Melbourne University Press, 1986.

Crawford, James. "The Legislative Power of the Commonwealth." In Gregory Craven, ed., *The Convention Debates 1891–1898: Commentaries Indices and Guide.* Sydney: Legal Books, 1986.

Crisp, L.F. *Australian National Government.* 5th ed. Melbourne: Longman Cheshire, 1983.

Cutler, Fred. "Government Responsibility and Electoral Accountability in Federations," *Publius* 34:2 (2004).

Crommelin, Michael. "The Federal Model." In Gregory Craven, ed., *Australian Federation: Towards the Second Century.* Carlton: Melbourne University Press, 1992.

Dafflon, Bernard. "Fiscal Federalism in Switzerland: A Survey of Constitutional Issues, Budget Responsibility and Equalisation." In Amedeo Fossati and Giorgio Panella, eds., *Fiscal Federalism in the European Union*. New York: Routledge, 1999.

Dehousse, Renaud. "Beyond Representative Democracy: Constitutionalism in a Polycentric Polity." In Joseph H.H. Weiler and Marlene Wind, eds., *European Constitutionalism Beyond the State*. Cambridge: Cambridge University Press, 2003.

Department of the Prime Minister and Cabinet. *Resolving Deadlocks: A Discussion Paper on Section 57 of the Australian Constitution*. Canberra: Commonwealth of Australia, 2003.

Deutsch, Karl W. *Die Schweiz als ein paradigmatischer Fall politischer Integration*. Bern: Paul Haupt, 1976.

Dicey, A.V. *An Introduction to the Study of the Law of the Constitution*. 8th ed. London: Macmillan, 1915.

Dinan, Desmond. *Ever Closer Union*. Boulder CO: Lynne Rienner, 1999.

—. "How Did We Get Here?" In Bomberg and Stubb, eds., *The European Union*.

Dion, Stéphane. "The Supreme Court's Reference on Unilateral Secession: A Turning Point in Canadian History." In Ronald Beiner and Wayne Norman, eds., *Canadian Political Philosophy: Contemporary Reflections*. Don Mills, ON: Oxford University Press, 2001.

Dixon, Sir Owen. *Commonwealth Law Reports* 85 (1952).

Donahue, John D. *Disunited States: What's at Stake as Washington Fades and the States Take the Lead?* New York: Basic Books, 1997.

Dougherty, Keith L. *Collective Action Under the Articles of Confederation*. Cambridge: Cambridge University Press, 2001.

Duckett, Stephen. "Commonwealth/State Relations in Health." In Linda Hancock, ed., *Health Policy in the Market State*. St Leonards, NSW: Allen and Unwin, 1999.

Dyck, Rand. *Canadian Politics: Critical Approaches*. 4th ed. Toronto, ON: Thompson Nelson, 2003.

Elazar, Daniel J. *Constitutionalizing Globalization: The Postmodern Revival of Confederal Arrangements*. Lanham, MD: Rowman and Littlefield, 1998.

—. *Exploring Federalism*. Tuscaloosa, AL: University of Alabama Press, 1987.

—. *Federalism and the Road to Peace*. Kingston, ON: Institute of Intergovernmental Relations, Queen's University, 1994.

—. "The United States and the Eurpean Union: Models for their Epochs." In Nicolaïdis and Howse, eds., *The Federal Vision*.

Elkins, David J. *Beyond Sovereignty: Territory and Political Economy in the Twenty-first Century*. Toronto, ON: University of Toronto Press, 1995.

Elwein, Thomas, and Joachim J. Hesse. *Das Regierungssystem der Bundesrepublik Deutschland*. Opladen: Westdeutscher Verlag, 1987.

Engelberg, Ernst. *Bismarck: das Reich in der Mitte Europas*. Berlin: Siedler, 1990.

Ferejohn, John A., and Barry A. Weingast, eds. *The New Federalism: Can the States Be Trusted?* Stanford, CA: Hoover Institution, 1998.

Fitzgerald, Edward A. "The Constitutional Division of Powers with Respect to the Environment in the United States." In Holland, *et al.*, eds., *Federalism and the Environment*.

Føllesdal, Andreas. "Survey Article: Subsidiarity." *The Journal of Political Philosophy* 6:2 (June 1998).

Forsyth, Murray. *Unions of States: The Theory and Practice of Confederation.* Leicester: Leicester University Press, 1981.

Franks, C.E.S. "The Canadian Senate in Modern Times." In Joyal, ed., *Protecting Canadian Democracy.*

Frey, Bruno S., and Reiner Eichenberger. *The New Democratic Federalism for Europe: Functional, Overlapping and Competing Jurisdictions.* Cheltenham: Edward Elgar, 1999.

Gabel, Matthew J. "The Endurance of Supranational Governance: A Consociational Interpretation of the European Union." *Comparative Politics* 30:4 (1998).

Galligan, Brian. "Amending Constitutions Through the Referendum Device." In Matthew Mendelsohn and Andrew Parkin, eds., *Referendum Democracy: Citizens, Elites and Deliberation in Referendum Campaigns.* Basingstoke: Palgrave, 2001.

—. *A Federal Republic: Australia's Constitutional System of Government.* Cambridge: Cambridge University Press, 1995.

—. *Politics of the High Court: A Study of the Judicial branch of Government in Australia.* St. Lucia: University of Queensland Press, 1987.

—. "The Republic Referendum: A Defence of Popular Sense." *Quadrant* (October 1999).

Gibson, Edward L., ed. *Federalism and Democracy in Latin America.* Baltimore, MD: Johns Hopkins University Press, 2004.

Gilbert, Mark. *Surpassing Realism: The Politics of European Integration Since 1945.* Lanham, MD: Rowman and Littlefield, 2003.

Glazer, Daryl J. "The Right to Secession: An Antisecessionist Defence." *Political Studies* 51:2 (2003).

Golay, John Ford. *The Founding of the Federal Republic of Germany.* Chicago, IL: University of Chicago Press, 1958.

Goldstein, Leslie Friedman. *Constituting Federal Sovereignty: The European Union in Comparative Context.* Baltimore, MD: Johns Hopkins University Press, 2001.

Gray, Gwendolyn. *Federalism and Health Policy: The Development of Health Systems in Canada and Australia.* Toronto, ON: University of Toronto Press, 1991.

Griffiths, Ann L., and Karl Nerenberg, eds. *Handbook of Federal Countries 2002.* Montreal, QC and Kingston, ON: McGill-Queen's University Press, 2002.

Hall, Kermit L. "Mostly Anchor and Little Sail: The Evolution of American State Constitutions." In Paul Finkelman and Stephen Gottlieb, eds., *Towards a Usable Past: Liberty under State Constitutions*. Athens, GA: University of Georgia Press, 1991.

Hamilton, Alexander, John Jay, and James Madison. *The Federalist*. Edited by George W. Carey and James McClellan. Indianapolis, IN: Liberty Fund, 2001.

Harrison, Kathryn. *Passing the Buck: Federalism and Canadian Environmental Policy*. Vancouver, BC: University of British Columbia Press, 1996.

Haysom, Nicholas. "Federal Features of the Final Constitution." In Andrews and Ellman, eds., *The Post-Apartheid Constitutions*.

Held, David, and Anthony McGrew, eds. *The Global Transformations Reader*. Cambridge: Polity, 2002.

Hesse, Joachim Jens, and Vincent Wright, eds. *Federalizing Europe? The Costs, Benefits, and Preconditions of Federal Political Systems*. Oxford: Oxford University Press, 1996.

Heun, Werner. "Supremacy of the Constitution, Separation of Powers, and Judicial Review in Nineteenth-Century German Constitutionalism." *Ratio Juris* 16:2 (2003).

Heywood, Paul. *The Politics and Government of Spain*. New York: St. Martin's Press, 1995.

Higgott, Richard. "Regionalism in the Asia-Pacific: Two Steps Forward, One Step Back?" In Richard Stubbs and Geoffrey R.D. Underhill, eds., *Political Economy and the Changing Global Order*. Don Mills, ON: Oxford University Press, 2000.

Hill, Christopher. *The Century of Revolution 1603–1714*. New York: Norton, 1982.

Hirschman, Albert O. *Exit, Voice and Loyalty: Responses to Decline in Firms, Organizations, and States*. Cambridge, MA: Harvard University Press, 1970.

Hirschman, Albert O. *Exit, Voice, and Loyalty: Responses to Decline in Firms, Organizations and States*. Cambridge, MA: Harvard University Press, 1970.

Hirst, John. *The Sentimental Nation: The Making of the Australian Commonwealth*. Melbourne: Oxford University Press, 2000.

Hobbes, Thomas. *Leviathan*. 1651; Cambridge: Cambridge University Press, 1992.

Holland, Kenneth M., F.L. Morton, and Brian Galligan, eds. *Federalism and the Environment: Environmental Policymaking in Australia, Canada, and the United States*. Westport, CT: Greenwood Press, 1996.

Howse, Robert. "Federalism, Democracy, and Regulatory Reform: A Sceptical View of the Case for Decentralization." In Knop, *et al.*, eds., *Rethinking Federalism*.

Hueglin, Thomas O. "Federalism at the Crossroads: Old Meanings, New Significance." *Canadian Journal of Political Science* 36:2 (June 2003).

Hueglin, Thomas O. *Early Modern Concepts for a Late Modern World: Althusius on Community and Federalism*. Waterloo, ON: Wilfrid Laurier University Press, 1999.

—. "From Constitutional to Treaty Federalism." *Publius* 30:4 (Fall 2000).

—. "Majoritarianism—Consociationalism." In Roland Axtman, ed., *Understanding Democratic Politics*. London: Sage, 2003.

Hurley, James Ross. *Amending Canada's Constitution: History, Processes, Problems and Prospects*. Ottawa, ON: Ministry of Supply and Services, 1996.

Inman, Robert P., and Daniel L. Rubinfeld. "Rethinking Federalism." *Journal of Economic Perspectives* 11:4 (1997).

Jeffrey, Charlie. "German Federalism from Cooperation to Competition." In Maiken Umbach, ed., *German Federalism: Past, Present, Future*. Basingstoke: Palgrave, 2002.

Johari, J.C. *Indian Government and Politics*. Delhi: Vishal Publications, 1976.

Johnson, Nevil. "Territory and Power: Some Historical Determinants of the Constitutional Structure of the Federal Republic of Germany." In Charlie Jeffrey, ed., *Recasting German Federalism: The Legacies of Unification*. London: Pinter, 1999.

Joyal, Serge, ed. *Protecting Canadian Democracy: The Senate You Never Knew*. Montreal, QC and Kingston, ON: McGill-Queen's University Press, 2003.

Juberías, Carlos Flores. "A House in Search of a Role: The Senado of Spain." In Samuel C. Patterson and Anthony Mughan, eds., *Senates: Bicameralism in the Contemporary World*. Columbus, OH: Ohio State University Press, 1999.

Junge, Kerstin. "Differentiated Integration." In Michelle Cini, ed., *European Union Politics*. New York: Oxford University Press, 2003.

Keating, Michael. *The Politics of Modern Europe*. Aldershot: Edward Elgar, 1993.

Kelemen, R. Daniel. *The Rules of Federalism: Institutions and Regulatory Politics in the EU and Beyond*. Cambridge, MA: Harvard University Press, 2004.

Kesselman, Mark, Joel Krieger, Christopher S. Allen, Stephen Hellman, David Ost, and George Ross, eds. *European Politics in Transition*. 4th ed. Boston, MA: Houghton Mifflin, 2002.

Kincaid, John. "American Experiences in the Theory and Practice of Fiscal Federalism." In Arora and Verney, *Multiple Identities in a Single State*.

—. "Confederal Federalism and Citizen Representation in the European Union." *West European Politics* 22:2 (1999).

—. "Devolution in the United States: Rhetoric and Reality." In Nicolaïdis and Howse, eds., *The Federal Vision*.

—. "Extinguishing the Twin Relics of Barbaric Multiculturalism—Slavery and Polygamy—From American Federalism," *Publius* 33:1 (2003).

—. "From Cooperative to Coercive Federalism." *The Annals of the American Academy of Political and Social Science* 509 (May 1990).

—. "Intergovernmental Costs and Coordination in US Environmental Protection." in Holland, *et al.*, eds., *Federalism and the Environment*.

Knop, Karen, Sylvia Ostry, Richard Simeon, and Katherine Swinton, eds. *Rethinking Federalism: Citizens, Markets, and Governments in a Changing World*. Vancouver, BC: University of British Columbia Press, 1995.

Kommers, Donald P. *The Constitutional Jurisprudence of the Federal Republic of Germany.* Durham, NC: Duke University Press, 1989.

—. *Judicial Politics in West Germany: A Study of the Federal Constitutional Court.* Beverly Hills, CA: Sage, 1976.

Konrad Hesse, *Der unitarische Bundesstaat.* Karlsruhe: C.F. Müller, 1962.

Krikorian, Jacqueline D. "British Imperial Politics and Judicial Independence: The Judicial Committee's decision in the Canadian case *Nadan v. The King.*" *Canadian Journal of Political Science* 33:2 (2000).

Kyvig, David E. *Explicit and Authentic Acts: Amending the U.S. Constitution 1776–1995.* Lawrence, KS: University Press of Kansas, 1996.

Lachance, R., and F. Vaillancourt. "Quebec's Tax on Income: Evolution, Status, and Evaluation." In D.M. Brown, ed., *Tax Competition and the Fiscal Union in Canada.* Kingston, ON: Institute of Intergovernmental Relations, 2001.

Laffer, Brigid, and Michael Shackleton. "The Budget." In Wallace and Wallace, eds., *Policy-Making in the European Union.*

Lane, P.H. *Introduction to the Australian Constitution.* Melbourne: The Law Book Company, 1990.

Laufer, Heinz, and Ursula Münch. *Das föderative System der Bundesrepublik Deutschland.* Opladen: Leske Budrich, 1998.

Lecours, André. "Belgium." In *Forum of Federations, Handbook of Federal Countries 2002.* Montreal, QC and Kingston, ON: McGill-Queen's University Press, 2002.

Leeson, Howard. "Section 33, The Notwithstanding Clause: A Paper Tiger?" In Peter Russell and Paul Howe, eds., *Choices* 6:4 (2000) Institute for Research in Public Policy.

Legislature of Alberta. *Strengthening Canada: Reform of Canada's Senate.* Edmonton, AB: Plains Publishing, 1985.

Lehmbruch, Gerhard. *Parteienwettbewerb im Bundesstaat.* Stuttgart: Kohlhammer, 1976.

—. "Party and Federation in Germany: A Developmental Dilemma." *Government and Opposition* 13:2 (1978).

Lehnig, Percy B., ed. *Theories of Secession.* London: Routledge, 1998.

Lemco, Jonathon. *Political Stability in Federal Systems.* New York: Praeger, 1991.

Leonardy, Uwe. "The Institutional Structures of German Federalism." In Charlie Jeffrey, ed., *Recasting German Federalism: The Legacies of Unification.* London: Pinter, 1999.

Lewis, Jeffrey. "National Interests: COREPER." In Peterson and Shackleton, *The Institutions of the European Union.*

Lijphart, Arend. *Patterns of Democracy: Government Forms and Performance in Thirty-Six Countries.* New Haven, CT: Yale University Press, 1999.

Linder, Wolf. *Swiss Democracy.* New York: St. Martin's Press, 1994.

Linder, Wolf, and Adrian Vatter. "Institutions and Outcomes of Swiss Federalism: The Role of the Cantons in Swiss Politics." *West European Politics* 24:2 (2001).

Lipgens, Walter, ed. *Documents on the History of European Integration: Continental Plans for European Union 1939–45*. 2 vols. Berlin: Walter de Guyter, 1984.

Lister, Frederick K. *The Early Security Confederations: from the Ancient Greeks to the United Colonies of New England*. Westport, CT: Greenwood Press, 1999.

—. *The Later Security Confederations: The American, Swiss, and German Unions*. Westport, CT: Greenwood Press, 2001.

Livingston, William S. *Federalism and Constitutional Change*. Oxford: Oxford University Press, 1956.

Lutz, Donald S. "The Iroquois Confederation Constitution: An Analysis." *Publius* 28:2 (1998).

Machiavelli, Niccolò. *The Prince*. 1532; Cambridge: Cambridge University Press, 1988.

Main, Jackson Turner. *The Antifederalists: Critics of the Constitution, 1781–1788*. 1961; Chapel Hill, NC: University of North Carolina Press, 2004.

Maioni, Antonia. "Federalism and Health Care in Canada." In Banting and Corbett, eds., *Health Policy and Federalism*.

Majeed, Akhtar, ed. *Constitutional Nation Building: Half a Century of India's Success*. New Delhi: Centre for Federal Studies, 2001.

Majone, Giandomenico. *Regulating Europe*. London: Routledge, 1996.

—. "Regulatory Legitimacy in the United States and the European Union." in Nicolaïdis and Howse, *The Federal Vision*.

Markovic, Mihailo. "The Federal Experience in Yugoslavia." In Knop *et al.*, eds., *Rethinking Federalism*.

Marx, Karl. "Moralizing Criticism and Critical Morality." In Karl Marx and Friedrich Engels, *Collected Works*, Vol. 6. London: Lawrence and Wishart, 1976.

McDonald, Forrest. *Novus Ordo Seclorum: The Intellectual Origins of the Constitution*. Lawrence, KS: University Press of Kansas, 1985.

—. *States Rights and the Union: Imperium in Imperio, 1776–1876*. Lawrence, KS: University Press of Kansas, 2000.

McGarry, John. "Federal Political Systems and the Accommodation of National Minorities." In Griffiths and Nerenberg, eds., *Handbook of Federal Countries*.

McKay, David. *Designing Europe: Comparative Lessons from the Federal Experience*. Oxford: Oxford University Press, 2001.

—. *Rush to Union: Understanding the European Federal Bargain*. Oxford: Oxford University Press, 1996.

McKinnon, Ronald, and Thomas Nechyba. "Competition in Federal Systems: The Role of Political and Financial Constraints." in Ferejohn and Weingast, eds., *The New Federalism*.

McMinn, W.G. *A Constitutional History of Australia*. Melbourne: Oxford University Press, 1979.

—. *Nationalism and Federalism in Australia*. Melbourne: Oxford University Press, 1994.

McRae, Kenneth D. *Conflict and Compromise in Multilingual Societies: Switzerland.* Waterloo, ON: Wilfrid Laurier University Press, 1983.

Meehan, Elizabeth. "The Belfast Agreement: Its Distinctiveness and Points of Cross-fertilization in the UK's Devolution Programme," *Parliamentary Affairs* 52:1 (1999).

Meekison, J. Peter, ed. *Constitutional Patriation: The Lougheed-Lévesque Correspondence.* Kingston, ON: Institute of Intergovernmental Relations, Queen's University, 1999.

Meyer, Michael C., and William L. Sherman. *The Course of Mexican History.* New York: Oxford University Press, 1979.

Michael Lusztig, "Federalism and Institutional Design: The Perils and Politics of a Triple-E Senate in Canada." *Publius* 25:1 (1995).

Michelmann, Hans J. "Germany and European Integration." In Matthias Zimmer, ed., *Germany: Phoenix in Trouble?* Edmonton, AB: University of Alberta Press, 1997.

Montesquieu, Charles de Secondat, Baron de. *The Spirit of the Laws.* Cambridge: Cambridge University Press, 1989.

Moore, Margaret, ed. *National Self-Determination and Secession.* New York and Oxford: Oxford University Press, 1998.

Moravcsik, Andrew. "Federalism in the European Union: Rhetoric and Reality." In Nicolaïdis and Howse, eds., *The Federal Vision.*

Morehouse, Sarah McCally, "The Governor in the Intergovernmental System." In O'Toole, ed., *American Intergovernmental Relations.*

Moreno, Luis. *The Federalization of Spain.* London: Frank Cass, 2001.

Morton, F.L. "The Constitutional Division of Powers with Respect to the Environment in Canada." In Holland, *et al.*, eds., *Federalism and the Environment.*

Mtshaulana, Patric Mzolisi. "The History and Role of the Constitutional Court of South Africa." In Andrews and Ellman, eds., *The Post-Apartheid Constitutions.*

Murray, Christina. "Negotiating Beyond Deadlock: From the Constitutional Assembly to the Court." In Andrews and Ellman, eds., *The Post-Apartheid Constitutions.*

Nagel, Robert F. *The Implosion of American Federalism.* New York: Oxford University Press, 2001.

Nathan, Richard P., and Thomas L. Gais. "Early Findings About the Newest New Federalism for Welfare." *Publius* 28:3 (Summer 1998).

Nicolaïdis, Kalypso, and Robert Howse, eds. *The Federal Vision: Legitimacy and Levels of Governance in the United States and the European Union.* Oxford: Oxford University Press, 2001.

Nielsen, Kai. "Liberal Nationalism and Secession." In Moore, ed., *National Self-Determination and Secession.*

Norrie, Kenneth, and L.S. Wilson, "On Re-Balancing Canadian Fiscal Federalism." In Harvey Lazar, ed., *Toward a New Mission Statement for Canadian Fiscal Federalism.* Montreal, QC and Kingston, ON: McGill-Queen's University Press, 2000.

O'Toole, Laurence J., ed., *American Intergovernmental Relations.* Washington, DC: Congressional Quarterly Inc., 1985.

Oates, Wallace E. *Fiscal Federalism.* New York: Harcourt Brace Jovanovich, 1972.

Obinger, Herbert. "Federalism, Direct Democracy, and Welfare State Development in Switzerland." *Journal of Public Policy* 18:3 (1998).

Öhlinger, Theo. "The Genesis of the Austrian Model of Constitutional Review of Legislation." *Ratio Juris* 16:2 (June 2003).

Painter, Martin. *Collaborative Federalism: Economic Reform in Australia in the 1990s.* Melbourne: Cambridge University Press, 1998.

Palmer, Kenneth T., and Edward B. Laverty. "The Impact of *United States v. Lopez* on Intergovernmental Relations: A Preliminary Assessment." *Publius* 26:3 (1996).

Parliament of Western Australia. *The Case of the People of Western Australia in support of their desire to withdraw from the Commonwealth of Australia established under the Commonwealth of Australia Constitution Act (Imperial), and that Western Australia be restored to its former status as a separate self-governing colony in the British Empire.* Perth: Government of Western Australia, 1934.

Patzelt, Werner J. "The Very Federal House: The German Bundesrat." In Samuel C. Patterson and Anthony Mughan, eds., *Senates: Bicameralism in the Contemporary World.* Columbus, ON: Ohio State University Press, 1999.

Peterson, George E. "Federalism and the States." In John L. Palmer and Isabel V. Sawhill, eds., *The Reagan Record.* Cambridge, MA: Ballinger, 1984.

Peterson, John, and Michael Shackleton, eds., *The Institutions of the European Union.* Oxford: Oxford University

Peterson, Paul E. *The Price of Federalism.* Washington, DC: Brookings Institution, 1995).

Phinnemore, David. "Towards European Union." In Michelle Cini, ed., *European Union Politics.* Oxford: Oxford University Press, 2003.

Pilz, Frank, and Heike Ortwein. *Das politische System Deutschlands.* München: Oldenbourg, 1995.

Pinder, John. *The European Union.* Oxford: Oxford University Press, 2001.

Posner, Paul. *The Politics of Unfunded Mandates: Whither Federalism?* Washington, DC: Georgetown University Press, 1998.

Proudhon, Pierre-Joseph. *The Principle of Federation.* Toronto, ON: University of Toronto Press, 1973. Originally published as *Du Principe fédératif et de la nécessité de reconstituer le parti de la révolution,* 1863.

Pusey, Merlo John. *Charles Evan Hughes.* New York: Macmillan, 1951.

Rack, Reinhard. "Austria: Has the Federation Become Obsolete." In Hesse and Wright, eds., *Federalizing Europe?*

Rakove, Jack N. *Original Meanings: Politics and Ideas in the Making of the Constitution.* New York: Knopf, 1996.

Rao, M. Govinda. "Indian Fiscal Federalism from a Comparative Perspective." In Arora and Verney, eds., *Multiple Identities in a Single State.*

Renzsch, Wolfgang. "Challenges and Perspectives for German Federalism." In Maiken Umbach, ed., *German Federalism: Past, Present, Future*. Basingstoke: Palgrave, 2002.

Richardson, Jack. *Resolving Deadlocks in the Australian Parliament*. Canberra: Department of the Parliamentary Library, Parliament of Australia, 2000.

Rickard, Carmel. "The Certification of the Constitution of South Africa." In Andrews and Ellman, *The Post-Apartheid Constitutions*.

Rieger, Elmar. "The Common Agricultural Policy: Politics against Markets." In Wallace and Wallace, eds., *Policy-Making in the European Union*.

Riker, William H. "European Federalism: The Lessons of Past Experience." In Hesse and Wright, eds., *Federalizing Europe?*

—. "Federalism." In Fred I. Greenstein and Nelson W. Polsby, eds., *Handbook of Political Science*, Vol. 5. Reading, MA: Addison-Wesley, 1975.

—. "The Senate and American Federalism." *American Political Science Review* 49:2 (1955).

Rodríguez, Victoria E., and Peter M. Ward, eds. *Opposition Government in Mexico*. Albuquerque, NM: University of Mexico Press, 1995.

Roemheld, Lutz. *Integral Federalism: A Model for Europe*. New York: Peter Lang, 1990.

Rose, Jürgen, and Johannes Ch. Traut, eds. *Federalism and Decentralization: Perspectives for the Transformation Process in Eastern and Central Europe*. Basingstoke: Palgrave Macmillan, 2002.

Rossum, Ralph A. *Federalism, the Supreme Court, and the Seventeenth Amendment: The Irony of Constitutional Democracy*. Lanham, MD: Lexington Books, 2001.

Rothmayr, Christine. "Towards the Judicialisation of Swiss Politics?" *West European Politics* 24:2 (2001).

Saunders, Cheryl. "The Hardest Nut to Crack: The Financial Settlement in the Commonwealth Constitution." In Gregory Craven, ed., *The Convention Debates, 1891–1898: Commentaries, Indices and Guide*. Sydney: Legal Books, 1986.

Saywell, John T. *The Lawmakers: Judicial Power and the Shaping of Canadian Federalism*. Toronto, ON: University of Toronto Press, 2002.

Sbragia, Alberta. "Environmental Policy: Economic Constraints and External Pressures." In Wallace and Wallace, eds., *Policy-making in the European Union*.

—. "Key Policies." In Bomberg and Stubb, eds., *The European Union*.

Scharpf, Fritz W. "Democratic Legitimacy under Conditions of Regulatory Competition: Why Europe Differs from the United States." In Nicolaïdis and Howse, eds., *The Federal Vision*.

—. "The Joint-Decision Trap: Lessons from German Federalism and European Integration." *Public Administration* 66 (1988).

Schattschneider, E.E. *The Semisovereign People: A Realist's View of Democracy in America*. New York: Holt, Rinehart and Winston, 1960.

Scheiber, Harry N, "The Condition of American Federalism: An Historian's View." In O'Toole, ed., *American Intergovernmental Relations.*

Schmitz, Georg. "The Constitutional Court of the Republic of Austria 1918–1920." *Ratio Juris* 16:2 (June 2003).

Schoutheete, Philippe de. "The European Council." In Peterson and Shackleton, eds., *The Institutions of the European Union.*

Schramm, Sandford, and Samuel H. Beer, eds. *Welfare Reform: A Race to the Bottom?* Washington, DC: Woodrow Wilson Center Press, 1999.

Senelle, Robert. "The Reform of the Belgian State." In Hesse and Wright, eds., *Federalizing Europe?*

Shapiro, Martin. *Courts: A Comparative Political Analysis.* Chicago, IL: University of Chicago Press, 1981.

Siemers, David J. *Ratifying the Republic: Antifederalists and Federalists in Constitutional Time.* Stanford, CA: Stanford University Press, 2002.

Simeon, Richard. *Federal-Provincial Diplomacy.* Toronto, ON: University of Toronto Press, 1972.

Simeon, Richard, and Christina Murray. "Multi-Sphere Governance in South Africa: An Interim Assessment," *Publius* 31:4 (Fall 2001).

Simeon, Richard, and David Cameron. "Intergovernmental Relations and Democracy: An Oxymoron If There Ever Was One?" In Herman Bakvis and Grace Skogstad, eds., *Canadian Federalism: Performance, Effectiveness, and Legitimacy.* Don Mills, ON: Oxford University Press, 2002.

Simeon, Richard, and Ian Robinson. *State, Society, and the Development of Canadian Federalism.* Toronto, ON: University of Toronto Press, 1990.

Skogstad, Grace. "Intergovernmental Relations and the Politics of Environmental Protection in Canada." In Holland, *et al.*, eds., *Federalism and the Environment.*

Smiley, Donald V. *Canada in Question.* Toronto, ON: McGraw-Hill Ryerson, 1980.

Smith, Jennifer. *Federalism.* Vancouver, BC: University of British Columbia Press, 2004.

Smith, Jennifer. "The Unsolvable Constitutional Crisis." In François Rocher and Miriam Smith, eds., *New Trends in Canadian Federalism.* Peterborough, ON: Broadview Press, 1995.

Snowiss, Sylvia. *Judicial Review and the Law of the Constitution.* New Haven, CT: Yale University Press, 1990.

Solozábal, Juan José. "Spain: A Federation in the Making?" In Hesse and Wright, eds., *Federalizing Europe?*

Souza, Celina. *Constitutional Engineering in Brazil: The Politics of Federalism and Decentralization.* New York: St. Martin's Press, 1997.

Spahn, Paul Bernd, and Wolfgang Föttinger. "Germany." In Teresa Ter-Minassian, ed., *Fiscal Federalism in Theory and Practice.* Washington, DC: IMF, 1997.

Stepan, Alfred. "Toward a New Comparative Politics of Federalism, (Multi)Nationalism, and Democracy: Beyond Rikerian Federalism." In Alfred Stepan, ed., *Arguing Comparative Politics.* New York: Oxford University Press, 2001.

Stevenson, Garth. "The Division of Powers." In Richard Simeon, ed., *The Division of Powers and Public Policy*. Toronto, ON: University of Toronto Press, 1985.

—. *Unfulfilled Union: Canadian Federalism and National Unity*. 2nd ed. Toronto, ON: Gage, 1982.

Stone, Alec. "The Birth and Development of Abstract Review: Constitutional Courts and Policymaking in Western Europe." *Policy Studies Review* 19:1 (1990).

Storing, Herbert J. *What the Anti-Federalists Were For: The Political Thought of the Opponents of the Constitution*. Chicago, IL: University of Chicago Press, 1981.

Stotsky, Janet G., and Emil M. Sunley. "United States." In Teresa Ter-Minassian, ed., *Fiscal Federalism in Theory and Practice*. Washington, DC: IMF, 1997.

Sturm, Roland. "Party Competition and the Federal System: The Lehmbruch Hypothesis Revisited." In Charlie Jeffrey, ed., *Recasting German Federalism: The Legacies of Unification*. London: Pinter, 1999.

Swift, Elaine K. *The Making of an American Senate: Reconstitutive Change in Congress, 1787–1841*. Ann Arbor, MI: University of Michigan Press, 1996.

Sylvia, Stephen J. "Reform Gridlock and the Role of the Bundesrat in German Politics." *West European Politics* 22:2 (1999).

Tassin, Etienne. "Europe: A Political Community?" In Chantal Mouffe, ed., *Dimensions of Radical Democracy: Pluralism, Citizenship, Community*. London: Verso, 1992.

Taylor, John. *Construction Construed and the Constitution Vindicated*. Richmond, VA, 1820.

—. *New Views of the Constitution of the United States*. Washington, DC, 1823.

Telford, Hamish. "The Federal Spending Power in Canada: Nation-building or Nation-destroying?" *Publius* 33:1 (2003).

Thomson, James. "Constitutional Authority for Judicial Review: A Contribution from the Framers of the Australian Constitution." In Gregory Craven, ed., *The Convention Debates 1891–1898: Commentaries, Indices and Guide*. Sydney: Legal Books, 1986.

Tiebout, Charles M. "A Pure Theory of Local Expenditures." *Journal of Political Economy* LXIV (1956).

Tilly, Charles. "Western State-Making and Political Transformation." In Charles Tilly, ed., *The Formation of National States in Western Europe*. Princeton, NJ: Princeton University Press, 1975.

Trudeau, Pierre Elliot. "The Theory and Practice of Federalism." In Michael Oliver, ed., *Social Purpose for Canada*. Toronto, ON: University of Toronto Press, 1961.

Tsoukalis, Loukas. "Economic and Monetary Union." In Wallace and Wallace, eds., *Policy-Making in the European Union*.

Usher, Dan. *The Uneasy Case for Equalization Payments*. Vancouver, BC: Fraser Institute, 1995.

Vaughan, Frederick. *The Canadian Federalist Experiment: From Defiant Monarchy to Reluctant Republic.* Montreal, QC and Kingston, ON: McGill-Queen's University Press, 2003.

Venables, Robert W. "The Founding Fathers: Choosing to be Romans." In Jose Barreiro, ed., *Indian Roots of American Democracy.* Ithaca, NY: Akwe:Kon Press, 1992.

Verney, Douglas C. "Are All Federations Federal? The United States, Canada and India." In Arora and Verney, eds., *Multiple Identities in a Single State.*

Vipond, Robert C. *Liberty and Community: Canadian Federalism and the Failure of the Constitution.* Albany, NY: State University of New York Press, 1991.

Volden, Craig. "Entrusting the States with Welfare Reform." In Ferejohn and Weingast, eds., *The New Federalism.*

von Beyme, Klaus. *Das politische System der Bundesrepublik Deutschland.* München: Piper 1987.

Waite, P.B. *The Life and Times of Confederation 1864–1867.* Toronto, ON: University of Toronto Press, 1965.

Walker, David B. *The Rebirth of Federalism: Slouching toward Washington.* 2nd ed. New York: Chatham House, 2000.

Wallace, Helen, and William Wallace, eds. *Policy-Making in the European Union.* 4th ed. Oxford: Oxford University Press, 2000.

Wallin, Bruce A. *From Revenue Sharing to Deficit Sharing: General Revenue Sharing and Cities.* Washington, DC: Georgetown University Press, 1998.

Wassener, Dietmar. "Federalism and the German Health-Care System." In Banting and Corbett, eds., *Health Policy and Federalism.*

Watts, Ronald L. *Comparing Federal Systems,* 2nd ed. Kingston, ON: Institute of Intergovernmental Relations, 1999.

—. *Executive Federalism: A Comparative Analysis.* Kingston, ON: Institute of Intergovernmental Relations, Queen's University, 1989.

Wehner, Joachim. "Fiscal Federalism in South Africa." *Publius* 30:3 (2000).

Weidenfeld, Werner, and Wolfgang Wessels. *Europe from A to Z: Guide to European Integration.* Luxembourg: Office for Official Publications of the European Communities, 1997.

Weiler, Paul. *In the Last Resort: A Critical Study of the Supreme Court of Canada.* Toronto, ON: Carswell/Methuen, 1974.

Weingast, Barry. "The Economic Role of Political Institutions: Market-preserving Federalism and Economic Development." *Journal of Law and Economics* 11 (1995).

Westmacott, Martin. "The Charlottetown Accord: A Retrospective Overview." In Martin Westmacott and Hugh Mellon, eds., *Challenges to Canadian Federalism.* Scarborough, ON: Prentice Hall, 1998.

Wheare, K.C. *Federal Government.* 4th ed. Oxford: Oxford University Press, 1963.

Williams, Melissa. "Toleration, Canadian-Style: Reflections of a Yankee-Canadian." In Ronald Beiner and Wayne Norman, eds., *Canadian Political Philosophy.* Don Mills, ON: Oxford University Press, 2001.

Wilson, James Q., and John J. DiIulio. *American Government*. Boston, MA: Houghton Mifflin, 1998.

Wolf, Christopher. *The Rise of Modern Judicial Review: From Constitutional Interpretation to Judge-made Law*. Rev. ed. Lanham, MD: Rowman and Littlefield.

Wood, Gordon S. *The Creation of the American Republic 1776–1787*. Chapel Hill, NC: University of North Carolina Press, 1969.

Young, Lisa, and Keith Archer, eds. *Regionalism and Party Politics in Canada*. Don Mills, ON: Oxford University Press, 2002.

Index